GREAT IRISH LIVES

Published by Times Books
An imprint of HarperCollins Publishers
Westerhill Road, Bishopbriggs,
Glasgow. G64 2QT
www.harpercollins.co.uk
times.books@harpercollins.co.uk

First published 2008
Second edition 2016
Paperback edition 2018

© Times Newspapers Ltd 2017
www.thetimes.co.uk

ISBN 978-0-00-826265-5

10 9 8 7 6 5 4 3 2 1

A catalogue record for this book is available from the British Library

Printed and bound by CPI Group (UK) Ltd, Croydon, CR0 4YY

Cover Image:
"From Everywhere and Nowhere (Seamus Heaney)"
Colin Davidson b. 1968 © Colin Davidson, 2013 Collection Ulster Museum

MIX
Paper from
responsible sources
FSC
www.fsc.org
FSC™ C007454

THE TIMES

GREAT IRISH LIVES

OBITUARIES OF IRELAND'S FINEST

EDITED BY CHARLES LYSAGHT

Charles Lysaght is a lawyer, biographer and long-time
contributor of obituaries to *The Times*.

TIMES BOOKS

CONTENTS

Introduction ix

INTRODUCTION

Charles Lysaght

WHEN DR JOHNSON proclaimed the Irish an honest race because they seldom spoke well of one another, he should have made it clear that it was the reputations of the living that he had in mind. In Ireland, speaking of the dead in the aftermath of their demise, the adage *nihil nisi bonum* applies not only among friends and acquaintances but in the media. Readers of Irish newspapers, national and especially local, are treated to accounts of the unprecedented gloom that settled over the district where the deceased lived, the largest and most representative gathering at a funeral within living memory, accompanied by eulogies reciting how the dear departed thought only of others and never of themselves, were never known to say an unkind word about anybody, were devoted to their family, were exemplary in their piety and charity and were universally loved and respected. Such undiscriminating eulogies lack credibility and do their subjects no favours.

It has been a signal service rendered by *The Times* to provide accounts of deceased Irish persons that aspire to more realism and more balance in their assessments while bringing out the exceptional achievements and positive qualities that make the deceased worthy of notice in a newspaper outside their own country. In the absence of a comprehensive dictionary of Irish biography they have sometimes been the best accounts of a person's life, at least for a period, and, as such, a valuable reference for historians.

It has been helpful to this process that many of these obituaries are prepared in advance and so allow for checking facts and for reflection unaffected by the immediate surge of sympathy surrounding a death.

It is conducive to frankness that obituaries are published anonymously and that the identity of the authors will not be disclosed by the paper in their lifetime, so keeping faith with the nineteenth century description of *The Times* as 'the most obstinately anonymous newspaper in the World'. It may add to the authority of a piece that it seems to represent the views of a great newspaper rather than an individual author. It probably puts some pressure on the individual authors to reflect a general view of a person rather than to indulge a personal experience or assessment.

Obituaries (especially major ones) may first be prepared when their subjects are relatively young and so need revision many times before publication. Apart from new facts, what is interesting about a person's life can change quite rapidly. In the nature of things, the subject some-times outlives the original author and what emerges on the final day is a composite work.

Historically, Irish obituaries in *The Times* reflected somewhat the troubled relationship that the paper had with Ireland from the days of Daniel O'Connell up to the creation of the independent Irish state. The difficulties in the relationship might even be traced back further to the incident when Irishman Barry O'Meara, who had been removed by the British Government from his role as physician to the captive Napoleon on St Helena, horse-whipped William Walter, mistaking him for his brother John who was one of the proprietors and the responsible editor of the paper. O'Meara had been affronted because *The Times* had dismissed as a lie a statement in his memoirs that he had been told by the deposed Emperor that *The Times* was in the pay of the exiled Bourbons. It ended up in court with O'Meara getting away with a fulsome apology.

The Times, under the editorship of Thomas Barnes (1817–41) supported O'Connell's campaign for Catholic Emancipation. But their relationship with O'Connell went sour not long after he entered parliament in 1830 when he accused the paper of misreporting him. As he espoused the repeal of the Union and brought the 'Romish clergy' into politics, they denounced him as an unredeemed and unredeem-able scoundrel and declared 'war to the political extinction of one of us.' One of the first assignments of the celebrated Irish-born reporter William Howard Russell was to report on O'Connell's monster meetings in 1843 and on his subsequent trial and conviction in Dublin – it took over 24 hours to get the news of the verdict to London.

After O'Connell's conviction had been set aside on appeal by the House of Lords, *The Times* returned to the fray, setting up what they called a commission in the form of a journalist sent to report on O'Connell's treatment of his own tenants in Kerry. They were found to be living in poverty without a pane of glass in any of their windows. Russell was sent to Ireland again and, despite being on friendly terms with O'Connell, confirmed that this was indeed the case. O'Connell, for his part, denounced *The Times* as 'a vile journal' which had falsely, foully and wickedly calumniated him every day and on every subject. Against this background it is not surprising that his obituary in 1847 is critical and reflects a hostile political viewpoint. But its recognition of the positive qualities of what it called an 'extraordinary man' shows admirable balance. It claimed to have shown a forebearance of which O'Connell himself was incapable and to have treated indulgently the memory of a man who in a long lifetime seldom spared a fallen adversary.

The confrontation between nationalist Ireland and *The Times* reached its apotheosis in the late 1880s when *The Times* published a series of articles entitled 'Parnellism and Crime' that were, in fact, largely written by a young Irish Catholic barrister and journalist, educated under Jowett at Balliol, called John Woulfe Flanagan – although anonymously as was still customary for all articles. Parnell was accused of having been complicit with terrorism and the organized intimidation of the Land War. The allegations were subsequently supported by letters said to have been written by Parnell that were proved before a judicial commission to have been forged by one Richard Pigott. The unmasking of Pigott before the commission by Sir Charles Russell, a former Irish solicitor who was then the leader of the English Bar, was an historic set-piece much recalled in the annals of the law as well as politics. Less remembered is that the commission, on the strength of evidence given by the Fenian informer Henri Le Caron, upheld the substance of most of the charges made in the articles. The events cast a long shadow, well beyond the obituary published on Parnell's death written by *The Times'* leader writer E. D. J. Wilson where this was pointed out. An account of the episode in a volume of the *History of The Times* covering the years 1884 to 1912, published in 1947, led to corrigenda in an appendix in the next volume credited to Parnell's surviving colleague and biographer Captain Henry Harrison MC. Attention was drawn to the role of Captain William O'Shea, the first husband of Mrs Parnell, as a witness before the commission and an admission made that the paper's association with O'Shea proved by Captain Harrison 'is not creditable' and should not have been ignored in the *History of The Times*.

In his main address to the commission Sir Charles Russell had admitted the terrorism associated with the Land League but claimed that the root cause of it was English oppression and that the fomentor of discord between the two peoples through several generations had been *The Times*. Sir Henry James, who appeared for *The Times*, answered by citing a long list of critical occasions in Irish history when the paper had supported the Irish popular cause often at the risk of alienating dominant opinion in England. It had helped to secure Catholic emancipation; it had argued for the endowment of the Roman Catholic seminary at Maynooth and the disestablishment of the Irish Church; it had taken a leading part in the relief of distress during the Irish famine and advocated the extension of the Irish franchise; it had highlighted evictions and supported legislation giving greater protection to tenants.

Because of its opposition to nationalist aspirations *The Times* was berated in nationalist Ireland as the enemy of all things Irish. In fact, this was not so. The unionism of *The Times* was an inclusive unionism and did not spill over into a general antipathy to the Irish or even the Catholic Irish. Tom Moore, the poet, had been a regular and valued contributor. Edmund O'Donovan, the son of the great Gaelic scholar John O'Donovan and old Clongownian Frank Power were two *Times* journalists who perished with General Gordon reporting the Egyptian campaign of the 1880s.

In the obituaries columns, as elsewhere, the Irish of all backgrounds got a good show. Just occasionally there was some stereotyping, although it was not unfriendly. In 1891, remarking that in his qualities and talents as in his defects Sir John Pope Hennessy was a typical Irishman, his obituary depicted him as 'quick of wit, ready in repartee, a fluent speaker, and an able debater but the enthusiasm and emotion which lent force and fire to his speeches led him into the adoption of extreme and impracticable views.' A few years later the obituary of the colourful Irish judge Lord Morris of Spiddal contained the observation that 'though an Irishman he was not given to verbosity.' Of Michael Davitt, the Land Leaguer, it was remarked that 'he was an Irishman of a somewhat unusual type dark and dour.' A more extensive indulgence in stereotyping is to be found in the obituary of Charles Villiers Stanford, the composer (not included in this collection), who was, it was stated, 'though an Irishman of the English occupation, every inch an Irishman; the quick acquisitive mind, the readiness of tongue, the appreciation of a good story and the power of telling it well, the ability to charm, and the love of a fight were qualities which endeared him to his friends but never left him in want of an enemy.' It must be said that this kind of thing was relatively rare, whether because many Irish obituaries were written by fellow Irishmen or because of a fastidiousness among those responsible in the paper itself.

The pattern of supporting beneficial reforms for the Irish majority, while defending the Union and the maintenance of law and order, remained the policy of *The Times* into the twentieth century. It was predictable that the paper should support the executions of the leaders of the 1916 rebellion and of Roger Casement, who was not even accorded an obituary, which could have recorded the achievements that had led to his being knighted. The treatment of Casement was a formidable challenge to the impartiality of a number of British institutions.

Whatever about the reaction to the 1916 rebellion, *The Times* tended to reflect the general acceptance even among unionists in the wake of the temporarily suspended Home Rule Act of 1914 that there would have to be some form of self-government for Ireland after the War. Significantly, after the peace in 1918 and the replacement of Geoffrey Dawson as editor by Wickham Steed, *The Times* originated the scheme that eventually found expression in the Government of Ireland Act,

1920 with its home rule parliaments for Northern Ireland and what was called Southern Ireland. Prior to that, the Ulster unionist demand was to remain fully integrated in the United Kingdom and they were slow to see the opportunities the Government of Ireland Act was to offer for establishing a protestant state for a protestant people. The latter history of the Act as the charter for that state has tended to obscure the fact that it explicitly envisaged a future date of Irish union and created overarching institutions such as a Council of Ireland and an All-Ireland Court of Appeal out of which it was hoped that this union would grow. It was the rejection of it by nationalist leaders now bent on achieving a totally independent republic that deprived the Act of its unifying possibilities.

The rejection of the Government of Ireland Act by the Sinn Fein leadership and the ongoing assassinations of policemen led the Government to allow free rein to their security forces, the Black and Tans and the Auxiliary cadets. *The Times* joined in a crescendo of criticism of their disgraceful behaviour and was also highly critical of the hardline reaction of the Lloyd George government to the 74-day hunger strike to death in November 1920 of Terence MacSwiney, the Lord Mayor of Cork. Editorials argued for a settlement along the lines of that eventually agreed in December 1921 granting dominion status to Southern Ireland.

Significantly, when the leading Irish negotiators of that settlement, Arthur Griffith and Michael Collins, died in the early months of independence the obituaries were uncritical. In the case of Collins there was virtually no reference to his part in the campaign of assassination from 1919 to 1921 that had led to his being demonised in Britain before the settlement. *The Times* had a special reason for being grateful to him as he had applied his ruthless efficiency to securing the safe return of their special correspondent A. B. Kay, who was kidnapped by the IRA in January 1922.

An important influence on the editorial policy of *The Times* in these years was Captain Herbert Shaw, a Dubliner who had served in the Irish administration and was one of the secretaries to the Irish Convention of 1917–18 where the moderate elements of unionism and nationalism had tried to broker a settlement. It was Shaw who penned *The Times* editorial entitled 'Playing the Game' on the occasion of the opening of the Northern Ireland Parliament in 1921 by King George V that was influential in pushing the Government towards negotiations with the Sinn Fein leaders. He was the author of a number of notable obituaries on Irish figures of that period, some of which, such as that on William T. Cosgrave, did not appear until well after his own death in 1946. Others were written by Michael MacDonagh, the journalist champion and historian of the Irish Party, and the unionist John Healy, editor of the *Irish Times*, and Dublin correspondent of *The Times* from 1894 until 1934.

The creation of an independent state covering most of the island of Ireland did not diminish the coverage of Irish affairs in *The Times*. The Irish were still regarded as part of the broader British family, albeit that their political leaders seemed to want to loosen their ties with it. Even the neutrality in the Second World War did not alter this, perhaps because the Irish of every tradition were such a presence in the British war effort. Churchill spoke for many in Britain when at the end of the war, having criticised Irish neutrality and paid tribute to 'the thousands of southern Irishmen who hastened to the battle-front to prove their ancient valour', he expressed the hope that the two peoples would walk together in mutual comprehension and forgiveness.

However, in the quarter of a century after the Second World War Irish political life, both north and south of the border, ceased to command attention in the British media. Even then, a fair coverage of Irish subjects was maintained in *The Times* obituaries columns. There may have been a bias towards individuals and institutions that retained to some extent a broader British identity or made an impact in Britain and might be presumed to be of more interest to the readership but it did not preclude coverage of significant figures from other strands of Irish life, especially those from the literary and artistic community. The outbreak of violence in Northern Ireland around 1970 brought Ireland centre stage once more and this has been reflected in an even more comprehensive coverage of Irish subjects in the obituaries columns.

Meanwhile, in the course of the twentieth century, there had been significant developments in the paper in the organisation of obituaries loosening the connection of that part of the paper with those who formulated editorial policy. From 1920 there was a separate obituaries department with its own editor. While obituaries had been prepared in advance since the editorship of John Delane (1841–1877), Colin Watson, who was obituaries editor from 1956 to 1981, embarked on a policy of commissioning advance pieces on a wider variety of living subjects than had been the case previously. Very often, those commissioned to write them were not journalists or even professional writers. In general, they were recruited having regard to their knowledge of the subject rather than with an eye to providing a particular viewpoint. In the case of Irish subjects the authors were generally found in Ireland. So it is that more recent Irish obituaries have often not reflected an English viewpoint, let alone that inside *The Times* – although the authors, if they were doing their job, have been conscious, when writing, that their readership would be largely English.

Despite this general trend, unexpected deaths of notable figures have, on occasion, still thrown the obituaries department back on its own resources. So, when Brian Faulkner died unexpectedly in 1978, Colin Watson ran up a superb obituary that reflected the paper's sympathy for Faulkner's brave effort to lead a cross-community executive. Three years earlier in 1975 the death at an advanced age of Eamon de Valera, which cannot have been unexpected, was marked by a much praised obituary involving substantial insider input by the celebrated leader writer Owen Hickey into a piece prepared originally by the former editor of the *Irish Times* Alec Newman. Hickey, born in Ireland and, incidentally, a grandson of the novelist Canon Hanney (George Bermingham), was an invaluable source of knowledge and understanding about matters Irish for *The Times* throughout most of the second half of the twentieth century.

The lack of total identification between the editorial policy of the paper and the obituaries that evolved through the twentieth century was never better illustrated than in the case of Sean MacBride, who died in 1988. He had been commander-in-chief of the IRA in post-independence Ireland before becoming a government minister and finally a human rights activist honoured by being awarded both the Nobel and Lenin peace prizes. An obituary prepared by the present writer that was quite laudatory but not uncritical, was followed a couple of days later by an editorial headed 'His infamous career' berating him as a man who was to the end of his days a cosmopolitan high priest of the cult of violence directed at British victims.

It is a problem in compiling a volume of Irish obituaries to decide who ranks as sufficiently Irish to be considered for inclusion. One thinks of the remark attributed, probably unfairly, to the Irish-born Duke of Wellington that a horse is not an ass because he is born in an ass's stable. Obviously, birth outside Ireland, as in the case of Eamon de Valera, would be an inappropriate reason for exclusion. On the other hand, some persons of immense distinction born in Ireland have little meaningful connection with the country. I have been disinclined to include them. In the case of others, of which William Orpen and George Bernard Shaw are examples, omission is referable to the failure of the obituary to do justice to the Irish dimension of the subject's life.

At the same time I have been concerned not to confine the selection to those who have spent their lives in Ireland or done their significant work there. In particular, it seemed to me important to represent those generally identified as Irish who made an impact not only in Britain but in the Empire and in the United States.

In choosing from a vast store of Irish obituaries over the years, I have sought to strike a balance between the significance of the subject and the quality of the piece. Clearly, any person opening a volume such as this would expect that there would be obituaries of Daniel O'Connell, Charles Stewart Parnell or Eamon de Valera in the political sphere or of William Butler Yeats or James Joyce among the writers. After persons of that calibre, the choices I have made have been affected by the quality of the obituary as well as the significance of the subject. Is it comprehensive or entertaining? Is it the best thing that has been written on a particular person? Is it too long? I have tended to favour those obituaries that give a picture of the person as well as an account of their life's work. I have also favoured those that paint the subject 'warts and all' over less discriminating eulogies. In older pieces I confess to having been attracted by those that betray contemporary attitudes and prejudices. In omitting certain obituaries I have had some regard to their being included in other anthologies of *Times* obituaries.*

I have sought to achieve a better gender balance than, for understandable reasons, was achieved in the actual obituaries in previous generations. I have also tried to represent a variety of spheres of Irish life, including in particular the arts, literature, business, sport, entertainment, science as well as the politicians, churchmen, lawyers, military men, public servants and academics that were preponderant in *The Times* obituaries of older vintage. In an earlier period other obituaries were often skimpy. In the case of the arts, literature and even science they were sometimes marred by an excessive preoccupation with the subject's work to the exclusion of their life and personality and not couched in terms readily understood by the general reader.

I have included a number of largely forgotten figures who have never been the subject of a full biography or have not made it even into the *Dictionary of National Biography*, which is sketchy in its recent Irish coverage. In one or two cases I have felt inspired by the observation of Brendan Bracken in the tribute he contributed anonymously to *The Times* in 1928 about his mother that 'one of the best services performed by *The Times* are the notices it publishes of gentle quiet lives which add much to the common stock but whose quality makes no appeal to the busy art of modern publicity.'

As the book celebrates links between *The Times* and Ireland, I have included a number of Irish persons who have worked for *The Times* beginning with William Howard Russell and culminating with William Casey, the editor from 1948 to 1952. In their different ways, their lives are illustrative of the infinite complexity of the British-Irish relationship.

I have felt deeply honoured by Ian Brunskill's invitation to edit this volume. It is the culmination of a happy association with the obituaries department dating back to 1969, when I was a young law lecturer and barrister in London. I have prepared more than a century of obituaries over the years. From the early days when Colin Watson, Peter Davies and Juliet Lygon were in charge to more recent times when Peter Strafford, Tony Howard and Ian Brunskill were the obituaries editors, I have been the recipient of much encouragement and unfailing courtesy from those working in the obituaries department. For that I am truly grateful. I am also grateful to the librarians and archivists in the paper for sourcing obituaries. I like to think that coverage of deceased Irish persons by *The Times* contributes to the mutual comprehension between the people of our two islands which is much to be desired.

* See Frank Roberts ed., *Obituaries from the Times 1961–1970* (1975); Frank Roberts ed., *Obituaries from the Times 1971–75* (1978); Frank Roberts ed., *Obituaries from the Times 1951–1960* (1979); David Heaton and John Higgins ed., *Lives Remembered: The Times Obituaries of 1991* (1991); David Heaton and John Higgins ed., *The Times Obituaries 1992: Lives Remembered* (1992); Anthony Howard and David Heaton, *Lives Remembered Obituaries from 1993* (1993); Ian Brunskill ed., *Great Lives: A Century in Obituaries* (The Times 2005); Ian Brunskill and Andrew Sanders ed. *Great Victorian Lives: An Era in Obituaries* (The Times 2007); Michael Tillotson and Guy Liardet ed. *Great Military Lives* (The Times 2008); Sue Corbett *Great Women's Lives: A Celebration in Obituaries* (The History Press 2014); Anna Temkin ed., *Great Lives: A Century in Obituaries*, 2nd edition (The Times 2015).

HENRY GRATTAN

WITH UNFEIGNED CONCERN we announce ... the much-to-be-lamented death of the Right Hon. Henry Grattan. The dissolution of this intrepid patriot would have been a subject of deep regret to the empire at large, had not the decline of his intellectual as well as vital powers been more recently observed. To his own immediate countrymen it is a source of profound and even filial sorrow ...

Mr Grattan came into Parliament about the year 1773. Towards the close of the American war he carried against both the English and Irish Government the repeal of those statutes which had given the British Parliament, and in some respects the Privy Council of England, an absolute control over the legislature of his native country. He has been since the year 1790 the strenuous, persevering, and powerful advocate for an entire abolition of the penal laws against the Catholics. This measure, in the separate Parliament of Ireland, he repeatedly declared to be essential to the complete deliverance of that country from the yoke of the British ministers, as, since the Union, he has, in the language of Mr Pitt, described Catholic emancipation to be a necessary step towards giving both countries the full benefit of that important measure. Mr Grattan has long laboured under dropsy of the chest. It is well known that he was conscious of his approaching dissolution; and that, when he devoted "his last breath to his country," he was sensible that his appearance in Parliament, for the pious purpose of recommending to the House of Commons the cause so near his heart, must tend to accelerate that mournful sacrifice. His enfeebled frame did not second the aspirings of his bold and fervent spirit: he was doomed to bequeath emancipation as a legacy – not to bestow it as a gift.

Mr Grattan's eloquence was peculiar and original. It resembled that of no speaker that we have ever heard. His voice was naturally feeble, but practice made it audible; and laborious effort, combined with a careful and studied articulation, rendered his high tones so piercing that none of them were lost. Mr Grattan had no wit, or rather, in Parliament, he did not exhibit any. He seldom discussed the details of any question, but fastened on a few of the leading principles, which he developed and illustrated with singular strength of language, and copious felicity of imagination. His sentences were full of antithesis; and, rather than lose that favourite structure of expression, he would build it up occasionally of common-place or even puerile matter. His arguments were frequently a string of epigrams. His retorts and personal invectives were distinguished by a keen and pithy sarcasm, which told upon every nerve of his ill-starred opponent. There was, nevertheless, an earnestness and solemnity, an innate and manifest consciousness of his own rectitude, about the man, which taught his hearers to respect and admire him when he most failed to convert them to the opinions of which he was the advocate. Mr Grattan, in society, was playful and simple as a child: irritable, perhaps, in a public assembly, he was elsewhere the very soul of courtesy, complacency, and cheerfulness.

Mr Grattan's property consisted for the most part of the sum of 50,000*l*, which had been tendered to him by his country, and it was honourably earned. He died at his house in Baker-street, Portman-square.

DANIEL O'CONNELL

24 MAY 1847

WE BELIEVE THERE is no doubt that Mr O'Connell expired on Saturday, the 15th of this month, at Genoa. He yielded up his latest breath at the distance of many hundred miles from the remains of the humble dwelling which became remarkable as his birthplace. In a remote part of the county of Kerry is a village called Cahirciveen, and within one mile of that obscure locality may be found a place bearing the name of Carhen. The latter was for many years the residence of Morgan O'Connell, father of the extraordinary man to an account of whose life and character these columns are assigned. In that most desolate region was Daniel O'Connell born, on the 6th of August, 1775 – a date which he was accustomed to notice with no small complacency, for he took much pleasure in reminding the world that he was born in the year during which our American colonies began to assert their independence, and he sometimes succeeded in persuading his admirers that that incident, taken in connexion with others, shadowed forth his destiny as a champion of freedom. Antecedently to his thirteenth year he received little instruction beyond what pedagogues of the humblest order are capable of imparting; but that class in Kerry are considerably superior to their brethren in other parts of Ireland, and upon the whole it could not be said that even his early education was by any means neglected. About this time his father's pecuniary circumstances began evidently to improve; his uncle, the owner of Darrynane, though long married, had no issue; he declared Daniel O'Connell to be his favourite nephew, and therefore the friends of "the fortunate youth" thought that no expense should be spared upon the intellectual culture of one whose acknowledged talents and brightening prospects rendered him what is called "the hope of the family." In those days the Irish members of the Church of Rome were just beginning to exercise a few of the privileges which they now most amply enjoy; and at a place

3

called Redington, in Long Island, one of their priests, a Mr Harrington, had opened a school. Thither young Daniel O'Connell was sent in the year 1788, and there he remained for about 12 months, when he and his brother Maurice took leave of Mr Harrington, with the view of proceeding to one of the Roman Catholic seminaries on the continent. Their first destination was Louvain, but immediately on their reaching that place it was found that Daniel had passed the admissible age; he, however, attended the classes as a volunteer, till fresh instructions could arrive from Kerry. At the end of six weeks the O'Connells proceeded from Louvain to St Omer, and finally to the English College at Douay, where the subject of this memoir pursued his studies with much distinction. Before he quitted St Omer the President of that College, in a letter still preserved, ventured to foretell that his pupil was "destined to make a remarkable figure in society." On the 21st of December, 1793, Mr O'Connell, being then in the 18th year of his age, quitted Douay, and reached England, without encountering any adventures, save those which sprang from the insults that the revolutionary party were accustomed to inflict upon every one whom they supposed to be an Englishman, or an ecclesiastic, or even a student of divinity. The scenes which he witnessed in France caused Mr O'Connell frequently to declare that in those days he was almost a Tory. He certainly was not then a revolutionist, for the moment he reached the English packet-boat he and his brother tore the tricolour cockades from their hats, and trampled them on the deck. Those sentiments, however, he did not long continue to cherish, for a year had not quite passed away when he exchanged them for doctrines which strongly savoured of Liberalism. It is understood that at a very early age he was intended for the priesthood. Those Irish Roman Catholics who evinced any aptitude for a learned profession found none other open to them in the days of O'Connell's boyhood. But it is difficult to imagine any one more incapable than he was of maintaining even those outward signs of holiness which are generally observed by the ecclesiastics of his persuasion. An overflow of animal spirits rendered him, not merely a gay, but an obstreperous member of society, and his riotous jocularity acknowledged no limits.

All idea, therefore, of his becoming a priest, if ever seriously entertained, must have been abandoned before he reached the age of 19, for he was then devoted to anything rather than the service of the altar. Hare hunting and fishing were amongst his darling pastimes; and these means of relaxation continued to fill his leisure hours, even when his years had approximated to three score and ten. From 17 to 70 the energy of his intellect and the ardour of his passions seemed to suffer no abatement. A large and well used law library, numerous *liaisons*, a pack of beagles, and a good collection of fishing tackle, attested the variety of his tastes and the vigour of his constitution. Before he had completed his 20th year he became a student of Lincoln's-inn, into which society he was received on the 30th of January, 1794. Previous to the year 1793 Roman Catholics were not admitted to the bar, and Mr O'Connell was amongst the earliest members of that Church who became candidates for legal advancement. His entrance upon the profession of the law, as a barrister, took place on the 19th of May, 1798, and it must be acknowledged that he spared no pains to qualify himself for that arduous pursuit. Though of a joyous temperament, self-indulgent, and in some respects sensual, he still was not indisposed to hard labour, so that he became almost learned in the law before he ever held a brief. Conformably with the custom of the Irish bar, Mr O'Connell prepared himself for any sort of business that might come within his reach, whether civil or criminal – whether at common law or in equity. There are men in the Temple who would laugh to scorn the best specimens of his special pleading; and conveyancers in Lincoln's-inn who hold very cheap his skill in their branch of the profession; but in 1798 there was no man of the same standing on the Munster circuit, or at the Irish bar, who knew more of his profession than young Mr O'Connell; and in a short time he became a very efficient lawyer of all-work. The sanguinary rebellion of that period was then at its height, and he probably cherished in his heart as much of the jacobinical principle as was consistent with the character of a thorough Roman Catholic. But he was a lawyer, and being also a shrewd politician, he foresaw that of those United Irishmen who escaped from the field many would be likely to perish on the scaffold; with great prudence, therefore, and most loyal valour, he joined the yeomanry and supported the Government. Again, when it became necessary to reorganize a yeomanry force in 1803, he once more took his place in "the Lawyers' Corps." Many anecdotes have been at various times retailed, showing the pains which he took to mitigate the atrocities of that period; and, however indifferent he might be as to the remote tendency of his political proceedings, he certainly manifested throughout his life a strong aversion to actual deeds of blood.

Mr O'Connell had been four years at the bar, and had entered upon the 28th year of his age, before he contracted matrimony. His father and his uncle pointed out more than one young lady of good fortune whose alliance with him in marriage they earnestly desired; but he felt bound in honour not to violate the vows which he had interchanged with his cousin, Mary, the daughter of Dr O'Connell of Tralee. Her father was esteemed in his profession, but her marriage portion was next to nothing; and great therefore was the displeasure which this union occasioned. It took place privately on the 23d of June, 1802, at the lodgings of Mr James Connor, the brother-in-law of the bride, in Dame-street, Dublin. This occurrence for some months remained a secret, but eventually all parties became reconciled. Mrs O'Connell was deservedly esteemed by her family and friends, while she enjoyed a large share of her husband's affection.

Having now reached that period when Mr O'Connell embarked in a profession and assumed the responsibilities of domestic life, we may arrest for a moment the current of his biography, in order to advert briefly to his family and connexions. Nothing is more frequent in society than a demand for "the real history of these O'Connells." It is often asked have they been "jobbers, hucksters, pedlars, smugglers, and everything base and beggarly? or are they the lineal descendants of the Sovereign Lords of Iveragh, and have they, through successive generations, preserved the purity of gentle blood and the reputation of honourable men?" Alas! who can tell? If there be one thing in this world less worthy of credence than another it is an Irish pedigree. In England the "visitations" are carefully preserved; the records of the Herald's College in this country, and the business of that office, are conducted quite in the manner of other public departments. Here all proceedings are so much according to law, that every family which preserves its land can prove its pedigree. But, amidst confiscations, burnings, rebellions, and massacres, the regularity of official records can never be maintained, and the evidences of succession degenerate into oral tradition. The ancient Greek, who happened to distinguish himself, usually traced his origin to a deified ancestor; the modern Irishman who makes a noise in the world, always avers that he is descended from a Sovereign Prince; while the world looks on, and with contemptuous impartiality pronounces both genealogies to be equally fabulous. Dismissing, therefore, all idle speculation respecting the early history of the O'Connells, it may be shortly stated that this family originally established itself in Limerick; that about the beginning of the seventeenth century they transferred their residence to the barony of Iveragh, in the western extremity of Kerry; but, being deeply implicated in the rebellion of 1641, they found it convenient to seek shelter in Clare. To this migration Daniel O'Connell, of Aghgore, formed an exception, and he contrived to keep his little modicum of land by not yielding to that appetite for insurrection. His son, John O'Connell of Aghgore and Darrynane, took the field in 1689 at the head of a company of Foot, which he raised for the service of James II., and having served at the siege of Derry, as well as at the battles of the Boyne and Aughrim, was included in the capitulation of Limerick. His eldest son died without issue, but his second son, Daniel, having married a Miss Donoghue, became the father of 22 children. The second of this gentleman's sons was Morgan, who married Catherine, the daughter of Mr John O'Mullane, of Whitechurch, in the county of Cork; and the eldest son of this Morgan was the extraordinary individual whose death we have now to record. Although nothing can be more absurd than to claim for him an illustrious descent, yet several of his relatives and connexions were respectable, and some of the number have served with distinction in the French and Austrian armies. But, sooth to say, his father was a most undignified person:- a very painstaking, industrious man, whose thoughts never wandered from the main chance; who held a good farm and kept a large shop, or rather a sort of miscellaneous store, which ministered to the limited wants of Cahirciveen and its rude neighbourhood; who is said to have been most adroit in the arts by which money may be acquired, not only in those of the fair dealer, but in those of the free trader. Almost every one who lived on the western coast of Ireland was, in those days, more or less of a smuggler; therefore Maurice of Darrynane and Morgan of Carhen were not much worse than their neighbours in carrying on the contraband or the wrecking trade; and thus did the elder brother keep his acres free from incumbrance, while the younger scraped together pence and pounds, till he was able to acquire a few additional acres at low rents and under long leases, by which means he ascended into that detested class known by the designation of Irish middlemen. He lived to see his son a prosperous barrister, and the acknowledged heir to Maurice of Darrynane; old Morgan therefore left at his death, which took place in 1809, a very considerable portion, if not the greater part, of all that he possessed to his second son, Mr John O'Connell, of Grena.

In the year 1802 Mr O'Connell found himself under the displeasure of his relatives, and obliged to contend with the difficulties which are inseparable from a growing family and a narrow income. The legislative union had then been only just consummated; his first popular harangue, however, was delivered at a meeting of the citizens of Dublin, assembled on the 13th of January, 1800, to petition against the proposed incorporation of the Irish with the British Parliament. The public have long been familiar with the grounds upon which Mr O'Connell was accustomed to urge the claims of his native country to the possession of an independent legislature. It is believed that he never urged those claims with more effect than in his earlier speeches; the very first of which has been extolled as a model of eloquence. It is a generally received opinion that, from the very starting point of his career, he displayed every quality, good and evil, of a perfect demagogue; and, those pernicious accomplishments being once known to the public of Ireland, his success at the bar ceased to be problematical. The great body of the Roman Catholics were only too happy to patronize an aspiring barrister of their own persuasion; the attorneys on the Munster circuit found that his pleadings were much more worthy of being relied on than those of almost any other junior member of the bar; and soon this description of business poured into his hands so abundantly, that he employed first one, and then a second amanuensis. At *nisi prius* his manner alone was enough to persuade an Irish jury that his client must be right. His anticipation of victory always seemed so unfeigned that, aided by that and other arts, he seldom failed to create in the minds of every jury a prejudice in favour of whichever party had the good fortune to have hired his services. His astonishing skill in cross-examination; the caution, dexterity, and judgment which he displayed in conducting a cause; the clearness and precision with which he disentangled the most intricate mass of evidence, especially in matters of account, procured for him the entire confidence of all those who had legal patronage to dispense. But his not being a Protestant excluded him from much valuable business. A Roman Catholic in those days was never heard in the courts of justice with that gracious approbation which encourages a youthful advocate; before a common jury, however, no man could be more successful than the subject of the present memoir, for this, among other reasons, that a large fund of the broadest humour usually enabled him to have the laugh on his side. In the Rolls Court also, where Mr Curran at that time presided, Mr O'Connell was in the highest favour.

During the few years which elapsed between 1800 and the death of Mr Pitt, two or three demonstrations were made in Dublin against the legislative union, in all of which Mr O'Connell continued to gain reputation as a popular leader; but he had not yet been recognized as the great agent of what was called "Catholic Emancipation." For some time after the extinction of the Irish Parliament it was believed that the expectations excited by Mr Pitt respecting a repeal of the penal laws would be realized. But three successive Ministries occupied the Cabinet without possessing ability, or perhaps inclination, to effect that object when at length Mr Perceval was annnounced as the head of the

Government amidst all the triumph of a grand No Popery agitation. Antecedently to this period, feeble efforts were occasionally made by the Roman Catholics, in which Mr O'Connell more or less participated, but it was not until the year 1809 that the struggles of that party became consolidated into a system and raised to the importance of a popular movement. The Orange party, of course, became alarmed; the measures of Government began to assume a definite and forcible character, obsolete statutes were called into activity, and fresh powers obtained from the Legislature. Some Roman Catholics of high rank, and others of good station, were prosecuted in the Court of King's Bench. Numerous *ex officio* informations were filed; and the Irish Attorney-General made war upon the newspapers of Dublin with unexampled vigour and pertinacity. It happened, however, that during the prosecutions of that period Mr O'Connell appeared more frequently as an advocate than in any other capacity. Amongst the most remarkable of his speeches, and probably the ablest that he ever delivered at the bar, was his defence of Mr Magee, the proprietor and publisher of the *Dublin Evening Post*, a gentleman whom Mr Saurin, the Attorney-General of that day, conceived it to be his duty to prosecute for a libel on the Government. It need scarcely be stated that in almost all the political trials which took place in Ireland during the early part of the present century, Mr O'Connell was counsel for the accused; and, although proceedings of that nature in Dublin are usually marked by extreme intemperance on both sides, yet this characteristic of Irish litigation was never carried beyond the height which it attained while Mr Saurin was first law officer of the Crown. His mode of conducting prosecutions betrayed feelings of such bitter animosity, that Mr O'Connell could never hope to attain the objects of his ambition if he allowed any opportunity to escape of vituperating the Attorney-General; and the public of the present age will readily believe that his modes of attack were such as would, in England, excite universal disapprobation. Almost every one recollects that these proceedings on the part of the Irish Government proved wholly unsuccessful. Roman Catholic delegates might be dispersed under the Convention Act, a committee of the Roman Catholics might be suppressed under some other statute, a new bill might be introduced to declare a certain mode of associating illegal; but Mr O'Connell made it his boast that "so long as the right of petition existed he should be able to manufacture some device" by means of which the war of agitation could still be successfully waged. Whether his followers were called Pacificators in Conciliation-hall, or Repealers on Mullaghmast; whether they went by the name of delegates or committee-men, associators or liberators; patriots or precursors; no matter what the name or the pretence might be, the purpose never was anything else than to carry on in Dublin a sort of sham Parliament, which in the first place was used to obtain a repeal of the penal laws; in the second, to collect and administer that annual tribute called "the rent;" and in the third, to cajole and amuse the ignorant portion of the Irish people with that pestilent dream – an independent legislature. Of this machinery Mr O'Connell was at all times the moving agent. Whoever could consent to become a puppet and permit the chief showman to pull the wires, might assure himself of occupation for all his leisure time, and flattery enough to satiate the grossest appetite; but woe be unto him that dared to have an opinion of his own; for the colossal agitator in ascending his "bad eminence" seemed to derive especial pleasure from trampling under foot his rash and luckless rivals. The history of the years which elapsed between the development of Roman Catholic agitation in 1809 and its signal victory in 1829 discloses just this much respecting Daniel O'Connell; that he was sometimes the mere mouthpiece, and occasionally the ruler, guide, and champion of the Romish priesthood; that he maintained a "pressure from without," which caused not only the Irish but the Imperial Government to betray apprehension as well as to breathe vengeance; and that he found or created opportunities, during this period of his life, to display in his own person every attribute of a democratic idol; and few readers require to be reminded that the history of all the men who form this class but too plainly shows in what a high degree the vices of their character predominate over the virtues. To sustain himself in the position which O'Connell held throughout the meridian of his career required great animal energy and unwearied activity of mind. He possessed both. Long before he reached middle life he had become the most industrious man in Ireland. As early as 5 o'clock in the morning his matins were concluded, his toilet finished, his morning meal discussed, and his amanuensis at full work; by 11 he was in court; at three or half-past attending a board or a committee; later in the evening presiding at a dinner, but generally retiring to rest at an early hour, and not only abstaining from the free use of wine, but to some extent denying himself the national beverage of his country.

He was often heard to say, "I am the best abused man in all Ireland, or perhaps in all Europe." Amongst those who delighted to pour upon him the vials of their wrath, the municipal authorities of Dublin were perhaps the most prominent. The old corporation of that city was so corrupt, so feeble, and so thoroughly Orange in its politics, that Mr O'Connell reckoned confidently upon "winning golden opinions" from his party, while he indulged his own personal vengeance, by making the civic government of Dublin an object of his fiercest hostility. In the year 1815 this feud had attained to its utmost height, and various modes of overwhelming their tremendous adversary were suggested to the corporators; but at length shooting him was deemed the most eligible. This manner of dealing with an enemy is so perfectly Hibernian, that in Dublin it could not fail to meet with entire and cordial acceptance. At that time a Mr D'Esterre, who had been an officer of marines, was one of those members of the Dublin corporation who struggled the hardest for lucrative office. The more knowing members of that body hinted to him that an affair of honour with O'Connell would make his fortune. To such advisers the death of either party would be a boon, for the one was a rival and the other an enemy. O'Connell had publicly designated the municipality of Dublin as a "beggarly corporation," and upon this a quarrel was founded by their champion, Mr D'Esterre, who walked about armed with a bludgeon, threatening to inflict personal chastisement on his adversary. The habits of thinking which then prevailed in Ireland admitted of no other course than that Mr O'Connell should demand satisfaction. Both parties, attended by their friends, met on the 31st of January, 1815, at a place called Bishop's Court, in the county of Kildare. It sometimes happens that a man displays unusual gaiety when he is sick at heart; and never did the jocularity of O'Connell appear more exuberant than on the morning of that day when he went forth to destroy the life of his adversary or to sacrifice his own. Sir Edward Stanley attended Mr D'Esterre, and Major Macnamara was the friend of Mr O'Connell. At the first fire D'Esterre fell mortally wounded. A gamester would have betted five to one in his favour. Familiarized with scenes of danger from early youth, his courage was of the highest order; practised in the use of the pistol, it was said that he could "snuff a candle at twelve paces," while Mr O'Connell's peaceful profession caused him to seem – as opposed to a military man – a safe antagonist, and this, added to D'Esterre's supposed skill as a shot, promised assured success to the champion whom the Orange corporation "sent forth to do battle" with the popish Goliah. But the lifeless corpse of the real aggressor bore its silent and impressive testimony to the imperfect nature of all human calculations. Mr O'Connell, though less culpable than his victim, still seemed conscious of having committed a great crime; and, influenced by a keen but imperfect remorse, he expressed the deepest contrition. It is, however, not the fact that he at that time "registered" his celebrated "vow" against the use of duelling pistols. On the contrary, he engaged in another affair of honour before finally abandoning the *dernier resort* of bullets and gunpowder. Mankind with one voice applauded his peaceful resolution the moment it was announced, but they were equally unanimous in condemning the license with which he scattered insult when he had previously sworn to refuse satisfaction. In a few months after the fatal event just recorded Mr O'Connell received a communication tending towards hostility from Sir Robert (then Mr) Peel, who at that time filled the office of Chief Secretary to the Lord Lieutenant of Ireland. Sir Charles Saxton, on the part of Mr Peel, had an interview first with Mr O'Connell, and afterwards with the friend of that gentleman, Mr Lidwell. The business of exchanging protocols went on between the parties for three days, when at length Mr O'Connell was taken into custody and bound over to keep the peace towards all his fellow subjects in Ireland; thereupon Mr

Peel and his friend came to this country and eventually proceeded to the continent. Mr O'Connell followed them to London, but the metropolitan police, then called "Bow-street officers," were active enough to bring him before the Chief-Justice of England, when he entered into recognizances to keep the peace towards all His Majesty's subjects; and so ended an affair which might have compromised the safety of two men who since that time have filled no small space in the public mind.

The period which this narrative has now reached was still many years antecedent to the introduction of the Roman Catholic Relief Bill. Down to that moment Mr O'Connell prosecuted with unabated vigour his peculiar system of warfare against the supporters of Orange ascendancy, while he pursued his avocations as a lawyer with increasing and eminent success. As early as the year 1816 his professional position quite entitled him to a silk gown, but his creed kept him on the outside of the bar, where he continued to enjoy the largest and most lucrative business that ever rewarded the labours of a junior barrister. Meanwhile that body, called the Catholic Association, with O'Connell at its head, carried on the trade of agitating the Irish populace. The latter years of the Regency were marked by a new and more soothing policy towards Ireland. Upon the accession of George IV. he visited that country; in the early part of his reign the principle of conciliating the O'Connell party was maintained and extended; the Liberalism of the Canning policy began to prevail; "Emancipation" was made an "open question," and even in 1825 the demand for religious equality seemed nearly established. Mr O'Connell declared himself willing to give up the forty-shilling freeholders – willing to sacrifice the lowest of his countrymen for the sake of the highest – to limit the democratic power in order that the aristocracy of the Roman Catholics should have seats in Parliament and silk gowns at the bar. The Parliamentary career of him – the "member for all Ireland" – now more immediately claims our attention; and it naturally takes its commencement from the first occasion upon which he was returned for Clare. A vacancy having occurred in the representation of that county, a gentleman called O'Gorman Mahon, seized by a sudden freak, posted off to Dublin, entered the Roman Catholic Association, and proposed a resolution calling on O'Connell to become a candidate, which was unanimously carried. Though legal success was impossible the scheme just suited the Irish character. It afforded the prospect of "a row," and – more acceptable still – a piece of whimsical agitation. The long continued labours of O'Connell, extending even then over a period of more than twenty years, had rendered a maintenance of the penal laws a matter which the Government of that day considered to be, if not unjust, at least exceedingly unsafe; but it is believed that the great Clare election was the first event that awakened them to a full sense of danger. Mr O'Connell had been so often engaged on the wrong side of a legal controversy that he did not, upon this occasion, hesitate to promise his adherents an easy triumph. He averred that he could sit without taking the oaths; and his legal doctrines were supported by Mr Butler – a member of the English bar – while his pretensions as a candidate were sustained by the influence of the priesthood and the agency of the mob. Mr (afterwards Lord) Fitzgerald had represented Clare for many years, he was one of the resident gentry in a land where not to be an absentee is a virtue; his ancestors had long been settled in that county: he had faithfully maintained the interests, and spoken the sentiments of the popular party, and he was the firm friend of Roman Catholic emancipation; though only a tenth-rate man in Parliament, he was a first-rate man on the hustings, but his exertions at the Clare election were wholly and signally unsuccessful. The combined influence of the Government, of his own connexions, of the squirearchy, were scattered and set at nought by the power of the priesthood; and Mr O'Connell was, on the 6th of July, 1828, returned to Parliament by a large majority of the Clare electors. He lost no time in presenting himself at the table of the House of Commons, and expressed his willingness to take the oath of allegiance, but refusing the other oaths he was ordered to withdraw. Discussions in the house and arguments at the bar ensued; the speedy close of the session, however, precluded any practical result. Agitation throughout every part of Ireland now assumed so formidable a character that Ministers said they apprehended a civil war, and early in the next session the Roman Catholic Relief Bill was introduced and carried: Mr

O'Connell was, therefore, in the month of April, 1829, enabled to sit for Clare without taking the objectionable oaths; but it was necessary that a new writ should issue, under which he was immediately re-elected.

His return for Clare was amongst the proximate causes of "emancipation," but the "rent" was another source of still more active influence. Whether the scheme for raising that annual tribute originated in the fertile brain of Daniel O'Connell, or sprang from the perverted ingenuity of some less conspicuous person, certain it is that he was ultimately the great gainer. One of the earliest effects, however, of this financial project was most materially to aggravate that threatening aspect of public affairs which coerced the Duke of Wellington into proposing the Roman Catholic Relief Bill. A due regard to the precise succession of events makes it necessary here to notice an occurrence in itself of no great amount. On the 12th of February 1831, Messrs. O'Connell, Steel, and Barrett, were brought to trial, under an indictment, which charged them with holding political meetings contrary to the proclamation of the Lord Lieutenant; they pleaded guilty, but the act of Parliament under which they had been prosecuted expired pending the general election, and before they were brought up for judgment; they therefore escaped punishment, and the partizans of Mr O'Connell pointed to this negative victory as one of the proudest proofs that could be furnished of his infallibility as a lawyer. The death of George IV. of course led to a new Parliament, when Mr O'Connell withdrew from the representation of Clare and was returned for the county of Waterford. In the House of Commons, elected in 1831, he sat for his native county (Kerry). Dublin, the city in which the greater part of his life was spent, enjoyed his services as its representative from 1832 till 1836, when he was petitioned against and unseated, after a long contest, before a committee of the House of Commons. He then for some time took refuge in the representation of Kilkenny; but, at the general election in 1837, he was once more returned for the city of Dublin, and in 1841 for the county of Cork. Mr O'Connell had a seat in the House of Commons for 18 years, under the rule of three successive Sovereigns, during six distinct Administrations and in seven several Parliaments.

Every reader is aware that he took an active part in all the legislation of the period, as well as in the various struggles for power and place in which the political parties of this country have been engaged during the last 20 years; and right vigorously did he bear himself throughout those changing scenes ... His position as mouth piece of the priesthood and populace of Ireland usually made it necessary that the tone of his speeches should harmonize with the feelings of a rude and passionate multitude; but on subjects distinct from the party squabbles of his countrymen scarcely any one addressed the house more effectively than did Mr O'Connell; and it is generally acknowledged that in his speeches upon the great question of Parliamentary Reform he was surpassed by very few members of either house. Although it cannot be denied that the faults of his character were numerous, and the amount of his political offences most grievous in the sight of the public, yet he enjoyed some popularity even in this country, for many elements of greatness entered into the constitution of his mind. Had he not belonged to a prescribed race, been born in a semi-barbarous state of society, been blinded by the fallacies of an educational system which was based upon Popish theology; had not his intellect been subsequently narrowed by the influence of legal practice, and the original coarseness of his feelings been aggravated by the habits of a criminal lawyer and a mob-orator, he might have attained to enviable eminence, legitimate power, and enduring fame. But he "lived and moved and had his being" among wild enthusiasts and factious priests. Who then can marvel that his great faculties were perverted to sordid uses? Apparently indifferent to nobler objects of ambition, he devoted herculean energies to the acqui-sition of tribute from his starving countrymen, and bestowed upon his descendants the remnants of a mendicant revenue, when he might have bequeathed them an honourable name. His Parliamentary speeches are numerous; but the events of his Parliamentary life have been few in number; for it can scarcely be said that by his personal efforts any series of measures were either carried or defeated; yet several propositions have been brought forward in the House of Commons by Mr O'Connell. Amongst the most remarkable of these was his motion for a repeal of the Irish union, submitted to Parliament on the 22nd of April, 1834. Upon that occasion he addressed the house with his usual ability for upwards of six hours; and Mr Rice (now Lord Monteagle) occupied an equal length of time in delivering a reply which might advantageously have been reduced within half its dimensions. After a protracted debate the house divided, only one English member voting with Mr O'Connell, the numbers being 523 to 38. Those who supported him on that remarkable occasion consisted of persons returned to Parliament by the Irish priests, at his recommendation, and pledged to vote as he directed; they were therefore called "the O'Connell tail," and no doubt, when political parties were nicely balanced, the 30 or 40 members whom he commanded could easily create a preponderating influence. Thus it was his power which from 1835 to 1841 kept the Melbourne Ministry in office. To reward such important aid, the greater portion of the Irish patronage was placed at his disposal; and, to a great degree, the Irish policy of the Melbourne Government took its tone and character from the known sentiments of the demagogue upon whose fiat their existence depended.

The return of the party called Conservatives to power in 1841 was the signal for renewed agitation in Ireland, and this led to a lengthened interruption of Mr O'Connell's Parliamentary labours; here, therefore, a fitting opportunity presents itself to state one or two circumstances which were not immediately connected with that portion of his career. In 1834 he received a patent of precedence next after the King's second Serjeant. When the Dublin corporation was reformed he was elected Alderman, and filled the office of Lord Mayor in 1841–2. Mr O'Connell was appointed a magistrate of Kerry in 1835, but during the violent excitement which prevailed in 1843 the Lord Chancellor thought it necessary to remove him from the commission of the peace. He had controversies with all sorts of people, and was charged with sundry crimes, public and private; with having taken bribes from the millowners of Lancashire to speak against all short time bills; with having, even in his old age, seduced and abandoned more than one frail member of the fair sex; with having neglected and oppressed his tenantry to an extent which justified his being described as one of the most culpable individuals belonging to the vilest class in all Europe – the middlemen of Ireland. The evidence on which the other two accusations rest is rather doubtful; but the clearest possible proofs of his misconduct as a landlord were, in the year 1845, given to the public by *The Times* Commissioner. His expectations of office, of patronage, of power, and even of titular distinction are understood to have been quite as ardent as those of men who made no pretension to the liberal or the patriotic. It has been said, and generally believed, that he aimed at a baronetcy, and even hoped for a seat on the bench. The present age may well felicitate itself on the fact that O'Connell was not raised to judicial authority; for, instead of displaying any quality approaching to the calm impartiality of a judge, it had always been his practice to place himself in a position of hostility to every class, or at least to the representatives of every class in the community except the lowest. If the reader will only take the trouble to cast a glance over the index of any periodical publication which records the events of these times, he will find in letter o, under the head "O'Connell," – "Abuse of the Wesleyan Methodists; abuse of the Free-masons (by whom he was expelled in April, 1838); abuse of the Chartists; abuse of the English Radicals," nay, even of the English women; "abuse of the King of Hanover, of the late Duke of York, of George III., of George IV., of the English aristocracy, of the Irish aristocracy, of the French Government, and especially of the French King;" to say nothing of his onslaughts upon Perceval, Liverpool, Wellington, Peel, and the head of every Tory Ministry; upon the established church, on the Dublin University, on the judges of the land, – upon every class and institution except the Irish populace and the church of Rome; thus labouring, day and night, to maintain the spirit of agitation just short of the point at which men are accustomed to burst forth into open rebellion. This peculiar system of his reached its culminating point in 1843. It is scarcely necessary to remind the reader that, to some extent, the subject of this memoir belonged to a political party, and, though at times he would call his political friends "base, bloody, and brutal Whigs," yet, usually, when the Liberals occupied the Cabinet, he endeavoured to keep Ireland in a state favourable to Ministerial interests; but on all occasions when the Tories were in the ascendant, the full might of democratic agitation was brought into the field. In the autumn of 1841 Sir R. Peel became First Lord of the Treasury. Early in the spring of the following year a repeal of the union was demanded by every parish, village, and hamlet, from the Giant's Causeway to Cape Clear, while a fierce activity pervaded the Repeal Association. In the course of the next year (1843) "monster meetings" were held on the royal hill of Tara, on the Curragh of Kildare, on the Rath of Mullaghmast, and in a score of other wild localities; the Irish populace were drilled, and marshalled, and marched under appointed leaders, whose commands they obeyed with military precision, while the master-spirit who evoked and ruled this vast movement announced to all Europe that he was "at the head of 500,000 loyal subjects, but fighting men." The Irish press enjoined "Young Ireland" to imitate the example of 1798, and open rebellion was hourly apprehended. At length the crisis arrived; the great Clontarf meeting was summoned; a Government proclamation to prohibit that assemblage went forth, the military were called out, and the grand repeal agitation shrank into nothingness at the mere sight of artillery and Dragoons. The intended meeting at Clontarf was fixed for the 8th of October, 1843; on the 14th of that month O'Connell received notice to put in bail; on the 2nd of November proceedings commenced in the Court of Queen's Bench; the whole of Michaelmas Term was consumed by preliminary proceedings, and the actual trial did not begin until the 16th of January, 1844. Twelve gentlemen of the bar appeared on behalf of the Crown, and sixteen defended the traversers; who then can wonder that this remarkable trial did not close till the 12th of February? At length Mr O'Connell was sentenced to pay a fine of 2,000*l*. and be imprisoned for a year. He immediately appealed to the House of Lords by writ of error, but pending the proceedings on the question thus raised, he was sent to the Richmond Penitentiary, near Dublin, where for about three months he seemed to spend his days and nights most joyously. On the 4th of September the House of Lords reversed the judgment against O'Connell and his associates, Lords Lyndhurst and Brougham being favourable to affirming the proceedings in the Irish

Queen's Bench, while Lords Denman, Campbell, and Cottenham were of an opposite opinion. Mr O'Connell was therefore immediately liberated, and a vast procession attended him from prison to his residence in Merrion-square. From the moment that proceedings were commenced against him in the preceding year he became considerably crest-fallen. By the result of those proceedings his supposed infallibility as a lawyer ceased to be one of the dogmas of his party; the utter failure of the repeal movement greatly impaired his credit as a politician; the enormous costs of his defence nearly exhausted the funds of the repeal association; and in the altered state of his fortunes it became no easy matter for him to devise new modes of agitation. In 1845 he expressed his determination to repair to London during the ensuing session, to support a repeal of the Corn Laws. When he re-entered the House of Commons in 1846 it became evident to every observer that he had not only suffered in purse and popularity, but very materially also in health; that though his mind was still unclouded, his physical energy had disappeared, and that he could never again hope to be the hero of a "monster meeting." Still a considerable portion of his ancient influence had not yet passed out of his hands, and when the Whigs once more came into office he was restored to the commission of the peace, and exercised no small authority over the Irish patronage of the Crown, of course giving Lord John Russell, in return, the full benefit of his support, to the great dismay of the "Young Ireland" party, who regarded his adhesion to any British Ministry as a traitorous "surrender of repeal." Long and loud was the controversy between those belligerents; but the reader may well be spared the trouble of perusing even an abstract of the gross invectives poured on his head by a swarm of indignant followers, or a detail of the concessions wrung from him by a hard necessity. Unfortunately for O'Connell's posthumous fame, he now betrayed "a broken spirit," though not "a contrite heart;" and the popular influence, as well as the moral courage, of the old agitator sank under the pressure of his youthful and vigorous assailants; then came the famine, the falling off of "the rent," thin audiences at Conciliation-hall, and the indefinite postponement of repeal. Successfully to contend with these disasters would have demanded the energy of O'Connell's early days; but old, infirm, and broken-hearted, he was alike incapable of a manly struggle or a dignified retreat; and when once more he attempted to take his seat in Parliament, he seemed to be only the *débris* of an extinuished demagogue. To amplify the tale of his decline and fall would be inconsistent with the general tone of a narrative which has treated indulgently the memory of one who in his long life-time seldom spared a fallen adversary. In thus closing his history it may be well to avoid the contagion of his example, and to practise a forbearance of which he was incapable; for though to the crowd of his adherents he always seemed a munificent patron, yet small is the number of those who could sincerely say he had ever been a true friend or a generous enemy.

* * *

MARIA EDGEWORTH

28 MAY 1849

OF MARIA EDGEWORTH it may be said – even more emphatically than of her sister-novelist, Miss Burney – that she lived to become a classic. Her decease in her 83rd or 84th year can hardly be felt as a shock in the world of letters though it bereaves her home-circle of one whose many days were but so many graces – so actively unimpaired did her powers of giving and of receiving pleasure and instruction remain till a very late period of her existence. The story of Miss Edgeworth's life was some years since told by herself in her memoir of her father. She was born in England – the daughter of Mr Richard Lovell Edgeworth, by the first of that gentleman's four wives – and had reached the age of 13 ere she became an Irish resident. Fifty years or more have elapsed since her *Castle Rackrent* – the precursor of a copious series of tales, national, moral, and fashionable (never romantic) – at once established her in the first class of novelists, as a shrewd observer of manners, a warm-hearted gatherer of national humours, and a resolute upholder of good morals in fiction. Before her Irish stories appeared, nothing of their kind – so complete, so relishing, so familiar yet never vulgar, so humorous yet not without pathos – had been tendered to the public. Their effect was great not merely on the world of readers, but on the world of writers and politicians also. Sir Walter Scott assures us that when he began his Scottish novels it was with the thought of emulating Miss Edgeworth; while Mr O'Connell at a later period (if we are to credit Mr O'Neill Daunt) expressed substantial dissatisfaction because one having so much influence had not served her country as he thought poor Ireland could alone be served – by agitation. Prudence will allay, rarely raise, storms; and Prudence was ever at hand when Maria Edgeworth (to use Scott's phrase) "pulled out the conjuring wand with which she worked so many marvels." Herein lay her strength and herein also some argument for cavil and reservation on the part of those who love nothing which is not romantic. "Her extraordinary merit," happily says Sir James Mackintosh, "both as a moralist and as a woman of genius, consists in her having selected a class of virtues far more difficult to treat as the subject of fiction than others, and which had therefore been left by former writers to her."

To offer a complete list of Miss Edgeworth's fictions – closed, in 1834, by her charming and carefully wrought *Helen* – would be superfluous; but we may single out as three masterpieces, evincing the great variety of her powers, *Vivian*, *Tomorrow*, and *The Absentee*. Generally, Miss Edgeworth was happier in the short than in the long story. She managed satire with a delicate and firm hand, as her *Modern Griselda* attests. She was reserved rather than exuberant in her pathos. She could give her characters play and brilliancy when these were demanded as in "Lady Delacour;" she could work out the rise, progress, and consequences of a foible (as in *Almeria*) with unflinching consistency. Her dialogue is excellent; her style is in places too solicitously laboured, but it is always characteristic, yielding specimens of that pure and terse language which so many contemporary novelists seem to avoid on the maidservant's idea that "plain English" is ungenteel. Her tales are singularly rich in allusion and anecdote. In short, they indicate intellectual mastery and cultivation of no common order. Miss Edgeworth has herself confessed the care with which they were wrought. They owed much to her father's supervision; but this we are assured by her, was confined to the pruning of redundancies. In connexion with Mr Edgeworth the *Essay on Irish Bulls* was written; also the treatise on *Practical Education* … This brings us to speak of that large and important section of Maria Edgeworth's writings – her stories for children. Here as elsewhere, she was "nothing if not prudential;" and yet who has ever suceeeded in captivating the fancy and attention of the young as her Rosamonds and Lucys have done? In her hands the smallest incident rivetted the eye and heart, – the driest truth gained a certain grace and freshness …

If Miss Edgeworth's long literary life was usefully employed, so also were her claims and services adequately acknowledged during her lifetime. Her friendships were many; her place in the world of English and Irish society was distinguished. Byron (little given to commending the women whom he did not make love to, or who did not make love to him) approved her. Scott, addressed her like an old friend and a sister. There is hardly a tourist of worth or note who has visited Ireland for the last 50 years without bearing testimony to her value and vivacity as one of a large and united home circle. She was small in stature, lively of address, and diffuse as a letter-writer. To sum up it may be said that the changes and developments which have convulsed the world of imagination since Miss Edgeworth's career of authorship began have not shaken her from her pedestal nor blotted out her name from the honourable place which it must always keep in the records of European fiction.

TOM MOORE

1 MARCH 1852

THE ELEGY OF TOM MOORE should not contain one mournful or distressing note! Flourishing in an age of poets – of men who have stamped their characters upon the literature of their country and earned undying fame – he takes his ground as fairly as the best of them. Within his sphere he is unapproachable. He has little in common with the stormy passion of Byron; the philosophical grandeur of Coleridge is unknown to him; the muse of Scott and his own are scarcely kindred cousins; his productions have as little of the dreamy and mystical splendour of Shelley as they are allied to the elaborate and fatiguing epics of Southey; but within the circle of his own uncontested dominion he has poured forth strains as exquisite as any fancy ever clothed in sparkling verse to delight the jocund heart of man. The mind of Moore, from the moment that he took pen in hand, may be said to have been always in a state of pleasure. He has written satires as well as songs, and dealt with themes both sacred and profane: he has described the loves of angels and the holy piety of erring mortals; but, whatever the employment, one condition of feeling is always manifest. Most musical, most happy was his genius, and music and joyousness are careering in almost every syllable that he spoke ...

Thomas Moore was born in Dublin on the 30th of May, 1780, the son of a small tradesman, who afterwards became a quartermaster in the army. It is not easy to decide when he first attempted verse. Upon looking back he could not discover when he was not a scribbler. In his thirteenth year he was already a contributor to a magazine; in his fourteenth he had addressed a sonnet to his school-master; and some three years before he sent his productions to the Irish periodical he had distinguished himself in another branch of art by undertaking principal characters in amateur theatricals. Moore was privileged to be precocious without paying the penalty of precocity. When he was 12 years old he accompanied his father, a Roman Catholic, to a patriotic dinner held in honour of the French Revolution, then a recent event, and regarded, as he himself tells us, as a signal to the slave, wherever suffering, that "the day of his deliverance was near at hand." Men's hearts, it has been written, are cradled into poetry by wrong. The early genius of Moore was, no doubt, nurtured by the sufferings of his race, and maintained in vigour and freshness until the decaying music of his native land came to claim him wholly as her own. The act of Parliament having opened the University to Roman Catholics in 1793, the young poet immediately availed himself of his opportunity. The year following his admission, while still a child, he wrote and published a paraphrase of Anacreon's fifth ode, and then proceeded to the translation of other odes by the same poet, for which he vainly hoped the university board might deem him "deserving of some honour or reward." Disappointed in his expectation he nevertheless continued his task, and occupied himself in improving his verses and illustrating them by learned annotations, until he reached his 19th year, when he quitted Ireland for the first time, and set out for London "with the two not very congenial objects of keeping his terms in the Middle Temple and publishing by subscription his translation of *Anacreon*." The translation duly appeared in 1800. It was dedicated to George IV., then Prince of Wales, who, we may remark, received no further honour at the poet's hands.

In 1803 Moore had the misfortune to obtain worldly advancement. He was promoted to an official situation in Bermuda. The duties of the office were performed by a deputy, and the consequence, was great personal anxiety and heavy pecuniary loss to the poetical principal ...

Moore's birth and origin made him a Liberal and something more. He came into the world one of a then oppressed race. He was the contemporary and schoolfellow of an ardent band who believed all things lawful to the struggler for liberty, and his spirit went with them in their most daring aspirations. The hapless victims of their own rash, ill conceived, and unwarrantable projects for national emancipation were his chosen and beloved associates, and when he saw them sacrificed to their wild enthusiasm he cherished the passion that had consumed them and embalmed their memory in matchless melody and verse. In middle life Moore, favoured by the friendship of the great Whig chiefs, soothed by the concessions that had been made to his country and his creed, and warned by sober experience of the vanity of egregious expectation, settled down into a constitutional Whig; but at the starting point of his career he had as little affection for Whigs as for Tories. In the preface to one of a series of solemn satires, he speaks of both "factions" as "having been equally cruel to Ireland, and perhaps equally insincere in their efforts for the liberties of England."

Moore had no cause to remember with pleasure either the prose or the poetry of these satirical exercises. Serious satire was at no time his forte – his lively and delicate hand could hardly wield the heavy weaponry of Dryden and Pope. Greater success attended his efforts when at a later period of his life he divested himself of his sombre attire, and became as joyous in hate as he had been in love. *The Fudge Family*, written in 1817, *The Twopenny Postbag*, and similar productions full of point, wit, and polish, are unrivalled as political lampoons, and preserve to this hour, their first exquisite relish. The generous fancy of the Irish poet could not be happy steeped in bitterness, and to affect sternness was to languish and die. The objects of Moore's squib warfare were no doubt sufficiently conscious of the sharpness of an airy weapon, never otherwise than most dexterously handled by their foe; but we question whether they suffered half as much pain as they enjoyed pleasure from his lively feats. How could men be seriously angry with an adversary who simply tickled when he pretended to strike?

The apprenticeship of Moore was served when he commenced *The Irish Melodies* which have rendered his name famous wherever music is cherished. From that hour his genius triumphed, and most deservedly. Moore attributes all his poetical success to his strong and inborn feeling for music. There can be no doubt that his obligations to nature in this respect were very great. Music and poetry were wedded in his heart, and were inseparable. So intimately, indeed, were they united, that the sight of *The Irish Melodies* crowded together in one volume, unaccompanied by the notes with which they were always associated in his own mind, inflicted upon him positive pain. It was as if he saw the skeletons of his children ranged before him, deprived of the warm flesh and breathing form. To the reader the verses have beauty of their own, and charm irrespective of the strains by which they were suggested. Moore could no more unbind melody and language than he could gaze on female beauty and separate the notions of body and soul.

The publication of *The Irish Melodies* commenced in 1807, and, continued at intervals, was concluded in 1834. They have been translated into Latin, Italian, French, and Russian, and are familiar as proverbs amongst the fellow-countrymen of the poet, and indeed wherever English is understood and music loved. It is difficult for the critic to refer to them in too high a tone of panegyric. It may be true that force and dignity are wanting to some of those lyrics, that occasionally fancy labours until art becomes too evident in strained and frigid similes, that ornament at times overlays sentiment until nature pants beneath the glittering encumbrance; but it is equally certain that universal literature does not present a lovelier and more affecting tribute to a nation's minstrelsy than is found in *The Irish Melodies* of Thomas Moore. The love of country that pervades and inspires his theme, his simple tenderness of feeling, that at once strikes the heart as instantly to melt it, his facility of creation, linked with the glad appreciation of all that is beautiful in nature – the grace, the elegance, the sensibility, the ingenuity, that are never absent – the astonishing and thoroughly successful adaptation of sense to sound, of sweetest poetry to thrilling music, – are claims to admiration which the most prosaic of his species will find it impossible to resist or gainsay.

The year 1812 found Moore, in his 32nd year, enjoying well-earned fame, but on circumscribed ground. He had not as yet given to the world a long and continuous work, and shown how well he could sustain the brilliancy that seemed too keenly elaborate for a protracted effort. In that year, however, the poet resolved to take the field against his most favoured competitors, and to attempt a poem upon an Oriental subject. In 1817 *Lalla Rookh* appeared ... The poem was hailed with a burst of admiration from sceptics as well as believers.

And no wonder! It was a triple triumph of industry, learning, and genius. The broad canvas exhibited a gorgeous painting; from beginning to end the same lavish ornament, the same overpowering sweetness, the same variegated and delicate tracery, the same revelling of a spirit happy in its intense enjoyment of beauty that characterized the miniatures and gems that heretofore had proceeded from the artist's pencil. So far from betraying a diminution of power, or an inability to maintain his high-pitched note, the poet pursued his strain until he fairly left his reader languishing with a surfeit of luscious song, and faint from its oppressive odours. We peruse the romance, and marvel at the miraculous facility of a writer who has but to open his lips to drop emeralds and pearls, like the good princess in the fairy tale. Nor does astonishment cease when we learn, that eager and all but involuntary as the verse appears to issue from its source, the apparently effortless composition is actually a labour performed with all the diligence of the mechanic and all the forethought of science. In his life of Sheridan, Moore informs us that many of the *impromptu* jokes of Richard Brinsley owed much of their point and off-hand brilliancy to the time and pains previously bestowed upon their manufacture. His own seemingly spontaneous and easy cadences were wrought most patiently at the anvil. But the time spent in the composition of *Lalla Rookh*, though it extended over years, was as nothing compared with the time given to preparation for the subject. For months Moore saturated his mind with Oriental reading, in order to familiarize himself with Oriental illustration, and with the view especially of educating his fancy for its essential and peculiar work. The research and industry of the poet were immense. He tells us himself that "it was amidst the snows of two or three Derbyshire winters, in a lone cottage amongst the fields, that he found himself enabled by that concentration of thought, which retirement alone gives, to call up around him some of the sunniest of his eastern scenes." He had devoured every book he could get relating to the East, and did not rise from his occupation until he positively knew more of Persia than of his own country, and until his acclimated genius found it as easy to draw inspiration from the influences of a land he had never seen as from the living and silent forms by which, in his own country, he had been from his childhood surrounded. Eastern travellers and Oriental scholars have borne testimony to the singular accuracy of Moore's descriptive pen ... The poem, translated into Persian, has found its way to Ispalian, and is thoroughly appreciated on the shores of the Caspian. In London the poem looks like an exotic; there it is racy of the soil.

In the autumn of 1817, and in the fulness of his triumph, Moore visited Paris with Mr Rogers, and picked up, as we have already noted, the materials of his *Fudge Family*, a satire written on the plan of the *New Bath* Guide, and intended to help the political friends of the satirist at the expense of their opponents. Time has taken away from much of the interest that attaches to these squibs of the hour, but age can never blunt the point of their polished wit or dull its brilliancy. The popularity of the *Fudge Family* kept pace with that of *Lalla Rookh*. In 1819 the poet went abroad again, this time with Lord John Russell. The travellers proceeded in company by the Simplon into Italy, but soon parted company, Lord John Russell to proceed to Genoa, Moore to visit Lord Byron in Venice. Moore had made the acquaintance of Byron in 1812, when the latter, then in his 20th year, had just taken the world by surprise with his publication of the earlier cantos of *Childe Harolde*. The poets took to each other as soon as they met, and their friendship continued unimpaired until death divided them. This tour yielded *Rhymes on the Road*, a volume of sketches which in no way added to the writer's reputation, since it lacks all that is chiefly characteristic of his genius. Nature in Italy charmed Moore much more than art. At Rome he visited the great collections with Chantrey and Jackson, but was a stranger to the lively impressions received by his companions. The glorious sunset witnessed in ascending the Simplon lingered on his spirit long after the united glories of Rome, Florence, Turin, and Milan were obliterated from his memory.

Returning from Rome, Moore took up his abode in Paris, in which capital he resided until the year 1822. The conduct of the deputy in Bermuda had thrown the poet into difficulties, and until he could struggle out of them a return to England was incompatible with safety.

There were not wanting friends to run to the rescue, but Moore honourably undertook to provide for his own misfortunes. Declining all offers of help, he took heart, and resolutely set to work for his deliverance. After much negotiation, the claims of the American merchants against him were brought down from 6,000 guineas to 1,000. Towards this reduced amount the friends of the offending deputy subscribed 300*l*. The balance (750*l*.) was deposited "by a dear and distinguished friend" of the principal in the hands of a banker, to be in readiness for the final "settlement of the demand." A few months after the settlement was effected Moore received 1,000*l*. for his *Loves of the Angels* and 500*l*. for the *Fables of the Holy Alliance*. With half of these united sums he discharged his obligation to his benefactor ...

In 1825 Moore wrote a *Life of Sheridan*, in 1830 he issued his *Notices of the Life of Lord Byron*, and in the following year the *Memoirs of Lord Edward Fitzgerald*, in all the biographies maintaining his well-earned position. In his *Life of Sheridan* he did not shrink from the difficulties of history. To borrow the language of a critic of the time, "he did not hide the truth under too deep a veil, neither did he blazon it forth." Of Byron, Moore thought more tenderly than the majority of his contemporaries. The character of the staunch ally, old associate, and brother bard, is finely painted in the *Notices*, and, to the honour of Moore be it said, he knew how to stand by his departed friend while fulfilling his obligations to the public, whom it was his business to instruct. The life of the amiable, but weak-minded and luckless Lord Edward Fitzgerald, is the least noteworthy of Moore's efforts of this kind. *The History of Ireland*, published from time to time in *Lardner's Cyclopedia*, we believe to be the latest, as it is the most elaborate and serious, of our author's compositions.

For many years in the enjoyment of a pension conferred upon him by his political friends, Moore quietly resided in his cottage near Devizes, in Wiltshire, from which he occasionally emerged to find a glad and hearty welcome among the best-born and most highly-gifted of his countrymen. During such separations from home it was the habit of the poet to correspond daily with his wife. The letters written at these times, are preserved, to be incorporated, we trust, in the diary of his life, upon which Moore was busily engaged. Mrs Moore survives her husband, but his four children have preceded him to the grave.

* * *

FATHER MATHEW

12 DECEMBER 1856

THE DEPARTURE OF a great and good man from among us, and the loss of one whose charity and good deeds were of more than European reputation, seem to call for a more extended notice than that which appeared in the columns of our Irish intelligence yesterday. The history of "Father Mathew" is strange and striking, and almost partakes of the character of romance. It has often been said, by way of reproach against Ireland, that her clergy are almost all chosen, not from the nobles or the landed gentry and middle classes of Ireland, but from "the lowest of the people," and that her priests have been chosen from the plough-tail and the pigstye. However this may be it was not the case with the subject of our memoir. Theobald Mathew was descended from a very ancient Welsh family, whose pedigree is carried in the records of the principality to Gwaythooed, King of Cardigan, in direct descent from whom was Sir David Mathew, standard-bearer to Edward IV., whose monument is to be seen in the cathedral of Llandaff. Edmund Mathew, his descendant in the sixth generation, High-Sheriff of Glamorgan in 1592, had two sons, who went to Ireland in the reign of James I. The elder son, George, married Lady Thurles, mother of "the great" Duke of Ormonde ...

We believe that Theobald Mathew, son of James Mathew, of Thomas-town, county Tipperary, was born at that place on the 10th of October,

1790 ... At the age of 13 he was sent to the lay academy of Kilkenny, whence he was removed in his 20th year to Maynooth to pursue his ecclesiastical studies, having shown signs of a clerical vocation. On Easter Sunday, 1814, he was ordained in Dublin by the late Archbishop Murray. After some time he returned to Kilkenny with the intention of joining the mission of two Capuchin friars there; but before long he removed to Cork. By a rescript from the late Pope Gregory XVI. he received the degree of Doctor in Divinity, together with a dispensation allowing him to possess property. From the moment of entering upon his missionary duties at Cork he began to show the sterling worth of his character. Ever diligent in his work of the pulpit, the confessional, and the sick man's bedside, he devoted all his spare time, not to violent agitation like Dr Cahill and other ecclesiastical firebrands, but to the temporal and spiritual wants of the poor, to whom he acted as counsellor, friend, treasurer, and executor. He acted as a magistrate as well as a minister, and thus composed feuds, secured justice to the oppressed, and healed the broken peace of many a family. His charities kept pace with his exertions, and were only limited by his means. Among other good deeds, Father Mathew himself purchased the Botanic Gardens of that city, and, allowing them to retain their former agreeable walks and statuary (the best specimens of Hogan's native genius), he converted them into a cemetery, not for Catholics alone, but for members of every other denomination. To the poor burial was allowed gratuitously, and the fees derived from all other interments were devoted to charity. About the same time he commenced building a beautiful Gothic church at the cost of about 15,000*l*.

Thus, by the force of his well-known character as a genuine Christian patriot, even before the commencement of the Temperance movement in the south of Ireland, Father Mathew had risen to the highest estimation among his people. The affability of his manners, his readiness to listen to every grief and care, and, if possible, to remove it, the pure and self-sacrificing spirit of his entire career, were eminently calculated to seize upon the quick, warm impulses of the Irish heart, and to make his word law. Some 20 years ago there was no country in which the vice of intoxication had spread more devastation than in Ireland. All efforts to restrain it were in vain. The late Sir Michael O'Loghlen's Act for the Suppression of Drunkenness was a dead letter; many even of the wise and good deemed it hopeless and incurable, and it was said that the Irish would abandon their nature before they abandoned their whisky.

There were those who thought otherwise. Some members of the Society of Friends and a few other individuals at Cork had bound themselves into an association for the suppression of drunkenness, but were unable to make head against the torrent. In their despair these gentlemen, though Protestants, applied to Father Mathew. Father Mathew responded to the call; with what success ultimately we suppose that our readers are all well aware. The work, however, was not the work of a day. For a year and a half he toiled and laboured against the deep-rooted degradation of the "Boys" of Cork, the ridicule and detraction of many doubtful friends, and the discountenance of many others from whom he had expected support. At length he had the satisfaction of seeing the mighty mass of obdurate indifference begin to move; some of the most obdurate drunkards in Cork enrolled their names in his "Total Abstinence Association." His fame began to travel along the banks of the Shannon. First, the men of Kilrush came in to be received, then some hundreds from Kerry and Limerick; until, early in the month of August, 1839, the movement burst out into one universal flame. The first great outbreak was at Limerick, where Father Mathew had engaged to preach at the request of the bishop; and the mayor of which city declared that within 10 months no less than 150 inquests had been held in the county, one half of which were on persons whose deaths had been occasioned by intoxication. As soon as the country people heard that Father Mathew was in Limerick they rushed into the city in thousands. So great was the crush, that though no violence was used the iron railings which surrounded the residence of "the Apostle of Temperance" were torn down, and some scores of people precipitated into the Shannon ... We have not the time or the space to follow Father Mathew in his

Temperance progresses. Some idea of their results may be formed when we state that at Nenagh 20,000 persons are said to have taken the pledge in one day; 100,000 at Galway in two days; in Loughrea, 80,000 in two days; between that and Portumna from 180,000 to 200,000; and in Dublin about 70,000 during five days. There are few towns in Ireland which Father Mathew did not visit with like success. In 1844 he visited Liverpool, Manchester, and London; and the enthusiasm with which he was received there and in other English cities testified equally to the need and to the progress of the remedy.

It only remains to add, that in Father Mathew the ecclesiastic was completely absorbed in the Christian, the man of goodwill towards all his fellow men. To him the Protestant and the Catholic were of equal interest and of equal value. Again, no man ever displayed a more disinterested zeal. He spent upon the poor all that he had of his own and reduced to bankruptcy his brother, a distiller in the South of Ireland, whose death followed shortly upon the losses resulting from the "Temperance" crusade. Yet this man, and other branches of the family, though extensively connected with the wine and spirit trade, not only bore their losses without a murmur, but even supplied Father Mathew with large sums of money for the prosecution of his work. A few years since, Her Majesty was pleased to settle upon Father Mathew an annuity of 300*l.* in recognition of the services which he had rendered to the cause of morality and order; but even this we understand was almost entirely absorbed in heavy payments on policies of insurance upon his life, which he was bound to keep up to secure his creditors.

WILLIAM DARGAN

8 FEBRUARY 1867

WILLIAM DARGAN, OF whose death we have just been informed by telegraph, was the son of a farmer in the county of Carlow. Having received a fair English education, he was placed in a surveyor's office. He obtained the appointment of surveyor for his native county, but soon after resigned, from a feeling that he could never in that position be able to advance himself as he thought he should do if he were free to do the best he could with his talents. The first important employment he obtained was under Mr Telford, in constructing the Holyhead road. He there learnt the art of road-making, then applied for the first time by his chief, the secret of which was raising the road in the middle that it might have something of the strength of the arch, and making provision for the effectual draining off of the surface water. When that work was finished Mr Dargan returned to Ireland and obtained several small contracts on his own account, the most important of which was the road from Dublin to Howth, which was then the principal harbour connected with Dublin. Soon after this he embarked in a career of enterprise which, owing to the state of the country at that time, and the nature of the works which he achieved, will cause him to stand alone as a leader of industrial progress in the history of Ireland. There was then on every hand a cry for "encouragement" and protection. In the name of patriotism people were invited to purchase certain articles, not because they were good, but because they were of Irish manufacture. To be personally engaged in business of any kind was considered vulgar. It was a thing to which no "born gentleman" would stoop, because if he did he would be put in Coventry by his class. The most wealthy manufacturer, no matter how well educated or gentlemanly, if he attended at his counting-house, or looked regularly after his business, would have been blackballed at any second or third rate club in Dublin. A gentleman might, indeed, amuse himself at some sort of work for the benefit of his health; but if it were for the benefit of his purse, and for so sordid a consideration as profit, he immediately lost caste. Trade might be a good thing in its way, but it should be left to men who were not born with gentle blood. Protestants of the middle classes, who had no pretensions to such blood, had imbibed from their "betters" much of the same contempt for industry and the same respect for idleness; while the Roman Catholics had not yet sufficiently recovered from the effects of the Penal Code to enter with self-reliance and persistent energy into any sort of industrial enterprise. It was under such circumstances that Mr Dargan applied himself to study the wants of his country, which, so far as the working classes were concerned, had derived so little benefit from political agitation. Such a man would naturally embrace any opportunity that opened for extending the benefits of the railway system to Ireland. Kingstown had superseded Howth as the Dublin harbour. It was increasing fast in population, and the traffic between it and the metropolis was immense. It was carried on chiefly on outside cars rattling away through stifling dust in summer and splashing mud in winter. Mr Dargan was then a young man comparatively unknown, except to a circle of appreciating friends. He inspired them with his own confidence; a company was formed, and he became the contractor of the first railway in Ireland – the Dublin and Kingstown line – a most prosperous undertaking, which has always paid better than any other line in the country. For several years it stood alone. People were afraid to venture much in railway speculation. Canal conveyance was still in the ascendant; a company was formed for opening up the line of communication between Lough Erne and Belfast and Mr Dargan became the contractor of the Ulster Canal, which was regarded as a signal triumph of engineering and constructive ability. Other great works followed in rapid succession; first the Dublin and Drogheda Railway, then the Great Southern and Western, and the Midland Great Western lines. At the time of the Irish Exhibition in 1853 Mr Dargan had constructed over 200 miles of railway, and he had then contracts for 200 miles more. All his lines have been admired for the excellence of the materials and workmanship.

Considering how completely untrained Irish workmen were at that time, and what perversity had been shown by some of the trades, it is a remarkable – indeed, a wonderful, fact that Mr Dargan in all his vast undertakings never had a formidable strike to contend with, and, though the ablest workmen flocked to him from all parts of the country, his gangs were never demoralized, as they have been under other contractors. Even the navvies looked up to him with gratitude as a public benefactor. He paid the highest wages, and paid punctually as the clock struck. So perfect was the organization he effected, so firmly were all his arrangements carried out, and so justly and kindly did he deal with the people, that he was enabled to fulfil to the letter every one of the numerous engagements with which he had entered. The result was that he was held in the highest respect by the whole nation, his credit was unbounded, and, as he once said at a public meeting, he "realized very fast." At one time he was the largest railway proprietor in the country, and one of its greatest capitalists. The secret of his success, as he once said himself, consisted in the selection of agents on whose capacity and integrity he could rely, and in whom he took care not to weaken the sense of responsibility by interfering with the details of their business, while his own energies were reserved for comprehensive views and general operations. When his mind was occupied with the arrangements of the Exhibition of 1853 he had in his hands contracts to the aggregate amount of nearly two millions sterling. To his personal character and influence that Exhibition was mainly due, and, although many of the first men in the country, including the highest nobility, co-operated with alacrity, and aided with liberal contributions, he was the man who found the capital. After the Exhibition a public meeting was convened by the Lord Mayor, in compliance with a requisition signed by 40 peers, six Protestant Bishops, 15 Roman Catholic Bishops, 49 members of Parliament, and a host of magistrates and professional gentlemen, amounting to 2,200 names. From this meeting resulted a suitable monument to Mr Dargan – the Irish National Gallery, erected on Leinster Lawn, with a fine bronze statue in front looking out upon Merrion-square. The Queen graciously honoured Irish industry in the person of its great chief. Her Majesty offered him a title, which he declined.

She shook hands with him publicly at the opening of the Exhibition, and with the Prince Consort paid a visit to Mr and Mrs Dargan. Wishing to encourage the growth of flax, Mr Dargan took a tract of land in Clara or Kerry, which he devoted to its culture; but owing to some mismanagement the enterprise entailed a heavy loss. He also became a manufacturer, and set some mills working in the neighbourhood of Dublin. But that business did not prosper. About a year ago he had a fall from his horse by which his system was so badly shaken that his recovery was for some time doubtful. Since that he had another fall, but not so serious. Probably the ill state of his health brought on a confusion in his affairs, which recently resulted in his stopping payment and in an arrangement with his creditors, though his assets, it is confidently said, will pay much more than 20s. in the pound. His embarrassments, however, seem to have deeply affected his health and spirits, and brought on a disease to which his powerful constitution has succumbed.

* * *

EARL OF ROSSE

2 NOVEMBER 1867

OUR OWN CORRESPONDENT in Dublin writes:-

The Earl of Rosse died yesterday, after a protracted illness, at his residence in Monkstown, County Dublin. In the world of science a death will leave a blank which the most distinguished of his associates will long view with painful concern. This was the sphere in which his great qualities could alone be appreciated, and where his genius shone amid the brightest of those who have adorned the age in which they lived. He was the eldest son of the second earl, and was born on the 17th of June, 1800, in the city of York. In 1818 he entered Trinity College, Dublin, and in the following year passed into residence in Magdalen College, Oxford, where he graduated in 1822. The bent of his mind was shown at this early period by the distinction which he obtained as a first-class honour man in math-ematics. About this time he was induced to enter public life, and, as Lord Oxmantown, was elected representative of the King's County, a position which he retained until the end of the first Reformed Parliament. He also sat for a while as a representative peer. His talents, however, had no congenial field in the Legislature, and his career was not marked by any brilliant feat of eloquence or states-manship. Though he shrank from the prominence of a Parliamentary debater, he occasionally spoke on subjects on which he felt it due to his constituents to express his opinions. Among the more remarkable was Mr Whitmore's motion for a committee of the whole House to consider the Corn Laws. He was opposed to the policy of repealing them, and showed the effect which it would have, especially as regards this country. He resisted Mr Hume's motion for the abolition of the Lord Lieutenent on the ground that it would increase absenteeism.... After retiring from Parliament Lord Rosse applied himself with greater zeal and assiduity to the pursuit of astronomical science. He conceived the noble purpose of surmounting the difficulties which stood in the way of a more accur-ate observation of the heavenly bodies, and with unexampled patience and persistent energy applied himself to the self-imposed task. His wonderful mechanical skill and scientific knowledge enabled him ultimately to achieve his object. It was not until after repeated experi-ments and failures, which would have daunted a less determined or enthusiastic worker, that he at last succeeded in producing those magnificent instruments which have won for him European fame. The art of making reflecting telescopes of vast compass and power may be said to have originated with him, and has certainly been brought by his unwearied diligence and inventive sagacity to a perfection which before he undertook the task would have been pronounced impossible. No work can be imagined of more exquisite delicacy, and his success in overcoming the complicated difficulties which arose at every step is a marvel of patient ingenuity. The mirror of Lord Rosse's largest telescope is a circular disc of metal weighing four tons, and measuring six feet in diameter; and a faint conception of the obstacles which he had to encounter may be formed when it is remembered that, in order to collect the utmost possible amount of light, which is the great object of reflectors, it must be slightly concave, about half an inch deeper in the centre than at the edge, and not exactly spherical, but varying from the spherical form only to the extent of the ten-thousandth part of an inch. The slightest variation of these conditions would produce a defective or distorted image. Lord Rosse not only succeeded in conforming to them, but attained to probably ten times greater precision. The shape, however, of the mirror is only one of the essentials. In adjusting the proportions of the copper and tin of which it is made, in guarding against the penetrating power of the molten mass which would make its way through the pores of cast iron – and wrought iron cannot be used, for the alloy would fuse with it – in the annealing, grinding, and polishing of the mirror, the latter process being performed by machinery, the resources of his inventive mind were displayed with marvellous effect. So completely did he master the minutest detail that those who desire to follow in his steps may pursue their course with perfect confidence. The value of the discoveries which his great instrument enabled him to make in the observation of nebuli, has been universally acknowledged. All the learned societies of Europe vied in doing him honour. In 1849 he was elected President of the Royal Society. He was elected a member of the Imperial Academy at St Petersburg, and was created a Knight of the Legion of Honour by the Emperor of the French, and a Knight of St Patrick by our most gracious Sovereign. He was *Custos Rotulorum* of the King's County and Chancellor of the University of Dublin. He was also a President of the British Association. In politics he was a moderate Conservative, but held independent views on some leading questions. Though English in his birthplace and descent, he was strongly attached to this country by the ties of family, property, and sympathy.

CARDINAL CULLEN

25 OCTOBER 1878

CARDINAL CULLEN, the Roman Catholic Primate of Ireland, died yesterday afternoon at his residence in Eccles-street, Dublin. It is supposed to have been caused by aneurism of the heart. His loss will give a severe shock to the Roman Catholic Church, of which he was the distinguished head in Ireland, and will be generally regretted, even by those who differed most widely from him on religious and political questions.

Of the early life of the Right Rev. Paul Cullen, D.D., but little is known beyond the fact that he was born about the year 1800, in the county of Meath, and was a member of a respectable family, engaged in agricultural pursuits. They are now among the most wealthy graziers in the country, and have considerable property in Meath and Kildare. His Christian name, which is not at all a common one in Ireland, would seem to denote an early dedication of his life to the priestly office to which especial honour is attached in a social as well as religious aspect by the Roman Catholic peasantry and industrial classes. Having been ordained for the ministry, he was sent to Rome, where he spent nearly 30 years of his life, and rose to a position of trust and eminence in the councils of the Vatican. He was officially connected with the management of the Irish College at Rome, but this was the only bond of connexion with his own country, and there can be no doubt that his ideas were deeply tinged by the impressions derived from foreign experience, and associated with the narrow circle in which he moved. In 1849 the death of Dr Crolly, Roman Catholic Archbishop of Armagh, created a vacancy in that important See, and, the Suffragan Bishops having been divided in opinion as to the choice of his successor, the Pope settled the dispute *suo more* by appointing Dr Cullen Primate of All Ireland. This exercise of Papal authority was regarded as an infringement of the elective rights or usage which had been previously recognized, and created much dissatisfaction at the time, though the supreme will of the Holy See was obeyed. To avoid scandal in the Church the bishops and clergy who had lived under a different regime suppressed their discontent, and the feeling gradually wore away. It was the first step, however, towards the enforcement of a despotic control which has since dominated the whole ecclesiastical system in Ireland. In pursuance of what seems to have been a deliberate purpose, the vindication of a principle which may be deemed essential to the preservation of unity and the concentration of power, the pre-existing plan of clerical government has been changed. The degree of independence which had been before enjoyed was taken away, and bishops and clergy were brought more into subjection to the direct authority of the Vatican. In furtherance of this policy, bishops were no longer elected by the clergy, and the old constitutional office of parish priest was superseded by that of administrator. The former possessed an independent parochial jurisdiction so long as he did not violate any canonical law, while the latter had no fixity of tenure, and might at any time be removed at the will of the diocesan, without being entitled to any compensation for even capricious disturbance. This change, which is being gradually and steadily worked out as opportunity offers, constitutes one of the most remarkable points of difference between the government of the Church of Rome in Ireland in the days of Cardinal Cullen and those of his predecessor. On the death of the late Dr Murray in 1851 Dr Cullen was transferred from the Primatial See of Armagh to the more important though less ancient and in an ecclesiastical sense, less dignified one of Dublin. No two characters could be more different than those of the mild and genial Archbishop Murray, whose liberal spirit conciliated many opponents of the Catholic claims and attracted the cordial esteem and friendship of the Protestant gentry, and the ascetic prelate who possessed no social sympathies, but looked, if not with suspicion and distrust, at least with cold and gloomy reserve, upon those of a heretical creed. He set up a new and strengthened by every means the old barrier of sectarian isolation and exclusiveness, and the result is the growth of a spirit in the country which may be more zealous and devotional but is also more narrow and illiberal than prevailed before his time. He was, as every one knows, an Ultramontane of the most uncompromising type, and though there were many, both of the clergy and laity, who dissented from his opinions, few had the courage to oppose them, enforced as they were by a systematic policy which made its influence felt and feared.

The name of Archbishop Cullen has been a foremost one in the history of Ireland for the last 28 years. No man in the kingdom has exercised a greater personal influence, or wielded more absolute power, by virtue of his high episcopal position as a Prince of the Church, Archbishop of the Metropolitan See, and legatee of the Pope. His authority, however, was not used for any selfish motive, or for the gratification of an arbitrary will, but in a conscientious and considerate spirit for the advancement of the interests of religion, according to his ideas of what was patriotic and right. It was not only implicitly obeyed, but was received with the respect and deference due to his office and his character … From the first the Cardinal has been unflinching and indefatigable in his advocacy of denominationalism, and there can be no doubt that the result of his persistent efforts has been to transform the national system into one, in fact, denominational. After a memorable struggle he succeeded in the famous Synod of Thurles by a majority of one vote in procuring the issue of an edict condemning the national schools. This has been a fruitful subject of contention ever since, and a severe embarrassment alike to the Church itself and to the State. This may be said to have been the only question of a political nature with which the Cardinal concerned himself, and it was only in consideration of the religious element that he took an active part in the agitation respecting it. He did not intermeddle in party strife or controversies, or countenance interference of his clergy in electioneering or other political movements. In this respect the Diocese of Dublin contrasted creditably with others in the country. All the thoughts and energies of his life were directed to the interests of religion, and he enforced, on the part of all who were subject to his authority, the strictest attention to their parochial duties. He was an earnest advocate and supporter of the temperance cause, and gave material help in promoting the Sunday Closing Act, and other social reforms. His loyal attachment to the Crown and constitution of England was shown with earnest and consistent firmness in trying times in spite of popular clamour and at the risk of personal odium. To none in Her Majesty's Dominions was the British Government more indebted for co-operation in extinguishing the flames of insurrection during the Fenian excitement, and restoring tranquillity and order in the country. His great influence was thrown heartily into the scale of constitutional authority, and he spared no exertions to put down every form of secret societies, which he believed to be incompatible with the duty of a citizen and a Christian. In private life he was most estimable, and, under a cold and stern exterior, had a warm and generous heart. In 1866 he was proclaimed a Cardinal priest, being the first Irishman who was invested with the purple and raised to the rank of a Prince of his Church; in 1859 he served as director to the Holy See by organizing an Irish Brigade, who went to assist in restoring the temporal sovereignty of the Pope. He was not present at the election of Leo XIII., although he left Ireland to attend.

CHARLES STEWART PARNELL

8 OCTOBER 1891

MR CHARLES STEWART PARNELL died at half-past 11 on Tuesday night at his residence, 10, Walsingham-terrace, Aldrington, near Brighton. The event was not, however, known locally until yesterday morning, when the news rapidly spread, causing everywhere the greatest astonishment. It had not even been known that Mr Parnell had been ill, and the suddenness of the event led to the dissemination of sensational rumours, which, so far as could be ascertained, were altogether without foundation. Neither before nor after their marriage were Mr and Mrs Parnell much known in Brighton and Hove. Walsingham-terrace, where before the marriage they occupied adjoining houses, and where they had since resided, is a lonely row of houses near the sea some two miles westward of the town. It is not, therefore, surprising that Mr Parnell's illness should have passed unnoticed. The facts, so far as they can be ascertained, appear to be as follows:- On Thursday Mr Parnell returned from Ireland to Walsingham-terrace suffering from a severe chill. As he was not unaccustomed to similar attacks little was thought of it at the time. The following day, however, he was so much worse that he did not leave his bed. On Saturday some improvement was visible in his condition, but on Sunday he suffered a severe relapse. A Brighton doctor was sent for, and found him, it is said, in the greatest agony, suffering from acute rheumatism. According to another account, however, death is ascribed to congestion of the lungs and bronchitis. Mr Parnell was nursed by his wife and one of her daughters, who happened to be staying at the time at the house next door, still kept up by Mr Parnell. In addition to the doctor already in attendance, two other medical men were called in. Mr Parnell remained, however, in the same condition until Tuesday afternoon, when a very rapid and startling change for the worse

46

occurred, and after lingering for some hours in pain he died, as stated, at half-past 11. With the exception of Mrs Parnell and her daughter, no relatives or immediate friends of the deceased were present. Mrs Parnell is completely overcome by this sudden and heavy blow, and yesterday absolutely refused to see any one ...

Charles Stewart Parnell, the eldest son of the late John Henry Parnell, high sheriff of Wicklow in 1836, was born at Avondale, in that county, in June, 1846. His mother was Delia Tudor, daughter of Admiral Charles Stewart, of the American Navy, who, as commodore, had been conspicuous in the naval struggle with England early in the century, when the United States struggled stoutly for the palm of naval supremacy. Mr Parnell's family had long been settled in Cheshire, and from their seat there his great uncle, Sir Henry Parnell, whose motion on the Civil List turned out the Wellington Government in 1830, and who was afterwards Secretary for War and Paymaster of the Forces under the Whigs, took his title of Lord Congleton. The Parnells belonged to the "Englishry" of Ireland; one of them, Dr Thomas Parnell, an author now best known by his poem "The Hermit," friend of Pope and Swift, and the subject of a sympathetic biography by Goldsmith, used to bewail his clerical exile among the Irish, and, indeed, consistently neglected his duties as Archdeacon of Clogher; others, later on, during the period of Protestant ascendency were Judges, officials, and members of Parliament; Sir John Parnell, who joined with Grattan and other patriots of that day in fighting for an independence that secured a monopoly of power to their own creed and caste, was Chancellor of the Exchequer just before the Union. Sir John Parnell's grandson was Mr John Henry Parnell, of Avondale, the father of the future chief of the Separatists, who thus inherited on the paternal side an antipathy to the Union, and on the maternal side the traditions of a bitter conflict with England. Mr Parnell nevertheless received, like many scions of the Irish landlord class, an exclusively English education at various private schools, and afterwards at Magdalene College, Cambridge, where, however, he did not take a degree, and where, it is said, he was "sent down" for some rather gross breach of academic discipline.

Some surprise was expressed in Ireland when, in 1874, Mr Parnell, then high sheriff of Wicklow, came forward to oppose in the county Dublin the re-election of Colonel Taylor, who had taken office as Chancellor of the Duchy of Lancaster in the Disraeli Government. He stood as an advocate of Home Rule, to which many of the Irish loyalists had temporarily attached themselves in their disgust at the success of Mr Gladstone's disestablishment policy. But Mr Parnell's "Nationalism" proved to be of another type. If it had a sentimental origin in his family traditions, it was qualified and dominated by the cold temper and the taste for political strategy which he seems to have inherited from his American kinsfolk. Defeated by a large majority in Dublin county, he was more successful a little more than a year later when a vacancy was created in the representation of Meath by the death of John Martin, one of the "Young Ireland" party and a convict of 1848, like his brother-in-law, John Mitchel. When Mr Parnell entered the House of Commons in April, 1875, the Liberal Opposition was disorganized, the Conservative Government was both positively and negatively strong, and the Home Rule party, under Mr Butt's leadership, was of little account. Mr Parnell immediately allied himself with Mr Biggar, who had struck out a line of his own by defying decency and the rules of Parliament, and, with more or less regular aid from Mr F. H. O'Donnell and Mr O'Connor Power, they soon made themselves a political force. How far Mr Parnell saw ahead of him at this time, what his motives were, and what secret influences were acting upon him may, perhaps, never be revealed. He found, as he believed, a method of bringing an intolerable pressure to bear upon the Imperial Parliament and the Government of the day by creating incessant disturbances and delaying all business, and he persisted in this course in spite of the protests and the denunciations of Mr Butt and the more respectable among the Irish Nationalists. To quote the triumphant language of one of his own followers, writing, almost officially, long afterwards, whereas obstructive tactics had been previously directed against particular Bills, "the obstruction which now faced Parliament intervened in every single detail of its business and not merely in contentious business, but in business that up to this time had been considered formal." The design was boastfully avowed that, unless the Imperial Legislature agreed to grant the Irish demands as formulated by Mr Biggar and Mr Parnell, its power would be paralyzed, its time wasted, its honour and dignity dragged through the dirt. In 1877, the whole scheme of obstructive policy was disclosed and exemplified in the debates on the Prisons Bill, the Army Bill, and the South Africa Bill. Speaking on the last measure, Mr Parnell said that "as an Irishman" and one detesting "English cruelty and tyranny" he felt "a special satisfaction in preventing and thwarting the intentions of the Government." On one occasion the House was kept sitting for 26 hours by the small band of obstructionists. The rules of the House, even when cautiously strengthened at the instance of Sir Stafford Northcote, proved entirely inadequate to control men, like Mr Parnell, undeterred by any scruples and master of all the technicalities of Parliamentary practice. Motions of suspension produced as little effect as public censure, nor was Mr Butt, though he strongly condemned the policy of exasperation and lamented the degradation of Irish politics into a "vulgar brawl," able to stem the tide. He was deposed in the winter of 1877 by the Home Rule Confederation of Great Britain, a body including most of the "advanced" wing of the Irish in England and Scotland; and though a modus vivendi was adopted in the Parliamentary party itself, and accepted by Mr Parnell, as he said, in Mr Butt's presence, on the ground that he "was a young man and could wait," it was felt that power had passed away from the moderates, of whom many were afraid to oppose the obstructives with a general election in sight, hoping, as the Parnellites said, to tide over the crisis and "survive till the advent of the blessed hour when the return of the Liberals to power would give them the long-desired chance of throwing off the temporary mask of national views to assume the permanent livery of English officials." History sometimes repeats itself with curious irony, and these words are almost textually the same as those lately used by Mr Parnell of those most intimately associated with him in his campaign against Mr Butt. The Session of 1878 emphasized the cleavage; Mr Butt practically resigned the lead to the extreme faction, and both spoke and voted in favour of the foreign policy of the Government. Mr Parnell pursued his course of calculated Parliamentary violence. In 1879 Mr Butt died, a broken man, and Mr Shaw was chosen to fill his place as "Sessional Chairman" of the party. But events were playing to Mr Parnell's hands. He had been associated with some of the Radical leaders in the attack on flogging in the Army, and he had been chosen as the first president of the Land League, which was started at Irishtown, in Mayo, a couple of weeks before Mr Butt's death, and which embodied the ideas brought back from the United States by Mr Davitt after his provisional release from penal servitude, with three other Fenian prisoners, at the end of 1877. Mr Parnell was at the head of the "Reception Committee" which presented an address to these patriots, and the list of those associated with him contains, besides the names of Mr John Dillon and Mr Patrick Egan, those of James Carey, Daniel Curley, and J. Brady.

Up to this point there was nothing known to the public to show that Mr Parnell was not pursuing a Parliamentary agitation by irregular and censurable methods. How far he had previously allied himself with those who had other objects in view and who worked by other methods remains obscure. At any rate, he quickly entered into the policy that Mr Davitt had devised in America in co-operation with Devoy and others, and after taking counsel with the leaders of the Clan-na-Gael and of the Irish Republican Brotherhood. That policy had been originally sketched by Fintan Lalor, one of the '48 men, and was intended to work upon the land hunger of the Irish peasantry in order to get rid of the British connexion. Davitt and Devoy brought over the revolutionary party to their views, including extremists like Ford of the *Irish World*, an open advocate of physical force, whether in the form of armed rebellion or of terrorist outrage. Proposals for co-operation with the Parnellites on the basis of dropping the pretence of federation and putting in its stead "a formal declaration in favour of self-government," of giving the foremost place to the land agitation, and adopting an aggressive Parliamentary policy generally were transmitted to Ireland, and, though not formally accepted either by Mr Parnell, for the moment, or by the

Irish Fenians became, in the opinion of the Special Commissioners, "the basis on which the American-Irish Nationalists afterwards lent their support to Mr Parnell and his policy." This "new departure," which Mr Davitt advocated as widening the field of revolutionary effort involved Mr Parnell's adoption of a more decided line on the land question and the opening up of closer relations with his allies beyond the Atlantic. In June, 1879, therefore, a few weeks after the establishment of the Land League, and in the teeth of the denunciations of Archbishop MacHale, Mr Parnell, accompanied by Mr Davitt, addressed a League meeting at Westport, told the tenantry that they could not pay their rents in the presence of the agricultural crisis, but that they should let the landlords know they intended in any case to "hold a firm grip on their home-steads and lands." He added that no concession obtained in Parliament would buy off his resolution to secure all, including, as Mr Davitt took care to say, the unqualified claim for national independence.

Mr Parnell's advances to the Revolutionists in America had an immediate reward, not only in the removal of any remaining obstacles in the path of his ambition, but in the supply of the sinews of war for the work of agitation and electioneering. Mr Davitt started the Land League with money obtained out of the Skirmishing Fund, established by O'Donovan Rossa in order to strike England "anywhere she could be hurt" and then in the hands of the Clan-na-Gael chiefs. But much more was needed, and in October, 1879, Mr Parnell started with Mr Dillon for the United States. During the voyage he imparted his views to the correspondent of a New York paper, afterwards a witness before the Special Commission, and told him, among other things, that his idea of a true revolutionary movement in Ireland was that it should partake both of a constitutional and an illegal character, "using the Constitution for its own purposes, but also taking advantage of the secret combinations." He was cordially welcomed by most of the extreme faction, and gratified them with declarations quite to their own mind. He told them that the land question must be acted upon in "some extraordinary and unusual way" to secure any good result and that "the great cause could not be won without shedding a drop of blood."

He went even beyond this point in the famous speech at Cincinnati, which he subsequently attempted to deny, but which was reported in the *Irish World* and was held to be proved by Sir James Hannen and his colleagues. He then said that the "ultimate goal" at which Irishmen aimed was "to destroy the last link which kept Ireland bound to England." The American wing were perfectly satisfied, and Mr Parnell, when he was summoned back to Ireland by the news of the dissolution, felt that he could rely on their support, pecuniary and other. It was not, at first, so easy to convince the Irish Fenians – who had distrusted and abjured any form of Parliamentary action – that they ought to vote for Parnellite candidates; and one or two Parnellite meetings were disturbed by this element. But Mr Parnell's speeches during the electoral campaign of 1880 showed them how far he was prepared to go in their direction, and how little inclined he was, to use his own phrase, "to fix the boundary to the march of a nation." It was at the time that Mr Parnell told, with great applause, the story which became very popular on Land League platforms, of the American sympathizer who offered him "five dollars for bread and 20 dollars for lead." The leading spokesmen and organizers of the League, Sheridan, Brennan, Boyton, and Redpath, were either known Fenians or used language going beyond that of Fenianism; and the same thing may be said of Mr Biggar, Mr O'Kelly, and Mr Matt Harris, members of Mr Parnell's Parliamentary following. The policy which Mr Davitt, acting as the envoy of the Irish extremists, thus used Mr Parnell to carry through, was developed in the announcement of the boycotting system in the autumn of 1880. Meanwhile, the alliance had already borne fruit at the general election of that year, when Mr Parnell, aided somewhat irregularly by Mr Egan out of the exchequer of the League, was returned for three constituencies – Meath, Mayo, and the city of Cork. He decided to sit for the last, and as "the member for Cork" he has since been known. The overthrow of the Beaconsfield Government, which had appealed to the country to strengthen the Empire against Irish disorder and disloyalty, was an encouragement to the Parnellites, who had a narrow and shifting majority in the ranks of the Parliamentary party. Mr Shaw was supplanted as chairman by Mr Parnell, and an open separation between the two sections ensued. The Parnellites took their seats on the Opposition benches; the Moderate Home Rulers sat on the Ministerial side below the gangway. To the latter Mr Gladstone seemed to incline most favourably, as he showed afterwards when he proposed to make Mr Shaw one of the Chief Commissioners under the Land Act. The Liberals, though they took the opportunity of dropping the Peace Preservation Act, were not disposed to reopen the land question, and it was only under pressure that Mr Forster hastily introduced the Compensation for Disturbance Bill, which was rejected in the House of Lords, and appointed the Bessborough Commission.

Mr Parnell and his party seized the opportunities afforded by the distress in Ireland and the Parliamentary situation to push on the operations of the League. The policy of boycotting had been expounded and enforced early in the year in Mr Parnell's speech at Ennis, a few days after Lord Mountmorres's murder, when he urged the peasantry if any man among them took an evicted farm to put the offender "into a moral Coventry by isolating him from the rest of his kind as if he were a leper of old." This doctrine was rapidly propagated by Mr Dillon, Mr Biggar, and the organizers of the League, and in the autumn the persecution of Captain Boycott and many other persons became a public scandal. This system of acting upon those whom Mr Parnell had described as "weak and cowardly," because they did not heartily join in the refusal to pay rent, has been pronounced on the highest judicial authority to amount to a criminal and illegal conspiracy, devised and carried out to lower the rental and selling price of land and to crush the landlords. Mr Parnell declared that he never incited to crime, but though he and his colleagues knew that boycotting and the unwritten law of the League led to outrages, wherever the organization spread, they took no effective measures to denounce and repress crime, and it is now plain that they could not do so without alienating the American support on which they were dependent. The ordinary law was shown to be powerless by the failure of the prosecution of Mr Parnell and others for conspiracy in Dublin in the opening days of 1881, when the jury disagreed, and Mr Parnell, in announcing the result to his American friends, telegraphed his thanks to the *Irish World* for "constant co-operation and successful support in our great cause." But the progress of unpunished crime, in which the American-Irish brutally exulted, and the paralysis of the law compelled Mr Gladstone's Government to act. Early in the Session of 1881 Mr Forster introduced his "Protection of Persons and Property Bill" and his "Arms Bill," of which the former empowered the Executive to arrest and detain without trial persons reasonably suspected of crime. At the mere rumour of this Egan transferred the finances of the League to Paris. It was a part of Mr Parnell's task, as he well knew, to fight the "coercion" measures tooth and nail, but, though he led the attack, the most critical conflicts were precipitated by the passion and imprudence of less cold-blooded politicians. We need not here recapitulate the history of that struggle, in which obstruction reached a height previously unknown, and in which the knot had to be cut for the moment by the enforcement of the inherent powers of the Chair. The Parnellite members were again and again suspended, and at length, after several weeks, both Bills were carried. Mr Parnell's party had by this time assumed an attitude towards the Government of Mr Gladstone which was highly pleasing to the *Irish World* and the Nationalist organs in Ireland, but was ominous for the prospects of the Land Bill. They did not, however, venture to offer a direct and determined opposition to a measure securing great pecuniary advantages to the Irish tenants. They could not go beyond abstaining on the question of principle and denouncing the whole scheme as inadequate. Of course, if the Land Act had succeeded in accordance with Mr Gladstone's sanguine hopes, it would have cut the ground from under Mr Parnell's feet and deprived him of the basis of agitation on which his alliance with the Irish Extremists rested, and from which his party derived their pecuniary supplies. No sooner, therefore, had the Land Act become law than the word went forth from the offices of the League that the tenants were not to be allowed to avail themselves of it freely, but that only some "test cases" were to be put forward. The penalties of any infraction of this addition to the unwritten law were well understood, for all this while terrorism and outrage were rampant. Mr Gladstone was more indignant at the rejection of his message of peace than at the proofs, which had been long forthcoming, of the excesses of Irish lawlessness. He denounced Mr Parnell at Leeds, in impassioned language, and declared that "the resources of civilization against its enemies were not yet exhausted." Mr Parnell replied defiantly that Mr Gladstone had before "eaten all his old words," and predicted that these "brave words of this English Minister would be scattered as chaff" by the determination of the Irish to regain "their lost legislative independence." A few days later he was arrested and imprisoned in Kilmainham with Mr Sexton, Mr O' Brien, the editor of his organ, *United Ireland*, and several others. Egan, on the suggestion of Ford, at once issued a "No-Rent" manifesto; the books of the Land League were spirited out of the jurisdiction of the Irish Executive, and as a natural consequence the Land League was suppressed. But the struggle was carried on, with little substantial change, during Mr Parnell's imprisonment. The Ladies' League nominally took the work in hand; American money was not wanting; boycotting was rigidly enforced, and was followed, as Mr Gladstone had shown, by crime. For this state of things the incendiary journalism subsidized and imported by the Parnellites was, and long after remained, responsible. The *Irish World*, with its advocacy of dynamite and dagger, was used to "spread the light" among the masses, and *United Ireland* was scarcely behind-hand. The *Freeman's Journal*, which had opposed Mr Parnell's extreme views on the Land Act, was compelled to come to heel, and the priest-hood, who never loved him, as a Protestant and as a suspected ally of the Fenians, found their influence waning in presence of the despotism of the League. The secret history of all that went on during Mr Parnell's imprisonment in Kilmainham is not yet revealed, though some light has been thrown upon it by the recent split among the Nationalists. Mr Parnell, for instance, said the other day in the last speech he delivered that "the white flag had been first hung out from Kilmainham" by Mr William O'Brien. Be that as it may, it is evident that in the spring of 1882 both the Government and the Parnellites were anxious to compromise their quarrel. Mr Gladstone was pressed by the Radicals to get rid of coercion, and the patriots were eager to be again enjoying liberty and power. Negotiations were opened through Mr O'Shea; Mr Parnell was willing to promise that Ireland should be tranquilized for the moment and in appearance – through the agency of the League; Mr Forster refusing to become a party to this sort of bargain with those who had organized a system of lawless terrorism, resigned; Lord Spencer and Lord Frederick Cavendish went to Ireland as envoys of a policy of concession, including a Bill for wiping out arrears of rent. How long Mr Parnell would have continued to give a *quid pro quo* for this can only be guessed at. A few days after the ratification of what became known as the Kilmainham Treaty, Lord Frederick Cavendish and Mr Burke were murdered in the Phoenix Park by persons then unknown. Mr Parnell expressed his horror of the crime in the House of Commons, but refused to admit that it was a reason for the Coercion Bill immediately introduced by Sir William Harcourt. This change of policy was forced upon Mr Gladstone by the imperious demands of public opinion, which was exasperated by the defiant attitude of the Irish party. The forces of obstruction, however, were for the moment broken by the shock. The Coercion Act became law, and was at the outset vigorously administered by Lord Spencer and Mr Trevelyan, who were, in consequence, attacked with the most infamous calumnies by *United Ireland* and other Parnellite organs. The authors of several wicked crimes were brought to justice in Ireland in spite of the clamour of the Parnellites against Judges and jurymen, and early in 1883 the invincible conspiracy, which had compassed the deaths of Lord Frederick Cavendish and Mr Burke, was exposed by the evidence of the informer, James Carey. Mr Forster made this the occasion of a powerful attack on Mr Parnell in the House of Commons, telling the story of the Kilmainham negotiations in the light of later disclosures, and pointing out that the language used without rebuke in Mr Parnell's organs and by his followers plainly sowed the seed of crime. Mr Parnell's callous defiance of the voice of public opinion shocked even those inclined to make allowance for him. Radical sympathy was withdrawn from him, while there was about this time also a widening breach with the Irish-Americans, who did not wish to have outrage even condemned by implication, and who were entering upon the dynamite campaign. Nevertheless, Mr Parnell's hold on his own party was unshaken; from time to time there were movements of revolt; he had to speak scornfully once of "Papist rats." Mr Dwyer Gray, Mr O'Connor Power, Mr F. H. O'Donnell, and Mr Healy at different times tried to thwart him, but he swept all opposition away, and reduced his critics to subjection or drove them out of public life. The Land League was allowed to revive under the name of the National League, and, operating more cautiously on the old lines, secured Mr Parnell's power. It was evident that the extension of the franchise would give Mr Parnell the power of nominating the representatives of three-fourths of Ireland. The priesthood, trembling for their influence, came round to him. But he was unable to induce the Government either to repeal the Coercion Act or to tamper with the land question. It was when the Franchise Bill was introduced that Mr Parnell's influence over the Government was first manifested. He insisted that Ireland should be included in the Bill and that the number of the Irish representatives should not be diminished, and on both points he prevailed. Meanwhile the alliance with the American-Irish had been renewed. The Clan-na-Gael captured the Land League in the United States, and in view of the elections in Great Britain funds were provided, Egan being now a member of the organization. Simultaneously a more active policy was adopted at home. As soon as the passage of the Franchise Bill had been made sure the Parnellites joined with the Conservatives to defeat Mr Gladstone. Towards the weak Salisbury Administration that followed Mr Parnell showed, during the electoral period, a benevolent neutrality, acting on the principle he had laid down several years before in Cork – "Don't be afraid to let in the Tory, but put out the Whig." He judged that he would be thus more likely to hold the balance of power in the new Parliament, and Mr Gladstone held the same opinion when he asked for a Liberal majority strong enough to vote down Conservatives and Parnellites together. In an address to the Irish electors on the eve of the struggle the Parnellites fiercely

denounced the Liberal party and its leader. Mr Parnell had even amused
Lord Carnarvon at a critical time with a deceptive negotiation.

The issue of the contest left Mr Gladstone's forces just balanced
by those of the Conservatives and Parnellites combined. He at once
resolved to secure the latter by an offer of Home Rule, though he had
up to that time professed his devotion to the Union, and though nine-
tenths of his followers had pledged themselves to it. His overtures
were, of course, welcomed, though without a too trustful effusiveness,
by Mr Parnell; the Conservative Government was overthrown on a side
issue; Mr Gladstone came into power and introduced his Home Rule
Bill. Much was made of Mr Parnell's unqualified acceptance of that
measure. It now appears that he objected to several points in it, being,
no doubt, aware of the view taken of it by his American allies, but he did
not press his objections, fearing, as he said since, that the insistence on
further concessions would deprive Mr Gladstone of other colleagues and
break up the Government. Mr Parnell's temporary forbearance, which
had no element of finality in it, did not save the Bill. In the Parliament
of 1886 his numerical forces were nearly the same as those he
previously commanded, but he was now allied with a greatly enfeebled
Gladstonian Opposition. It was necessary to affect the most scrupulous
constitutionalism, and for a time Mr Parnell played the part well.
The Irish-Americans took the cue from him, and were willing to wait.
Dynamite outrages had ceased. But the necessities of the case urged
him to insist on reopening the Irish land question, and in Ireland the
National League continued to work on the old system. Boycotting and
its attendant incidents increased, and, during Mr Parnell's temporary
withdrawal from active politics, Mr Dillon and Mr O'Brien committed
the party to the Plan of Campaign, which involved a pitched battle with
the Executive and the law. The introduction of the Crimes Bill was the
direct result of this policy, which Mr Parnell privately condemned.
His opposition to the Bill was of the familiar kind. But the tactics of
obstruction which were then pursued were overshadowed in the public
eye by the controversy on "Parnellism and Crime" that arose in our
own columns. Seeing that the alliance between Mr Parnell and the

Gladstonian Opposition was growing closer and closer, that it was employed to obstruct the Executive Government and to set at naught the law, and that the success of Home Rule would deliver over Ireland to a faction tainted by association with Ford and Sheridan, we thought it right to call public attention to some salient episodes in Mr Parnell's career and to draw certain inferences from them. We also conceived it to be our duty to publish some documentary evidence that came into our hands, of the authenticity of which we were honestly convinced, and which seemed to us perfectly consistent with what was proved and notorious. Mr Parnell gave a comprehensive denial to all our charges and inferences, including the alleged letter apologizing to some extremist ally for denouncing the Phoenix Park murders in the House of Commons. He did not, however, accept our challenge or bring an action against *The Times*, nor was it till more than a year later, after Mr O'Donnell had raised the question by some futile proceedings, that he demanded a Parliamentary inquiry into the statements made on our behalf by the Attorney-General. We need not here recite the story of the appointment of the Special Commission and its result. The evidence of Richard Pigott broke down, and with it the letters on which we had in part relied, and Mr Parnell's political allies claimed for him a complete acquittal. But the Report of the Commissioners showed that, though some other charges against Mr Parnell were dismissed as unproved, the most important contentions of *The Times* were fully established. The origin and objects of the criminal conspiracy were placed beyond doubt; the association for the purposes of that conspiracy with the Irish-American revolutionists was most clearly made manifest, as well as the reckless persistence in boycotting and in the circulation of inflammatory writings after it was known in what those practices ended. Nor was it without significance that a confession was extorted from Mr Parnell that he might very possibly have made a deliberately false statement for the purpose of deceiving the House of Commons. Indeed, on more than one point where Mr Parnell's sworn testimony had to be weighed against that of other witnesses – as in the case of Mr Ives and Major Le Caron – the Commissioners rejected it. Nevertheless, the Gladstonians went out of their way to affirm their unshaken belief in the stainless honour of Mr Parnell, to accept him as the model of a Constitutional statesman, and to base upon his assurances their confidence that a Home Rule settlement would be a safe and lasting one. Mr Parnell received the honorary freedom of the city of Edinburgh. He was entertained at dinner by the Eighty Club; Mr Gladstone appeared on the same platform with him; his speeches were welcomed at Gladstonian gatherings in the provinces as eagerly as those of the patriarchal leader himself; and, finally, he was the late Premier's guest at Hawarden Castle, where the details of the revised Home Rule scheme, which has never been disclosed even to the National Liberal Federation, was discussed confidentially as between two potentates of co-equal authority.

But a cruel disappointment was in store for credulous souls. Mr O'Shea, whose intervention had brought about the Kilmainham Treaty, instituted proceedings against Mr Parnell in the Divorce Court. It was denied up to the last that there was any ground for these proceedings; it was predicted that they would never come to an issue. But when, after protracted and intentional delays, the case came on in November last, it was found that there was no defence. The adultery was formally proved and was not denied, nor was it possible to explain away its treachery and grossness. The public mind was shocked at the disclosure; but those who were best entitled to speak were strangely silent. Mr Gladstone said nothing; the Roman Catholic hierarchy in Ireland said nothing; Mr Justin M'Carthy, Mr Healy, and the rest of the Parliamentary party hastened to Dublin to proclaim, at the Leinster-hall, their unwavering fidelity to Mr Parnell. Mr Dillon and Mr O'Brien telegraphed their approval from America. On the opening day of the Session Mr Parnell was re-elected leader. Meanwhile the Nonconformist conscience had awakened, and Mr Gladstone responded to its remonstrances. His letter turned the majority round, and, after a violent conflict in Committee Room No. 15, Mr Parnell was deposed by the very men who had elected him. He refused to recognize his deposition, and has fought a daring, but a losing, battle in Ireland ever since. The declaration of the Roman Catholic hierarchy against him, however, sealed his doom. The clergy have worked against him as they never worked in politics before. Mr Dillon and Mr O'Brien have taken the same side. He has been defeated in North Kilkenny, North Sligo, and Carlow, and though he has been battling fiercely down to a few days ago, the ground has been visibly slipping away from him. Even his marriage with Mrs O'Shea, the only reparation for his sin, has been turned against him in a Roman Catholic country, and was the excuse for the defection of the *Freeman's Journal*. It is not surprising that a feeble constitution should have broken down under such a load of obloquy and disappointment.

* * *

SIR JOHN POPE HENNESSY

8 OCTOBER 1891

SIR JOHN POPE HENNESSY, M.P. for North Kilkenny, died early yesterday morning at his residence, Rostellan Castle, from heart failure. Sir John, who was 59 years of age, had been suffering from anaemia, which may be traced to his long residence in tropical climates.

The death of Sir John Pope Hennessy removes a man who might have played a more important part in politics had he been differently or less brilliantly gifted. In his qualities and talents, as in his defects, he was a typical Irishman. He was quick of wit, ready in repartee, a fluent speaker, and an able debater; but the enthusiasm and the emotion which lent force and fire to his speeches led him into the adoption of extreme and impracticable views. He was one of the most independent of private members in the House of Commons. He might fairly be described as eccentric and crotchety; and the Colonial Office had reason to mistrust a subordinate who, as it might be charitably presumed, with the best intentions, was always stirring up troubles abroad and landing his chiefs in hot water. In short, we must believe that Sir John Hennessy, with a super-abundance of brain, had an unfortunate deficiency of ballast. The son of a Kerry landowner, he was born in 1834, educated at Queen's College in his native city of Cork, and called to the Bar of the Inner Temple in 1861. His pursuit of the legal profession was somewhat perfunctory, for two years previously he had turned his attention to politics and taken his seat in the House of Commons. It must be confessed that he had the courage of his originality, for he had presented himself to the constituency of King's County and carried the election in the novel character of a Catholic Conservative. We may presume that the clever young man was commissioned by the more worldly-wise members of his Church to prove there were possibilities of coming to an understanding with a party which had hitherto been antipathetical to them. From the first Sir John Hennessy took politics very seriously, and showed the ambition and resolution to get on. His Parliamentary record was an active one, and nowadays it would be difficult for a novice and a private member to achieve half so much. An Irish Catholic and a Conservative, he was at once patriotic and politic; and, moreover, he made sundry valuable contributions to the cause of practical philanthropy. The young member received a flattering compliment when he was formally thanked by the Roman Catholic Committee of England for his successful exertions in the Prison Ministers Act. He was thanked likewise by the Association of British Miners for useful amendments introduced in the Mines' Regulation Bill, which showed he had carefully studied the subject. He was less practical when he urged upon the Government the propriety of making Irish paupers comfortable at home by reclaiming the swamps and the bottomless bogs. Generally he supported the Government on questions relating to the English Church Establishment; but, on the other hand, he took strong exception to the denominational system of education they had introduced in Ireland under what he declared to be the misnomer of a "national" system.

Had he been content to go more quietly, and to be more amenable to party discipline, the Conservatives might have found him a useful ally, and, like the King of Moab with the recalcitrant prophet Balaam, they would willingly have promoted the *protégé* of the priests to great honour. As it was, they thought it prudent to give him the government of distant Labuan, the future of which seemed to be bound up with the existence of coalfields; and we suspect that it was his poverty rather than his will which reconciled him to that honourable exile. Few men have done more official travelling or seen more varied service in tropical climates. From Labuan he went to West Africa, to be transferred in the following year to the Bahamas; and after a short subsequent sojourn in the Windward Islands he governed cosmopolitan Hongkong and the semi-French island of Mauritius. We must add that Sir John Pope Hennessy's colonial career says very little for the intelligence or discretion with which the Colonial Office exercises its patronage. He ought never to have been placed in charge of such colonies as Hongkong or the Mauritius, where the pretensions of the natives threatened to make trouble. The sympathizer with the down-trodden Catholics of West Ireland was an enthusiast with regard to the equal rights of men. And at the Mauritius, to make matters worse, that strong-willed martinet, Mr Clifford Lloyd, whose Irish antecedents associated themselves with peremptory suppression, was assigned to Sir John as Secretary and colleague. Of course, they quarrelled, like two jealous dogs, locked together in couples beyond the master's sight and reach. The experience of Sir Hercules Robinson was called in to arbitrate. Sir John did not come very creditably out of the business, though the final decision was given in his favour. He returned to the colony, to be retired on a full pension when the term of his administration had expired. He had the satisfaction, however, of being formally congratulated by the Secretary of State on his successful administration. He might have been content to rest on his honours, and to interest his leisure with literature. But it was never in his nature to be idle. It is an affair of yesterday, and in everybody's recollection, how he chanced to be put forward as a candidate for North Kilkenny in the very crisis of Mr Parnell's career, and on the eve of Mr Parnell's political collapse. When the choice was between the Protestant dictator and the priests, the choice of the devoted son of the Church could not be doubtful. With the whole influence of the Kilkenny clergy to back him, he carried the election by two to one. At that time he finally broke with the Conservative party by resigning his membership of the Carlton; but since then, owing probably to failing health, he had made no such figure in the House as formerly, and, indeed, had seldom been seen there. It only remains to say that he married a daughter of Sir H. Low, and that it was in 1880 he was created a Knight Commander of St Michael and St George. He showed his good taste by buying as his residence the picturesque and historical mansion in Youghal which had been given to Sir Walter Raleigh by his Gloriana; and, whether it were cause or effect, it was consequently appropriate that Sir John Hennessy should have published some years ago a volume on "Raleigh in Ireland, with his Letters on Irish Affairs and some Contemporary Documents."

* * *

MRS CECIL ALEXANDER

14 OCTOBER 1895

MRS CECIL FRANCES ALEXANDER, so well known as "C.F.A.," died at the Palace, Londonderry, at 6 o'clock on Saturday evening after a few weeks' illness. She was born in county Wicklow in 1818, and was the daughter of Major John Humphreys, who served with distinction at the battle of Copenhagen and was afterwards a landed proprietor and extensive land agent in Ireland. In 1847 she married the Rev. William Alexander, who became Bishop of Derry and Raphoe in 1867. In all religious and charitable works in Londonderry and the diocese she took a wise and energetic part. She possessed a simple and straight-forward dignity of manner, which gave a peculiar distinction to her in social relations. Among the poor and aged she was loved with pathetic intensity. It is, however, upon her writings that Mrs Alexander's extended fame is built. She had a natural bent for poetry, and her early intimacy with Keble and Hook stamped her mind with a lasting impression. Her "Hymns for Little Children" and "Moral Songs" have had an immense circulation. Her less widely known "Poems on Old Testament Subjects" reach a loftier practical standard, but it is by certain of her hymns especially that she will be remembered, not only within the Anglican Church, but by all Christian communities. Of several of these Gounod said that they seemed to set themselves to music. Six only need be indicated- "The roseate hues of early dawn," "When wounded sore the stricken soul," "His are the thousand sparkling rills," "Jesus calls us o'er the tumult," "All things bright and beautiful," and "There is a green hill far away." The "Burial of Moses" is her best known poem. Of this Tennyson observed that it was one of the poems by a living writer of which he would have been proud to be the author. The Rev. F. A. Wallis, of the Universities' Mission to Central Africa, preaching in Londonderry Cathedral yesterday, mentioned that he had heard Mrs Alexander's hymns sung by half-clad Africans in a language she had never known.

OSCAR WILDE

1 DECEMBER 1900

A REUTER TELEGRAM from Paris states that Oscar Wilde died there yesterday afternoon from meningitis. The melancholy end to a career which once promised so well is stated to have come in an obscure hotel of the Latin Quarter. Here the once brilliant man of letters was living, exiled from his country and from the society of his countrymen. The verdict that a jury passed upon his conduct at the Old Bailey in May, 1895, destroyed for ever his reputation, and condemned him to ignoble obscurity for the remainder of his days. When he had served his sentence of two years' imprisonment, he was broken in health as well as bankrupt in fame and fortune. Death has soon ended what must have been a life of wretchedness and unavailing regret. Wilde was the son of the late Sir William Wilde, an eminent Irish surgeon. His mother was a graceful writer, both in prose and verse. He had a brilliant career at Oxford, where he took a first-class both in classical moderations and in *Lit. Hum.*, and also won the Newdigate Prize for English verse for a poem on Ravenna. Even before he left the University in 1878 Wilde had become known as one of the most affected of the professors of the aesthetic craze and for several years it was as the typical aesthete that he kept himself before the notice of the public. At the same time he was a man of far greater originality and power of mind than many of the apostles of aestheticism. As his Oxford career showed, he had undoubted talents in many directions, talents which might have been brought to fruition had it not been for his craving after notoriety. He was known as a poet of graceful diction; as an essayist of wit and distinction; later on as a playwright of skill and subtle humour. A novel of his, "The Picture of Dorian Gray," attracted much attention, and his sayings passed from mouth to mouth as those of one of the professed wits of the age. When he became a dramatist his plays had all the characteristics of his conversation. His first piece, *Lady Windermere's Fan*, was produced in 1892. *A Woman of no Importance* followed in 1893. *An Ideal Husband* and *The Importance of Being Earnest* were both running at the time of their author's disappearance from English life. All these pieces had the same qualities – a paradoxical humour and a perverted outlook on life being the most prominent. They were packed with witty sayings, and the author's cleverness gave him at once a position in the dramatic world. The revelations of the criminal trial in 1895 naturally made them impossible for some years. Recently, however, one of them was revived, though not at a West-end theatre. After his release in 1897, Wilde published "The Ballad of Reading Gaol," a poem of considerable but unequal power. He also appeared in print as a critic of our prison system, against the results of which he entered a passionate protest. For the last three years he has lived abroad. It is stated on the authority of the *Dublin Evening Mail* that he was recently received into the Roman Catholic Church. Mrs Oscar Wilde died not long ago, leaving two children.

* * *

LORD MORRIS OF SPIDDAL

9 SEPTEMBER 1901

WE REGRET TO record the death of Lord Morris and Killanin, which occurred yesterday morning at 4 o'clock, at his residence, Spiddal, county Galway ...

Irishmen have in considerable numbers made their mark in the profession of the law, but those with whom, on this side of the Channel, we are familiar have usually been members of the English Bar, like Baron Martin, Lord Cairns, Lord Macnaghten, and the late Lord Chief Justice. But in the last 30 years the two Irish Chancellors who have been peers,

Lord O'Hagan and Lord Ashbourne, and the Irish Lords of Appeal, Lord Fitzgerald and the late Lord Morris, have served to bring more closely together lawyers of the two nationalities. Lord Morris and Killanin may be said to have had a singularly fortunate career, and up to the time of his resignation in the summer of 1900 he had filled judicial office for 33 years, a whole generation. Born on November 14, 1827, Michael Morris was a member of an old Irish family descended from one of the ancient 13 tribes of Galway, the city with which he was throughout his life associated. An ancestor, Richard Morris, was Bailiff of Galway in 1486. The family, it would appear, were always Catholics, and the father of the late peer was in 1841 the first of that faith who had been High Sheriff since 1690. He was a landed proprietor in the county. His distinguished son, whose career we have now to record, was always attached to his native place, and spent a great deal of his time at the family residence, Spiddal, about a dozen miles west of Galway, on the northern shore of the bay, a pleasant "oasis of civilization," as its owner used to call it, amid some of the wildest tracts of Connaught. Educated at Erasmus Smith's school in Galway, Michael Morris, like many other Catholics of that day, went up to the University of Dublin, despite its "Protestant atmosphere," and it is right to say that he was always loyal to his Alma Mater. He entered Trinity College while still a mere boy and took his degree before he had completed his 20th year, graduating as Senior Moderator and gold medallist in Logic and Ethics in the summer of 1847 ... He was called to the Irish Bar in 1849, and soon won a large practice on circuit and at *nisi prius*, especially in cases connected with his own province. His force of character and his racy wit, founded always on a strong basis of sterling common sense and an undisguised contempt for sentimentality and phrase-making, were rapidly recognized. He took silk in 1863, when he was a little over 35 years of age. In Galway, where he always enjoyed an extraordinary personal popularity, he attained to a position which enabled him to secure his return for that city, at the general election of 1865, at the top of the poll, obtaining the votes of over 90 per cent of the electors, though he issued no formal address and attached himself to no party.

At no time, however, was it doubtful that Morris was a conservative in the broad sense of the word. He distrusted democratic institutions, particularly as applied to an imperfectly developed community like Ireland, and he scorned the sounding platitudes of professional patriots. No Irishman, however, had the best interests of his country more sincerely at heart, or worked more vigorously for them. Morris took up an independent attitude in the House of Commons. But on the change of Ministers in June, 1866, he was offered by Lord Derby and accepted the office of Solicitor-General for Ireland, being the first Roman Catholic who had received such promotion under a Conservative Administration. His acceptance was referred to in complimentary terms by the Prime Minister in the House of Lords. That it was not distasteful to his constituents in Galway was clearly shown when his seat was challenged on his seeking re-election after his appointment. He was returned by a majority of five to one, and when he became Attorney-General a few months later no one ventured to come forward against him.

In April, 1867, when he was little more than 39, he became a puisne Judge of the Court of Common Pleas, ... On the retirement of Lord Chief Justice Monahan, in 1876, Mr Justice Morris succeeded him and was the last Chief of the Common Pleas. Eleven years later he was placed at the head of the Irish Common Law Bench as Lord Chief Justice of Ireland. Meanwhile he had done much public service of a non-judicial character. He was a leading member of the Royal Commission on Irish Primary Education in 1868–70; was one of the Commissioners of National Education in Ireland from 1868 ... In 1885 he was created a baronet. In 1889 he attained the culminating point of his professional success, becoming Lord of Appeal in Ordinary and entering the Upper House as a life peer with the title of Lord Morris of Spiddal. At the same time he was sworn of the Privy Council in England, and shortly afterwards became a bencher of Lincoln's Inn. This was the first occasion – apart from the complimentary admission of Royal and princely personages – in which one who had never been called to the English Bar was placed upon the governing body of one of the Inns of Court.

As a puisne Judge, as Chief Justice of the Common Pleas, and as Lord Chief Justice of Ireland, Morris showed high judicial qualities. He was not, and he never professed to be, a lawyer deeply read in the reports and eager to associate his name with subtle developments of case law. But he was a most capable and careful Judge in *nisi prius* cases and on circuit, where his inborn sagacity, his scorn for shams, his rapidity in mastering facts, his knowledge of the national character, and his genial humour gave him a controlling power over all save the most incorrigible of juries. Yet it would be wrong to say that afterwards, when Lord Morris became a member of the Supreme Appellate Tribunal, he was not capable of dealing ably with judicial principles. Though he was an Irishman, he was not given to verbosity, and he was frequently content to record his concurrence with others of the legal members of the House of Lords. When he pronounced his judgments, however, he spoke always to the purpose, if briefly. Perhaps the public, and even his profession, cannot realize how valuable a check is the presence of incarnate common sense and good-humouredly cynical contempt for the extravagances of hair-splitting and logic-chopping on the part of some eminent lawyers. Of the House of Lords as an abode of liveliness, whether regarded from the political or from the legal point of view, Lord Morris had not a very high opinion. It is even whispered that he used to talk of the august Chamber, irreverently, as "the graveyard." He sometimes could not resist the temptation to supply the quality that was lacking. The proceedings were occasionally diversified by a sally, delivered in the brogue which he never sought to modify, and which, indeed, he frankly declared had been his fortune. One of these interruptions to grave argument was in the prolonged appeal of "Allen v. Flood," the trade union case decided in December, 1897, after a two years' sojourn in the House of Lords. The late Lord Herschell had been frequent in rather petulant interruption of the counsel for the respondent. Lord Morris took the opportunity of saying, in a pretty loud voice and in a way which made laughter irresistible:- "I think we can all understand from the present proceedings what amounts to molesting a man in his business." ... The late Lord's humour was not of the literary kind which finds its way into judgments, but it does bubble up now and again. In the decision of the Judicial Committee in "Cochrane v. Macnish" the question was of the lawful and unlawful use of the term "club soda," and Lord Morris, who gave the decision of the tribunal, remarked:- "In the manufacture of soda-water there is no secret, and frequently no soda." Perhaps his best judgment was the admirable one which he delivered in the Privy Council in "McLeod v. St Aubyn" in 1899. The decision was referred to in these columns in comment on the case in which grossly disrespectful language was used in a Birmingham newspaper of Mr Justice Darling, and the writer was subjected to a fine. Lord Morris, while affirming the existence, deprecated the exercise, of the jurisdiction to commit for contempt of Court on account of scandalous matter published with respect to the Court or Judge ... On Lord Morris's retirement in the summer of 1900 a hereditary peerage, the barony of Killanin, was bestowed upon him. He preferred, however, to be known by his old name.

Perhaps the most signal triumph, from a personal point of view, that Lord Morris had to boast of in his long and successful career was won shortly after his resignation of the Law Lordship in the early part of 1900. While he filled a judicial office, Lord Morris felt that it was not right for him to take an active share in party politics and political controversy. His eldest son contested the borough of Galway unsuccessfully in 1895, and, though he was chosen a member of the first county council of Galway under the Irish Local Government Act in 1899, the only Unionist elected west of the Shannon, it seemed that he had not much prospect of victory when he presented himself again as a candidate for the borough after the dissolution of last year. But, in the meantime, his father had been "unmuzzled." Lord Morris had never lost touch with the people of Galway. He lived much among them, and enjoyed living among them. He knew them all, and rarely forgot a face. When the Local Government Bill was before the House of Lords, he fought manfully, and for the moment successfully, to preserve for Galway a privileged position as a county borough, and by his individual energy carried an amendment to this effect against the Government, in the Upper House, which was set aside in the House of

Commons. Lord Morris, during the interval before the strict "electoral period," when it was permissible for him as a peer to engage in political conflict, threw himself with characteristic energy and humour into the fray. It was largely due to his personal influence that Mr Martin Morris won his seat – the only one outside Ulster for which a Unionist was returned last autumn – by a satisfactory majority against a singular combination of adverse forces. All the sections of the Nationalists combined to work for the Separatist candidate, Mr Leamy, a popular and able man apart from politics. The Roman Catholic Bishop was Mr Leamy's proposer, and, with hardly a single exception, the clergy, parish priests and curates alike, were active partisans on the same side. But Lord Morris appealed successfully to the memories and the kindly feeling of his old friends and neighbours, his former constituents. He reminded them that he had never severed his interests from theirs, and that he had always lived among them, dealt with them, knew almost every man by name, and was ardent for their welfare. He repelled in vigorous speeches the attacks upon him and his son as representatives of Toryism and landlordism. He roused the enthusiasm of the fishermen of "the Claddagh" by speaking to them in Irish, though he used to confess that he could no more read a line in that language than the majority of the professional patriots could understand it, whether spoken or written. Mr Martin Morris's victory was creditable to himself; but it was even in a higher degree a personal triumph for his father and a tribute to the unique place he had won in the hearts of the people of Galway.

Perhaps Lord Morris's social gifts were even more remarkable than his legal and political successes. What he enjoyed most of all things in the world was talk; and he talked admirably – not least because he chose to express himself in what he used to call "my broadest Doric" – whether he was strolling with a single companion through the rough moorland region behind Spiddal or was the life and soul of the company at a country house party or a London dinner. His humour was of a far higher quality than the fine-drawn subtleties of the professional wit. It was always rooted in a sturdy and fearless common sense. It may perhaps be said that in politics Lord Morris was a pessimist, like so many other brilliant humourists. He had not, at any rate, a very high opinion of either the intelligence or the straightforwardness of politicians. His reply to some one who asked him, somewhat inaptly, to explain "the Irish question" in a few words is well known. "It is the difficulty," he said, "of a stupid and honest people trying to govern a quickwitted and dishonest one." Yet he was by no means of opinion that the government of Ireland was impracticable, though he was full of scorn for the incurable optimism which professed to believe that Irish separatism would be weakened rather than strengthened by the extension of the franchise and, at a later date, the introduction of local government of the broadest democratic kind in Ireland. How the loyal minority could hope to win in an electoral fight he could not understand. "If it was to be fought out with fists," he said, "I could understand it, but at the ballot-box, when the rebel party are ten to one, don't ask me to believe that we can beat them." When a distinguished Radical, begged to be informed how long the struggle against the law in Ireland would be maintained, after "resolute government" had been really instituted, Lord Morris's answer was "one hour!" If the prediction has not been realized, it is because the condition precedent has never been fulfilled.

A whole chapter of legend has grown up about Lord Morris's name and his reputation as a wit. Countless stories are told of his sharp sayings, some of them authentic and most of them characteristic. Perhaps none are more striking than some of the utterances attributed to him when he sat on the Bench in Ireland. During the earlier developments of Fenianism some Irish Judges expended a vast amount of rhetorical indignation on the puny traitors of that day. Morris dealt with them in a different fashion. He wasted no words upon them, but dismissed their futile folly with a moderate sentence and with cutting contempt. In a case where some young farmer's sons were tried on a charge of illegal drilling and carrying arms by night, Morris said:- "There you go on with your marching and counter-marching, making fools of yourselves, when you ought to be out in the fields, turning dung." On another occasion, when an eloquent advocate had extenuated some criminal act on the ground that "the people" were in sympathy with the offenders, the Chief Justice remarked, "I never knew a small town in Ireland that hadn't a black-guard in it who called himself 'the people.'" Of trial by jury in the sister island he had no very high opinion. "In the West," he said, "the Court is generally packed with people whose names all begin with one letter, Michael Morris on the Bench, ten men of the name of Murphy and two men of the name of Moriarty in the jury-box, and two other Moriartys in the dock, and the two Moriartys on the jury going in fear of their lives of the ten Murphys if they don't find against their own friends."

As Chief Justice he had a high regard for the dignity and independence of his own Court, and especially resented any claim on the part of the Treasury to interfere. Once, it is said, a most distinguished official was sent over from Whitehall to Dublin, after a long correspondence on the side of the Department about the expenditure of fuel in the Court-rooms and Judge's chamber, to obtain the answer that the vigilant guardians of the public purse had failed to extract in writing. He was received politely by the Chief Justice, who said that he would put him in communication with the proper person; and, ringing the bell, which was answered by the elderly female who acted as Court-keeper, he remarked, as he turned on his heel and left the room, "Mary, this is the man that's come about the coals." Shortly after the Land Act of 1881 became law a very important case was carried to the Court of Appeal, of which Morris, as Chief Justice of the Common Pleas, was an *ex officio* member. Morris was not summoned, and, meeting the Lord Chancellor in the street, he expressed his surprise. The Chancellor, with some embarrassment, explained that he had not wished to put the Chief Justice to inconvenience, that he had summoned a sufficient number of Judges to constitute the tribunal, and that, in fact, there were not chairs enough on the bench of the Court of Appeal to accommodate any more. "Oh!" (said Morris, according to this story). "That need make no difference. I'll bring my own chair out of my own Court, and I'll form my own opinion and deliver my own judgment, Lord Chancellor!" In the early days of the Home Rule policy the Chief Justice, it is said, was a guest at a great official banquet in Dublin, where a lady of high position, full of enthusiasm for Mr Gladstone's latest transmigration, asked him whether the great majority of those present were not ardent Home Rulers. "Indeed, Lady," said Morris, "I suppose that, with the exception of his Excellency and yourself, and, perhaps, half a dozen of the servants, there aren't three in the room!"

Lord Morris and Killanin married, in 1860, Anna, daughter of the Hon. G. H. Hughes, Baron of the Court of Exchequer in Ireland. By her he had four sons and six daughters. The eldest son, Martin Henry FitzPatrick, a graduate of the University of Dublin, a barrister of Lincoln's Inn, succeeds, on his father's death, to the Barony of Killanin and to the baronetcy. The life peerage of Lord Morris of Spiddal ceases, of course, to exist.

* * *

ARCHBISHOP CROKE

23 JULY 1902

DR THOMAS WILLIAM CROKE, Roman Catholic Archbishop of Cashel and Emly – perhaps the most remarkable Irish ecclesiastic since the death of Cardinal Cullen, though there was little in common between the two men – was born close to the town of Mallow, county Cork, on May 19, 1824. His people were well-to-do farmers. Though his mother was a Protestant, he was destined from an early age by his uncle, who took charge of his education, for the priesthood. He was never in Maynooth, the great training college of the Irish priesthood, but spent ten years in colleges on the Continent established during the operation of the Penal Laws for the education of priests intended for the mission in Ireland and Great Britain. At the age of 14, he entered the Irish College in Paris, and spent six years there; another year was passed in a college in Menin, in Belgium, and after an additional three years in the Irish College in Rome he obtained the degree of Doctor of Divinity, and was ordained priest in 1848. Then for brief periods he was Professor in the Diocesan College, Carlow, and in the Irish College, Paris, after which he returned to his native diocese of Cloyne, Cork, as a missionary priest. In 1858 he was appointed president of St Colman's College, Fermoy; after seven years he returned to the mission as parish priest of Doneraile. In 1870, when he was 45 years of age, he was appointed by the Pope, on the nomination of Cardinal Cullen, to the bishopric of Auckland, New Zealand. In 1875 the bishopric of Cashel and Emly became vacant. The parish priests of the see met, as usual, to propose three names – *dignissimus, dignior, dignus* – from whom the Pope was to select the Archbishop. But on the recommendation of Cardinal Cullen the three names were set aside by the Holy See, and Dr Croke was recalled from New Zealand to take charge of the Archdiocese of Cashel and Emly. He was received with extreme coldness by the priests; but a patriotic oration he delivered at the O'Connell Centenary in August, 1875, made him extremely popular. He was thence known as "the patriot Archbishop."

In the early fifties, while he was a curate in the diocese of Cloyne, Dr Croke took an active part in the land agitation for "the three F's" – fixity of tenure, fair rents, and free sale – conducted by Gavan Duffy. The movement did not long survive. It was deserted by most of those who had created it. Gavan Duffy, describing Ireland as like "a corpse on the dissecting table," resigned his seat in Parliament and emigrated to Victoria. Before his departure Dr Croke wrote him a letter, which thus concluded:- "For myself I have determined never to join any Irish agitation, never to sign any petition to Government, and never to trust to any one man or body of men, living in my time, for the recovery of Ireland's independence. All hope with me in Irish affairs is dead and buried. I have ever esteemed you at once the honestest and most gifted of my country-men and your departure from Ireland leaves me no hope." In 1879, clean on a quarter of a century after that despairing letter had been written, Mr Parnell went down to the little market town of Thurles, in Tipperary, where Dr Croke resided, to request the Archbishop to give his support to the Land League agitation which had just been inaugurated. Dr Croke stated some years afterwards that he was at first reluctant to join the movement and that he only yielded his consent when Mr Parnell actually went on his knees before him, saying, "I must have the Bishops at the head of this movement, else it will not succeed." However, Dr Croke soon became the most active Land Leaguer among the Roman Catholic hierarchy. He supported the agitation in vigorous letters and speeches. But he thought the no-rent manifesto, issued on the proclamation of the Land League by Mr W. E. Forster, in 1881, was going too far. He wrote an address to the people of Ireland denouncing it, not, indeed, so much because it was immoral, as because it was illogical. He said that the trim reply to the proclamation of the Land League was to refuse to pay taxes rather than to repudiate debts due to a number of individuals, who had no responsibility for the action of the Government. Two years later he sent another letter to the Press advocating a national testimonial to Mr Parnell for his services to Ireland. Pope Leo XIII issued an encyclical letter condemning the tribute, but this had the effect of increasing the subscription, and ultimately Mr Parnell was presented with a cheque for £40,000. Dr Croke and a number of other Bishops were summoned to Rome to explain their conduct to the Holy See. When he returned he received a most enthusiastic welcome, and in a speech at a public meeting declared he was "unchanged and unchangeable."

In 1890 it fell to the lot of Dr Croke to draw up, on behalf of the Roman Catholic hierarchy of Ireland, an address to the Irish people declaring that Mr Parnell was not a fit man to be their leader, because of the disclosures of the O'Shea divorce case. This address was not issued until after the publication of Mr Gladstone's letter stating that his efforts on behalf of Home Rule would be fruitless if Mr Parnell were retained as chairman of the Irish party. The charge was subsequently made against the hierarchy that they had postponed taking action until they saw how things were going decisively, but Dr Croke explained, five years later, that the delay was due entirely to the fact that the document had to be sent to Bishop after Bishop for signature. After the fall of Mr Parnell Dr Croke retired from public life. Appeals were frequently made to him to try to settle the differences between Parnellites and anti-Parnellites, O'Brienites and Healyites, but he refused absolutely to intervene.

Dr Croke, physically, was over 6ft. high and well made in proportion. In his youth and early manhood he had been a champion athlete in leaping and jumping, and was distinguished also in the hurling and football fields. All through life he took the keenest interest in the national sports and pastimes of the Irish people. On the foundation of the Gaelic Athletic Association in 1885 for the revival of Irish games he became its president. In his address on the subject he said:-

"Ball playing, hurling, football kicking, according to Irish rules, 'casting' (or throwing the stone), leaping in various ways, wrestling, handy-grips, top-pegging, leap-frog, rounders, tip-in-the-hat, and all such favourite exercises and amusements amongst men and boys may now be said to be not only dead and buried, but in several localities to be entirely forgotten and unknown. And what have we got in their stead? We have got such foreign and fantastic field sports as lawn tennis, polo, croquet, cricket and the like. Very excellent, I believe, and health-giving exercises in their way, still not racy of the soil, but rather alien to it."

There might be, he added, "something rather pleasing to the eye in the get-up of the modern young man who, arrayed in light attire, with party-coloured cap on, and racket in hand, is making his way, with or without a companion, to the tennis ground," but he preferred the youthful athletes of his early years – "bereft of shoes and coat and thus prepared to play at hand-ball, to fly over any number of horses, to throw the sledge of winding-stone, and to test each other's mettle and activity by the trying ordeal of three leaps, or a hop, step, and jump."

Dr Croke was of a genial and warm-hearted nature. He delighted in hospitality at his palace in Thurles, and after dinner was fond of regaling his guests with humorous Irish stories and Irish comic songs. He had a contempt for books, but especially abhorred collections of sermons.

He did not hesitate to declare that Irish history was too cheerless a chronicle for him to study. It was infinitely better, he also said, to try to make history, even in a small way, than to write volumes about it.

* * *

MICHAEL DAVITT

31 MAY 1906

MR MICHAEL DAVITT died early this morning at a private hospital, in Lower Mount-street, Dublin, where he had been lying in a critical condition for some days. Michael Davitt, probably the most resolute and implacable enemy of the connexion between Great Britain and Ireland that has appeared in modern time, was born at Straid, a small village in county Mayo, in March, 1846, a few weeks before the birth of Charles Stewart Parnell, his associate in after life, though coming from a very different social stratum. Davitt's father was a petty peasant farmer, who was evicted in 1851 for non-payment of rent, which, however, it is alleged, had not been raised during the period of his tenancy. The family then migrated to Lancashire, and settled in the small manufacturing town of Haslingden, where the boy found employment in a cotton mill, and, though a Roman Catholic, got his elementary education at a Wesleyan school. When he was 11 years old a machinery accident deprived him of his right arm, but he got casual occupation as a news-boy, as an assistant letter-carrier, and ultimately as an employé in a small printing office. Reading widely if not wisely, he drifted rapidly into the ranks of the Fenian Brotherhood, which became actively aggressive in 1865. When an abortive attempt was made by the Fenians to capture Chester Castle, early in 1867, Davitt, according to an admiring

79

biographer, "though unable to shoulder a rifle with his single arm, carried a small store of cartridges in a bag made from a pocket-handkerchief." When the baffled band of conspirators broke up, Davitt escaped detection and returned to Haslingden, where he immediately resumed "active operations," arranging for the secret export of firearms to Ireland. This led to his arrest in 31 May, 1870, on a charge of "treason felony," on which he was tried at the Old Bailey, with a confederate, before Lord Chief Justice Cockburn, and convicted, without hesitation, by the jury. A letter in Davitt's handwriting was produced and sworn to, a passage in which, the Chief Justice said, in passing a sentence of 15 years' penal servitude, showed that there was "some dark and dangerous design against the life of some man." Towards the close of 1877, however, Davitt was released, after serving half of his sentence in Dartmoor Convict Prison, and a few months later he visited the United States, where his mother, herself of American birth, though of Irish blood, had settled with other members of the family. Before crossing the Atlantic he had rejoined the "Irish Republican Brotherhood," the branch of the Fenian organization established in Ireland, and was elected a member of the "Supreme Council," which practically admitted him to confidential relations, as the Special Commission found, with the Clan-na-Gael and the whole body of American-Irish Fenians. He told the Commissioners himself that he had "a well-defined purpose" in visiting the States, which, as his further evidence showed, was to "make the Land Question the stepping-stone to national independence." With another Fenian and ex-convict, John Devoy, Davitt, during his stay in America, studied the methods of revolution through agrarian agitation devised 30 years before by Fintan Lalor, and on his return to Ireland the confederates launched the "new departure," with the assent and co-operation of the emissaries of the Clan-na-Gael, the aim being to combine the physical force faction and the agrarian revolutionists in a common policy, embracing an attack on rents and the acquisition of complete control over local elected bodies. Into this policy Mr Parnell was gradually drawn, and the Land League, originally started at Irishtown, in Mayo, early in 1879, developed, half a year later, into a "national organization," with its seat in Dublin, Parnell as president, and Davitt as one of the secretaries. In view of the anti-clerical developments of Davitt's later career, it is worthy of notice that the Irishtown meeting was called to denounce a landlord who was also a parish priest, one Canon Burke. Parnell's visit to America, his violent speeches there, the assurances given to the physical force party that their methods were not to be interfered with were among the first results of the foundation of the Land League. Davitt himself crossed the Atlantic in May, 1880, just after the general election, and for several months acted "as the link between the two wings of the Irish party," explaining to the Fenians that the aims of the two sections did not clash and that they might be of mutual aid to one another.

The earlier course of the Land League did not bring Davitt into any peculiar prominence, though he defended the organization against charges of crime, which soon were only too notoriously established; but in 1881 the Parliamentary conflict became intense, and Davitt, though not an M.P., was one of the first to feel its effects. He had made some violent speeches in favour of the League in Ireland, and in February it was announced in the House of Commons that Davitt's ticket-of-leave had been withdrawn, that he had been arrested, and sent to Portland Prison. The action of the Government was fiercely challenged, and the energetic reply of the Home Secretary, Sir William Harcourt, who declared that Davitt's freedom had been abused to the ruin of the peace of Ireland, and that his continued avowal of Fenian aims was incompatible with the indulgence of the Crown, almost provoked an open riot. The loud cheers of the Liberals were met with a howl of Nationalist rage, but Sir William Harcourt was firm, and Davitt was detained at Portland, while Parnell and the rest, after Mr Gladstone's discovery that the resources of civilization were not exhausted, found their headquarters in Kilmainham Gaol, and continued their endeavours to nullify the Land Act by the issue of the famous "no rent" manifesto. Not many months after, the perennial dreams of conciliation had their hour of triumph; Davitt's freedom was apparently one of the articles of the so-called "Kilmainham Treaty," and on May 6th, 1882, the ominous day on which Lord F. Cavendish and Mr Burke were stabbed to death in the Phoenix Park, Parnell and other friends escorted the released prisoner from Portland to London, where his first work was to compose a denunciation of political assassins, of which the unction must have surprised his "guide, philosopher, and friend" – so described by himself – Mr Patrick Ford, of the *Irish World*. But before the year was over Davitt was again at cross purposes with the law and the Gladstonian Government, was prosecuted for seditious speeches in 1883, and again imprisoned, but for three months only. Up to this time Davitt, though a potent force in the Nationalist party, had never sat in Parliament. He was elected for Meath in 1882, but, being still a convict, was held disqualified.

At the general election of 1885 Davitt had the offer of several Nationalist seats, but declined them all, on the ground that he could not, consistently with scruples of conscience, consent to take the oath of allegiance. At this time his relations with Parnell were becoming somewhat strained, though they had much in common, including a rooted distrust of clerical influence and a contempt for the febrile excitability of some of their comrades in arms. Davitt, too, during his years of prison seclusion and afterwards, had studied the works of Henry George, and became an advocate of land nationalization, inclining in later years to sympathy with other forms of socialism; while Parnell, though willing to transfer property from one set of owners to another, was, like the vast majority of Irishmen of all classes, opposed to placing any restrictions on the rights of the new owners for the benefit of the general community. While Davitt thus occupied a somewhat ambiguous and at times isolated position, and when he had not yet conquered his scruples about the oath of allegiance or sought a Parliamentary seat, the proceedings before the Special Commission appointed to inquire into the "charges and allegations" in the article on "Parnellism and Crime" brought him again into a conspicuous place in the public eye as one of the "respondents." He appeared in person before the Commission, and showed much ability both in argument and in cross-examination, meriting the complimentary notice of Sir James Hannen and his colleagues. His speech in his own defence occupied five days. He told the tribunal a great many things which threw light on the events and agencies that led up to the foundation of the Land League and influenced its subsequent operations and their consequences. But, as the report of the Commissioners points out, he declined to answer several important questions, especially those connected with the visits to Ireland, in 1879 and 1880, of persons representing the Clan-na-Gael, who were intimately associated then with Davitt himself. The Commissioners found that Davitt, in common with Parnell and others, "established and joined in the Land League organization with the intention, by its means, to bring about the absolute independence of Ireland as a separate nation"; and that he shared the responsibility of the other respondents for neglecting to denounce the intimidation that led to outrage, and for even inciting to that intimidation; for disseminating the *Irish World* and other newspapers inciting to sedition and to crime; for inviting the pecuniary assistance of the physical force party in America, and, in consideration of that support, abstaining from condemnation of the acts of those allies. Two personal charges, moreover, against Davitt were held to be proved in substance – that he was a Fenian and convicted as such, and that he received money out of an "outrage fund" to help in starting the agitation out of which the Land League sprang. Further-more, it was held to be proved – and was, indeed, admitted by him – that he was in close and intimate alliance with the party of violence in America, and was mainly instrumental in bringing about an alliance between that party and the Parliamentarians. It was significant that these proved facts do not seem to have injuriously affected Davitt's influence with the Irish Home Rulers generally.

His recognition as a leader was, however, retarded for the moment by the line he took at the close of the year 1890, when "the Nonconformist conscience" and the imperious will of Mr Gladstone compelled the Irish party to eject Parnell from the leadership. Davitt did not hesitate a moment in separating himself, the instant the question of the divorce scandal came up, from his former ally; he said, having been grossly duped by false assurances, no matter what the party decided, "I will have nothing more to do with him as long as he lives," and he censured the Roman Catholic Bishops severely for shrinking from speaking out. Thenceforward Davitt became a leading spirit in the anti-Parnellite camp, until, long after Parnell had passed away, "unity" was temporarily achieved under Mr John Redmond. At the general election of 1892 Davitt was returned to the House of Commons for the first time as member for North Meath, but was unseated on petition. Shortly after he was elected for North-East Cork unopposed, but became bankrupt owing to the North Meath petition costs, and had to vacate his seat. In 1895 he was returned for West Mayo, but before the next dissolution he had retired from Parliamentary life for reasons of health. Then and on former occasions he travelled much and wrote several books, all deeply coloured with antipathy to England and the Empire. His sympathies with the Boers, the Sudanese, and all other nationalities whom he could contrive to regard as the enemies of the British race were never concealed, and his anti-British bias was so strong that he had not, during his comparatively brief career in the House of Commons, anything like the position he might have enjoyed if he had been less rancorous and unfair. He was an Irishman of a somewhat rare type, dark and dour, though not without a good deal of astuteness. Far more than the voluble phrasemonger who coined the expression, he represented "the unchangeable passion of hate" which, it has been said, is the permanent attitude of the Celtic and Catholic Irishman towards the British power. His intimacy with the Labour party in Great Britain was close, and he exulted over their victories in the late elections. Towards the end of his life Davitt grew more and more to distrust the domination of the priesthood, which in turn excluded him from many fields of influence. One of his latest efforts in controversy was the publication of a long and vigorous letter attacking the educational policy of the Bishops, and particularly the ideas of Dr O'Dwyer. On this ground he failed to secure much public support in his native land, but it is known that many Roman Catholic laymen were thankful for his courageous denunciation of the clerical boycott of Trinity College. He was a journalist wielding a ready, if somewhat rough, pen, who contributed largely not only to

Irish, but to British, American, and colonial newspapers. His books were too manifestly partisan to be worth serious study. Anything more misleading than his presentation of what he calls "The Boer Fight for Freedom" cannot be imagined, unless it be his still wilder travesty of history, grotesquely named "The Fall of Feudalism in Ireland."

Our Dublin Correspondent writes:-

"To the generation which is now reaching manhood in Ireland much of what has been recorded above is ancient history. Older Irish Unionists cannot forget Davitt's bitter and dangerous part in the anti-English agitation, but the younger men found something to admire in his later political activities. He enjoyed among them a reputation for courage and sincerity which they refused to many of his associates, and it pleased them to see the cautious and time-serving party leaders embarrassed by his candid criticisms. He did not fear the priests, and his temper, with all its faults, was free from any trace of hypocrisy or meanness. These qualities made him singular; and, while they were a cause of constant uneasiness to his colleagues, they inspired in his political opponents a feeling not far removed from respect. His keen sense of humour and his large knowledge of men and affairs made him in private life an entertaining companion. In the course of his quarrels with the priests he was often denounced as an atheist, but there is no reason to believe that he was not a sincere Roman Catholic. On his deathbed he received the last ministrations of his Church."

THE O'CONOR DON

2 JULY 1906

THE RIGHT HON. Charles Owen O'Conor died on Saturday, after a brief illness, at his residence, Clonallis, Castlerea, co. Roscommon.

Charles Owen O'Conor, commonly known as The O'Conor Don, the head of one of the most ancient and renowned of Irish septs, the O'Conors of Connaught, was born on May 7, 1838. Left fatherless at an early age, he inherited relatively large estates in the counties of Roscommon and Sligo, the relics of the vast possessions held by his family in the West of Ireland, from the days when anarchy, just before the Anglo-Norman invasion, produced in Roderic O'Conor the last and unfortunate titular monarch of the Irish race. The descent and title of The O'Conor Don had always been recognized by the Celtic population and, to a certain extent, by successive Governments of both political parties. Adhering to the Roman Catholic faith and generally associated with the Liberal connexion, as it existed before the Parnellite deluge swept away the ancient landmarks, the family was credited with an impregnable position in Connaught, and few deemed, during the late fifties and early sixties, that the chief of the house would, during the last quarter of a century of his life, be a political outcast in his own land. He received, with his brother, his early education in St Gregory's, Downside – a school which turned out many brilliant men trained by the scholarly and accomplished Benedictine order. In those days Roman Catholics were practically excluded from the older Universities. Accordingly, in 1855, The O'Conor Don matriculated in the University of London, then a purely examining institution, but did not proceed to take a degree.

He was naturally drawn into politics while still quite young, and in 1858 he was returned at a by-election for the county Roscommon, which his father had represented for several years. By this constituency he was again sent to the House of Commons, without opposition, at the general elections of 1865, 1868, and 1874. In the last two Parliaments his younger brother, Denis, held one of the two seats in the neighbouring county of Sligo, regaining it, though by a narrow margin, even in the *débâcle* of 1880, when the elder of the two succumbed, never regaining a Parliamentary seat. The O'Conor Don, three years later, contested Wexford against Mr William Redmond, but was beaten by more than two to one.

During his Parliamentary career, from 1860 to 1880, The O'Conor Don won no conspicuous place in debate, though his ability as a master of detail and a hard-headed reasoner gave him a considerable degree of authority. He was able to carry one or two important legislative measures – an achievement of which few private members, especially when in Opposition, are able to boast. He had a principal share in placing on the Statute-book the Irish Industrial Schools Act of 1868, and the Irish Sunday Closing Act of 1879. His most remarkable interference in politics was the part he took in the development of the Irish University controversy in 1879. He had always been an advocate of a Roman Catholic teaching college or University, but the Bill which he presented in May, 1879, was in the nature of a "half-way house," proposing the creation of a new University Senate, in many ways resembling that of the Royal University, but obtaining powers of paying results fees to denominational colleges ... The Home Secretary, Mr Cross, speaking for Lord Beaconsfield's Government, said that they could not accept The O'Conor Don's Bill, but would, at once, introduce a measure of their own, which was brought forward by Lord Cairns in the Upper House, and out of which the Royal University, now universally condemned as unsatisfactory, emerged on the ruins of the Queen's University.

But The O'Conor Don's advocacy of a Catholic University had little influence over the rising storm of agrarianism. He, like many others of his class, was destined to show that the most illustrious Celtic blood, the purest Catholic orthodoxy, and the most faithful Liberalism were not to protect any landlord who did not surrender every claim of right, against the proscriptions of the Land League, founded by Michael Davitt about the time that The O'Conor Don was meditating his University Bill.

Roscommon was swept, after the dissolution of 1880, by a carpet-bagger barrister from Liverpool and by Mr O'Kelly, an avowed revolutionary, and, indeed, a Fenian. Thenceforward, The O'Conor Don's work – for he was never an idle man – lay outside the House of Commons. He was selected by Mr Gladstone as one of the members of Lord Bessborough's Commission on the Irish Land Question in 1880. The appointment was regarded as a solatium for his defeat by the Land League, and was very bitterly attacked by the extreme followers of Parnell and Davitt. Many years later he was placed on the Royal Commission appointed to inquire into the Financial Relations between Great Britain and Ireland, and on the death of Mr Childers, in 1896, he became chairman of that body, and, as such, was responsible for the final report. In recent years, the activity of The O'Conor Don has been chiefly displayed in the incessant discussions on changes in the land laws and on educational controversies ... As a leading and industrious representative on the executive committee of the Irish Landowners' Convention, The O'Conor Don's sagacious and temperate criticisms were very highly valued by his colleagues during the anxious consideration which had to be given to a succession of Land Bills, all of them containing many doubtful and dangerous elements. His minutes and speeches were always clear, frequently pointed, and sometimes very forcible, though never pretending to eloquence. Besides his work on the history of the O'Conors of Connaught, published in 1891, which is founded on O'Donovan's manuscripts in the possession of the family, The O'Conor Don published several pamphlets and fugitive essays on Irish taxation, land tenure, and education. He was twice married and leaves issue.

SIR W. H. RUSSELL

11 FEBRUARY 1907

SIR WILLIAM HOWARD RUSSELL, the veteran War Correspondent of *The Times*, died yesterday morning at his London residence, 202, Cromwell-road, S.W., in the presence of the members of his family ...

It was in 1821 that the future War Correspondent was born at Lilyvale, in the county of Dublin ... His parents were people of small means, and had not the power, if they had the will, to spend much on his education. All that is known is that he was a pupil for some time at a school in Dublin kept by Dr Geoghagan; and that he entered Trinity College, Dublin, as an exhibitioner in 1838. His name does not appear in the list of graduates, and we fancy he never took a degree or distinguished himself greatly in academic studies. But his intellect was too bright and too keen not to take in knowledge by a sort of instinctive process; and though we should doubt his ever having been a profound scholar, or even having studied literature very seriously, he undoubtedly contrived to pick up all the learning which ... was requisite to enable a man to hold his own as a gentleman amidst gentlemen. In the years when the Repeal agitation was at its height, when the monster mass-meetings of Tara and Clontarf were supposed to be the fore-runners of a revolution which was only prevented by the arrest of O'Connell, Russell, who after leaving college had drifted into journalism, took an active part as a reporter of the Repeal meetings. He himself in later years gave the following account of how he first came to report for *The Times*:-

My brother-in-law was in 1841 a reporter for *The Times* in Ireland, the election was coming on at Longford, and my brother-in-law was ill, so he said to me, "Billy you've got to report the election for *The Times*." Well, I was under 20, and I'd never written a line in my life; but my Irish wit told me that in an Irish election most of the free and independent electors generally had to come to hospital.

So I sat there until they all came in to get their heads bandaged, and so I got quite a dramatic account of it all, and posted over to London with it. When I got to *The Times* Office and was waiting in a dark passage a man came out of a room, "Are you the chap who wrote this?" and I said, "I did, Sir, but it wasn't my own fault, and I'll apologize"; but he then and there offered me £4 a week, and from that day to this they've never stopped paying me liberally more than I was worth.

... He was ... for some years a constant visitor to the gallery of the House of Commons as a Parliamentary reporter, and soon acquired the reputation of a very active and clever young journalist. He kept his terms at the Middle Temple, was called to the Bar in 1850, and obtained a fair amount of practice for a youthful barrister who had no special connexion with solicitors, and whose attention was mainly devoted to other pursuits. Journalism and the law have this much, at any rate, in common, that they are both jealous mistresses and expect single-hearted service from those who would win their favour.

The year 1853 was the turning-point of Russell's career. On the outbreak of the Crimean War the barrister journalist was selected to represent *The Times* during the impending campaign. Since that date war correspondence has become so recognized a part of journalistic enterprise that it is difficult to realize the fact of Russell's mission to the East having constituted at the time a new departure in the Press ... Great was the outcry of the service clubs and military circles when it was announced that war correspondents were to be allowed to accompany our Army to the East. Discipline, we were assured, would become impossible if the action of our generals, the plans of our campaign, and the condition of our troops were to be criticized by newspaper reporters on the field of battle. These apprehensions were not, perhaps, as absurd as we deemed in the days when, as it now seems to us who write, all the world was young. War correspondents might well have become an evil instead of a boon if the first and greatest of the body had not set an example at the outset how the most zealous discharge of the duties of a purveyor of war news could be made consistent with the most perfect loyalty to the Army whose achievements and experiences it was the correspondent's mission to record. On his first joining the Army in the East, Russell was an unknown and almost an unwelcome visitor, tolerated rather than accepted by the military authorities. In a short time, however, his cheery good-humour, his manifest liking for military men and military matters, rendered him a *persona grata* throughout the British camp. To enter into any elaborate recital here of the part played by *The Times* during the Crimean campaign would be unfitting the occasion. Suffice it to say that the letters which appeared in our columns from our Special Correspondent brought home the vicissitudes of the war with marvellous vividness to our fellow-countrymen. Some of his descriptions, such as that of the battle of Inkerman, when "the thin red line" of the British troops withstood the onslaught of the Russian columns, of the charge of the Light Brigade, and of the chaos of Balaclava Harbour, have long outlived the ordinary span of existence allotted to journalistic literature even of the highest order. Without reviving worn-out controversies, we may say that all subsequent investigation has justified the substantial accuracy of the judgments, opinions, and views in connexion with the Crimean campaign to which Russell called the attention of the British public in his letters to this journal. He was mainly responsible for the popular outcry against the mismanagement of our Army during the terrible winter of 1854 – an outcry which created the most intense excitement at home and which contributed more powerfully than perhaps any other single cause to the downfall of the Aberdeen Ministry. Nothing has occurred since to throw doubt on the justice of Russell's Balaclava letters, or to cause us to regret the action taken by *The Times* with the view of exposing and redressing the sufferings inflicted upon our troops, partly by incompetence, still more by a too rigid adherence to old fashioned routine.

Whatever controversy there may have been at the time as to the soundness and accuracy of Mr Russell's criticisms, there was a well-nigh universal consensus of opinion as to the brilliancy of his descriptions. Though there have been eminent war correspondents since the days of the Crimean War, none of them can lay claim to have experienced the same difficulties, surmounted the same antagonism, and achieved the same position as the first and chief of military journalists.

The special correspondents of latter-day journalism have not the time, even if they have the power, to describe what has passed before their eyes in language so graphic, so happily chosen, so full of nervous vigour, as that which rendered Russell's letters from the Crimea masterpieces in their own class of literary composition ... All newspaper work is of its nature ephemeral. Mr Russell, however, could have said truly that he had accomplished a feat unparalleled in the annals of journalism, that he had written newspaper articles which would be remembered as long as Englishmen interest themselves in the records of English valour, English heroism, English disasters, and English victories.

When Mr Russell returned to London after the Crimean War he found himself famous. The almost unknown reporter had become the first of journalists in his own special department, and had got his name associated with a campaign which the British public still regarded with passionate admiration. Those who desire to realize the sentiments entertained at the time with regard to the Crimean War by the great mass of Englishmen ... will understand something of the peculiar position occupied at the time by the prince of war correspondents, whose writings had brought home to us all the gallantry of our soldiers, the cruelty of their sufferings, and the errors which had dimmed, though they had not hidden, the fulness of their triumph.

Balaclava Russell, as he was then popularly called, might, had he been so minded, have been the lion of the London season. But somehow social distinction was not a matter in which he took any keen interest. About this time he had been elected a member of the Garrick Club, and he cared much more for the society he met with there than he did for fashionable gatherings. No man was ever more popular in a club where popularity was not easily to be acquired, and where friendships once made were not lost easily. Thackeray's saying that he would anyday pay a guinea to have Russell dine with him at his table in the club was characteristic, not only of the great novelist, but of the general feeling with which Russell was regarded by his fellow-members. To devotees of the game of whist some idea of Russell's charm may best be given by the statement that few men ever played whist so badly and yet few men were so invariably welcome at the whist-tables of the club.

In 1857 the war broke out in India, and Russell was sent out as the representative of this journal. He had lived down the jealousy with which war correspondents were regarded in the Crimean era, and was received as a personal friend by the then Sir Colin Campbell and all his old acquaintances during the Russian war. Perhaps the letters Russell wrote from India were the best he ever contributed to *The Times*. There must be many amidst the elder generation of our readers who still remember his marvellous description of the night march to Lucknow. But the story of the Mutiny and its suppression had not the attraction for English readers possessed by the narrative of the Crimean War.

It should be recorded here to his credit that though then, as always, Mr Russell's sympathies were on the side of military authority, he went out of his way, fearless of any offence he might give, to protest in his letters against the indiscriminate reprisals which followed the defeat of the mutineers; in the outcry against "Clemency Canning" Mr Russell refused to join. Yet then and afterwards we cannot doubt that it went against his feelings to take up a view not in harmony with military sentiments. No man, not a soldier born, was ever fonder or prouder of the British Army. His dearest friends and most intimate associates were, as a body, British officers with whom the fortunes of his life had thrown him into intimate relations; and we are convinced that in his own heart he would have been prouder of having earned distinction as a British officer than he was of being the greatest of war correspondents. Yet in the controversy as to the policy that ought to be pursued in regard to the mutineers, he took a side which at the time was unpopular with the Army. Few men have ever made less fuss about their principles, few men were less addicted to sentimental humanitarianism, but when it came to a question on which Russell believed that right was on one side, no consideration of personal friendship or professional interest could deter him from declaring his opinion.

His independence of judgment was also illustrated during the American Secession War, in which he again acted as representative of *The Times*. Popular sentiment in England, especially in the classes from which our officers are mainly recruited, was strongly enlisted on the side of the Southerners. If Mr Russell had thought solely of what was likely to please his readers, his letters would have displayed a strong partisanship for the Confederate cause. It would be absurd to say that Mr Russell was an ardent abolitionist. Indeed, the whole tone and bias of his nature rendered him far more sympathetic towards the Southerners than towards the Northerners. But his good sense and clearness of mind showed him that in the end the North must win, and, more than that, deserved to win. In his letters from the seat of war, which attracted perhaps even greater attention on the other side of the Atlantic than they did in England, he gave no encouragement to the belief, which was then so popular at home, and of which Mr Gladstone was, perhaps, the most prominent exponent, that ultimate victory was assured to the Confederate armies. At the same time, his unionist proclivities were not sufficiently pronounced to satisfy the jealous susceptibilities of the North, and the candour with which he criticized the defects of the new levies, who, under General McClellan, formed the army of the Potomac, gave intense offence to the public of the Federal States. His description of the stampede of the Northern armies in their early battles caused the most extreme irritation throughout the North; and for some time "Bull Run" Russell was the best abused and the most maligned of Britishers north of Mason and Dixie's line. The outcry against him was so violent that he felt it better to return home in the first years of the Secession War. Later experience, however, proved the justice not only of Mr Russell's prognostications of the ultimate triumph of the North, but of his exposition of the defects of the Northern military organization which only became effective when the raw Federal levies had developed into trained soldiers under the leadership of Grant and Sherman and Sheridan. It is characteristic of the man that, though Russell incurred an amount of abuse in America which might easily have biased a less sound judgment and a less kindly nature, he yet formed any number of personal friendships in the Northern States. There must still be left many of these friends to whom the news that Russell is no more will recall the memories of the "Bold Buccaneers Club," which relieved the gloom of social life in Washington during the dreary winter of 1861–62, and of which Russell was the life and soul ...

In 1866 Russell acted as Correspondent of *The Times* with the Austrian armies under General Benedek and was present at the disastrous defeat of Sadowa in the seven weeks' campaign by which Prussia won for herself the hegemony of Germany. In 1870 Russell accompanied the army of the then Crown Prince of Prussia in the Franco-German war, and remained at Versailles during the latter part of the siege of Paris. Of his many journalistic triumphs we should class amongst not the least remarkable his description of the burning of Paris by the Communards, as seen from the lines of the German Army. On one occasion Russell had reported a long interview with the Crown Prince (Frederick), some expressions in which gave umbrage to Bismarck. Bismarck sent for him, lost his temper, and said:-

"I suppose you couldn't resist showing your importance by reporting all that that 'Dunderhead' confided to you."

Russell replied:- "Your Excellency knows that I always respect confidence; there is much that you have said to me yourself that I have not reported."

Bismarck:- "Pouf! Anything I say to you you may bawl from the top of St Paul's."

Russell:- "I thank your Excellency. I shall use that permission to record your opinion of the Crown Prince."

The year 1871 witnessed practically the close of Russell's active career as the War Correspondent of *The Times*. On the occasion of the present King's visit, as Prince of Wales, to India, Russell, for whom His Majesty had always a great regard and affection, was appointed honorary private secretary to his staff, and accompanied him throughout his long and arduous journey. In 1879 Russell went out to South Africa with his friend Lord Wolseley on the occasion of the Zulu war, and acted as correspondent to one of our contemporaries. The conditions of the campaign however, were not favourable to journalistic description; Mr Russell, who was then close upon 60, felt, as we have reason to believe, that the time had gone by, in so far as he was concerned, for work requiring such exuberance of physical health and mental activity as are necessary for a modern war correspondent.

At any rate, from the period of his return to England after the unsatisfactory termination of the Zulu war, Russell practically abdicated his functions as a chronicler of campaigns. He was present in Egypt during the bombardment of Alexandria, the battle of Kassassin, and the occupation of Cairo by the British troops, but, though he took an extreme interest in the operations of our Army, he did not, so far as we are aware, record his impressions in writing. There has seldom been a successful journalist who cared less than Russell about writing for writing's sake; he had no desire to rush into print, and, as a past-master in the craft of journalism, he had none of the uneasy craving to keep his individuality before the public which characterizes so many of the profession.

Indeed, the actual bulk of his published writings is very small compared with that produced by many authors of far smaller note. The majority of his books were in the main republications of the letters which originally appeared in our columns. His most serious attempt at independent literature consisted in a novel, "The Adventures of Dr Brady," which was brought out more than a score of years ago. The novel, which was supposed to be more or less founded on the experience of his own life, was undoubtedly clever, and had what the French call a success of esteem. But its reception by the general public was not such as to encourage him to a repetition of the experiment. Nor is this, we think, to be wondered at. The attainment of very high success in journalism almost of necessity presupposes the possession of certain qualities which are well-nigh inconsistent with great proficiency in other classes of literature in which condensation is a defect, not a merit. Aptitude in compressing a gallon of news into a pint pot of print is a disadvantage, not an advantage, if your task is to expand a pint of news into a gallon of printed matter.

Russell during the last years of his life was content to rest upon his laurels ... He went frequently to Egypt in the winter months and was a well-known figure in London society during the season and in country houses at those periods when London is out of town. Everybody liked him; everybody, from the oldest of our statesmen to the youngest of our subalterns, found him interesting as a companion. In 1895 he had the honour of a knighthood conferred upon him on the recommendation of Lord Rosebery, and the King conferred on him the Companionship of the Victorian Order in 1902. The University of Oxford also, some years ago, gave him the degree of Hon. D.C.L. Among other foreign decorations he received the orders of the Medjidieh and the Osmanieh, the ribbon of the Legion of Honour in 1869, and the Iron Cross in 1871. He contested Chelsea in 1869 in the Conservative interest, but was not successful; he never again tried to enter Parliament. In politics Mr Russell was a strong unionist, and, though greatly attached to Ireland, he always resented the idea of separation as a sort of personal affront as well as a material injury to his native land.

During the last few years frequent attacks of gout, disappearance by death of one old friend after another, the physical infirmities well-nigh inseparable from old age, and the occupations of a harassing business precluded his mixing much in general society. But on the rare occasions when he visited his clubs or assisted at social gatherings he was as bright, as high in spirits, as full of humour, as genial as ever ...

Mr Russell was twice married – in the first instance, as a very young man, to Miss Burroughs, who died many years ago; secondly, after he had attained an advanced age, to the Countess Pia Malvezzi, who survives her husband. Of his private life there is little that need be said, save that it was honourable, independent, and worthy of his high professional repute. He had his full, perhaps more than his full, share of the troubles to which all human careers, and especially all journalistic careers, are liable, but nothing ever dimmed his cheery brightness and genial Hibernian humour. His latter years were, we are glad to think, exceptionally happy; and if anything can attenuate the grief of his family at his loss, it must be the knowledge that, if by honours we mean not

97

official distinctions, but regard, esteem, and love, the husband and father whose loss they now deplore died not only full of days, but full of honours also.

* * *

JOHN MILLINGTON SYNGE

25 MARCH 1909

THE NEW DRAMATIC movement in Ireland has received a heavy blow in the death of perhaps its most brilliant exponent, Mr John Millington Synge. He died to-day in Dublin, having just completed his 37th year.

Mr Synge was born in Dublin, and educated at Trinity College. After he took his degree he divided his life curiously between the Continent and the remoter Irish districts. He was frequently in Paris, where in 1899 he first came under the influence of Mr W. B. Yeats. For some months of the year he lived in the Arran islands and acquired an intimate knowledge of the Irish language and of the primitive manners and customs of the people. Two years ago he published a book on these islands which is full of descriptive passages of great poetical charm. Mr Synge first came into prominence in connexion with the Irish National Theatre Society with the two plays *Riders to the Sea* and *In the Shadow of the Glen*, which were produced in 1905. In the same year he wrote *The Veil of the Saints*. His most remarkable – certainly his most sensational – work, *The Playboy of the Western World*, was produced three years ago at the Abbey Theatre, Dublin. The first performance ended in a riot, and for some weeks afterwards a piquant controversy, half personal and half literary, raged in the Irish Press. It is said that Mr Birrell, who made his first appearance in Ireland about this time, was astonished to find Dublin obsessed not with any matter of Home Rule or the land, but with the question whether Mr Synge's play was or was not an insult to Irish womanhood. In England and elsewhere Mr Synge's dramatic merits were more calmly appreciated, and our own critic referred to the *Playboy* as being, perhaps, the most remarkable play of its year. At the time of his death Mr Synge was engaged on another Irish play called *Deirdre*. He published last year a play called *The Tinker's Wedding*, which is especially characteristic of his candid, yet exceedingly subtle, dramatic method. It has not been, and is not likely to be, produced in Ireland. As an Irish dramatist, both in his conception and treatment of the problems of rural life, Mr Synge was greatly in advance of his time. The general public failed to appreciate the extraordinary delicacy of his style. The audacity of his attacks on Irish institutions and conventions provoked bitter resentment in some political and religious quarters.

* * *

SIR LUKE O'CONNOR

V.C. hero of the Crimea

2 FEBRUARY 1915

MAJOR-GENERAL SIR Luke O'Connor, V.C., K.C.B., who rose from the ranks to command the regiment in which he enlisted some 65 years ago, and was one of the first to receive the Victoria Cross, died in London yesterday, in his 84th year. He had been seriously ill for some time.

Born in February, 1831, at Elphin, County Roscommon, O'Connor enlisted in the 23rd Royal Welsh Fusiliers at the age of 17. With his regiment he landed in the Crimea early in 1854, and they came under fire immediately afterwards on the heights of the Alma. O'Connor had at this time attained the rank of sergeant, his promotion having been exceptionally rapid for those long-service days. Scarcely had the closely contested action of the Alma begun – the 23rd had but just come within range of fire – when Lieutenant Anstruther, carrying the Queen's Colour, fell mortally wounded. O'Connor, marching by his side as one of the Colour party, was struck in the breast, and had also fallen. Finding, however, that the officer's condition was hopeless and the position demanded prompt action, the young sergeant picked himself up, pulled himself together, took the Colour, rushed forward with a desperate effort in face of a murderous fire, and planted the emblem of victory on the redoubt before those of the enemy who were near at hand could realize their peril. The effect on the advancing battalion was instantaneous. Seeing what had been done by the valour of one man, all ranks of the gallant 23rd pressed onward to his support, and within a few seconds the position had been carried at the point of the bayonet.

This having been accomplished, O'Connor was urged to place himself under medical care; but he pleaded so earnestly to be allowed to do his duty to the end that his wish was acceded to. Thus he and the Colour he had borne so nobly did not part company until the battle was over and he had received the praise and thanks of Sir George Browne and General Codrington on the field, before his assembled comrades, and been told that he would be recommended for a commission. His own simple comment on his exploit in later years was that he "only did a soldier's duty." He was gazetted to an ensigncy whilst in hospital. But an honour was to come which he valued even more than his promotion: that was the Victoria Cross, conferred upon him when the decoration was created, largely as the result of his own act of valour. The Cross was pinned on his breast by Queen Victoria at a great military parade in Hyde Park in June, 1857.

O'Connor obtained his lieutenancy in February, 1855, and had returned to duty in time to be present at the siege and fall of Sevastopol, the attack on the quarries, and the assaults of June 18 and September 8. On the latter occasion he again distinguished himself by what was spoken of as his "cool heroism and the splendid example he set to all about him." But he was again seriously wounded – this time in both thighs. For his service in the Crimea, besides receiving his commission and the Victoria Cross, he was decorated with the medal and two clasps, the Sardinian and Turkish medals, and the 5th Class of the Medjidieh.

The 23rd, which had returned home at the close of the war, at once embarked for India when the Mutiny broke out in 1857, and there O'Connor had the good fortune to see service under Sir Colin Campbell in the operations for the relief of Lucknow. He was present at the defeat of the Gwalior contingent at Cawnpore, at the siege and capture of Lucknow, the operations across the Gomtee under Outram, and in several minor affairs. For the Mutiny Captain O'Connor – he was promoted in August, 1858 – received another war medal with clasp. After several uneventful years he accompanied the 2nd Battalion Royal Welsh Fusiliers to the Gold Coast for Sir Garnet Wolseley's expedition to Kumasi at the end of 1873, having then reached the rank of major. For this service he received a brevet lieutenant-colonelcy, and the medal with clasp.

On June 24, 1884, he succeeded to the command of the 2nd Battalion Royal Welsh Fusiliers, and in 1886 he went on half-pay with the rank of colonel. He was granted a Distinguished Service reward, and retired on March 2, 1887, with the rank of major-general. He was made a C.B. in 1906, and K.C.B. in 1913; and only last year he had the satisfaction of being appointed honorary colonel of his old regiment.

JOHN REDMOND

A Great Irish Leader

7 MARCH 1918

MR REDMOND, WHOSE death yesterday we announce in another page, was born in 1851, of a Roman Catholic family long established in Co. Wexford, Anglo-Norman by origin and Whig rather than nationalist in political tradition. His father, however, was a conspicuous Home Ruler, who sat for some years in Parliament under Isaac Butt. The young Redmond was educated at Clongowes, and displayed early histrionic talent and the gifts of oratory. He was called to the Bar; but instead of practising he took up the position of a clerk in the Vote Office of the House of Commons at £300 a year. He would have been well suited by temperament and training for membership of Butt's party; but before his opportunity came Butt's influence had declined, and the application for an Irish constituency had to be made to Parnell. It is said that William Redmond (then an officer in the Militia), on hearing of his brother's intentions, telegraphed, "For God's sake, don't disgrace the family." Mr Redmond took his seat in 1881 as member for New Ross. Mr T. M. Healy has since claimed, or rather accepted, the responsibility for introducing the future leader of the Irish race into public life. It was he who assured Parnell that Mr Redmond was a very clever young man. "Who is he?" asked Parnell. "The chap who hands out the programmes." "Oh, that fellow!" said Parnell, grudgingly. However, the dignified oratory of the new recruit was at once recognized as an asset by the party, and Mr Redmond was sent next year to collect funds in Australia.

There he met with and married Miss Dalton. The mission was a success; £15,000 was collected; and many obstacles were overcome; chief of them the suspicion under which the Parnellite movement had fallen after the Phoenix Park murders. Mr Redmond used moderate language in putting the Home Rule case before his colonial audiences, omitting all Separatist sentiment from his speeches. In America, whither he proceeded, Home Rule had to be represented as a means towards national independence. But even in those days the real Mr Redmond was a man whose ingrained respect for British civilization was never really shaken by a rhetorical devotion to the Irish or, rather, the Anglo-Irish tradition of nationalism. He did not easily adopt the *rôle* of the rebel or fanatic; his natural pose was that of the eighteenth-century patriot, a Grattan or a Flood.

However, in 1887, he followed the custom of the times by getting imprisoned – a five weeks' sentence. It was during Mr Balfour's *régime*, and under the Crimes Act; the charge against him, one of intimidation, was brought by a landlord in Co. Wexford. He had not taken an important part in the debates of 1886; but his credit stood high, and he was recognized during the domestic crisis of 1891 as quite the ablest of the minority which refused to throw Parnell to the "wolves of English Liberalism." But the relations between Parnell and Mr John Redmond had never been close. On Parnell's death the leadership of the minority passed by common consent to Mr Redmond. The elections of 1892 ended in disaster, and Mr Redmond's group in Parliament consisted of but 12 members. In Ireland he had rather equivocal support from the hillside men or old Fenians. It was, no doubt, in obedience to this element that he described the Home Rule Bill of 1893 as "a toad, ugly and venomous," which yet wore a jewel in its head, taking particular objection to the clauses which provided for Irish representation in the Commons.

One advantage Mr Redmond had over the leaders of the anti-Parnellite organization; being, as it were, a free lance, he could dispense with old shibboleths and take part with his unionist fellow-countrymen in movements of a non-political and regenerative character. He gladly accepted an invitation to the Recess Committee, and signed its famous Report. He was, also, well disposed towards the Land Purchase and Local Government Acts (1896–7).

Peace negotiations between the two Irish parties were opened in 1898, and finally, in 1900, the leadership of a reunited party was entrusted to the chairman of the Parnellite minority. The hillside men and neo-Fenians never forgave Mr Redmond for accepting the "bribe"; but public opinion generally approved of Mr Redmond's elevation, although the task of preserving the new-found unity seemed to require the highest powers. From that day to this no fatal division appeared in the ranks of the Irish Parliamentary movement. Not that Mr Redmond had his way in all things. At times he led his army from behind. It is likely that he disapproved of the anti-English demonstrations made by nationalists during the South African war, but could not check them. In the autumn of 1901, as "leader of the race at home and abroad," he made a successful tour in the United States and Canada. Three years later he played a decidedly weak part over the Land Conference of 1903, and its sequel, the Wyndham Land Act. He sat on the Land Conference as chief representative of the tenants' interest, and was a signatory to the Report upon which Mr Wyndham founded his far-reaching measure of Land Purchase. Mr Redmond sold a small property of his own in Co. Wexford on "Conference" terms – 24 years' purchase; but he made scarcely an effort to repress the agitation against the Act, an agitation which drove Mr William O'Brien, who kept to his bargain with the landlords, out of the party.

The numbers with which the Liberals returned to power in 1906 diminished the value of Mr Redmond's alliance. But Mr Birrell, who became Chief Secretary in 1907, favoured the Nationalists. He satisfied the long outcry for a National University; his Land Bill of 1909 pleased the agrarians, and it was preferred to the Wyndham Act. The party also succeeded in obtaining Sir Horace Plunkett's dismissal from the post of Vice-President of the Department of Agriculture; it enjoyed many minor triumphs of this sort. Protests came from Ireland, first from unionists, then from Mr William O'Brien's All-for-Ireland Party, and thirdly from the Sinn Feiners; but nothing disturbed Mr Redmond's amicable relations with the Government. Leader and party were completely out of touch with the new ideas, issue of the Gaelic League and Sinn Fein. Mr Redmond despised, because he could not comprehend, Young Ireland, and he made no attempt to guide or restrain it.

The General Elections of 1910 and 1911 showed that, widespread as was the criticism of Mr Redmond's leadership, the party had full control of the political machine. He was bitterly criticized for supporting the Budget of 1909, but the events of 1910 and 1911 proved that his word was law at election times. Never before had an Irish leader such influence in English affairs. Mr Redmond held the balance in the House of Commons, and directed the policy of the Liberal Party. He demanded a definite assurance from Mr Asquith that if the Lords rejected the Veto resolutions the Government would either get guarantees from the King or resign. Mr Asquith refused, on the plea that he wished to keep the King out of party politics. A great excitement was only relieved when, early in March, the Prime Minister announced that the Government had adopted the method for the destruction of the Veto recommended by Mr Redmond, of first introducing resolutions in the Lords and Mr Redmond's credit rose in Ireland; even the Sinn Feiners withdrew their criticism. He had also greatly increased his reputation with the English Radicals. On the other hand, to moderate unionists, who a few years before might have considered favourably some friendly settlement of the Irish question, it seemed improper that a great constitutional issue affecting British destinies should be decided by the votes of Nationalists, to whom the abolition of the Veto of the House of Lords was only a means to an Irish end. The determination of Ulster to resist Home Rule at all costs was greatly strengthened.

The Home Rule Bill of 1912 Mr Redmond described as a final settlement, better than the Bill of 1886, "the greatest charter ever offered to Ireland"; and the audience at the National Convention were warned "to keep their amendments in their pockets." Then came the Ulster movement, surprising the Nationalists, who had long professed to regard the Covenant and the Ulster Volunteer Force as "bluff." The opposition of Ulster crystallized into a demand for the exclusion of the Province, and Mr Redmond characterized this solution as an "unthinkable" one. In the autumn of 1913 a group of Independent Nationalists proposed, without asking Mr Redmond's leave, to establish a body of Irish Volunteers: this retort to Ulster was not in Mr Redmond's line of policy; but the movement became popular, and he had no option but to capture it. Events in Ulster during the spring and early summer of 1914 – the Larne gun-running and the evident disinclination of the Army to coerce Ulster – made Mr Redmond ready to consider an amendment whereby the Ulster Counties might, if they so decided by vote, remain for six years outside of Home Rule; but Sir Edward Carson rejected the compromise. It was understood that the Nationalists had reached the limit of concession. In July the King invited the party leaders, English and Irish, to a conference at Buckingham Palace. It failed; hostile parties stood again face to face. There was an attempt on the part of the Nationalists, accompanied by some loss of life, to emulate the achievements of the Ulstermen at Larne; then, of a sudden, the European War approached. Sir Edward Grey outlined the position of the Allies in relation to Germany, and Mr Redmond promised unconditional loyalty on behalf of Nationalist Ireland. He spoke with genuine emotion, and his words came as a great relief to British opinion. In an eloquent speech he assured the House of Commons that Great Britain could in the event of war "remove all her troops from Ireland"; Irishmen, both of North and South, would then combine to defend the shores of Ireland against foreign aggression. But Mr Redmond seemed to hesitate before throwing himself whole-heartedly into the recruiting campaign. He had a scheme for bringing the Nationalist Volunteers under Government control as a body for home defence; he was also much occupied with negotiations over the Home Rule Bill. This measure finally reached the Statute-book on September 17, 1914; but it was accompanied by a Suspensory Bill postponing the operation of the Act until the close of the war, and the Ulster minority received from Mr Asquith the promise of an amending Bill. Mr Redmond's success in bringing Home Rule to the Statute-book in no way conciliated the revolutionary Nationalist and Sinn Fein groups. The Ulstermen were angered, and the high hopes of those who had looked on the war as a healer of ancient feuds were dashed to the ground. On the other hand, Mr Redmond's coup, such as it was, did tend towards the encouragement of recruiting in Nationalist Ireland. But

Mr Redmond underestimated the strength of his Irish opponents, whom he described in American Press interviews as a handful of pro-Germans and shirkers. He deprecated action against seditious writing and seditious speeches on the ground that the Sinn Fein movement, if treated with contempt, would die of inanition. Unionists disagreed with this view, but they recognized the sincerity of Mr Redmond's effort to promote recruiting and the very fair success that attended it. Events in England rather than in Ireland gave Mr Redmond his chief anxiety. The formation of a Coalition Government seemed likely to weaken his hold on nationalist opinion.

In consideration, no doubt, of the changed circumstances, Mr Asquith offered the Irish leader a place in the new Cabinet; but the offer was rejected, and Mr Redmond, in an appeal to his supporters, spoke of dangers ahead and of the necessity of strengthening the party organization. The crisis passed; there was no General Election; and Mr Redmond secured the exclusion of Ireland from the Registration and Military Service Bills. Motives of expediency prevented him from expressing the current English view, namely that the inclusion of Ireland might mean more trouble than it was worth, and he redoubled his efforts to encourage voluntary recruiting; even intimating that Home Rule itself might be conditional on the number of men obtained. He also condemned the agitation against the application of war taxes to Ireland. Though he must have been aware of the increase of general disaffection in Ireland, the revolution of Easter Week, 1916, took him completely by surprise. He condemned it in the strongest terms. He was assured, as he afterwards confessed, that the result would be an agitation for the repeal of the Home Rule Act. No one was more surprised than he when the Government proceeded to institute negotiations for a provisional settlement by consent. He took part in those negotiations, he accepted the terms and the principles of Mr Lloyd George's settlement, but the scheme was wrecked by the Sinn Feiners, whose movement from the first was directed as much against Mr Redmond and the Nationalist Party as against Great Britain. He approved the calling together of the Convention, which held its first meeting last July and still maintains a precarious existence; and he took a prominent and authoritative part in its proceedings, and always in the direction of securing if possible an all-round agreement. In spite of ill-health and growing doubts as to how far he represented the operative opinion of Nationalist Ireland, he was strenuous in his efforts to make the great experiment a success, and, whatever the upshot of the Convention – and particularly in the event of its breakdown – Ireland will grievously miss his sagacious and conciliatory counsels.

Mr Redmond's personal charm was acknowledged by all. By his death the House of Commons loses one of its best-known figures, who both by his appearance and his oratory had long been its ornament. His eloquence was founded on natural genius, real feeling, and a classical choice of language. He could always be relied upon as a speaker to raise the tone of current political debate; and on occasions of state, when the subject was not political, few if any in the present Assembly could compete with him.

CARDINAL GIBBONS

26 MARCH 1921

JAMES, CARDINAL GIBBONS, Archbishop of Baltimore, whose death we announce on another page, was born in Baltimore of Irish parentage in 1834. Before taking him to Ireland in 1837, his father, Thomas Gibbons, once lifted him in his arms to see President Andrew Jackson passing through Baltimore.

The future Cardinal acquired a life-long love of the Classics at Ballinrobe, in Mayo, from the glorified hedge school-masters of the time. He preserved vivid memories of the Irish Famine, of Archbishop MacHale, by whom he was confirmed, and of Isaac Butt fighting an election. In 1853 he returned to America with his family, after suffering ship-wreck off the Bahamas, and entered the dry-goods business in New Orleans.

At a mission conducted by members of the newly formed Order of Paulists under Father Isaac Hecker he felt the divine call, and made his way to Baltimore. Educated at St Charles's College and St Mary's Seminary under the French Sulpicians, he was ordained priest by Archbishop Kenrick in the cathedral of his baptism, 1861. With the outbreak of the Civil War he served as chaplain to Fort McHenry, and, though the sympathies of Maryland were Southern, he continued to pray Archbishop Carroll's prayer that the people "might be preserved in union." His own heart was, he said, with the South, but his head was with the North, and he was one of the two priests who dared follow the body of the assassinated Lincoln through the streets of Baltimore. On Good Friday, 1865, a few hours before the crime, he preached a famous sermon picturing in presentiment a just ruler slain by a subject as a type of the Crucifixion.

In 1868, at the age of 34, Gibbons was consecrated as Bishop of North Carolina. Bishop Gibbons served through the stormy period of Southern Reconstruction and Negro Emancipation. His flock was limited to a few hundred and he claimed to know them all by name. To reach them his life was spent in saddle, steamboat, and stage. He lived like a pioneer, sheltering in the lowliest shanties. He shared in bearing the white man's cruel burden after the war, and was once even ordered to pull down a frame building by a negro official. From the forlorn struggle against "carpet-baggers" in the South he was summoned to attend the Vatican Council, where, as the youngest present, he deemed silence his wisest contribution.

His zeal and sympathy fitted him to become Bishop of Richmond, the ex-Southern capital, in 1872. Meantime Archbishop Spalding had requested his succession from his deathbed, and in 1877 he was made coadjutor to Archbishop Roosevelt Bayley, whom he succeeded in Baltimore that year, being the last of Pius the Ninth's Archbishops. In 1884 he presided as Apostolic Delegate over the Third Plenary Council at Baltimore, and two years later was raised to the Sacred College by Leo XIII. Soon after, he celebrated the centenary of his diocese and founded the Catholic University at Washington, of which he became first Chancellor.

The war opened the most strenuous chapter of his life. Through a private letter to Mr Redmond he was in the unique position of being the first American to endorse the Allied cause. His appointment as Grand Officer of the Legion of Honour testified to French gratitude ... Through him Austria made a last despairing appeal for a separate Peace, which he promptly communicated to the President, but so strict was his American attitude that he felt unable to answer the congratulations of Cardinal von Hartmann at the time of his jubilee.

His ecclesiastical life was unique in America, and perhaps was the most important of any Cardinal of recent times. He was the link between the past and the present, between the old Southern life and modern American Imperialism, between the Vatican Council and the democratized Papacy. He outlived three generations of episcopal contemporaries. His episcopacy covered the total rise and fall of the German Empire. Presidents came and went, but he seemed to remain for ever. The secret of his success was a sweet temperance in all matters save of vital principle, appeal to which alone tempered his diplomatic temperament. His American popularity was due to his poverty both of wealth and ambition. He did not fear opposition, but he preferred compromise and peace. He bowed before attack and disarmed criticism and by out-living both generally secured the acceptance of his views. He upheld negro suffrage, while advising a gentle tutelage of the weaker race. He fought Prohibition by opposing to it temperance. He criticized the American public school but lost no means of Americanizing the Catholic immigrant through Church agency. He favoured Irish freedom faithfully, but he joined Cardinals Logue and Vaughan in their far-sighted appeal for international arbitration after the Venezuela trouble in 1896. His most effective work, "The Faith of our Fathers," was so because it was the least controversial of such books. He became a legend in his lifetime in a country which is more disposed to hero-worship than canonization and a force where the strenuous is invariably preferred to the saintly.

MICHAEL COLLINS

Romantic Career
Hairbreadth Escapes

24 AUGUST 1922

SINCE THE DARK days of 1916, Michael Collins, the son of a County Cork farmer, has been one of the most interesting and romantic figures in Irish public life.

Thirty years ago he was born at Woodfield, Clonakilty, Co. Cork the youngest of a family of eight children. Educated at the local national school, he entered the Civil Service at the age of fifteen as a boy clerk, and later spent three years as a clerk in a London bank, after which he joined the branch of a New York bank in the same city. Before entering the service of the banks he was in the employ of the Post Office in London, where his sister is also employed. During his residence in London he took the keenest interest in Irish affairs, and before his return to Ireland at the time of the Rebellion he is said to have drilled with other Irishmen at Wormwood Scrubs. On Easter Monday, 1916, he was one of those who seized the General Post Office in Sackville-street, Dublin, and towards the end of the week he was taken prisoner, with others, in the building. He was deported to Stafford Gaol, and was later sent to Frongoch, from which place, with the other interned men, he was released at Christmas.

Since that time he had been the most assiduous of workers for Irish freedom, and in time came to occupy a high place in the Sinn Fein organization. In 1918 he was imprisoned in Sligo Gaol for a seditious utterance, and after his release he disappeared completely from official view. North and south the country was searched for him, but he eluded all the efforts of the police and military to secure him. When he was elected to Dail Eireann, in 1918, as the representative of his native county, he was in England, and soon afterwards he took a leading part in the escape of Mr de Valera from an English gaol. He was next heard of as Finance Minister of the Dail. Through his energy loans amounting to very large sums were subscribed in Ireland, Great Britain, and America, and although the authorities many times tried to lay hands on the money, they succeeded in seizing only a very small part of the whole.

At this time the hunt for Michael Collins was pursued up and down the country. A price was said to have been put on his head, and raids were constantly made in Dublin and the provinces by the Constabulary, the Military, and the Auxiliary Police Force. At times they had him almost in their grasp, but he slipped through their fingers at the last moment, and so the hunt went on until the Truce was signed. On one occasion he was in his office in Harcourt- street, Dublin, when a raiding party burst into the building and arrested several of those who were in it. Collins escaped through a skylight and got into an adjoining hotel and drove away on a hackney car. The stories of his hairbreadth escapes at this period would fill a volume. Some of them have little foundation, but that he was often almost within the fingers of his pursuers and escaped by a hair's breadth is true. On two occasions he made his way from hotels in Dublin when raids were carried out, and, standing in groups of civilians in the street, watched the Crown Forces' work. It is told of him that when the chase was hottest he boarded a tramcar in Dublin and sat down beside a detective, who immediately recognized him. Collins, after a brief conversation, advised the man not to leave the tramcar until the terminus was reached. Collins broke his journey and disappeared long before the tramcar reached its destination.

His visit to London as one of the plenipotentiaries, his fight for the Treaty with Arthur Griffith in the Dail in the face of the most determined opposition, and his fearless advocacy of it in all parts of the country at the elections will be remembered by everyone. He was greatly grieved when the trouble began in Dublin with the seizure of the Four Courts, and did all that he could to stave off the evil days that followed. Last month he was appointed Commander-in-Chief of the Army, and since that time he had travelled the country up and down, paying flying visits to Dublin for consultation with Mr Griffith and other leaders. Mr Griffith's unexpected death was a severe blow to him, and all who saw him at the funeral last week recognized how deeply he was moved.

* * *

ERSKINE CHILDERS

25 NOVEMBER 1922

ROBERT ERSKINE CHILDERS, whose execution in Ireland is recorded elsewhere, was an Englishman, the son of an Irish mother.

He was the author, early in the century, of "The Riddle of the Sands," an excellent story on the theme of a German invasion plot, and when the war came he did good service and won a coveted decoration. It was afterwards that his hostility to his father's country, possibly fostered by his Irish connexions, came to a head, and he joined the extreme wing of the Sinn Fein movement.

Ever since the peace negotiations in London in 1921, Childers had been one of the most intelligent and subtle opponents of the Irish Free State. He was the real author of the famous Document No. 2, which was attributed to de Valera, and which contained the alternative oath; and to his cool, calculating brain and knowledge of the art of war were chiefly due the organization of the Republican forces and their persistence in their policy of destruction.

He had already, as far back as 1911, published a book on "The Framework of Home Rule," in which he propounded the Dominion solution, and in 1917–18 he was a member of the Secretariat of the Irish Convention. The failure of the Convention undoubtedly hastened the development of a mind already attuned to extremist policy. Childers belonged to the type of man who, accepting premisses without sufficiently careful examination, pursues them rigorously to their logical conclusion.

In March, 1920, the police received information that Sinn Fein meetings were being held and arms were stored in his house in Dublin, which was accordingly searched, and a large number of documents were found. Childers was himself detained, but soon released.

Childers's family connexions were English squires and officers of the Navy and Army; his mother was Irish–Anna, daughter of Thomas Barton, of Glendalough House, Co. Wicklow. There was another link with the same family. His father's sister, Agnes, married his mother's brother, Charles William Barton, of Glendalough House; her eldest son is Robert Childers Barton, Sinn Fein M.P. for Wicklow, who was a signatory of the Treaty, but afterwards declared that he had signed it under duress. It was at Barton's residence, Annamoe House, that Childers was himself captured on November 10 last.

Childers's father, Robert Cæsar Childers was a great Oriental scholar and the author of the first Pali dictionary. Robert Erskine Childers was the second son, born on June 25, 1870. His father died when the boy was only six years old. Erskine Childers was sent to school at Haileybury, and in due course went up to Trinity, Cambridge. Later on, he obtained an appointment as junior clerk in the House of Commons. He served in the South African War, an experience which bore fruit in his book, "In the Ranks of the C.I.V." (1900), and "The H.A.C. in South Africa," which he wrote with Mr Basil Williams.

But his most important work was Volume V. of "*The Times* History of the War in South Africa," published in 1907. In view of later events, Childers's editorship of this book is particularly interesting, for it covers the period of the guerrilla war. It was his conviction that regular war and guerrilla war have much in common, for they both pursue the same end and are both governed by the same fundamental principles. The peculiar interest of guerrilla war, he said, is that it illuminates much that is obscure and difficult in regular war, and reveals, stripped of secondary detail, the few dominant factors which sway the issue of great battles and great campaigns. Childers continued his studies of the art of war, for he published in 1910 "War and the Arme Blanche," with an introduction by Lord Roberts, and "German Influence on British Cavalry" in 1911.

All this time Childers had been making many friends by his personal charm as well as his ability, which found expression in articles and other writings. He had long had a strong love of the sea, and was never so happy as when sailing in small craft. He owned the ketch Asgard, built in 1905 and berthed at Southampton. To this taste of his was due his rise to fame as the author of "The Riddle of the Sands." This book, which appeared in the summer of 1903, was not so much a novel as an apologue about a possible German invasion from the mesh of Frisian islands and sand banks with an objective in the Wash. Two young men, one a Foreign Office clerk and the other a yachtsman, exploring the sands and channels, discover a British traitor in German service and all the secrets of the projected invasion. Childers thoughtfully provided his readers with two maps and two charts, without which, in truth, the book could hardly have been understood.

Childers married in 1904 Mary Alden, daughter of Hamilton Osgood, of Boston, U.S.A., and had two sons.

THOMAS CREAN V.C.

Irish International's Bravery.

27 MARCH 1923

MAJOR THOMAS JOSEPH CREAN, V.C., D.S.O., Hon. F.R.C.S.I. (Fellow of the Royal College of Surgeons in Ireland), died on Sunday at 13, Queen-street, Mayfair.

The son of Michael Theobald Crean, barrister, of the Irish Land Commission, he was born in 1873, was educated at Clongowes College, and qualified as L.R.C.P.I. (Licentiate of the Royal College of Physicians of Ireland) and L.R.C.S.I. (Licentiate of the Royal College of Surgeons in Ireland). In 1891 he gained the Royal Humane Society's testimonial for saving life at sea. From 1894 to 1896 he was a member of the Irish International Rugby XV., and of the English team in South Africa in 1896. He settled at Boxberg, in the Transvaal, and practised there. When the South African War broke out he enlisted as a trooper in the Imperial Light Horse, and was appointed captain in March, 1900, but in June, 1901, he abandoned squadron rank and became a surgeon-captain. He was wounded at Elandslaagte, while at Tygerskloof in December, 1901, he was awarded the V.C., "for great gallantry in attending to the wounded under a heavy fire at 150 yards' range, although himself wounded, only desisting when he received a second and what was thought to be a mortal wound." He was a captain in the R.A.M.C. (Royal Army Medical Corps) from 1902, when he won the Arnott gold medal, till 1906.

In 1914 he rejoined as major in the R.A.M.C., and served first with the 1st Cavalry Brigade, being "mentioned" and receiving the D.S.O., then as officer commanding the 44th Field Ambulance in France, and lastly as medical officer in charge of the hospital established at the Royal Enclosure at Ascot. After the war Major Crean struggled to carry on his practice, but in spite of his magnificent physique, the strain of his war service had broken down his health. He married in 1905 Victoria, daughter of Don Tomas Heredia, of Malaga, and had one son and one daughter.

LORD PIRRIE

Dominant Figure in Shipbuilding

9 JUNE 1924

IN LORD PIRRIE ... the country loses one of its greatest business men. If captains of industry are classifiable, as no doubt they are, as a type of their own, then it is in such men as he that we should look for the prototype. Primarily he was known as head of Harland and Wolff, Limited, but his interests in shipowning were extremely wide. Only the other day Lord Kylsant regretted his absence from the meeting of the African Steamship Company, of which he was chairman. He was also a director of Elder, Dempster, and Co., Limited, and he has exercised, although not always seen by the public, a very powerful influence on shipping. Last year, it will be recalled, an agreement was concluded between the White Star and Cunard companies for alternate sailings of the biggest trans-Atlantic ships during the "off season." There is good reason to believe that this arrangement was largely due to the farsighted-ness of Lord Pirrie, who is a director of the White Star Line. Lord Pirrie had the vision to see that shipbuilding and shipowning could be closely connected with each other, and to this policy the remark-able success of Harland and Wolff in recent years has been largely due.

In spite of his age Lord Pirrie was in manner a young man. He was an extremely hard worker, and at the time of his death he was returning from South America, where he had been on a visit in connexion with the port facilities available for the large new ships which are now being built for the Royal Mail Steam Packet Company by Harland and Wolff. It was evidently his enjoyment of work which took him on that mission. On the occasion of the recent trip of the new P. and O. liner Mooltan from Belfast to London Lord Pirrie seemed to be one of the youngest and happiest men on board. His buoyancy has long been the subject of admiration by younger business men, who envied him his possession of optimism and brilliancy. On various occasions Lord Pirrie has publicly paid tribute to the help which he has obtained throughout his career from Lady Pirrie, from whom he was very rarely separated. She proceeded with him on his visit to South America, and accompanied him wherever he went, and is known to have taken the closest possible interest in his work and to have helped him vastly.

William James Pirrie was born in Quebec in 1847, the son of J. A. Pirrie, of Little Clandeboye, Co. Down, an Ulsterman, of Scotch extraction; his mother was the daughter of another Ulster family, the Montgomerys. After his father's death in Canada, his mother brought him back to Ireland and sent him to the Belfast Royal Academical Institution. When only 15 he entered as a premium apprentice the engineering and shipbuilding firm of Harland and Wolff, at Belfast. Of it he was destined to become the chief, and the firm in its turn under his leadership one of the greatest in the world.

The times were favourable. The most prosperous era which British industry has ever known, or perhaps will ever know, was mounting towards its zenith. In particular transatlantic traffic of every description was growing in volume year by year. In this traffic Harland and Wolff largely specialized, and from its earliest days they were associated with the White Star Line. Most of the White Star fleet were built by them from the first Oceanic of 3,000 or 4,000 tons in 1871 down to many of the monster ships of recent times.

In 12 years from his entry into the firm Pirrie had risen to a partnership, and thereafter played a dominant part in its affairs. He was admirably suited in spirit to the age in which he lived. The sympathies of his temperament flowed in much the same courses as the whole trend of human affairs at that period, and he was therefore able perfectly to appreciate the opportunities and liabilities of his business, with the result that he made on its behalf many shrewd moves and but few serious errors. Big ship followed big ship. The Britannic in 1874, the Teutonic in 1889, the second Oceanic in 1899 of 17,000 tons, the Celtic in 1902 of 20,000 tons, the Cedric in 1903, and the Baltic in 1904, of more than 23,000 tons were all the largest or amongst the largest vessels of their time. Later still, came the Adriatic, followed in 1910 by the Olympic and her more famous and tragic sister, the Titanic. He was extraordinarily successful in getting business. Of his ability to secure orders the following story is told. On one occasion a well-known shipping company asked, towards the end of a week, for tenders for the construction of a new liner from a number of leading shipbuilding companies. On the Monday morning there were written replies from all the shipbuilding companies with the exception of Harland and Wolff. When the letters were received, Lord Pirrie was closeted with the head of the company and secured the contract. He never allowed the grass to grow below his feet. In the industrial and mechanical sphere, therefore, Pirrie's name must always be identified with a half-century of most remarkable adventure and progress, though it is as yet too soon to estimate the true value of its contribution to civilization as a whole.

A Conservative at heart, although he favoured the Home Rule cause – a circumstance which once, at least, brought him into violent conflict with the Orangemen – Lord Pirrie never sat in the House of Commons, though he played a considerable part in local affairs. He was Lord Mayor of Belfast, 1896–7, High Sheriff of Antrim, 1898, and of Down, 1899, and he had the distinction of becoming the first honorary Freeman of Belfast in 1898. He was also at various times Pro-Chancellor of Queen's University, Comptroller of the Household to the Lord Lieutenant of Ireland, a member of the Road Board, and a member of the Committee on Irish Finance. In 1911 he was made Lord Lieutenant of the County of the City of Belfast.

During the latter part of the war he was Controller of Mercantile Shipbuilding, and the task of drawing up the programme for repairing the losses which our merchant shipping had suffered fell in large measure to him. Merchant shipbuilding in the United Kingdom was then in a very unsatisfactory state, and a stimulus to increased production was urgently needed. He went to the Admiralty without any staff, and, as a war measure, a large number of standard cargo steamers were built in British yards under his authority and with his active management. The standard ships, for which the original programme had been laid down by the Shipping Controller, were built for account of the State, and were subsequently sold to the shipping industry. Lord Pirrie, on his appointment, gave close attention to the speedy repairing of torpedoed ships, and improved the organization.

Lord Pirrie was made a Privy Councillor in 1897 in Ireland and in 1918 in Great Britain, was created a baron in 1906, and was raised to a viscounty in 1921. He was also a Knight of St Patrick.

Lord Pirrie married, in 1879, Margaret M., daughter of John Carlisle, of Belfast, but leaves no issue, and his peerage in consequence becomes extinct.

* * *

LORD MacDONNELL

Indian and Irish Administration.

10 JUNE 1925

THE DEATH OF Lord MacDonnell removes an administrator of extraordinary ability and industry, who both in India and in Ireland exercised an important influence on the events of his time.

Antony Patrick MacDonnell, son of the late Mark G. MacDonnell, a Roman Catholic of the middle class, was born in county Mayo on March 7, 1844, and was sent to a small boarding school at Athlone. Disregarding the ecclesiastical censure on "mixed education," he became a student in Queen's College, Galway, graduating with honours in modern languages in 1864. He early showed the qualities which brought him to eminence – great industry, rapidity in learning, and sturdiness of will and frame. In the Indian Civil Service examination of 1864 he was fifth on the list, and went out to Bengal at the end of 1865. At once he saw something of the mismanaged relief works in the Orissa famine. Seven years later he helped to cope with the Bengal famine of 1873.

His sympathy with the tenantry of Ireland provided a keynote to the strong influence he exercised on agrarian policy in India. Appointed in 1884 Revenue Secretary to the Bengal Government, he pressed forward, with the assistance of an Irishman of like mind, the late Mr Michael Finucane, legislation for the protection of the Bengal cultivators. Stoutly resisted by the zamindars, the Bengal Tenancy Act, 1885, led the way in the greater protection the law now provides in the various Indian provinces against arbitrary ejectment, rack-renting, and other tenant grievances ...

Next he was for two years a member of the Government of India, and at the end of 1895 Lord Elgin selected him for the Lieutenant-Governorship of what are now the United Provinces of Agra and Oudh. He had come to the rule of four of the greatest Indian Provinces, one after the other, by great capacity consecrated to the public service, and by application that was unwearying and intent on things both great and small. A natural gift of language and of dignified exposition, whether oral or written, led him to state his conclusions with admirable clearness and decision. What is much more rare, he had a remarkable power of giving practical effect to his conclusions, down to the minutest details.

But this rugged man of beetling, shaggy brows and determined manner had the defects of his qualities. He was feared, he was admired, but he was not loved, either by his colleagues, his subordinates, or the Indian public. His six years in the United Provinces – for there was a 12 months' extension – were marked by the spectacle of a long string of capable officers, of all sorts and temperaments, anticipating their day of retirement. The Moslems on their part were much aggrieved that he insisted on introducing the Nagri (Hindi) script in the Courts and public offices, where Urdu had previously held the field without rival. To the agitation this step aroused may be traced the beginnings of Moslem participation in politics against Government measures.

The chief characteristic of the MacDonnell administration was its extreme centralization. In the terrible famine of 1897 the head of the province conducted the campaign in person, and was famine commissioner and divisional commissioner in one. Yet the vigour and consistency of "the L.G.'s" relief measures won admiration even from unfriendly critics. When he accepted the presidentship of the Famine Commission of 1901, he refused Lord Curzon's offer to relieve him for the time being of his administrative responsibilities in the United Provinces. The report, prepared after a tour through India with remarkable celerity, has taken the place of a batch of predecessors, and remains to this day the standard authority. On the basis it laid down, the famine codes were thoroughly revised in every province, and it constitutes the coping-stone of Indian famine policy, which it removed from the domain of controversy.

MacDonnell's governorship ended in 1901, and, returning to England, he was appointed in January, 1903, a member of the India Council and received a Privy Councillorship. He might have looked forward to further service in India, such as the Governorship of Bombay, but a different call came. Mr Wyndham, the new Chief Secretary for Ireland, was in search of a strong man as Under-Secretary. In India MacDonnell had settled vast agrarian difficulties, had had to deal with hostile races and classes, and had made a great administrative reputation. Accordingly, Lord Lansdowne, his former Chief, warmly recommended him to Mr Wyndham, and MacDonnell, impelled by the hope of serving his native country, accepted the post. But he was by no means on the footing of an ordinary official. He had, in fact, as was afterwards disclosed in Parliament, a position of independent influence over administration and a right to exert an authority far above "mere secretarial criticism."

At first, with the Land Conference and the Wyndham Land Act, he seemed successful, but soon he had aroused, not only the passive hostility of the Irish civil servants, but the active hostility of the Irish Unionists. His plan for setting up a college for Roman Catholics within the University of Dublin broke down mainly owing to the opposition of the Hierarchy. Then came Lord Dunraven's Devolution scheme, of which MacDonnell was regarded as the real author. Mr Wyndham was obliged to disavow it, but disavowal did not save him. He had to resign, and was succeeded by Mr Walter Long. When matters were explained, after much delay, in both Houses of Parliament, it became plain that the exceptional conditions of service conceded to MacDonnell would have to be withdrawn, and Mr Long's language on this point was explicit. But the prolongation of MacDonnell's appointment, even after they had been withdrawn, was much criticized ... In the opinion of Irish Unionists, he had in no way justified his exceptional powers; their case was that he had not improved the administrative machinery of the country, and had not expedited the working of land purchase, that he had weakened and disheartened the Royal Irish Constabulary, and that he had encouraged the Nationalist movement by his clandestine support of the "Devolution" scheme, and in other ways.

Sir H. Campbell-Bannerman's great victory at the general election of 1906 brought Mr Bryce, soon succeeded by Mr Birrell, to the Chief Secretaryship. The change was doubtless welcomed by MacDonnell, but it cannot be said that the remainder of his term of office enhanced his reputation. He must, presumably, be held responsible for the refusal of the Government in 1907 to renew the Arms Act of 1887, and for the breaking-up of the political detective service, a policy which was to have disastrous results later. Yet when he visited America in 1907 he was vigorously denounced by the United Irish League there for his share in Mr Birrell's timid and half-hearted Irish Councils Bill, as well as for certain exceptional measures which the Government had been forced to take in Ireland owing to the breakdown of the ordinary law. MacDonnell had little or no idea of compromise; and he was perhaps too apt to apply in Ireland methods similar to those by which he had achieved great results in India ... He resigned in 1908, as his ideas of governing Ireland did not agree with Mr Birrell's. He was rewarded with a peerage, and took the title of Lord MacDonnell of Swinford, after a small estate in the West which had belonged to his father, and which he sold to the tenants under the Land Acts.

MacDonnell was the first Indian civilian since John Lawrence to be elevated to the peerage, and though Ireland was his main interest, he did not forget India ... While unreservedly accepting the 1917 declaration of policy, he was a strong critic of the diarchic solution, and subsequent events went far to justify his apprehensions as to the effect of the changes on recruitment for his old service.

To the discussion on the Home Rule Bill of 1912 he contributed some useful criticisms, chiefly on the financial provisions, which he maintained were not sufficiently generous. When the Irish Convention of 1917–18, of which he was a member, was obviously about to split on the fiscal difficulty, he made a valiant effort to save it. He proposed that Customs and Excise should be left under the Imperial Parliament during the war, and thereafter till the question had been decided by the Imperial Parliament, such decision to be taken not later than seven years after the conclusion of peace. This was carried, but by only four votes, and not long afterwards the Convention dissolved. He was a member of the Irish Peace Conference, which assembled in Dublin in August, 1920, and in a letter to *The Times* in November urged that the Government should enlarge their proposals so as to meet the constitutional demands of moderate Home Rulers. Not long before, in the House of Lords, he had strongly condemned the policy of reprisals, and supported the movement for a comprehensive measure of self-government for Ireland ... Later on, he supported the proposals for a truce with Sinn Fein, and intervened occasionally in the discussions on the Irish Free State (Consequential Provisions) Bill.

Lord MacDonnell married, in 1878, Henrietta, daughter of Mr Ewen MacDonell, of the Keppoch family, well known in the Highlands. He leaves an only daughter, and the peerage becomes extinct.

KEVIN O'HIGGINS

11 JULY 1927

MR KEVIN CHRISTOPHER O'HIGGINS, Minister for Justice in the Irish Free State Government ... was murdered in Ireland yesterday:-

Mr O'Higgins, who was aged 35, was the youngest surviving son of the late Dr T. Higgins, of Stradbally, Queen's County, who was murdered in 1923 in his own house by unknown men. The late Minister was the first of the family to use the prefix O'. One of his brothers was killed in the war. Another is at present a surgeon-lieutenant in the Navy.

Educated at Clongowes and St Patrick's College, Carlow, and in the National University of Ireland, where he took his arts degree, he originally intended to enter the Roman Catholic priesthood, but changed his mind. He was apprenticed to his uncle, the late Mr Maurice Healy, solicitor of Cork, but did not complete his course for admission, being caught up in the Sinn Fein movement shortly after the rebellion of Easter week, 1916. He was interned by the British Government, and while he was in gaol, he was elected member for Queen's County at the election of 1918. On his release he met Michael Collins, who recognized his talents and appointed him Assistant Minister for Local Government to Mr Cosgrave. He was a strong supporter of the Treaty, and became a member of the Provisional Government in the early months of 1922. He then was appointed Minister for Justice and Vice-President of the Executive Council, a post which he filled with distinction until last month, when he undertook the Ministry for External Affairs in addition to his old Ministry. Perhaps his greatest achievement was the establishment of the Civic Guard, the unarmed police force which now keeps the peace of the Free State. As Minister for Justice he was largely responsible for the administration of the law during 1922–23, when 77 Irregulars were executed. He was afterwards called to the Irish Bar. During the recent election campaign he made a tour of the country, speaking in practically every constituency in support of the Government candidate. He headed the poll in his own constituency. Mr Higgins married, in 1921, Miss Bridget Mary Cole, of Dublin, and leaves two children.

B. B. [Brendan Bracken] writes: Your correspondent's account of the death of Mr Kevin O'Higgins at the hand of assassins shows that even under the pain of his grievous wounds his native fortitude, magnanimity, and patriotism never forsook him. Mr O'Higgins was, on many grounds, one of the most remarkable men of his time. Inflexible integrity, constancy, directness, and fidelity were the distinguishing marks of his short but memorable life. The notice of his career you publish to-day does justice to his many eminent public services, and stresses his diligence and firmness in administering the law during 1923, when 77 Republicans were executed. This seeming ruthlessness was not due to any inherent harshness of temperament or lack of sensibility of heart. Much otherwise. Many can bear witness to his affectionate nature, the fascinating charm of his manners, and his steadiness in friendship. But his inherent gentleness of disposition was not weakened by sentimentality. He knew that intolerable misery would have been inflicted upon his fellow-citizens had he interposed his compassion to preserve the lives of men (some of them friends) who were plunging the Free State into anarchy. He knew that order and freedom could not be established in Ireland unless a strong hand – much stronger than that of former British Governments – was used to suppress lawlessness.

Perhaps you will permit me to recall some interesting observations on the future of Ireland which Mr O'Higgins made at a private gathering in London during the Imperial Conference. Though he intensely disliked the partition of Ireland, he nevertheless came to believe that a united Ireland could only be obtained when the Free State had shown Ulster that its government was firmly established and secured by well-constructed and well-tried institutions, and that justice was administered without fear or favour in every part of its territory. He thought that years of strict economy in public administration would enable the Free State Government to reduce taxation to such a level that it would be greatly to the advantage of Ulster to join it in the formation of a "Kingdom of Ireland" constitutionally associated with Great Britain in the Empire, but politically free. The King of England was to be King of Ireland after the pattern of the former Austro-Hungarian Empire.

Mr O'Higgins's death is a public calamity. Many hoped that this young statesman would have played a large part, not only in the management of Irish affairs, but in the larger affairs of the Empire. But if these hopes have been dissipated by death, there is at least the consolation that he has left behind him a memory and an example which Ireland will not lightly let die.

* * *

COUNTESS MARKIEVICZ

16 JULY 1927

THE DEATH OCCURRED in Dublin yesterday morning of Mme. Constance de Markievicz, Fianna Fail member of Dail Eireann for South Dublin.

Mme. de Markievicz, who was a daughter of the late Sir Henry Gore-Booth, Bt., of Lissadell, Co. Sligo, married in 1900 Count Casimir de Markievicz, a Pole, who had estates near Kiev. Having settled in Dublin, Mme. de Markievicz, or, as she was commonly called, "The Countess," became identified with the Larkinite Labour movement of 1913, and when her husband returned to Poland on the outbreak of war to join the Russian Army she joined the militant wing of Sinn Fein. In the Easter rising of 1916 she commanded the volunteers who occupied the College of Surgeons in Dublin, and was sentenced to death for her part. The sentence was commuted to penal servitude for life, but Mme. de

Markievicz was released at the amnesty in 1917. A year afterwards she was elected as the first woman member of the House of Commons, but never took her seat. She was imprisoned on several occasions.

Mme. de Markievicz acted as Minister for Labour in the Shadow Cabinet, which was formed by Mr de Valera to conduct the campaign against the British Government in 1919, and during the Treaty debates she opposed the acceptance of the Articles of Agreement, declaring that her object was the establishment of a Workers' Republic in Ireland. She was one of Mr de Valera's staunchest supporters in the troubled times that followed the setting up of the Free State. Again she was imprisoned, this time by the Government of the Free State, but at the two General Elections of 1922 and 1923 she was returned by comfortable majorities for her old constituency of South Dublin. She was again a successful candidate at the General Election last month, but fell ill almost immediately after the declaration of the poll. Having seen her daughter Mme. de Markievicz rallied and hopes were entertained for her recovery. She died in the presence of her husband, who had travelled to Dublin from Warsaw, and of Mr de Valera.

Mme. de Markievicz originally was a Protestant, but she was received into the Roman Catholic Church after the 1916 rebellion.

JOHN DEVOY

1 OCTOBER 1928

MR JOHN DEVOY was the oldest of Irish revolutionaries and the most bitter and persistent, as well as the most dangerous, enemy of this country which Ireland has produced since Wolfe Tone, the organizer of the United Irish Movement at the end of the 18th century, brought about the attempted invasion of Ireland by the French under Hoche. For 60 years Devoy was unremittingly engaged in conspiracies, both in Ireland and in America, for the establishment of an Irish Republic.

Born in Dublin, Devoy, while a mere youth, served for some years in the French Foreign Legion in Algeria. Returning to Dublin in the early sixties, he was given control of the department of the Irish Republican Brotherhood, or Fenians, concerned with the enrolment in the conspiracy of Irish soldiers in the British Army. One of his most successful agents was John Boyle O'Reilly, a sergeant of the 10th Hussars, then stationed in Dublin. The plan was to assemble on the day appointed for the insurrection 2,000 sworn men of the Dublin garrison, who were said to be ready to turn out, fully armed, within an hour of summons, divide them among the three principal railway stations in Dublin, seize trains, and go down the country to capture the three main military arsenals. The plan was discovered before the time had come for action. Devoy was sentenced to five years' penal servitude. O'Reilly, tried by Court-martial and sentenced to be shot, was reprieved and transported; having escaped from the penal settlement in Western Australia – carried off, by a steamer sent out for the purpose from America by Devoy – he lived to become editor of the Boston *Pilot* and a well-known poet and novelist.

Devoy, who likewise took to journalism, was foreign editor of the *New York Herald* for many years. As a member of the "Revolutionary Directory" of the Clan-na-Gael, the most widely extended and powerful of the advanced nationalist organizations in America, he was associated with Michael Davitt, in the later seventies, in forwarding "the New

Departure," a plan for the co-operation of the physical force men in the constitutional movement under Parnell. For more than 30 years afterwards Devoy kept alive the Fenian idea in his weekly paper, the *Gaelic American*. During the War he was associated with German agents in America in stirring up trouble in Ireland, and he aided and abetted the Dublin Rebellion of Easter, 1916. He was also prominently associated with the mission of de Valera to the United States, but when de Valera in February, 1920 suggested a grant of Irish independence by England, with a Monroe doctrine policy, or English protectorate, Devoy broke with him and declared that the Irish in America would not agree to any compromise with England. Nevertheless, he supported the treaty under which the Irish Free State was set up, and when he visited Ireland in July, 1924, after an absence of 45 years, Mr Cosgrave invited him to consider himself the guest of the Irish people. Devoy was met on arrival by the Minister for External Affairs, and the freedom of several Irish cities was conferred on him during his stay.

JOHN WOULFE FLANAGAN

A great servant of The Times

BY THE DEATH of Mr J. W. Flanagan, which we announce to-day with
the most profound regret, *The Times* loses one of the oldest members
of its editorial staff and one of its most brilliant and devoted servants.

Scholar, lawyer, historian, and student of international affairs, Mr
Flanagan brought to his work a mind exceptionally well furnished,
a balanced judgment, and a rare grace of style. Though he had long
passed the age when he might honourably have sought relief from daily
attendance at the office, he steadily refused any lightening of his labours.
For him life meant work, and work meant his writing in Printing House-
square and the wide reading and concentrated thought which gave
that writing its pre-eminent value and distinction. In spite of pain and
increasing weakness he continued to work almost to the end, and it can
truthfully be said that he died as he had lived, in the active service of the
paper he loved and served so well.

John Woulfe Flanagan was born on April 6, 1852, the eldest son in
a large family of six boys and five girls. He came of good legal stock
which traces its descent from an old Irish family long settled in County
Roscommon. This family was one of that not very numerous but, in
proportion to its numbers, highly distinguished class – those old Irish
stocks which were at once strong Roman Catholics and strong Loyalists.
Both characteristics were marked in Flanagan. He was throughout life
a devout member of his Church, and – until his spirit was broken by
what he regarded as successive English surrenders to Home Rule and
Sinn Fein – a fierce Loyalist. His father, the Right Hon. Stephen Woulfe
Flanagan, Q.C. (1817–91), was eminent as Judge of the Irish Landed
Estates Court, and was sworn of the Privy Council both in Great Britain
and in Ireland. His mother was a daughter of John R. Corballis, LL.D.,

Q.C., and his uncle, also named John Woulfe Flanagan, of Drumdoe, J.P. and D.L., married a daughter of the Right Hon. Sir Michael O'Loghlen, Bt., Master of the Rolls in Ireland. The name of Woulfe came into the family by the marriage of his grandfather, Terence Flanagan, of St Catherine's Park, Leixlip, to Johanna, daughter of the Right Hon. Stephen Woulfe, of Tiermaclane, Co. Clare, Lord Chief Baron of the Irish Exchequer Court.

Flanagan was sent to school at Oscott, and went up to Balliol College, Oxford, in 1871. There he did well, taking his two firsts in the classical schools, and winning the Stanhope prize in 1874 for an essay on "The Portuguese in the East." ... He was called to the Bar by Lincoln's lnn, in 1877, and was also a member of the Irish Bar. He practised as a conveyancer. In 1881 he served in the office of High Sheriff of Roscommon, where he had a property, Rathtermon, and was a magistrate for that county and for Co. Sligo. He joined the staff of *The Times* just after the split in the Liberal Party caused by Gladstone's acceptance of Parnell's Home Rule policy, and was a protagonist in the sustained campaign which the paper waged against the new departure. While he had nothing to do with accepting and publishing the so-called "Parnell Letters," he was in fact the author of the series of articles on "Parnellism and Crime," which brought out in relentless detail the truth of W. E. Forster's charge that "Crime dogged the footsteps of the Land League." He warmly supported Lord Balfour's policy as Chief Secretary, and had a great admiration for Lord Carson.

While his earliest writing was mainly about Ireland, his chiefs and his colleagues soon discovered his deep interest in, and considerable knowledge of, many European countries, their languages, history, and literature. Accordingly he became more and more diverted to writing on foreign policy, and gradually became the principal leader-writer of *The Times* in this sphere. His versatility was indeed remarkable. By disposition and education a thorough scholar, he had also the lawyer's power of cool, analytical thought, and he possessed in a high degree the lawyer's capacity for rapid mastery of a brief. These qualities enabled him swiftly to marshal the most intractable array of discordant facts, to find his way with unerring certainty to the heart of the matter, and, with his fastidious pen, to express the policy of the paper in finely chiselled prose. But his versatility would have been of little effect if it had not been securely founded upon an encyclopaedic knowledge and sustained by a reading which was at once wide and selective. All the principal political treatises in half a dozen languages passed under his review, and his daily reading included the leading journals of France, Italy, Spain and Germany. Nothing but a daily timetable carefully ordered and strictly observed could have enabled him with profit to cover so wide a field.

In addition, he was the master of a superb style – not the chipped and clear but somewhat "snappy" style which, through a corrupt following of Macaulay, has been generally prevalent in high-class British journalism; but rather a style deriving from Burke, whom he greatly admired, with colour and sweep and glow, filling and satisfying the ear and eye as well as the mind. It was typical of the strenuousness which he put into his work at the office that he used to take off his coat and waistcoat before beginning, and sit down to write in a costume suitable to active outdoor exercise or heavy physical labour. Always he nourished his spirit on the greatest authors, on whom, when occasion offered, he wrote memorable articles. He was a lifelong student of Dante, and he used to keep a Shakespeare in his room at the office to read while waiting for instructions.

Mention must also be made of his love of art. He was an ardent admirer of the great Italian painters and never lost an opportunity during his visits to Italy of studying their masterpieces. He was, indeed, familiar with most of the important galleries of Europe, and his last foreign journey was made in order that he might refresh his knowledge of the art treasures of Spain. These Continental visits gave him great delight, and they bore fruit in articles in which his critical taste was reinforced by his wide historical knowledge.

In a life so completely devoted to work there was naturally little time for recreation, and still less for the common amenities of social life, and his close friendships were necessarily few, but to work with him day by day in intimate association was a joyous and stimulating experience.

Passionately devoted to liberty and detesting tyranny in any form, he lived to see the supersession of liberal institutions in many lands and the rapid growth of democratic pretensions, which he feared because he believed them to be rooted neither in liberty nor in knowledge. So it came about that in the later days his outlook upon life was a little saddened. But it was never cynical. His religious faith was too secure and too robust to allow him to despair of the future, though he felt that the full reaction and the day of regeneration would not come in his lifetime.

In the face of regrets and disappointments, the flame of his patriotism was at all times ardent and pure and illuminated some of the most eloquent of his leading articles. For at heart he was ever young. Age could not quench his indomitable courage and independence of mind, or curb his eagerness of heart; and to his loyalty to the paper and to his colleagues there were no bounds. To the privileged few who were admitted to the inner circle of his friendship there will ever remain the memory of a character of singular beauty and overflowing kindness. They will not find it easy to speak of their privilege and of their loss. Let it suffice to say that for them life will henceforth be less abundant, for his death leaves a void which no new friendship can ever fill.

Flanagan married, in 1880, Mary Emily, second daughter of Major-General Sir Justin Sheil, K.C.B., and niece of the famous Irish orator, Lalor Sheil, and had a son, John Henry, born in 1881, and a daughter, Jane Mary, born in 1883. Mrs Flanagan was a cousin, for her mother was a daughter of Lord Chief Baron Woulfe. She was a lady of singular beauty and charm, and her death in 1888 was, as his friends knew, an abiding sorrow. Flanagan's fourth brother, James, who was the most courteous, kindly, and popular resident magistrate for Newry district, was shot by three young men on June 4, 1922, as he was leaving Newry Cathedral after Mass. He died soon afterwards. At the inquest the jury found that he had been brutally and callously murdered. The criminals were never caught, though the Government of Northern Ireland offered a reward of £1,000. Among Flanagan's other brothers are Mr Stephen Woulfe Flanagan, J.P., D.L., of Lecarrow Lodge, Boyle; Colonel Richard

John Woulfe Flanagan, D.S.O., The Royal West Kent Regiment; and Lieutenant-Colonel Edward Martyn Woulfe Flanagan, C.M.G., D.S.O., and Legion of Honour, The East Surrey Regiment.

* * *

T. P. O'CONNOR

Father of the House of Commons

19 NOVEMBER 1929

THE RIGHT HON. Thomas Power O'Connor, politician and journalist, whose death at the age of 81 was announced in our later editions yesterday, was the most versatile, and also the most widely known Irishman who has appeared in public life for many years. He had remarkable gifts, both as writer and as talker, which he exercised with unwearied industry and amazing productiveness for more than half a century, and he has his place in the separate annals of Ireland, the House of Commons, and the British Press. O'Connor first entered the House of Commons in 1880, and had remained a member of it without a break ever since. Save for the first five years of his Parliamentary career, he sat, paradoxically enough, for an Irish constituency in England which is called Scotland – the Scotland Division of Liverpool. O'Connor was for many years the "Father" of the Irish Parliamentary Party, and survived for years its dissolution and the establishment of the Irish Free State, and when Thomas Burt, the venerable Labour leader, retired, O'Connor succeeded him as "Father" of the House of Commons, by right of having the longest unbroken period of service as a member.

Thomas Power O'Connor was born on October 5, 1848, at Athlone, on the Shannon. His father was of the small shopkeeping class; his mother was the daughter of a non-commissioned officer of The Connaught Rangers; and the boy, having the run of the barracks at Athlone, was brought up – as he used to, say – to the strains of "The British Grenadiers," "Rule, Britannia," and "The Red, White and Blue." He first went to the College of the Immaculate Conception at Athlone, and afterwards entered Queen's College, Galway, a constituent college of the old Queen's University. In 1866, at the age of 18, O'Connor graduated and secured a senior scholarship in history and modern languages, with the aid of which he made his way to Dublin, and obtained the post of junior reporter on *Saunders' Newsletter*, an old and staid Conservative daily paper.

In 1870, he arrived in London, friendless and obscure. The Franco-Prussian War had broken out, and his knowledge of French and German obtained for him a post as sub-editor on the *Daily Telegraph*. After a few years of this work he earned a precarious livelihood as a "free lance." He also began to take an active part as a Radical in politics, addressing workmen's clubs, and exercising wherever he could his talent for debate.

It was during this period that he wrote his first book, a life of Lord Beaconsfield. His first intention was to describe notable and historic scenes in the House of Commons, and he went to the British Museum for an account of the howling down of Disraeli during his maiden speech and his declaration that the day would come when the House would listen to him. But O'Connor was so fascinated by the picture of ringletted Disraeli in cambric shirts, embroidered waistcoats, and gold chains during his first candidature for High Wycombe in 1832, as presented in the file of the *Bucks Herald*, that he changed his mind and decided to write a biography. The book appeared in serial numbers anonymously during 1876. It was so unsparing an attack upon the Prime Minister and took so unfavourable a view of his career, that it attracted attention, and when O'Connor put his name to it on its appearance in book form in 1879 it gave him his first lift into public notice.

O'Connor had worked in the Reporters' Gallery of the House of

Commons, and had seen with sympathy the rise of the obstruction policy of Biggar and Parnell. But when towards the end of 1879, a General Election came in view, and he decided to make a bid for a seat in Parliament, he was disposed to stand as a British Radical rather than as an Irish Nationalist. Having obtained a promise of nomination for an English borough, he went to Parnell to enlist the support of the Irish voters and mentioned that he was known to Frank Hugh O'Donnell, a member of the Nationalist party. The upshot was that O'Connor stood for the borough of Galway as a Home Ruler and was returned as the junior member, but with a margin of only six votes.

The old Irish Party, a mere tail of the Whigs, or Liberals, had come to an end. The new Nationalist member was also an entirely different type from the old. "The best member that Ireland ever sent to Westminster," said Palmerston, "was Cornelius O'Brien from Clare, for he was in the House 30 years, and never once opened his mouth." The young men whom Parnell led – the O'Connors, the Healys, the Redmonds, the Sextons, the Dillons – were astonishingly and relentlessly fluent of speech when they wished to delay business. A fortnight after the assembling of Parliament O'Connor made his maiden speech, advocating the suspension of the landlords' right of eviction for two years, as a temporary measure for the alleviation of the then acute agrarian trouble in Ireland. John Bright told Justin McCarthy that he was charmed by the young man's brogue. It is probable, however, that O'Connor's mellifluously flowing voice soon grew tiresome to the House, for he was one of the most voluble and pertinacious talkers among the Parnellites, unaffected by the atmosphere of the Assembly, whether it was chillingly indifferent or hot with resentment. In a character sketch of the time he is described as "lean and arrogant." He was conspicuous in many a scene in those days. The most memorable was the 41 hours' sitting, prolonged from January 31 to February 2, 1881, by the obstruction of the Parnellites to the Coercion Bill of Mr Forster, the Chief Secretary. It was only closed by Speaker Brand's putting the question, though no authority to do so was vested in him by the then existing rules, and resulted in the introduction of the closure. The sitting, Thorold Rogers suggested, ought to be commemorated by a statue of brass with the Nationalist members for the raw material.

In 1883 O'Connor was appointed president of the Irish Nationalist organization in Great Britain. At the General Election of 1885 he wrote the address of the Irish Party to the Nationalist voters in Great Britain, urging them to defeat the Liberal oppressors of Ireland by supporting the Conservatives. At the General Election of 1886, when Gladstone had committed himself to Home Rule, he wrote another address in still more moving terms to the same electors to vote for the Liberals.

All this time he continued his journalistic activities. John Morley, when editor of the *Pall Mall Gazette* in the early eighties, engaged him to write a sketch of the proceedings in Parliament, and thought that no journalist excelled him in depicting the personal and dramatic aspects of the party conflict in the House of Commons. O'Connor published in 1886 "The Parnell Movement," which, while frankly intended as a vindication of the Nationalist agitation, both agrarian and political, is of value as a piece of historical writing, and is probably the one book from his fertile pen which will be found of service to future historians.

The adoption of Home Rule by the Liberals had the effect of reviving the early associations of O'Connor with Radicalism, so much so indeed that he was able to obtain sufficient financial support to found in 1887 the *Star*, an evening newspaper with an advanced Radical and democratic programme. He was always very proud of the leading article he wrote for the first number. "The policy will appear to us," it declared, "worthy of everlasting thanks and of ineffaceable glory that does no more than enable the charwoman to put two pieces of sugar in her cup of tea instead of one, and that adds one farthing a day to the wage of the seamstress or the labourer." He broke away from the old traditions under which newspapers had become dull and insipid, and inaugurated the "new journalism" with "the human touch." In a few years, however, differences arose between him and his proprietors, and his interest was bought out for £15,000 on the condition that he should not start another evening paper for three years. When he was free he established the *Sun*, but, though it was conducted on the same principles as the *Star*, it was not successful.

In the early years of his career O'Connor was "Tom" to his friends, and whenever he rose to address the House Mr Speaker Peel invariably called on him as "Mr Thomas O'Connor." One night, however, as he was making one of his trenchant speeches in denunciation of the Government, a countryman in the gallery broke in with the fervidly admiring exclamation, "Glory to you. Tay Pay, me fine man!" and with that incident began the glorification of O'Connor's initials as distinct from his family name. So it was that he founded *T.P.'s Weekly*, a popular pennyworth of literary and artistic culture, which flourished for many years, and was revived in 1923. The "Book of the Week" was its principal feature, which consisted rather of quotation than of criticism. He started other weekly newspapers – such as *M.A.P.* (Mainly About People) and *P.T.O.* (Please Turn Over) – both devoted chiefly to personal gossip – and tried his hand also at a monthly called *T.P.'s Magazine*.

Later on the facsimile of his signature, "T. P. O'Connor," was for years seen by millions of people daily (including Sunday) on the certificate of the Board of Film Censors which precedes the presentation of every film in the cinemas. O'Connor was appointed president of the Board at the beginning of 1917 – a position conferred by the cinematograph trade, but independent of any control in the acceptance or rejection of films.

Another of O'Connor's journalistic activities was the writing of obituaries for the *Daily Telegraph*. His own depreciatory reference to these articles as "T.P.'s Meditations among the Tombs" was not at all apt, for there was little that was funereal about them. They dealt at large with the drama and comedy of life, with a strict observance of the injunction to say nothing of the dead but what is good. His conversation was also of the same quality of kindly reminiscence and anecdote.

In later years O'Connor did not often speak in the House, and, having mellowed with age, his part was usually to soften asperities or to get his comrades out of a fix in which tactless and indiscreet statements had landed them. He had not, however, entirely controlled his native impulsiveness, which had led to the most violent scene that ever took place in the Commons. Chamberlain had made a fierce attack on

Gladstone and the Liberal subserviency to him. "Never since the time of Herod," he declared, "has there been such slavish adulation." "Judas! Judas!" cried O'Connor, and immediately there was uproar, and blows were struck for the first time in the House. Mr Speaker Peel was sent for and succeeded in calming the excitement. Explanations followed, and the proceedings ended in loud laughter when Mr Condon, an Irish member standing up to defend O'Connor, spoke of him by a slip of the tongue as "the hon. member for Scotland Yard."

O'Connor was president of the United Irish League from 1883, and ruled it at its annual conferences with unchallenged sway. In that capacity his chief aim was to soften the asperity of the political relations between Ireland and England. His other rôle was that of plenipotentiary of the Nationalists to foreign countries. He was instrumental in arousing in France widespread sympathy with the Home Rule movement. But the United States was the chief field of his exertions. He paid frequent visits to raise funds for the Parliamentary Party, and reaped an abundant harvest. In later years O'Connor visited the United States on another mission – that of appealing to Americans of Irish birth that the greatest service they could do for Ireland was to help America in the War.

In O'Connor's 75th year, 1923, all parties in the House of Commons united in testifying their esteem and affection for the Father of the House. At a luncheon to which he was entertained at the House, the Speaker, who presided, presented him, on behalf of his colleagues, with a gold snuff-box of the George III. period – O'Connor being one of the few members who continued the old Parliamentary custom of snuff-taking – and also with the original of the cartoon of himself by "Spy," of *Vanity Fair*, and both the Prime Minister, Mr Baldwin, and the Leader of the Opposition, Mr Asquith, spoke of him as a Parliamentary institution. Nor were the Lords behindhand in paying their tribute. Lord Curzon of Kedleston, presiding at a dinner at the Savoy Hotel, supported by Lord Derby, and Lord Carson, said of their guest, "the Parliamentary free-lance has grown into a British statesman." In 1924, when the first Labour Government was in office, O'Connor was made a member of the Privy Council. This was an honour he highly appreciated, and he was wont also to boast that, in recognition of his services to the cause of Greece after the War, a street in Athens was named after him. On his 80th birthday a dinner was given in his honour, at which a telegram conveying "heartiest congratulations" from the King was read. Last July, after he had been once more returned for the Scotland Division of Liverpool, O'Connor was presented on the Terrace of the House of Commons, on behalf of friends of all political parties, with a declaration of trust making financial provision for him. Mr MacDonald, the Prime Minister, presided.

O'Connor continued his journalistic activities almost to the last, though in his later years he became physically more and more feeble and was unable to use pen or type-writer. Last spring he published two substantial volumes, "Memoirs of an Old Parliamentarian," which provided for the first time a complete and intimate account of the original Parnellite Party.

SIR HORACE PLUNKETT

28 MARCH 1932

SIR HORACE PLUNKETT, whose death we announce with much regret this morning, has left an achievement as enduring as his work for the single cause of its attainment was devoted. His influence on the economic development of Ireland can only be described as historic. Before him Irish agriculture was in the depths of depression; what was worse, the Irish peasant was without the ability or even the desire to improve himself. After his ideas had been put into execution the Irish agriculturist was firmly set on the way, if not to flourishing prosperity, at any rate to self-help, contentment, and security. Cooperation, education, and the encouragement of enterprise were his principles. But the virtue of these would not have been enough without his own unstinted and unselfish work, drawing its force from a lively sympathy. And not the least thing he did, by his mistrust of pure State action and his refusal to recognize sectional disagreement, was to remove the cause of Irish agriculture as far as it could be removed from politics. His death now will be mourned by men of all parties in Ireland. His beautiful house at Foxrock was burned in the civil tumults, and his indomitable mind fought an increasingly severe battle with bodily illness, but his later years had their compensations. The man whose independent patriotism had incurred in turn the hostility of Irish unionists and of the old Nationalist Party, lived to be acclaimed by unionists and nationalists alike as a great Irishman and a great benefactor of his country. He lived to see his principles of agricultural cooperation embodied in the programme of a Free State Government, and to win warm tributes from a Free State Minister for Agriculture. Only two of his fellow-pioneers, the Rev. T. A. Finlay and Mr R. A. Anderson, survive him, but he died in the knowledge that his work has been established and will shape his country's future. Ireland to-day is the poorer by the loss of a son who combined apostolic zeal and a deep and delicate sense of humour with the best qualities of an Anglo-Irish aristocrat. The third son of the sixteenth Lord Dunsany and of Anne, daughter of the second Lord Sherborne, Horace Curzon Plunkett was born on October 24, 1854, at Sherborne House, Gloucestershire. He was uncle of the present Lord Dunsany, the poet and dramatist. He belonged to one of the oldest of the pre-Cromwellian Anglo-Irish families, for the Dunsanys were counted in medieval Ireland among the Lords of the Pale, who were a moderating influence in Irish life, standing between the native Irish Party on the one hand and the Cromwellian interest on the other.

Plunkett was sent to Eton in 1868 and was in Mr Oscar Browning's house. Then he went up to University College, Oxford, where he obtained a second class in modern history. At the age of 25 he took the step which was to determine the whole course of his life. A lover of outdoor life, with the temperament of a pioneer, he bought a ranch in Montana. In 10 years he had acquired a fortune, and when he returned to Ireland, in 1889, he carried back with him the new ideas of American agriculturists and a mass of practical knowledge, and he left behind him a local reputation as a promoter of many fortunate projects of land cultivation and extension. He continued to visit his ranch annually, but henceforth his main activities were concerned with Ireland.

The disillusionment of 1890–91 was Plunkett's opportunity. The sudden collapse of Parnellism transformed the Irish situation. The country generally was tired of mere politics. It was a moment for the philosopher and the prophet. New energies in Irish life released themselves – economic and social, literary and intellectual. They ran into various movements which composed the Irish Revival, as it was called. Already Plunkett's propaganda had had visible results. Dairy farming in Ireland had become an organized industry, and in principle the co-operative movement resembled, with certain modifications, the similar movement already established in England. In April, 1894, the Irish Agricultural Organization Society (I.A.O.S.) was formed with Plunkett as the first president, and the presence of Mr (now Lord) Carson and of Mr John Redmond on the same platform emphasized the non-political character of the enterprise. Plunkett himself had sat for South County

Dublin as a Unionist since the election of 1892, a fact which, if it involved the hostility of Mr John Dillon and his Nationalists, recommended the movement to the Unionists. On August 27, 1895, in a letter to the Press, Plunkett propounded the "need for economic legislation which would encourage individual enterprise and promote practical education, but must be removed from the region of political controversy." As a result the "Recess Committee" of Irishmen was formed to inquire how far State aid was essential for giving technical instruction to the agricultural, commercial, and industrial producer. Orangemen, Jesuits, the old Parnellites, Protestant landlords, and Roman Catholic unionists sat together on the committee; and the Bill which became law in 1899 was based on their report. It established a Department of Agriculture and Technical Instruction, with an income of £166,000 drawn almost exclusively from Irish sources. A Council of Agriculture, part-elected and part-nominated, assisted the heads of the Department. Plunkett, on being appointed vice-president, immediately resigned his position at the head of the I.A.O.S., but made it clear that the status and the duty of the society were unimpaired. It would continue its efforts to alter the complexion of Irish rural life and to gain acceptance for the doctrine of self-help and cooperation. The value of Plunkett's work was now recognized. In 1897 he had been appointed an Irish Privy Councillor; in 1902 he was elected a Fellow of the Royal Society; and in 1903 he was made K.C.V.O. when King Edward visited Ireland. He had been appointed a member of the Congested Districts Board in 1891, and so continued till 1918.

It was said that when Plunkett began the cooperative movement he had to address 50 meetings before he could form a single rural association. Apathy on the part of the peasant was the obstacle. But when his ideas had become a force in Ireland a coherent opposition was organized in nationalist circles. The word went forth that the building up of a self-reliant and independent movement outside all parties was not to be tolerated. Nevertheless the first attack came from a unionist quarter. Plunkett was associated in the minds of extreme Irish Conservatives with Mr Gerald Balfour and his policy of "killing Home

Rule by kindness." He had appointed Mr T. P. Gill, an ex-Nationalist member, general secretary of the Department; and he was in friendly relations with the independent Home Rulers. When, in 1900, he again stood for South County Dublin, a second Unionist candidate appeared, and the Nationalist was victorious. It was the end of Plunkett's Parliamentary career, but he was retained in the post of vice-president of the Department with the approval of independent Irish opinion. Mr Redmond, however, who had been elected leader of the Nationalists, withdrew his support from the cooperative movement. In 1904, in "Ireland in the New Century," Plunkett was able to report that the turnover of the rural societies is now £2,000,000, a figure large, indeed, when one remembers that many of the associated farmers are in so small a way that in England they would scarcely be called farmers at all.

With the advent of a Liberal Government to power in 1906 ... Plunkett was succeeded by the Nationalist nominee, Mr T. W. Russell, who had become a Liberal Home Ruler. In December Plunkett was elected president of the I.A.O.S. for the second time. These events suggested to his Irish admirers (among whom were many nationalists of the independent varieties) that the time had come for him to receive a material token of their respect and affection. Sir Horace asked that it should be such as to serve the future of the I.A.O.S. and produce a permanent monument, not to himself, but to his work. Three thousand pounds were quickly subscribed, and on November 11, 1908, 84, Merrion-square, Dublin, formally entered into Plunkett's possession. The house, one of the finest in the Irish capital, was immediately made into the headquarters of the cooperative movement.

The formation in 1911 of a body known as the United Irishwomen was another illustration of the wide scope of Plunkett's ideals. It was an organization for the promotion of "industries peculiarly associated with womankind" for the clothing of the "dry bones of economics" with humanity. A few years before he had similarly appealed to Irish landlords. His pamphlet, "Noblesse Oblige," was a stirring call to the gentlemen of Ireland to share in the regenerative experience of the nation ... The Parliamentarians, however, remained unreconciled, and in 1912 Mr John Dillon set forth in a letter to *The Times* a summary of his objections to the cooperative movement as conducted by Plunkett.

In a long letter to *The Times*, published in February, 1914, Plunkett proposed a scheme for an agreed settlement of the Irish problem. By this Ulster was to accept Home Rule with the right of secession after a number of years, and the Ulster Volunteers were to become a Territorial Force. He followed this up by publishing in July a pamphlet entitled "The Better Way" in which he announced his conversion to Home Rule, appealed to Ulster to give Home Rule a chance, and proposed a conference of Irishmen on the Bill. The War broke out immediately afterwards, but in 1917, the year after the Easter rebellion, the idea of a conference of Irishmen was adopted by Mr Lloyd George, and took shape as the Irish Convention. The members themselves paid Plunkett the compliment, at their first meeting, of choosing him unanimously as chairman. But Sinn Fein, steadily gathering strength, stood aloof, the general feeling in Ireland was sceptical, and, in spite of the unwearied and devoted efforts of Plunkett ... the Convention proved abortive. In 1919 Plunkett created and endowed the Horace Plunkett Foundation in Bloomsbury as a trust for the promotion of agricultural development. In 1920–21 he was prominent as an advocate of Dominion Home Rule, and when the State of Southern Ireland was set up he was for a time a Senator.

Plunkett was an old and valued correspondent of *The Times*. In 1920, owing to a mistaken report of his death by a news agency, he had the privilege of reading his obituary notices in British and Irish newspapers. He was unmarried.

LADY GREGORY

Irish playwright and poet

24 MAY 1932

WE ANNOUNCE WITH much regret that Lady Gregory, the Irish playwright and poet, died on Sunday night at her home at Coole Park, Gort, Co. Galway, at the age of 73.

The seventh and youngest daughter of Dudley Persse, D.L., of Roxborough, Co. Galway, Augusta Persse was Irish to the backbone. In childhood her love of the Irish people and their history and legend drew her to learn the language and to go about among the cottages of her father's tenants – heedless of the suspicion that she was trying to convert them to Protestantism – picking up from their lips the old stories of saints and wonders. Thence came her first impulse to make literature. She was writing down the legends of Ireland before she began writing plays; and her earliest plays were written round the legends of Ireland, and more or less with the idea that they should be acted by the peasants and their children.

But in those days the literature, and especially the drama, of Ireland were being fostered into new life and vigour by Douglas Hyde and others; Augusta Persse, though not directly connected with the movement, was caught up in its efforts, and given opportunities of which her marriage, in 1881, with the widowed Sir William Gregory, F.R.S., lately Governor of Ceylon, enabled her to make full use. Her influence upon the Anglo-Irish literature of her time is difficult to estimate, because a great deal of it was exercised within the walls and grounds of her beautiful home at Coole Park, in talks with the poets and novelists and playwrights who were her guests. But, apart from her own writings, her most eminent achievement was the foundation and control, which she shared with Mr W. B. Yeats, of the Irish Players and the Abbey Theatre, Dublin. She came just at the moment when the Irish Literary Theatre was expiring and the much more practical and human Irish National Theatre was coming into being. She was a good organizer, with a strong, if not imperious, will; and with Mr Yeats's help she ruled the enterprise, and slaved for it and fought for it, and backed it through many storms and calms, until it achieved fame far outside the borders of Ireland, and produced a drama which is unique in the history of the English-speaking peoples.

As author she began to write in prose, wrote well in verse, and went back to prose. Of her plays the most distinctive and the best written, as well as the most popular, were the one-act comedies of modern Irish life, such as *Hyacinth Halvey*, *The Workhouse Ward*, and *Spreading the News*. She wrote tragic plays of modern or recent Ireland as well: *The Gaol Gate*, for instance, and *The Rising of the Moon*. In these plays, comic and tragic, she used with great effect the Anglo-Irish speech of the peasants which she was proud to know herself the first to present in literature. She called it "Kiltartan" and one of her most characteristic and lively productions was the translation of certain plays of Molière into this Kiltartan tongue. Her plays included also some folk-plays and tragedies of Irish legend, and in her "Book of Saints and Wonders," her "Cuchulain of Muirthemne," her "Gods and Fighting Men," and other books, she told anew the old stories which she had heard from her people. Her writing was best when the chosen form kept it within rather narrow limits; and it is not too much to say that her one-act plays – so humorous, so wise, so moving, so poetical even when most homely – are among the best in the language. Other writings to be remembered are a beautiful little book (her last) about her home at Coole and its library, and her life of Sir Hugh Lane, who was the son of one of her sisters.

Lady Gregory had one son, William Robert Gregory, a painter of great promise, who was killed in the War. Her husband, who died in 1892, was Conservative member for Dublin from 1842 to 1847 and was elected for Co. Galway in 1857 as a supporter of Palmerston; but he was best known as a scholar and Orientalist and a great benefactor of the national art collections. He left his best pictures to the National Gallery.

GEORGE MOORE

23 JANUARY 1933

GEORGE MOORE, WHOSE death on Saturday we regret to announce, is an instance – rare in English literature – of absolute devotion to a self-imposed task, the task of becoming a writer. Nearly all his life lies in his books, and his assumptions of personality outside them enhanced his reputation but little.

George Augustus Moore was born on February 24, 1852, the eldest son of George Henry Moore, M.P., of Moore Hall, Co. Mayo, who became one of the leaders of the tenant right movement in the fifties, and grandson of a George Moore who wrote but never published a History of the French Revolution. A great-uncle, John Moore, joined the Rebellion of 1798 and was elected President of the Republic of Connaught. Moore's father loved horses and racing (forsaking the stables at length for politics), and George himself showed the family passion for horses, both before and after an attempt to educate him at Oscott had been abandoned. His own story was that it was abandoned because he had already found Catholicism abhorrent and himself at heart a Protestant; and so he returned to Moore Hall and half-enchanted idleness with a Shelley in his pocket.

An attempt to train him for the Army gave place to an attempt to make himself a painter, and after the sudden death of his father, in 1870, when he succeeded to Moore Hall, he went to Paris to study art, at about the end of 1872. For ten years he remained in Paris, learning French, haunting schools and cafés, discovering that he could never become a painter, and meeting Manet, Degas, Renoir, Zola, Verlaine, Mallarmé, and a dozen other famous men of whom he never tired of writing, at first in "Confessions of a Young Man" and then in other books. He looked back variously upon those ten years, sometimes seeing in them his initiation into the world of art, sometimes charging them simply with making his task as an English writer almost impossible.

The effects of the Land League agitation recalled him from Paris to London, and he remembered with pride his impoverished years in a Strand lodging, writing reviews and articles and his first novel, "A Modern Lover." That novel brought him preposterous praise and the opposition of the libraries, and from then (1883) to the day of his death he fostered, while deploring, an atmosphere of contention and wrath. In those days he quarrelled well and loudly, and even his later books showed that he never relinquished a grievance. His second novel, "A Mummer's Wife," repeated the offence to the libraries, but its success freed him from dependence upon them, and thereafter he could write as he chose; luckily he chose to write better, and "A Drama in Muslin" was the result. So book followed book, until "Esther Waters," in 1894, declared him master of the English naturalistic novel. He wrote nothing better in the naturalistic manner, but he followed it with worse books: "Evelyn Innes" and "Sister Teresa," for example, which were ambitious, exotic, and vulgar.

Not until the South African War drove him to Ireland in search of a Celtic Renaissance (the statement was his own) did he recover his better self, the immediate sign being "The Untilled Field" and "The Lake," which formed the first essays of an Irish Turgenev. His sojourn in Ireland lasted some ten years (during which, in 1905, he was High Sheriff of Co. Mayo), and was ended by formal renunciation, or rather denunciation, of Catholicism and everything Celtic. But that decade produced his unique work, the romantic autobiography called "Hail and Farewell," the three volumes of which developed the style first revealed in "Memoirs of My Dead Life" (1906), and a rich confusion of reminiscence, imagination, satire, and defamation of friends and enemies alike. He subjected most of his books to scrupulous revision years after they had become familiar to the public, and the writing of prefaces (reminiscent or critical) to the revised texts became an endless delight.

Moore's later work displayed his passion for exploring new worlds. "The Brook Kerith" was an imaginative life of Jesus with romance poured in and faith strained out. Two revised editions were issued, the revision being an effort to secure a yet more exact and delicate prose. A series of privately printed books began in 1918 with the half-delightful, half-lamentable "Story-Teller's Holiday," followed by "Avowals," "Heloise and Abelard," "Conversations in Ebury Street," "In Single Strictness," "Ulick and Soracha" (a Celtic romance), and a translation of "Daphnis and Chloe." In these volumes Moore professed to despise the public. Only after the limited editions became exhausted did he relax his rule and allow cheaper editions to gratify more numerous readers.

He wrote plays at various times, but, with the exception of *The Passing of the Essenes*, they do not take rank with his major work. To this play closely associated in subject with "The Brook Kerith," he devoted all his powers, and was rewarded – it was a great reward to him – by seeing its run at the Arts Theatre prolonged by general demand. In only one of his pieces for the theatre, *The Making of an Immortal*, a one-act play of Queen Elizabeth and Shakespeare, did his comic genius run true on the stage. Both these plays were work of his old age.

Moore was a great worker, a fine artist, a fond talker, with a self-conscious touch of wantonness in much that he said and wrote. His personality was striking, capricious, quarrelsome, preserving, nevertheless, for some, a certain affectionate loyalty. He loved art supremely and would sacrifice everything and everyone to it. Partly for this reason and partly because he cultivated a repute for uncharitableness which should save him from the trouble of suffering fools gladly, he was lonely in his later years. But to believe him to be bitter or cruel was to misunderstand him. His asperities sprang from his moods rather than from his character, and whoever was patient enough to smile at them and remain his friend would be rewarded by an almost childlike eagerness to "make it up" next morning and by a continually increasing comprehension of the man. Not to be interested in his craft of writing or in his peculiar views and delusions on the subject of feminine behaviour was to find him tedious, for he was ever true to his favourite themes.

When he was out walking, he would turn suddenly into the shop of a French chemist to demand of its astonished owner a French word to displace another which, in a translation of his writing, had failed to express his thought. The *mot juste* was on the tip of his tongue; he would stand in the shop, careless of the other customers, careless too of the chemist's embarrassment – for the word was not a comfortable one, waving his hands despairfully at mankind who had thought for other things. And when, after a long struggle with sickness and discomfort, the limited edition of "Aphrodite in Aulis" came at last to his table, he was at once discontented with it. Even before it had been published and while he was helpless in a nursing home, he was planning a new end to it. "I am famous for my endings," he said, "and now I have seen that this book has no ending. I have improvised another. My last book must end with a flourish. Then I am done." And he was half afraid to revise that improvisation, lest he should spoil it, for he liked to think of himself, not as a stylist, a manipulator of words, but as a master of narrative. He was fond of saying, not only for the sake of being contradicted, that he "could not write," and would cite Landor as proof by contrast. But he could "invent incident" and "compose a pretty story"; after a dozen false starts, he could "begin in the right place" and shape a tale "like a vase."

In person he was of middle height, with fresh complexion, sloping shoulders, long, sensitive hands which he employed continually in limp gestures, hair once yellow and afterwards white, and a moustache that partly hid the arrogant, sensual mouth; but nothing hid the changes of his eye, which was now soft and gentle, and anon – at a challenging thought – sharp as a hawk's. He was never a great reader or a tolerant one. It pleased him to insist on unexpected preferences and he was delighted if anyone would dispute his claim that the first half of "The Tenant of Wildfell Hall" was superior to anything else written by the Brontës. No reputation, not even Shakespeare's, awed him, except, perhaps, Landor's and, on occasion, Milton's; and there were few books – if we exclude Shelley's, which he loved – that he spoke of with greater enthusiasm than Trelawny's Recollections of Shelley and Byron. But as his age increased he read less and less, and in the room of his nursing home, not a book was to be seen. "I think," he said, "and tell myself stories. Then I doze a little until I have a better story to tell."

George Moore did not marry. His brother, Colonel Maurice George Moore, C.B., has had a distinguished military career and is a Senator of the Irish Free State. Colonel Moore lived at Moore Hall until about 1912. From that date it was vacant until, in 1923, it was burned by Republicans.

* * *

EDWARD CARSON

The chosen champion of Ulster

23 OCTOBER 1935

IN LORD CARSON OF DUNCAIRN, who died at Cleve Court, Minster, yesterday at the age of 81, a great figure disappears from public life. To Englishmen it seemed strange that a Southern Irishman should become the hero and the chosen leader of Ulster, commanding the absolute confidence and the passionate devotion of the self-willed and mistrustful Northern democracy as no man had commanded them before. But to his own countrymen the growth of Carson's influence and authority in Ulster seemed perfectly natural and intelligible. He belonged to a class which has played in England and in the Empire a part out of all proportion to its small numbers in Ireland. He was a Southern Protestant of the middle class, wholly educated in Ireland, but sharing in large measure the opinions held by British Liberals before the rise of the Home Rule controversy. Men of that order, with negligible exceptions, regarded the Union as the irrevocable and necessary foundation of progress and of civilization in Ireland. When the Gladstonian Liberals went over to Home Rule the Southern Protestants of all shades were inevitably drawn more closely to their fellow-Protestants of Ulster, among whom hatred and fear of Southern and Roman Catholic supremacy obliterated all distinctions between Church of Ireland and Presbyterian, Conservative and Liberal. Carson, haunted by the same feelings and the same dread, naturally turned to Ulster. As naturally, the Unionist democracy of the North welcomed him as a champion, and soon hailed him as their unquestioned chief.

It will long be debated whether he was the evil genius who seduced them into the slippery path of hypothetical rebellion, or whether he was the wise leader who moderated and guided to safety the fiercest racial and religious passions. He did not originate the idea of organized resistance in Ulster. When he was still an unknown junior at the Bar organization had begun and arms were imported. Colonel Saunderson, who had begun, like Carson, as a Liberal, had discovered that there were only two parties when it came to the "push of pike"; John Morley, not yet a full-blown Home Ruler, had warned his friends that Home Rule, forced on a recalcitrant Ulster, might result in "a reduced and squalid version of the Thirty Years' War"; and Lord Randolph Churchill had felt his ground carefully before declaring that "Ulster will fight." Carson's achievement was to weld together the elements of resistance with a masterly hand and an iron control. What in weaker hands would have led only to isolated riots and street fighting became a coherent movement which won the support of the Conservative Party in England and ultimately secured what Ulster regarded as the essential conditions: no separation from England and no subordination to a Dublin Parliament.

Two great qualities, courage and single-mindedness, could not be denied to Carson by his bitterest enemies – though indeed it is almost true to say that he had no enemies among those who knew him personally and not merely as a figure-head and a political symbol. His private friendships were deep and permanent: in spite of all his apparent severity as an advocate and a leader he had an extraordinarily tender heart. As a public man he had imagination, extraordinary personal magnetism, a missionary enthusiasm controlled by a clear and powerful intellect, intense sincerity and conviction, and a steady, life-long fidelity to a great ideal. With the cause of the Union he passionately believed the whole welfare of his native country stood or fell, and to that cause everything else seemed secondary. Hence it was that party politics really had little meaning for him save in their bearing on his ideal. He began as a Liberal, even a member of the National Liberal Club, but the same political evolution which threw the Liberals into the arms of the Nationalists threw Carson into the Unionist fold. Ireland was always first.

In the War he did great service, and might have done more were it not that, in spite of himself, he was still obsessed by the Irish problem, and also because any kind of teamwork was difficult to him. He had for too long been accustomed to his uncrowned kingship, and was little versed in the ways of compromise. At the Bar he will be remembered as one of the greatest advocates in the whole legal annals of England. His power of oratory and his gift of searching cross-examination were aided by his curiously impressive countenance, long, lean, hatchet-shaped, with burning, piercing eyes, and by the height of his thin, sinewy frame. With juries he was an acknowledged master, and he made up for any deficiencies in legal profundity by his quickness of apprehension and an almost uncanny knack of penetrating other men's minds, whether he was dealing with a recalcitrant witness or an unconvinced Judge or the counsel on the other side.

Edward Henry Carson was born on February 9, 1854, the second son of Edward Henry Carson, a civil engineer, of Dublin, sometime vice-president of the Royal Institute of Architects, by his marriage to Isabella, daughter of Captain Lambert, of Castle Ellen, Co. Galway. He was sent to Portarlington School, where he was early known as a fighter, thrashing a bigger boy who had proved objectionable. From school he went to Trinity College, Dublin, where he took his degree at the age of 22, and a year later was called to the Irish Bar. For some 10 years he practised with continually increasing fame in the Irish Courts, and his experiences at this time help to explain the vehemence with which, later on, he denounced the Nationalists and all their works.

Two years after his call to the Bar he married Sarah Annette Foster, daughter of Mr H. Persse Kirwan, of Triston Lodge, Co. Galway. The young couple were not at all well off, and the first years at any rate were a hard struggle. But by her sympathetic and earnest character and womanly charm, Carson's wife gave him the support that he needed, both in those early years and later, when he was making his way at the English Bar and in Parliament. She died in April, 1913. Her elder son, who was in the Army, died in May, 1930; her younger son is in the Navy. The younger of her two daughters died in 1925.

Fortunately for Carson, an early application for an Irish County Court Judgeship was unsuccessful. In 1887 Mr Arthur Balfour began his historic Chief Secretaryship, and Mr Edward Carson was made counsel to the Attorney-General for Ireland, and later senior Crown Prosecutor. In the work of putting into operation the Crimes Act, Carson fought the National League at the hourly peril of his life. Armed detectives watched over him as he went about securing convictions for the agrarian and other outrages that had terrorized large districts. It was an experience that was enough to test the bravest, but Carson came out of it unmoved save only that his political convictions were if anything strengthened. Mr Balfour, who had formed a high opinion of Carson, obtained for him the appointment of Irish Solicitor-General. This was in June, 1892, only three months before Lord Salisbury's second Administration came to an end. At the General Election in the autumn of that year he entered Parliament as one of the members for his old university. At Westminster he quickly confirmed the good opinion of his political chiefs, and the fate of Mr Gladstone's second Home Rule Bill was in no small degree due to Carson's ready wit, skill in debate, and unfailing knowledge of the weak points in his opponent's armour, as well as to the impassioned fervour of his eloquence.

In 1893 he was called to the English Bar by the Middle Temple. He was already a Q.C. in Ireland and a Bencher of the King's Inns, and in 1894 he became an English Q.C. and was in due course elected a Bencher of his Inn. On the accession of the Unionists to power, in 1895, Carson did not accept office. At this period he was at the zenith of his great powers as an advocate, and especially as a cross-examiner, and he doubtless felt it necessary to devote himself, at least for a time, to his professional career. In that career he went from triumph to triumph.

After the General Election of 1900 Carson joined the Unionist Ministry as Solicitor-General (for England), receiving the customary honour of knighthood. Though the Courts took up much of his time, he was enough in the Commons to consolidate his position as the man to whom the Ulster Unionists could look as their future leader. He would have no paltering with nationalist aims, and was constant in keeping his own leaders on the strait path of unionism. Thus he would have none of the Devolution scheme which attracted Mr Wyndham and Lord Dudley; the Lord Lieutenant even protested against the violence of Carson's views. On the fall of Mr Balfour's Government, at the end of 1905, Carson was sworn of the Privy Council, and, retaining his seat after the General Election, he appeared in the new Parliament once more in opposition.

While he maintained his position at the Bar, his influence within his party and in the House grew steadily. In one striking instance he broke away from Ulster opinion; he strongly supported Mr Birrell's Irish Universities Bill, which owed its passage largely to his advocacy. But this defection was excused. He was chosen as leader of the Irish Unionists. When Mr Balfour later on resigned the leadership of the Opposition, Sir Edward Carson was one of the four men who were mentioned as possible successors. But he refused to be a candidate, preferring to devote all his energies to the service of Irish unionism. In the battles over the Parliament Act Carson's speeches were chiefly directed to showing the effect the measure might have on the Irish problem; he frankly declared that not only would Home Rule be resisted by force, but that such resistance was constitutionally justified. It must not be forgotten that in this estimate of the situation he was both guided and supported by the most intense demonstrations of Ulster feeling. It was known that he was ready for any personal sacrifice, that he counted his professional advancement at the Bar and his career in politics as weighing less than nothing in the balance. He urged the Lords to throw out the Bill, and when they rejected his advice he considered that the die was cast. The veto of the Lords had gone, and the passage of Home Rule was assured.

The Ulster Unionist Council thereupon appointed a Commission "to take immediate steps, in consultation with Sir Edward Carson, to frame and submit a Constitution for a Provisional Government for Ulster." Ulster would never submit to the domination of a Dublin Parliament, and, she must therefore arrange for her own administration. Preparations to this end were made, a large force of Volunteers, armed at first with dummy rifles but admirably drilled, was enrolled, and Carson himself, by speeches at spectacular demonstrations in Ulster and elsewhere, and by his marked powers of organization, firmly consolidated his position, and roused his followers to an intense fervour of devotion. Both Liberals and Nationalists endeavoured to ridicule him as an "elderly lawyer" and his followers as prospective and conditional rebels. The Government were even urged to indict him for high treason, but to his disappointment they refrained.

In the spring of 1912 Mr Asquith's Home Rule Bill was introduced and the Ulster movement grew apace, until in September a solemn Covenant of resistance to Home Rule was signed at Belfast by hundreds of thousands. In the following year the Ulster Unionist Council was actually organized into a Provisional Government with Carson at the head. Ministers now began to be seriously uneasy, and made overtures which Carson did not altogether reject.

Down to the autumn of 1913 Mr Asquith had entirely refused to consider the exclusion of Ulster even for a time, but in October he was inviting a settlement by consent, and in the following March he proposed that any Ulster county might vote itself out of the Bill for six years. This was refused by Carson ... The famous incident at the Curragh followed, when the officers, on being sounded as to their attitude if they were ordered to suppress Ulster's resistance, immediately tendered their resignations. These they withdrew on receiving assurances from the War Office which were strongly repudiated by the Liberal Party, and Mr Asquith himself had to take over the War Office from General Seely. Moreover, Mr Churchill, who had already propounded a vast devolution scheme for the whole kingdom, was charged by the Unionists with endeavouring, by a concentration of naval strength in the Irish Sea, to incite Ulster to armed resistance.

On April 25, 1914, the public were startled by the "gun-running" incident. During the previous night a large quantity of rifles and ammunition was landed at Larne and on the coast of the County Down. They were brought over in an unknown steamer, and distributed over North-East Ulster by motor in the course of a few hours. The skill with which the operation was planned and the complete success with which it was executed were striking proofs of the degree to which Carson's organization had been disciplined and developed. Although some 12,000 men were engaged in the landing, no whisper of the scheme reached the authorities until many hours after it had been carried out. Carson had outwitted and defied the King's Government. That made him for the time nearly as popular among Southern Sinn Feiners as he was among Northern unionists. Sober Irishmen shook their heads at the grave character of the step, but its humour was irresistible.

In the Lords the Home Rule Bill was amended by the permanent exclusion of Ulster. This was refused by the Government, and Mr Asquith then advised the King to convene a small conference of English and Irish leaders, including Carson, at Buckingham Palace. This last hope of procuring an agreed settlement failed on July 24, 1914, and its failure was attributed by his enemies to Carson's obstinacy. But it may be doubted whether, in view of Ulster's profound conviction that her religion and her liberties would never be safe under any form of Home Rule, any real agreement was possible.

All domestic controversies were, however, swept aside by the outbreak of the War, in the course of which Carson played a notable part. While protesting vehemently against Mr Asquith's decision to keep Home Rule in a state of suspended animation, he worked loyally for recruiting in Ulster; his Volunteers hastened to enlist, and in the famous Ulster Division rendered conspicuous service in the field. Carson was naturally all in favour of the most strenuous war measures, and in the summer of 1915 he joined Mr Asquith's Coalition Ministry, with the other Unionist leaders, as Attorney-General. But in October he resigned, partly because he desired a stronger recruiting policy, but more immediately because of the Government's policy in the Balkans, which, he considered, involved the desertion of Serbia, then in grave peril, and which was not coordinated with the Gallipoli adventure, undertaken before he joined the Ministry.

In January, 1916, Carson, now the most outstanding figure among private members of Parliament, accepted the chairmanship of a War Committee formed to support the most vigorous prosecution of the War. To this object he devoted all his powers, ever urging the ideal of complete national unity. He supported Mr Lloyd George's efforts that summer for a settlement of the Irish problem by consent, and when the Asquith Government fell in December, he joined Mr Lloyd George's Coalition as First Lord of the Admiralty. In March, 1917, he delivered an important speech in which he clearly set forth the U-boat menace in its true proportions, while declaring that he would neither interfere with the sailors himself nor allow anyone else to interfere with them. He would have no amateur strategists. In July, 1917, he resigned from the Admiralty and became a member of the War Cabinet without portfolio. In September he went to the front in France and studied the ground on which the Ulster Division had made their historic attack on July 1, 1916. Throughout this period he did great service in countering premature talk of peace.

For some time Carson had been obviously uneasy, and in January, 1918, he again resigned, this time because, in view of the assembling of the Irish Convention, he felt bound to be free to act on his pledges to Ulster ... Soon afterwards Carson, in a speech at Belfast, explained that he did not want to "burst" the Convention, any more than he wanted to break his covenant with Ulster. Both Mr Asquith and Mr Lloyd George had agreed that the coercion of Ulster was "unthinkable," and she would willingly consider any settlement that did not mean surrender. He was still all for conscription applied all round, but resented the attempt to mix it up with Home Rule. "The Nationalists," he declared, "are not likely to be appeased by the offer of conscription as a price for Home Rule, and the Ulster Unionists are not likely to be appeased by the offer of Home Rule as the price for conscription." But his intense conviction that everything else remained secondary to the great object of winning the War inspired his denunciation of the proposed introduction in April 1918 of a Home Rule Bill for the whole of Ireland. It prompted also his accusation that Sinn Fein was in alliance with Germany, and a characteristic speech in Belfast in which he described himself as "disgusted with the filth of politics."

After the War Carson gave up his seat for Dublin University and was returned at the General Election for the Duncairn Division of Belfast. At first he strongly supported the Coalition Government, and declared that Ulster's policy must be a still closer union with Great Britain. He demanded the repeal of the Home Rule Act, and met the proposal of Dominion Home Rule, fathered by Sir H. Plunkett, with a threat of armed resistance. Later on he bitterly denounced the movement for an Irish peace promoted by *The Times.* But when this movement took shape in Mr Lloyd George's Bill for establishing Parliaments in both Dublin and Belfast, linked by a Federal Council, he refrained from active opposition, and even undertook that Ulster would do her best to make the new scheme a success. He refused, however, to accept the leadership, which meant the Premiership, in the Parliament of Northern Ireland. In the struggle with Sinn Fein and the policy of reprisals which followed he took up a position of sombre acquiescence, and when the Downing Street policy was reversed he could find no good word for negotiations with Sinn Fein.

In May, 1921, he accepted the appointment of Lord of Appeal in Ordinary ... and received a life peerage. But he did not consider himself precluded by his judicial position from all intervention in politics, and we find him in January, 1922, attacking the Coalition, in which the Unionists had been "strangled." Such interventions brought down on him a severe rebuke from Lord Birkenhead, who, as Mr F. E. Smith, had been his "galloper" in the stirring days in Ulster before the War. Carson defended himself in the Lords in an able disquisition on the whole question of the relations of the Judiciary to party politics. "I am now willing to resign if I have done anything wrong. What do you think I care about office and salary, as compared with my honour?"

He did not resign then, but kept in touch with Ulster and intervened from time to time when he thought her interests were assailed, as in the boundary question. He was also ever ready to plead the cause of the Loyalists in Southern Ireland. In November, 1929, he resigned his office of Lord of Appeal in Ordinary, which he had held for more than eight years. His acute, clear intellect and long experience of affairs undoubtedly proved of value in the decisions of the supreme tribunal ...

A tour of his old constituency of Duncairn was made in November, 1932, by Lord Carson, who had been in Belfast for the visit of the Prince of Wales. In July of the following year he received a great ovation in Ulster when he attended the unveiling of his statue in front of the new Parliament Buildings at Stormont, Belfast. Some 40,000 of Lord Carson's old supporters were present at the ceremony, including 15,000 Orange-men from Belfast and 3,000 from other parts of the province.

Soon after his eightieth birthday, last year, Lord Carson fell seriously ill with bronchitis, and was for a time in grave danger. Not long before, to a meeting of the India Defence League held at his home in London, he had explained his opposition to the India Bill, pouring scorn on "that safeguard business" in the light of our experiences in Ireland.

For the last 20 years of his stormy life Lord Carson found great happiness in his second marriage, in September, 1914, to Ruby, daughter of Lieutenant-Colonel Stephen Frewen, formerly commanding 16th Lancers. By this marriage he leaves a son, born in 1920, who is now at Eton.

WILLIAM BUTLER YEATS

A great Irish poet and dramatist

30 JANUARY 1939

THE DEATH OF Mr William Butler Yeats, which our Cannes Correspondent telegraphs took place at Roquebrune, Cap Martin, on Saturday,
at the age of 73, deprives Ireland of one of the greatest of her poets
and dramatists, whose labours did very much to bring about the revival
of Irish letters at the opening of this century, and to open new fields,
especially in the theatre, for her national genius.

Like Emmet, Parnell, and other of the great champions of Irish
nationality, Yeats belonged by birth to the Protestant Anglo-Irish. He
was a son of J. B. Yeats, the painter, and his grandfather on that side
had been a clergyman of the Irish Church. The family came from Sligo,
and to the same county belonged the poet's mother, by birth a Pollexfen,
who passed on to him a streak of Cornish blood that reinforced the
dreaming mysticism he drew from the setting of his youth. Although he
was born near Dublin on June 13, 1865, he spent much of his childhood
in Sligo in the company of his grandfather, William Pollexfen, a retired
shipping owner, with the bluffness and violence of the expert mariner,
and an uncle, George Pollexfen, who combined business shrewdness
with the pursuit of astrology, and whose servant, Mary Battle, was gifted
with second-sight, and saw in vision the fairies and the giant dead of
Ireland. How powerful was the impression of such companionship
and of the haunted countryside upon the sensitive imagination of the
brooding boy he has shown in the delicate pages of his "Reveries Over
Childhood and Youth."

It is not surprising that when, at the age of eight or nine, he was sent
to London to Godolphin School, Hammersmith, he was unhappy and
felt the cleavage between his own traditions and those of his English
schoolfellows. In 1880 he was moved back to Dublin, where he went

to the Erasmus Smith School and then to the Metropolitan School of Art. By the time, however, that the family returned to London, in 1887, to live at Bedford Park, he had pretty well decided that his vocation was for letters, not for painting. He now came under the patronage of Henley and his group, and under the influence (in some sense lasting with him) of Morris and the Pre-Raphaelites. He had certain natural affinities with their view of life and art, and, as he has confessed, was "in all things Pre-Raphaelite." The enemies of his soul, he believed, were Huxley, Tyndall, Carolus Duran, and Bastien-Lepage, who frustrated his craving for spiritual unity by dissolving the simplicity of religion and asserting not only "the unimportance of subject, whether in art or literature, but the independence of the arts from one another."

Yeats's passion for occult studies, the influences of Mme. Blavatsky, and the esoteric Buddhism of the Theosophists, had steadily developed the mystical seed in his character. It had been first nurtured in the atmosphere of Irish folk-lore, and he was already seeking to catch the voice of the *Anima Mundi*, the mysterious One that lies behind the multiplicity of phenomena. His association during the nineties in London with the men of the Rhymers' Club, with Arthur Symons, Lionel Johnson, Ernest Dowson, and Oscar Wilde, as well as his interest in the French Symbolists, in Mallarmé and in Verlaine, might easily have led him to pursue his quest along the paths of more and more paradoxical speculation, more and more subtlety and refinement of verbal expression. But he could not, he felt, "endure an international art, picking stories and symbols where it pleased." Had not, rather, he asked, "all races had their first unity from a mythology that marries them to rock and hill"? The speech and legends of the folk were nearer to the primal source of Being; in them would be found the naked and majestic symbols that might transmit its gleam, and only a style of individual simplicity, free from the accretions of borrowed culture, could serve to rejuvenate their ancient potency.

Such were the ideas that with increasing definiteness inspired Yeats's first poetical writings. He had published in 1886 *Mosada*, a play on a Spanish subject, and "John Sherman," an autobiographical novel in 1891. But, beginning with "The Wanderings of Oisin" in 1889, a mythological narrative poem, he produced a series of ballads and other poems, including "The Secret Rose" and "The Wind Among the Reeds," which when collected in 1906 provided a volume of poetic achievement that established him as a great lyric poet. Among these early pieces was "The Lake Isle of Innisfree," "my first lyric," he afterwards said, "with anything in its rhythm of my own music," the haunting melody of which has made it probably the best known of all his poems.

But lyric poetry was not the only product of these busy, ardent years. In 1893, with his friend Mr E. J. Ellis, he published his large edition of Blake, whose mystic symbolism he intimately appreciated; in the same year came out "The Celtic Twilight," a volume of peasant lore and fairy magic; in 1903 a number of essays, contributed to various periodicals of the day, on his philosophic and artistic beliefs were collected under the title "Ideas of Good and Evil."

He had, however, come to feel that the true starting-point for such a revival of Irish and Celtic culture as he desired (a nationalism of the sort that interested him far more than the political nationalism, which he yet firmly embraced) was the theatre. Drama, by its nature, demanded that simplification – and directness – which was the heart of Yeats's poetic ideal, and poems, after all, were made to be spoken, not read. In 1892 and 1894 he published two plays, *The Countess Cathleen* and *The Land of Heart's Desire*, and in 1899 the Irish Literary Theatre, which had been founded as part of that remarkable "Celtic renaissance" to which Mr George Russell ("A. E."), Mr George Moore, Lady Gregory (Yeats's firm friend and helper), Mr Edward Martyn, and other eminent writers in various ways contributed at this time, produced the first of the two in Dublin. It was a notable day in dramatic history, and in 1902 *The Countess Cathleen* was followed by *Cathleen ni Houlihan*, Yeats's greatest play, in which his symbolism, his mysticism, and his patriotism are all expressed with austere pathos in what makes only a few pages of printed dialogue.

Yeats also wrote for the same Irish Theatre (which became in 1904 the famous Abbey Theatre) *The Shadowy Waters, The King's Threshold, The*

Deirdre, and *The Golden Helmet,* besides assisting in the management of the theatre and founding and contributing lavishly to *Samhain,* the organ of the work. His dramatic fame was rivalled, if not over-shadowed, by the discovery of J. M. Synge, whose *Playboy of the Western World,* produced in 1907, had a riotous reception and led to dissensions in the Nationalist movement, in which Yeats strenuously defended his friend. His own *Countess Cathleen* had offended ecclesiastical sentiment, and he became conscious of the gulf between his ideals and the narrower strains of religious and political passion. In a speech defending Synge he declared characteristically that his fellow-countrymen should inquire "what a man is, and be content to wait a little before we go on to that further question: 'What is a good Irishman?'" In a volume of poems called "Responsibilities," published in 1914, he spoke very plainly of the disappointing side of nationalism, as he contrasted it with the Stoic idealism of the Fenian leader, John O'Leary, who had inspired him in his boyhood:-

Romantic Ireland's dead and gone.
It's with O'Leary in his grave.

He had, nevertheless, by his own poems and plays added liberally to her romantic heritage; and the influence of the Abbey Theatre, not only through its lofty aims and great plays, but through its exquisite diction, and simplicity of acting and scene-craft, has radiated widely beyond its immediate orbit. The name of Mr Sean O'Casey is enough to show that the impulse is not exhausted. Yeats's differences with his own countrymen seem insignificant when we take into view not merely what he gave Ireland but what Ireland, through him, has given to the world.

In 1922 Mr Yeats became a Senator of the Irish Free State. In 1923 he was awarded the Nobel Prize for Literature. He received the degree of D.Litt. at Oxford in 1931, and the Goethe plaque of the city of Frankfurt in 1934. In his later years, besides an occult treatise, "Vision," and his autobiography printed in 1922 under the title, "The Trembling of the Veil," which is a masterpiece of serene beauty, he wrote "Four Plays for

Dancers," "Wheels and Butterflies," a religious drama, *The Resurrection*, and the collections of poems entitled "The Tower" and "The Winding Stair." In 1935 he published "A Full Moon in March," a new volume of poems; and in 1936 "Dramatis Personae," another volume of auto-biography. In the latter year "The Oxford Book of Modern Verse" appeared, the contents of which were chosen by him. He contributed some of the finest poems and an introduction, which was a brilliant and penetrating essay on English poetry during the last half century. Last year he published two new plays, *The Herne's Egg* and *Purgatory* (in the form of a monologue in which an aged man relives his life in retrospect); and "Essays, 1931 to 1936," which were mainly introductions to various books. The essays also included Mr Yeats's talk on modern poetry, which was broadcast from London in October, 1936.

On the occasion of his seventieth birthday Yeats received telegrams of congratulation from all over the world. He was also the guest of honour at a dinner organized by the P.E.N. Club at which the other guests included Mr John Masefield, the Poet Laureate, who presented Yeats with an original drawing by Dante Gabriel Rossetti on behalf of the writers and artists of England. In 1917 he married Georgie, only daughter of the late Mr W. G. Hyde Lees, of Pickhill Hall, Wrexham, and had a son and a daughter.

SIR JOHN LAVERY

A famous portrait painter

11 JANUARY 1941

SIR JOHN LAVERY, R.A., the famous portrait painter, died at Rossenarra House, Kilkenny, yesterday at the age of 84.

Lavery was specifically a painter, expressing himself and building up his compositions in values of colour, in which tonal rather than decorative relations are the first consideration. With resemblances to Whistler and Manet he, like them, derived ultimately from Velazquez. He was not a great draughtsman – actual drawings by him must be extremely rare – and, below their broad and fluent brushwork, most of his full-sized portraits are found to be flimsy in construction. A noteworthy exception was his portrait of Lord Melchett, in the Academy of 1930. In solidity, as well as in depth of characterization, it was probably the finest portrait he ever painted.

Though he is generally associated with the Scottish school, Lavery was born in Belfast in March, 1856. He was early transplanted from farm life to Saltcoats, where during five years he acquired that intimate knowledge of the sea which was to appear in his paintings. At the age of 15 he went to Glasgow as a clerk in the mineral department of the Glasgow and South-Western Railway, but soon returned to Ireland to work for four years on a farm, drawing at the same time. Then he went back to Glasgow, where he found work as assistant to a photographer, and attended the Haldane Academy of Art. In 1881 he exhibited his first picture, "The Courtship of Julian Peveril," at the Royal Scottish Academy, and the same year went to Paris, where he studied under Bouguereau and Fleury, laying the foundations of the broad and fluent style by which he was to become known. About that time he became acquainted with the late Sir James Guthrie and the group of artists who formed the "Glasgow School," which had its first conspicuous success in 1885 at the Glasgow Institute, where Lavery exhibited his "Bridge at Gretz" and "On the Loing – an Afternoon Chat."

In his larger compositions Lavery was always at his best when, upon a general ground of black or grey, he could work in an arabesque of brighter colours in comparatively small touches, gold, emerald, or rose. When he composed in more positive colours over larger areas, as in "A Game of Chess," in the Academy of 1930, the result was apt to be a collection of colours rather than a colour scheme. He seemed to need tone as a reconciling element. He had some important official commissions, "Queen Victoria's Visit to the Glasgow International Exhibition of 1888" and a portrait group of the Royal Family at Buckingham Palace among them; but, though these were carried out in a workmanlike manner, it is in his smaller studies of interiors with figures, such as those of "The House of Lords" and "The House of Commons," and the many impressions of jockeys in the weighing room, that his more characteristic powers are to be seen. He had the gift of preserving a characteristic likeness when the head was reduced to a patch of tone. Among his best portraits on a larger scale, besides "Lord Melchett," are those of Mr R. B. Cunninghame Graham, Mr Fitzmaurice Kelly, Miss Mary Burrell, and the Ladies Hely Hutchinson.

Lavery was extremely generous with his work. To Leighton House he gave his "The House of Commons in Session, 1929," and to the new Municipal Art Gallery and Museum, Belfast, a collection of 35 of his paintings, now housed in a "Lavery Room," receiving the freedom of the city in recognition of his gift. To the Dublin Municipal Art Gallery he gave 33 of his pictures in memory of Lady Lavery, and was made an honorary freeman of the city. Lavery was elected A.R.A. in 1911, knighted in 1918, and elected R.A. in 1921. He was also R.S.A., R.H.A., and a member of several foreign academies. He was hon. LL.D. of Belfast.

In 1890 he married Kathleen, daughter of Mr L. MacDermott. She died in 1891. There was one daughter of the marriage, who married Colonel Lord Sempill. She died in 1935. Sir John Lavery married secondly in 1910, Hazel, daughter of Mr E. J. Martyn, of Chicago, and widow of Dr E. L. Trudeau, of New York. She was a lady of great beauty and charm and was known as a painter of character and distinction. She died in 1935.

JAMES JOYCE

Author of "Ulysses"

14 JANUARY 1941

MR JAMES JOYCE, an Irishman whose book "Ulysses" gave rise to much controversy, died at Zurich yesterday. The extremes of opinion on Joyce's work are represented by Sir Edmund Gosse, who wrote to the *Revue des Deux Mondes* on "the worthlessness and impudence of his writings," and Arnold Bennett, who said of "Ulysses" "the best portions of the novel are immortal"; while the middle, puzzled state of mind is typified by A. E.'s remark on meeting the author: "I don't know whether you are a fountain or a cistern." It would seem, however, that the appreciation of the eternal and serene beauty of nature and the higher sides of human character was not granted to Joyce – or at least did not appear in his work.

James Augustine Aloysius Joyce was born in Dublin on February 2, 1882, one of a large and poor family. He went to the National University of Ireland and graduated in 1902. Joyce had strong literary tendencies in adolescence. For Ibsen he had such a passion that he learnt Norwegian so as to read the original. In his student days he was so self-opinionated and vain that he said to W. B. Yeats: "We have met too late; you are too old to be influenced by me," to which the poet made answer: "Never have I encountered so much pretension with so little to show for it." There was, indeed, not much to show for 12 or 14 years. Joyce was in Paris during 1903–04, engaged first in medical studies and later in having his voice trained for the concert platform, and in 1904 he returned to Dublin. He published a few stories, but could not make a living, so he and his wife went off to Trieste, where he taught English. He had a great talent for languages and learnt Italian so well that he was able to contribute articles on Irish politics to the *Piccolo della Sera*. In 1912 he went back to Dublin to start the Volta cinema theatre, but on its failure he resumed his teaching in Trieste. Thus far his only book had been one of lyrics called "Chamber Music." In 1914 appeared "Dubliners," delayed nine years by haggling with publishers owing to their demand that he should make certain excisions.

When the last War was declared Joyce had to suspend his teaching, but the Austrians allowed him conditions of "free arrest." "A Portrait of the Artist as a Young Man" was serialized by Ezra Pound in the *Egoist* from February, 1914, to September, 1915. In due course he was allowed to go to Zurich, where he formed a company of Irish players, who performed his play called *Exiles*, on the model of Ibsen. He had already begun "Ulysses" at Trieste in 1914. He continued it at Zurich, and it began to appear serially in the *Little Review*, New York, from March, 1918, to August, 1920, at which date it was stopped by a prosecution initiated by the Society for the Suppression of Vice. At Zurich his sight began to fail. A few years after the War ended he settled in Paris. "Ulysses" came out in book form in Paris and London in 1922, but owing to its alleged obscenity it was not allowed to circulate in England or America. Editions were, however, printed in Paris, and thousands of copies were smuggled into this country by individual bibliophiles. Joyce's next task was a large work which he entitled "Work in Progress," which began to appear in 1927, in sections under various titles. In it the word-coinages that were a feature of "Ulysses" were multiplied and extended to the point of unintelligibility.

Joyce's book "Ulysses" purports to relate the whole mental and physical history of Leopold Bloom, Jewish advertisement canvasser, and Stephen Dedalus, scholar-philosopher, during one single day in Dublin. Its settled principle is to omit nothing, however trifling or scabrous, and it makes extensive use of what has been called the "interior monologue," a literary device which Joyce claimed to have discovered in Edouard Dujardin's forgotten novel, "Les Lauriers sont coupés" (1888): Proust, of course, used it, as did Miss Dorothy M. Richardson and others in this country, and it has had a far-reaching influence on the technique of many modern writers. "Ulysses" has many repellent or merely boring passages. It is steeped and soaked in the rough life of Dublin city. It is, however, intensely alive, fundamentally Irish, full of Rabelaisian "humour," with a highly developed sense of time and a fantastic imaginative faculty.

In person Joyce was gentle and kindly, living a laborious life in his Paris flat tended by his devoted, humorous wife. There were a son and a daughter of the marriage. Joyce's favourite diversion was music.

* * *

SARAH PURSER

17 AUGUST 1943

MISS SARAH PURSER, R.H.A., died at Mespil House, Dublin, on August 7, at the age of 95. Herself an accomplished artist, she did much for art in Ireland, and she was famous for her hospitality and wit.

Sarah Henrietta Purser, the daughter of Benjamin Purser, of Dungarvan, was born on March 22, 1848. Her brother Louis Claude, who became Vice-Provost of Trinity College, Dublin, was a Greek scholar of international repute; another brother, John, became Regius Professor of Medicine at the same university. Sarah Purser studied art at Julien's, in Paris, sharing a studio with the late Louise Breslau, a Swiss artist who afterwards became a close friend of Degas, and with Marie Bashkirtseff.

"When I came back from Paris I joined the Ladies' Literary. There I met Mrs Coffey and I painted that portrait of her that you have seen. It is a very good portrait and everybody liked it. Mrs Coffey was a Miss Lestrange from Sligo, and she got Lady Gore, to have me down to Lisadell to paint Con and Eva. And that went well. Then Lady Gore's brother being at the [Viceregal] Lodge I was called in there, and he got me a few commissions for portraits in London. They were hung in the

Royal Academy, and from that I never looked back – I went through the British aristocracy like the measles."

That is a summary of Sarah Purser's early career in approximately her own words. The Mrs Coffey referred to was the beautiful wife of a well-known Irish archaeologist. Lady Gore was the wife of Sir Jocelyn Gore-Booth and Con and Eva were her daughters, Constance Markievicz, painter and revolutionary, and Eva Gore-Booth, the poet. Lady Gore-Booth's brother was the Marquis of Zetland, who as Viceroy of Ireland occupied the Viceregal Lodge in those far-off days.

In her later working years Miss Purser, when she was painting portraits of friends, liked to honour them by wearing an overall that Marie Bashkirtseff had given her in return for one she, Marie, had accidentally burned. In the famous Bashkirtseff diaries Sarah Purser is referred to as a *grande philosophe irlandaise*. If she was not a great philosopher she was certainly, at the end of her days especially, a *philosophe* in the French sense, in the sense, that is to say, that she reasoned closely, if usually rather cynically, about practical problems.

Miss Purser always collected famous people, and as she was a great traveller they were from all over the world. She made close friends of most of them. In her handsome eighteenth-century house, famous for its stucco ceilings, which stands in its own small but beautiful park in the heart of Dublin, she entertained simply but frequently. Almost everybody who was anybody, living in Ireland or visiting it, was likely to be found at her "Second Tuesdays."

Ireland owes it to Miss Purser that the modern Irish stained glass movement, initiated by her good friend Edward Martyn, the "dear Edward" of George Moore's trilogy, was put on its feet, financially and artistically. She it was who, 40 years ago, persuaded a reticent young artist named Michael Healy to come into the Tower of Glass, as the new industry was called, to study stained glass technique, and, alternately encouraging and scolding, enabled him to develop into the original and distinguished artist he had become before he died in September, 1941. Fortunately other good artists appeared as well, and the Tower of Glass still flourishes.

Similarly encouraging and scolding Hugh Lane, Miss Purser helped him to found the admirable Dublin gallery of modern art, and it was she herself who, a dozen or so years ago, first thought of having its collections of pictures, statuary, and engravings permanently housed in their present beautiful quarters at Charlemont House in Parnell Square. It was about the same time that she initiated the movement for the launching of the society of "Friends of the National Collections of Ireland," which, in its modest way, fulfils a similar function in Ireland to that of the National Art Collections Fund in Great Britain. She argued about pennies, but the whispered stories of her generosities are numerous. "I will not spend money," she said, "because if I were to spend all I have it could not buy me the one thing I want – and that is to be 25 years of age again."

* * *

JOHN McCORMACK

18 SEPTEMBER 1945

MR JOHN McCORMACK, who died at his Dublin home on Sunday night, aged 61, ... has only been heard in recent years on a few gramophone records, which gave but the shadow of the quality of his singing in his younger days. He won an international reputation first as an opera singer before the first German war. After that war and his estrangement from this country he returned in 1924 and was heard in recitals and in the "international celebrity" type of concert. Most of his career has been made in America, where he became a citizen of the United States in 1917.

John McCormack was born at Athlone on June 14, 1884, and there he might have remained undiscovered but for the existence of the Irish national festival, known as *Feis Ceoil*. He was encouraged to take part in the competition held at Dublin in 1902, when he was just 18, and the beautiful quality of his tenor voice and the charm of his untutored singing won for him the gold medal. He was clearly marked out for the career of a singer, and for the next two years he sang in the Roman Catholic Cathedral choir in Dublin until circumstances enabled him to go to Milan to study under Sabbatini. His first appearances in London were as a concert singer early in 1907, but he came out on the stage of Covent Garden during the autumn season of that year singing the part of Turiddu in *Cavalleria Rusticana*. A greater opportunity, however, awaited him in the same season, for it happened that a couple of performances of *Don Giovanni* were given and he was cast for the part of Don Ottavio. His singing of the two big arias of that part created the highest impression of his powers, showing that besides the possession of a voice of great beauty, less commanding in volume than those which Italy produces but more sympathetic in quality, he had the gift of realizing the lyric charm of Mozart's melody in his spontaneous phrasing of it.

It was not long after this that he was chosen by Felix Weingartner to sing his part at the Mozart festival in Salzburg and his success there brought about his European reputation as one of the first tenors of the day. He had arrived just in time to take part in what is remembered as the "Tetrazzini boom," the few years in which *La Traviata* and *Lucia di Lammermoor* could not be played too often so long as the *prima donna* trilled her way through them. McCormack was associated with her in many of these performances, and the old-fashioned type of Italian opera was certainly what suited him best. Writing of *Lucia* in 1908, *The Times* reminded its readers that "it is well worth waiting until the final scene for Mr John McCormack's admirable singing of the famous tenor song." He was also the ideal partner to Melba's Mimi in *La Bohème* in the seasons up to 1914.

He made his first appearance in America in 1910, when he sang at the Manhattan with Tetrazzini in *La Traviata*. Subsequently he sang with the Boston and Chicago Opera Companies, returning to London each season to fulfil his engagement with the Royal Opera Syndicate up to 1912. He also appeared on the concert platform, notably at the Birmingham festival of that year, when he sang in *Elijah*. Unfortunately, his Italian training had not equipped him thoroughly for the difficult art of singing the English language, and the pleasure to be got from the purely vocal side of his art was modified by his failure to produce with any appearance of naturalness the vowel sounds contained in such a phrase as "If with all your hearts." Fortunately Italianate vowels did not contaminate the Irish intonation of his native folk-songs, which he began to include in his recitals along with the *Lieder* of Hugo Wolf, which somewhat surprisingly won a large place in his affection. He was made a Count of the Papal Court in 1928.

* * *

DOUGLAS HYDE

First President of Eire.

14 JULY 1949

DR DOUGLAS HYDE, the first President of Eire, who died on Tuesday in Dublin at the age of 89, was a most eminent Gaelic scholar. Known in Ireland as *An Craoibhin Aoibhinn* (the delightful little branch), which he sometimes used as a pen-name, he was the author of a number of books, poems, and plays in Gaelic as well as English, and was in addition an able translator. He was also the founder and for many years president of the Gaelic League for the revival of the ancient language, music, art, and customs of Ireland and thus started an enthusiasm among his fellow-countrymen which was eventually to overflow into politics and supply much of the driving force of the advanced nationalist movement. Never himself a politician in the ordinary sense of the word and sprung from the Protestant and landed class, he was in 1938 unanimously elected for the office of President of Eire which had been created under the new Constitution of that country.

Douglas Hyde was born on January 17, 1860, the youngest son of the Rev. Arthur Hyde, rector of Frenchpark, Co. Roscommon. Delicate in his youth, he was educated at home by his father and as a boy used to wander about a neighbourhood in which Irish was still spoken. Through the friendships he made there with humble people he learned and came to love the language. Then as a young man he was sent to Trinity College, Dublin, and with a view to taking orders entered the Divinity School; but he also read widely in modern languages and Gaelic, obtaining in 1884 a first Senior Moderatorship and Large Gold Medal and in 1887 the degree of LL.D. To speak Gaelic was a rare accomplishment in the Trinity of his day, and Hyde could not only do so, but could think and write in it as the living language of the West from which he came. In 1891 he was appointed Interim Professor of Modern Languages at the State University of New Brunswick, and while in the Dominion studied the folklore and customs of the Red Indians. He did not, however, stay there long and, returning to Ireland, founded the Gaelic League in 1893, and the year after became president of the Irish National Literary Society.

It was Dr Hyde's belief that the nationality of a people found a fuller and truer expression in its own language and traditions than it could in any separate legislature, and for many years he succeeded in keeping politics out of the Gaelic League, on behalf of which he toured the United States and collected some £11,000 in 1906. By 1915 Ireland, infected by the general excitement of the times, was in a high political fever, and an insurgent nationalism was seeking every means of advancing its aims. In these circumstances the leaders of Sinn Fein, realizing the political possibilities of the instrument Dr Hyde had forged, demanded that political independence should be included in the objects of the Gaelic League. Hyde, on the other hand, insisted that Sinn Fein should confine itself to its own field of activities. A resolution for a "free

Ireland" was carried against him and he resigned his presidency. Hyde thereupon confined himself to his duties as Professor of Modern Irish in the National University, a chair which he held for many years, and to research work. In 1925, however, he was coopted a Senator in the Free State Senate, but he took no part in political affairs.

In 1938 a conference of representatives of the Eire Government and Opposition agreed to invite Dr Hyde to accept nomination for the new office of President of Eire. He was 78 but still extremely active both physically and intellectually. At his first Christmas in an office which it was the Eire Government's desire to invest with the utmost dignity, he broadcast to the United States, but he dealt principally with the Irish language which was still his chief preoccupation. In 1940 he had a serious illness. He recovered and continued to perform the duties of his position, but announced in 1945 that he would not seek re-election.

In 1939 his wife, who was a daughter of Mr Charles Kurtz, a German manufacturing chemist and art collector, by an English mother, died. One daughter of the marriage survives him.

EDITH SOMERVILLE

Flurry Knox's chronicler

10 OCTOBER 1949

DR E. Œ. SOMERVILLE, the surviving figure in the celebrated literary partnership of Somerville and Ross, authors of "Some Experiences of an Irish R.M.," and a woman of strikingly individual character and wit, died on Saturday at her home in County Cork. She was in her ninety-second year.

Edith Oenone Somerville was born in Corfu – hence her second name – the daughter of the late Lieutenant-Colonel Somerville, D.L., of Drishane, Skibbereen. Her mother was Adelaide, daughter of Sir Josiah Coghill, Bt., and her maternal grandfather the "silver-tongued" Charles Kendal Bushe, Chief Justice of Ireland. She was one of what has been described as a "severe and heavy family" of sons, and, since the family exchequer was limited, her youth, except for a term or two at the Alexandra College in Dublin, was spent at home, where old-fashioned governesses educated her as best they could. Her first intention was to become an artist, and she attended the studios of Colarossi and Délécluse in Paris. Later she was to achieve distinction and success as a painter in oils and as an illustrator both in black and white and in colour. She gave several one-man shows in London and in New York. She might indeed have confined herself entirely to art if her cousin, Miss Violet Martin, of Ross, had not encouraged her to develop her literary gifts. Hers, however, was an astonishingly versatile endowment, and an unbounded energy to match. She was, for instance, an extremely good musician among other things. And there was always, an expression of the entirely different side of her life and interests, her sportsmanship. Edith Somerville's love of horses, dogs, and hunting was the first of her passions, and the time of her mastership of the West Carbery hounds – she took them over in 1903 – was probably the happiest of her life.

The most famous of the books that came from the collaboration between Miss Somerville and Miss Martin (who on the title-page adopted the name of Martin Ross) was, of course, "Some Experiences of an Irish R.M." But the collaborators, who almost from the start were likened to a superlatively well-matched pair of horses, had already demonstrated their abilities to excellent purpose in a number of volumes. "The Real Charlotte," their fifth novel, published in 1894, reached a level of imaginative penetration which they never afterwards surpassed. The "Experiences," however – the product, it appears, of a sketching holiday at Etaples, when the weather was first too wet and then too hot for painting – were on a plane of comedy not attained by any Irish writer before or since. Even in their most boisterous moments these stories hold an essence which flows deeper than the laughter. "Dan Russel, the Fox" (1911) and "In Mr Knox's Country" (1915) followed, and then, in the latter year, the wonderful partnership was dissolved by the death of Martin Ross.

For the rest of her long life the surviving partner wrote on, as it seemed to all except herself, alone. She, however, was confident that her dead friend still helped and inspired her work, and, in witness of her consoling faith, the name of Martin Ross continued to appear upon the title-page of most of her books. Among them were "Mount Music" (1919), in which she created the powerful and impressive figure of Dr Maugan; "Stray-aways" (1920), in which she wrote about herself and her collaborator; "An Enthusiast" (1921), a novel written in the melancholy Ireland of that period and all but haunted by a strain of lament. One of her most admirable essays in fiction was "The Big House of Inver" (1925), a vivid and finely comi-tragic reconstruction of a vanished Irish past. "The States through Irish Eyes" (1931) – she illustrated it herself – described a visit to America, where Miss Somerville was much at home with American fox-hunting folk. There was also "The Smile and the Tear" (1933), a volume of essays; "The Sweet Cry of Hounds" (1936), a small series of hunting vignettes; "Sarah's Youth" (1938), a hunting novel in entirely characteristic strain; and "Notions in Garrison" (1941), a conversation piece, in which the author pursued, among other themes, a favourite idea of hers that dogs converse telepathetically. Few, it may be said, knew more about them than she, and her last book "Maria and Other Dogs," a collection of pieces of her earlier writing with some new illustrations by her, was in the hands of the publishers at the time of her death. Miss Somerville was an Hon. D.Litt. of Trinity College, Dublin, and in 1941 the Irish Academy of Letters conferred on her their principal literary honour, the Gregory Medal.

* * *

JOHN DULANTY

Loyal servant of Ireland

12 FEBRUARY 1955

MR JOHN W. DULANTY, C.B., C.B.E., who represented successive Irish Governments in London as Commissioner for Trade, as High Commissioner, and finally, for a few weeks before he retired in 1950, as Ambassador, died in hospital in London yesterday.

For a quarter of a century he was well known and much liked by people in all walks of London life, official and unofficial, as a man who knew both Britain and Ireland from the inside and was loyal to both countries. Successive Irish leaders, from Mr Cosgrave through Mr de Valera to Mr Costello, relied on him, in spite of their acute mutual distrust. British Ministers, including Sir Winston Churchill, turned to him with confidence when they were bewildered by the latest inexplicable twist in Dublin policy. He kept open house for all comers concerned with Ireland in his office perched above Piccadilly Circus. Writers and artists found him as good company as did politicians and business men, and when he spoke at a public dinner no one was ever bored.

John Whelan Dulanty was born at Manchester in 1883, his father coming from Tipperary and his mother from Limerick. He was educated at St Mary's, Failsworth, and at Manchester University, where he read law and later became secretary of the faculty of technology. In 1910 he was appointed educational adviser to Indian students in the northern universities of England. Three years later he entered the Civil Service, and quickly rose to positions of responsibility. Having started as an examiner of the Board of Education in 1913, by 1917 he was principal assistant secretary at the Ministry of Munitions, and by 1920 assistant secretary at the Treasury. Next year he gave up his Civil Service career (which had earned him the C.B. and C.B.E.) to become deputy chairman and managing director of Peter Jones, Ltd.

When in 1926 the Irish Free State Government appointed him Commissioner for Trade in Great Britain he had not lived for any length of time in Ireland. But there was no mistaking that he was an Irishman, and he had been a leader of the United Irish League of Great Britain under John Redmond and had been busy behind the scenes at the time of the Treaty of 1922. He succeeded Professor T. A. Smiddy as High Commissioner in 1930 and represented the Irish Free State on the Imperial Economic Committee and the Empire Marketing Board. He played a prominent part in the negotiation of the "Coal-Cattle Pact" of 1938 and helped the British Government with his advice when the question of introducing conscription in Northern Ireland was being considered early in the war.

The change in formal relations between the United Kingdom and the 26 counties, brought about by the Irish External Relations Act of 1949, was marked the following year by Dulanty's title being changed from High Commissioner to Ambassador. Bernard Shaw, whose birthday happened to occur that day, July 26, sent him a message saying: "My birthdays are an unmitigated curse to me ... but this one has one consolation; it has been chosen for giving John Dulanty official recognition of the position he really occupies. . . . His Excellency has been a

fact so long that it is only diplomatic decency to make it a form as well."
But the form, for Dulanty, was not to last long, for within two months
he had retired. He then became a director of the National Bank and
he continued frequently to be seen in London. He was made honorary
doctor of laws at Leeds University in 1939, and of the National University
of Ireland, Dublin, in 1940.

He married, in 1909, Ann, younger daughter of the late George
Hutton, of Chorlton-cum-Hardy. She died in 1952, and he is survived
by two sons and one daughter.

* * *

EVIE HONE

15 MARCH 1955

MISS EVIE HONE, who died in Dublin on Sunday at the age of 61, was
one of the most distinguished artists in stained glass.

Born in 1894, she was crippled in early life by infantile paralysis,
yet with great fortitude pursued vigorously her chosen subject, studying
in London under Bernard Meninsky and Walter Sickert and in Paris
under André L'Hôte and Albert Gleizes. On her return to Ireland in
1927 she first made a reputation as an abstract painter, but by 1934
hereditary influence had begun to take effect, for she numbered among
her ancestors a well-known Victorian landscape painter, a foundation
member of the Royal Academy, and, significantly, Galyon Hone, glazier
to King Henry VI.

It was, therefore, appropriate that, on the advice of Sir Kenneth
Clark, she should have been commissioned to design the glass of the
great East Window in Eton College Chapel, to replace the unregretted

Victorian glass destroyed by a bomb in 1941. Its jewelled splendour of sapphire, ruby, emerald, and topaz vividly recalls Wordsworth's injunction, written in another foundation by the same monarch: "Tax not the royal Saint with vain expense." This window is, perhaps, her masterpiece, though there are many both before and after it, in Ireland and in England, which manifest her strong and various genius, notably at Tullamore and Kingscourt in Ireland and at Lanercost, Downe, Highgate, and Farm Street, London, in England.

* * *

WILLIAM FRANCIS CASEY

Former Editor of "The Times"

22 APRIL 1957

MR W. F. CASEY, Editor of *The Times* from 1948 until 1952, died in London on Saturday at the age of 72. His long and varied career as a journalist, beginning in 1913 and covering two world wars and two phases of uneasy peace, was all spent in the service of *The Times*. He was unique among editors of *The Times* in his first-hand knowledge of all branches of the paper's journalistic activities at home and abroad. No editor of *The Times* has been more well or more widely loved.

William Francis Casey was born in Cape Town on May 2, 1884, the son of Patrick Joseph Casey, of Glenageary, Co. Dublin. He was educated in Ireland at Castleknock College and Trinity College, Dublin, where he spent two years at the medical school. But, abandoning medicine for the law, he was called to the Irish Bar in 1909. While he was reading for the law he acted briefly, in a part-time capacity, on the business side of the Abbey Theatre of which Yeats and Lady Gregory were then directors. Casey used to dismiss this brief legal phase of his career characteristically – summing it up as "One year, one brief, one guinea."

He decided to seek his fortune in London, having, before doing so, won the reputation of being a young dramatist of promise. Two of his plays, *The Suburban Groove* and *The Young Man from Rathmines*, were produced at the Abbey Theatre. An introduction to Sir Bruce Richmond led to writing reviews for *The Times Literary Supplement*. Then, shortly before war broke out in 1914, the future editor was offered work during the holiday season as a sub-editor in the sporting room. After a spell as a foreign sub-editor he was posted as acting correspondent in Washington in 1919 and transferred to Paris in 1920, where he remained for the next two years. From 1923 until 1928 he was chief foreign sub-editor and was then promoted to the foreign leader writing staff. He attended many sessions of the League of Nations at Geneva and followed events in Europe in a spirit of sympathy towards French rather than German aspirations. He became an assistant editor in 1935 and, on the retirement of Geoffrey Dawson in 1941, he was appointed by the new editor, R. M. Barrington-Ward, as his deputy. After the sudden death of Barrington-Ward in 1948 Casey succeeded him. Increasing ill-health handicapped him through his last years in Printing House Square. But he continued, until his retirement, to keep a close watch on affairs and to make the influence of his poise and fairmindedness felt in the policies of the paper.

Many qualities go to make a responsible journalist, and Casey possessed most of them, above all the most fundamental one of principle. Whatever his own views on any subject, he was inflexibly insistent that the facts, however disagreeable they might be to him, were fully and accurately reported. He could form a judgment on the spur of the moment, as is sometimes inevitable in such work as his, and he seldom had reason afterwards to regret what he had decided. Tactful in the handling of the work of other men, he would alter it, with speed and felicity, when he felt that lucidity, truth, or common sense required it. As a writer he had the gifts of clarity and of an easily read style, and in his time he handled with distinction a remarkably wide range of subjects.

Those who knew his early work in the theatre felt that he should not have allowed the pressure of other responsibilities to combine with an easy-going temperament to discourage him from tackling more ambitious plays. The keen watch he kept on the comedy of life, his warm heart, and his freedom from sentimentality might have stood him in good stead had he chosen to explore his own possibilities as a dramatist. He wrote two novels, *Haphazard* in 1917 and *The Private Life of a Successful Man* in 1935, but neither of these gave evidence of more than some talent for the writing of fiction. The wit and the relish for political and social scenes which were so marked and so delightful a feature of Casey's personality found easy expression in conversation at the clubs where he delighted to relax. The Athenaeum, the Garrick, the Beefsteak, and the Savile have lost in him a member who kept up, almost until the last, the art of good talking which is so often said to be on the wane. Casey could "rattle" – his own word for himself off duty – with the best of civilized men. But he never ceased to be a serious student of home and foreign politics. Controversialists who mistook his bland, modest air for the mark of a lightweight frequently found themselves out of their depths and worsted in argument with him. Eminent public figures no less than the rank and file went through that experience.

He married, in 1914, Amy Gertrude Pearson-Gee, daughter of the late Henry Willmott. There were no children of the marriage. He was an honorary LL.D. of his own university, Dublin.

MARGARET BURKE SHERIDAN

18 APRIL 1958

MARGARET BURKE SHERIDAN, an Irish soprano who won considerable success in Britain and the Continent, died in a Dublin nursing home on Wednesday. She was in her sixties. She was born in Castlebar, Co. Mayo, the youngest of seven children and, orphaned at the age of four, she was placed in the care of the Dominican Nuns at Eccles Street, Dublin, where she received her first singing lessons from Mother Clement, who was a noted music teacher. She won a gold medal at the *Feis Ceoil* and showed so much promise that a benefit performance was given in the old Theatre Royal in Dublin to help her to study at the Royal Academy of Music.

In London she met people like Howard de Walden, Lady Millicent Parker, T. P. O'Connor, and other members of the old Irish Parliamentary Party, but the man who most influenced her future career was Marconi, whom she met at a party. After hearing her sing Marconi decided that she should go to Italy. In Rome at the age of 21 she made a brilliant début in *Madam Butterfly*. Shortly afterwards she accepted a five-year contract for the international season at Covent Garden, and this was followed by eight seasons at La Scala, Milan. There, singing under the direction of Toscanini, she transformed Catalini's *La Vallee*, previously a failure, into a success, and the directors of the theatre struck a special medal to commemorate her performance.

She was chosen to sing at the wedding of the Italian Crown Prince Umberto. She stopped singing in public over 20 years ago and later came to live in Dublin.

ARCHBISHOP GREGG

4 MAY 1961

THE MOST REVEREND Dr J. A. F. Gregg, C.H., Archbishop of Armagh and Primate of All Ireland from 1939 to 1959, died at his home at Rostrevor, Co. Down, on Tuesday. He was 87.

He was Archbishop of Dublin from 1920 to 1939 and at the time of his retirement from the See of Armagh 1959 he had been a bishop of the Church of Ireland for 44 years. His grandfather, Dr John Gregg, was Bishop of Cork from 1862 to 1878, and his uncle, Dr Robert Gregg, was Archbishop of Armagh from 1893 until 1896. His father, a clergyman of the Church of England, was vicar of St Nicholas's, Deptford, where Gregg was born, in July, 1873.

His influence and prestige within the Anglican communion were great; some indication of this can be given by quoting a remark made a few years ago by a Bishop of the Church of England: "When we are confronted with a difficult problem, we always say, 'we can ask the Archbishop of Armagh'." But he was also held in no small esteem by those not of his flock; when the names of possible candidates for the presidency of Ireland were being discussed a Dubliner remarked, "If they're serious about it, there's only one living Irishman with the qualifications for the job and that's Dr Gregg." Such good opinions were won not solely by his scholarship, which was of a high order, but by his gifts as an administrator, his native wisdom, and his warm and kindly nature.

John Allen Fitzgerald Gregg was educated at Bedford School, Christ's College, Cambridge (he was an honorary Fellow of the college from 1934 to 1959), and Ridley Hall. He did brilliantly, taking a first class in Part I Classical Tripos of 1894 and a first in Part II the following year. He was Stewart of Rannoch scholar in 1894 and Hulsean prizeman in 1896.

He was appointed curate of Ballymena and in 1899 went to Cork as a curate at St Finbarr's Cathedral. He became rector of St Michael's Blackrock, Co. Cork, in 1906, and in 1911 went to Dublin as Archbishop

King's Professor of Divinity in Trinity College and a Canon of St Patrick's Cathedral. He was chaplain to the Lord Lieutenant from 1912 to 1915.

In 1915, at the age of 42, Gregg was elected Bishop of the diocese of Ossory, Ferns and Leighlin from whence he was translated in 1920 as Archbishop of Dublin. His translation took place at a difficult time in the history of the Church. The Sinn Fein troubles which had the country in turmoil were probably at their worst, and the Protestant community was experiencing great anxiety about the future. With the setting up of the Free State Government fears were entertained that the Church might be divided, but the calm leadership and the wise counsel of Gregg was a big factor in bringing it through the crisis. Not the least of the problems which confronted the Church of Ireland was the decreasing membership, particularly in the south and west, and it was due largely to his guiding hand that the Church survived a very difficult period.

A strong individualist, Dr Gregg often took his own line on subjects of Irish controversy; and on matters affecting the welfare of his Church he never hesitated to speak with candour and forcefulness. In particular he protested about the Irish Government's policy of teaching Gaelic and about matters contained in the new history books ...

He bore some facial resemblance to Mr de Valera. When in 1921 the Irish leader was on the run, Gregg was questioned by British soldiers who thought he was Mr de Valera disguised in clerical garb.

After the death of Archbishop D'Arcy in 1938 Dr Gregg was invited to succeed him at Armagh. He decided, however, to remain in Dublin but, after the death of Dr D'Arcy's successor, Dr Day, the House of Bishops turned once more to Dr Gregg and his enthronement took place in Armagh Cathedral in 1939.

Gregg took a prominent part in the oecumenical movement working towards better relations between the Anglican Churches and such communions as the Greek Orthodox Church and the Old Catholic Churches in Europe, but he never allowed any departure from the principles of the Reformed Church. As Professor T. A. Sinclair put it when presenting him for the degree of D.D. at Queen's University Belfast in 1949: "He has always been a doughty fighter in the cause of church and of truth. Yet there was no bitterness in his polemics and his integrity and honesty of purpose earned the admiration of his opponents."

Gregg, who was made a Companion of Honour in 1957, was author of *Decian Persecution* (1897); *Epistle of St Clement of Rome* (1899); ...

He married first in 1902, Anna Alicia, daughter of F. M. Jennings, by whom he had two sons and two daughters. His wife died in 1945 and in 1947 he married Lesley Alexandra, younger daughter of the late Very Rev. T. J. McEndoo, then Dean of Armagh. The Dean, who performed the ceremony in Armagh Cathedral, had thus the unique distinction of marrying his daughter to his Archbishop.

* * *

SEAN O'CASEY

21 SEPTEMBER 1964

MR SEAN O'CASEY, the Irish playwright, died in a Torquay nursing home on Friday night. He was 84.

A writer of acknowledged genius, his professional life was threaded with misunderstandings that brought about a neglect of his plays which never altogether ceased to trouble the theatrical conscience. There was a time when the general public eagerly expected him to go on working indefinitely in the style of his famous Dublin trilogy – *The Shadow of a Gunman, Juno and the Paycock* and *The Plough and the Stars*. He insisted on his right as an artist to develop in his own way. Neither politically nor stylistically were the developments in his middle period popular. The consequence was that when he had mellowed politically and critics were in a position to appreciate that his real preoccupation as a dramatist had not been with the destruction of society but with the destruction of dramatic realism it was too late. O'Casey could no longer count on getting the plays he continued to publish adequately performed, if at all. Any of his later fantasies that happened to be taken up were apt to present difficulties that might not have been there if the author's contact with theatrical conditions had remained close and constant. His superbly evocative autobiography in six volumes abounds in scenes from plays that he did not write.

Shaun O'Cathasaigh, the son of Michael and Susanna O'Cathasaigh, was born on March 30, 1880, in a Dublin tenement. He was the last of 13 children, eight of whom had already died in infancy. He himself contracted a chronic eye affliction, and his early years of dire poverty and much pain were a prelude to a young manhood of deprivation and insecurity. Till he was 30 he worked as a casual labourer with long periods of unemployment.

He had taught himself at the age of 14 to read, and he read all that came his way, getting to know some of the English classics, steeping himself in Shakespeare and the melodramas of Dion Boucicault. His imagination was fired by Jim Larkin, the fiery orator who organized the unskilled labourers of Dublin into the newly formed Irish Transport and General Workers' Union. O'Casey became an active member of the union and served as one of the Chief's assistants during the 1913 strike. He learnt and taught Gaelic. He became secretary of the Irish Citizen Army in 1914. It was during the war years that he began to do a little utilitarian writing and at the same time tried his hand at one or two plays. "Your strong point is characterization," Lady Gregory told him after reading *The Crimson in the Tricolour*. *The Shadow of a Gunman* (1923) was the first of his plays to be accepted. Rather to the surprise of the Abbey's directors, it filled the theatre night after night. During its run he was still working as a labourer, mixing cement on a road repair job. Next year came *Juno and the Paycock* that was to win the Hawthornden Prize of 1926. These two plays restored the failing fortunes of the Abbey and enabled the author to start his professional career as a playwright.

Though Lady Gregory made him welcome at Coole and taught him, among other things, to use "divers tools at food" the celebrity from the tenements found more to poke fun at than to admire in the city's *literati*. *The Plough and the Stars* (1926) duly provoked the riot and the subsequent newspaper controversies with which Dublin customarily greets its masterpieces, and in the midst of his turbulent success O'Casey left Ireland for England.

The three plays were widely acclaimed as masterpieces of realism. There was misunderstanding here that was to persist. The condition of Dublin at the time of the Easter Rising and during the Troubles is certainly depicted with extraordinary vividness, but the spirit of the plays is far from being realistic. The Paycock, Joxer, Fluther and the Covey use language that was never spoken by mortal tenement dwellers. These unforgettable rapscallions come, like Falstaff, out of the sea of poetry, and the natural development of their creator was not along realistic lines. In 1928 the Abbey received *The Silver Tassie*, an anti-war play which sought to achieve unity through a diversity of styles and its rejection gave rise to a public dispute between the angry author and Yeats.

The decision not to produce this play had serious consequences alike for the author and for the theatre, which lost its greatest modern playwright. In 1929 *The Silver Tassie* was put on in London and, though a commercial failure, won high critical praise as a bold experiment in theatrical method. Its symbolic middle act dominated by a great howitzer and the figure of a man, chanting, is still memorable. *Within the Gates* (1934), a modern morality set in Hyde Park, carried the method still further with even less public acceptance. Its mingling of styles was thought by some critics to open up a new country of the imagination to a theatre then shut in by rigid literalism: but the audiences that might have appreciated O'Casey's intentions had yet to come into being. *Within the Gates* was the last of his plays automatically to command production on a central stage. During the years of neglect he published *Windfalls* (1934), a collection of early poems, short stories and one act plays, *The Flying Wasp* (1937), essays on the London theatre, and in 1939 the first volume of his autobiography, *I Knock at the Door* appeared. It was followed by *Pictures in the Hallway* (1942), *Drums under the Windows* (1945), *Inishfallen, Fare Thee Well* (1949), *Rose and Crown* (1952) and *Sunset and Evening Star* (1954). And he continued to write plays in his own highly personal style. Of these *The Star Turns Red* (1940), a piece of communist propaganda, and *Oak Leaves and Lavender* (1946), celebrating England at war, are perhaps best forgotten, but *Red Roses for Me* (1943), a piece about a doomed Dublin idealist who sees the shame of a new world in the shilling-a-week for which railwaymen are striking, was brought to London in 1946 and had some success. After visiting America in the late thirties O'Casey had settled in Devonshire, and as he grew older Ireland seemed to grow more and more real to the exile.

How far his Ireland corresponded with present-day Ireland has been hotly disputed, and after the rejection of *The Drums of Father Ned* by the second Dublin Theatre Festival in 1958 O'Casey indignantly banned the presentation of any of his plays in Dublin – a ban that was relaxed earlier this year, when he permitted the Abbey Theatre company to stage a limited run of *The Plough and the Stars* and *Juno and the Paycock* before their presentation in London.

Purple Dust (1940), *Cock-a-Doodle Dandy* (1949), *The Bishop's Bonfire* (1955) and *The Drums of Father Ned* (1958) all have an Irish setting. The first three have a common theme – the arraignment of all established institutions, the Church among them, as enemies of the free mind, especially as they are leagued together to fill youth with a superstitious dread of life and a distrust of happiness. Their interest for the student of the drama is that they show that out of his ceaseless experiments, some of them rash and stumbling, O'Casey had succeeded in evolving out of the juxtaposition of different techniques a sort of kaleidoscopic play which re-introduces the song and the dance which the drama since Ibsen has lost and restores the flamboyance that is natural to it. Imperfect as they are, they sustain the impression of bigness of mind that is inseparable from O'Casey's tragi-comic vision of life.

He married in 1927 Eileen Reynolds (Eileen Carey), an Irish actress, and they had two sons and a daughter.

JIMMY O'DEA

8 JANUARY 1965

MR JIMMY O'DEA, whose death occurred in a Dublin hospital yesterday, was unquestionably Ireland's greatest comedian. He was in his mid-sixties. There were and are many actors who could get the precise Dublin accent, the rich and often savage satire of the Dubliner's conversation. But none of them could approach O'Dea's deeper insight into character, the magic that conveyed satire and the more subtle kindly tolerance in one simple gesture. He was, by any standards, a first-class actor.

He was born near the Coombe, in the very heart of Dublin, and this was as significant an influence on his career as was the sound of Bow Bells on Dan Leno's. It produced the character of Biddy Mulligan, a rare harridan whose rich colloquialisms delighted Sean O'Casey and every other Dubliner for over 40 years. Jimmy O'Dea's early life was as conventional as most other comedians of that time. While he was qualifying as an optician he provided light entertainment at rugby dinners and seaside towns. In the early 1920s he was induced to play Buttons in the annual pantomime in the Queen's Theatre (now occupied by the Abbey Theatre) and was an immediate success.

After other engagements, and having abandoned his profession, he began his partnership with Harry O'Donovan, who was to write most of his scripts for the remainder of his career. At about this time he married Miss Bernie Fagan, his best man being his boyhood friend and now the Prime Minister of the Irish Republic, Mr Sean Lemass. His quite phenomenal range of comedy immediately established him as one of the greatest artists on the Irish stage. He was content to remain mainly based in Dublin with occasional tours of the Irish provinces and to Manchester and Liverpool.

It was commonly said of him that his style was so particularly Irish that it would scarcely translate to wider audiences. Nevertheless it was clear to many critics that his scope could have been universal if he had had a mind to it. His performance as Bottom in *A Midsummer Night's Dream* during the war, with Micheál Mac Liammóir, and his brilliant caricatures of Churchill and Stalin were clear evidence of his talent.

In 1959, after the death of his first wife, he married Miss Ursula Doyle. There were no children of either marriage.

* * *

WILLIAM T. COSGRAVE

17 NOVEMBER 1965

MR WILLIAM T. COSGRAVE, President of the Executive Council of the Irish Free State from 1922 to 1932, died yesterday at his home in Dublin at the age of 85.

An advanced nationalist from his earliest days, he fought in the Rising of 1916 and then, devoting himself to politics, became a leader of the extremist movement. On the issue of the Irish Treaty of 1921 he stood with Arthur Griffith for its acceptance, and on Griffith's death, was elected head of the government which established the new regime. Confronted by the tremendous difficulties and fierce passions of that time he proved himself during the ensuing decade to be a statesman of resource, wisdom, and good-will. In spite of the opposition of a large and formidable section of his fellow-countrymen who regarded him as false to the true nationalist tradition he continued with persistence to seek within the Commonwealth a closer economic relationship with Great Britain. In this, however, he failed to carry his country against the force of Mr de Valera's appeals and personality, and, once defeated, was never again returned to power.

William T. Cosgrave

William Thomas Cosgrave was born in Dublin in 1880. He was the son of a licensed trader there, and after education at a neighbouring Christian Brothers' School himself became an assistant in a public house. He took an active part in the formation of the Sinn Fein movement during the early years of the century, and in 1909 was selected as a Sinn Fein candidate for a seat in the Dublin Corporation.

In the rising of 1916 Cosgrave fought under Eamonn Ceannt in the South Dublin Union, was taken prisoner and condemned to death, but the sentence was commuted to Penal servitude for life. Of this he served one year in Portland prison and was then released under the general amnesty. Back in Ireland he devoted himself to the Sinn Fein movement, and was elected to Parliament by an overwhelming majority at a by-election in Kilkenny City, though as a Sinn Fein he refused to take his seat. Then in 1918 he was returned unopposed for North Kilkenny.

In the following year, when the Sinn Fein members of Parliament formed their first Republican Dail Eireann, Cosgrave became Minister of Local Government and also a hunted man. He was twice imprisoned; but he succeeded nonetheless in formulating a new system on the Sinn Fein model. After the Truce he stood by Arthur Griffith, who had succeeded Mr de Valera as leader, and, resuming his old position as Minister for Local Government, faced the bitter animus which the extreme Republicans directed against those of their fellow-countrymen who accepted the Treaty.

When in 1922 the Provisional Parliament, after its confirmation by a general election, met to consider the situation which had arisen owing to the sudden deaths of Griffith and Michael Collins, Cosgrave was chosen to be President of Dail Eireann. He also accepted the portfolio of finance. As President of the Executive Council of the Irish Free State, a title which soon replaced his earlier one, he was in a position of great difficulty. His government consisted of untried men. Militant republicanism was both strong and relentless and, owing to its refusal to sit in the Dail, one-third of the country was virtually disfranchised. The whole country, moreover, was torn by the passions engendered by the civil war. But the people came together behind him, and an increased majority confirmed this.

He was assisted and inspired by the late Kevin O'Higgins; together they decided to bring the new Dominion into an intimate relationship with Great Britain and thus to serve the mutual interests of both countries. He became as time went on far less inclined than he had been at first to placate his Republican opponents by anti-British gestures. He continued, however, to insist on Ireland's independent status and at the two Imperial conferences at which the Free State was represented during his presidency its delegates were protagonists of Dominion independence.

The period of the fourth Dail, 1923–27, was one of great progress. The Legislature became efficient and reputable, the mechanism of local government and the judiciary was established. In the country, however, the Republicans having abandoned militancy were carrying on a vigorous propaganda campaign against the government. Cosgrave decided boldly to attack this issue and introduced the Electoral Amendment Bill under which all candidates for an election were compelled to give a guarantee that they would take their seats. He thus presented Mr de Valera with the alternatives of participation or political extinction. Cosgrave knew that this policy was more likely to help his opponents than himself. But he was satisfied that he would obtain a sufficient majority to carry on and took a risk in what he believed to be the national interest. Shortly before the 1927 election in which he stood for Cork, he predicted that his own party would win by 61 seats. The forecast proved exactly accurate. As a result Mr de Valera decided to treat the oath as an "empty formula" and with his supporters entered the Dail.

Also in 1927 Cosgrave went to Geneva where he delivered a speech in Irish. The next year he visited the United States and Canada. He was indeed at the height of his prestige: but it was not long before the foundations of his authority began to crumble. Mr de Valera's arguments pointed by the 1930–31 fall in British prices exerted an increasing effect. Terrorism raised its head once more, and Cosgrave's measures against it told against him with the result that in 1932 he was defeated and

Mr de Valera's party found itself with the assistance of Labour in office.

Cosgrave's qualities were those of a sound and resourceful administrator rather than leader of an opposition. He was up against a man of a far more arresting personality than his own who understood the Irish temperament even more deeply than he. There was another election in 1933 but Cosgrave's "whirlwind" campaign failed to reverse the result.

True to the convictions of his career Cosgrave continued to plead for a settlement with Great Britain and a relationship with the Commonwealth. With the outbreak of the Second World War, however, the attitude of Eire to the war became the absorbing political interest of her people, and, although all parties were agreed upon neutrality, Mr de Valera, whose steadfastness on points of principle had become a legend, was generally regarded as the obvious and remained the chosen leader. The election of 1943 did reduce his majority, but it in no way brightened the prospects of his chief opponent, who also suffered a considerable loss of seats. Cosgrave, moreover, wearied by his long struggle and deeply disappointed in the hopes he had placed in the Irish people, had begun to show increasing signs of strain. His health began to fail, and in January, 1944, he retired finally from public life.

In 1919 he married Louise, daughter of Alderman Flanagan of Dublin. They had two sons. His wife died in 1959. His elder son, Mr Liam Cosgrave, became leader of Fine Gael, the main opposition party, in April of this year.

FRANK O'CONNOR

Master of the short story

11 MARCH 1966

MR FRANK O'CONNOR, the Irish writer, died yesterday at his home in Dublin. He was 64.

By his death English literature has lost a master of the short story. But Ireland is worse deprived, for incomparably he revealed to Irishmen and the world the splendour and vitality of an ancient literature known only to a handful of scholars in Irish.

A revolutionary by nature, who at 19 was fighting in the Civil War, the strange rapture and naivety of the lonely child of Cork were in him to the end. At 25, after an apprenticeship with Lennox Robinson (at that time library adviser to the Carnegie Trust), he moved from a librarianship at Cork to another in Dublin, where he soon carried on his own civil war with everyone whose ideas on literature conflicted with his. In this contest, A. E. (George Russell) was his one point of rest. Yeats's friendship was more austere, but not less appreciative of a remarkable talent for both story and verse, and persuaded him towards an Abbey Theatre directorship during a critical period. O'Connor later resigned in anger at the anti-Yeats group. Librarianship, too, he abandoned for literature. The war brought him to London, where he did some memorable broadcasts while working with the Ministry for Information.

His first book, *Guests of the Nation* (1931), won immediate recognition just when the short story was reaching a peak of refinement as a literary form. *Bones of Contention* (1936) and *Crab Apple Jelly* (1944) followed; but in the interval there were poetry translations for the Cuala Press; *The Big Fellow* (1937), a life of Michael Collins; and five unpublished plays of his Abbey period (three in collaboration with Hugh Hunt) which elevated the theatre he was trying hard to save. The novel, too, had excited him, but neither *The Saint and Mary Kate* (1932) nor *Dutch Interior* (1940) was conspicuously successful. He returned to the story in *The Common Chord* (1947), *Travellers' Samples* (1950), and *Domestic Relations* (1957). Later there were collected editions and volumes of selections.

The academic approach of the critics to Shakespeare drove him to *The Road to Stratford* (1948), a practising writer's analysis of another's workmanship. The same inspiration produced *The Mirror in the Roadway* (1956), where he examined the style and technique of some great novelists. But he was curious about every art and craft, and on "discovering" Irish architecture he mounted a bike and toured the country to see its ruined monuments. *Irish Miles* (1947) remains a refreshing and intelligent guide for the tourist in Ireland. In another guide of a different kind, *The Book of Ireland* (1958), he allowed Ireland to speak magnificently for herself in the prose and poetry of native and foreign writers since the ninth century. The story-tellers got a volume to themselves, *Modern Irish Short Stories* (1957) in the World's Classics series.

A few years of lecturing and teaching in America were terminated in the 1950s by a longing for Dublin. But the tranquillity he sought there was disturbed by the mediocrity of Irish writing and the antics of place-seekers in society whose most notable contribution to a new Ireland was the mortal wound it had inflicted on literature with a state censorship. Perhaps it is significant that he was becoming more absorbed at that time with the medieval poetry; it is certain that his reputation will be hallowed by the superb translations as by the greatest of the stories. The first collected edition, *Kings, Lords and Commons* (1961), was promptly banned for containing the seventeenth-century satire *The Midnight Court* (1945), already proscribed by state order (1946). It was later revoked on formal and tedious submission by some friends to the Appeals Board. A second collection appeared in *The Little Monasteries* (1963).

LADY HANSON

A famous Dublin hostess

29 AUGUST 1970

LADY HANSON, WIDOW of Sir Philip Hanson, C.B., formerly chairman of the Commission of Public Works in Ireland, died on Thursday at the age of 90. Constance Geraldine Hanson, the "Deena" of George Moore and his circle, was born in Dublin, a younger daughter of Robert Yelverton Tyrrell, sometime Professor of Greek in Dublin University, and remembered as scholar, man of letters, and wit. She came of a noteworthy stock. On her father's side she was related to the Rev. George Tyrrell, S.J., and to Lord Tyrrell of Avon. Through her grandfather, George Ferdinand Shaw, sometime Senior Fellow of Trinity College, Dublin, she was related to a vast family of Shaws, overtopped and overshadowed later by George Bernard.

Dublin in the decade of the Victorian golden jubilee retained much of the fading splendour of an historic metropolis, and Deena Hanson with her three brothers and two sisters formed a typical social group in a constellation that included Mahaffy, Salmon, the Pursers, the Orpens, the Yeatses, the Gwynns, and the Starkies, at a time when good claret and good conversation were everyday amenities. In 1914 she married the late Philip Hanson, a Commissioner of Works, knighted in 1920, by whom she had twin sons.

For many years the Hansons' house in Dublin was a social landmark. As a hostess, Lady Hanson was exceptionally gifted, and she maintained her circle undimmed through the darkest years of Irish civil strife and confusion; indeed, hers may be said to have been among the last surviving salons of Dublin culture. Generous, impetuous, dignified and elegant, she inherited from her father a clarity of vision and delicacy of speech that gained forcefulness from the charm and beauty of her elfin personality. The tenderness with which she encouraged the humble and meek was matched by the almost surgical skill with which she punctured the proud and overbearing. Meredith would have been glad to have included her among his heroines; but she was more than a Victorian heroine; for in times of adversity and distress she showed herself to be a great lady. Her husband died in 1955.

* * *

SEAN LEMASS

Better Anglo-Irish relations

12 MAY 1971

MR SEAN FRANCIS LEMASS who was premier of the Irish Republic from 1959 to 1966 has died at the age of 71.

Lemass became premier after Mr Eamon de Valera, the founder of the Fianna Fail party, had relinquished the post to become the country's third president. Under the Lemass leadership the country took on a more outward-looking approach. Economic problems became the priority and he strove diligently to get Ireland into the European Community as he saw in it the greatest prospect for the advancement of agriculture and industry. Departing sharply from the de Valera attitude towards Northern Ireland he travelled to Belfast in 1965, passed through the gates of Stormont, the Northern Ireland Parliament, to exchange greetings with Captain Terence O'Neill. It was the most dramatic event in Irish politics since the advent of Fianna Fail to power and it might have led to a better understanding between North and South had the process not broken down in the northern turmoil of later years.

Lemass also had a cordial relationship with Mr Harold Wilson and was instrumental in having the remains of Roger Casement returned to Ireland, thereby ending another 40-year-old controversy. The working out of the Free Trade Area Agreement (1965), brought the two prime ministers to a very close understanding, and the two countries to closer ties than had existed since the Treaty of 1921.

Lemass, who had been Minister for Industry and Commerce in successive Fianna Fail Governments since 1932, was born in July, 1899, and became identified with the Irish revolutionary movement at an early age. In the Easter Week Rising of 1916, not yet 17, he served in the garrison at the General Post Office in Dublin. When caught by British soldiers ... they told him to "go back to mother". This did not please him; he had already seen action, and no longer looked on himself as a boy.

His enthusiasm for the cause burned fiercely, and later he rejoined the Irish Republican Army. After the Anglo-Irish Treaty he threw in his lot with its opponents under Mr de Valera and was captured and imprisoned when the Four Courts fell at the beginning of the Civil War.

He was elected to the Dail in 1924 but like other members of the Anti-Treaty block did not take his seat. A year later he proposed to Mr de Valera the formation of a new party, Fianna Fail, which would take over the policies of Sinn Fein and apply them constitutionally. Fianna Fail came to Government in 1932 and Lemass became its youngest minister and incidentally the youngest Cabinet minister in Europe.

De Valera, with whom he was on the terms of closest friendship, although the two men differed radically in character and temperament, called him the Benjamin of the Government. As Minister for Industry and Commerce, his uncommon grasp of practical matters served the country well, acting as a counter-balance to the visionary qualities of his leader. Under him the concept of state enterprise, which has successfully taken on tasks which are too risky to attract private capital without encroaching on the preserves of private enterprise, was worked out at first in the development and extension of electricity supplies and the establishment of air companies.

The narrow ideas of economic self-sufficiency fostered by Sinn

Fein which were responsible for the period of economic war which embittered relations with Britain in the 1930s were thrown overboard when he negotiated the trade agreement in 1965. In a country where ideology of any sort is frowned on, and Lemass himself was an avowed pragmatist, he saw the need for a shift to the left, embracing better social services and educational facilities.

What may be counted as one of the first fruits of this policy of moderate direction by the state, the national wages agreement worked out by employers and unions under the aegis of the Government in 1964, was not an unmitigated success. The unions, having won a general rise in wages of 12 per cent, proceeded to press for a reduction of working hours. Economic troubles followed and there was not to be a repeat of the experiment for a number of years.

Lemass was the prime mover and architect of the Republic's economic programmes. These were launched under his direction and those which ran through his period of office were largely successful.

He was intimately associated with the difficult period when the state was founded, when emotions dominated men's actions, but nevertheless Lemass attended primarily to the business end of politics and looked to the future. Therefore, when the time came to replace the older men of the revolutionary period, he was the bridge by which young men of ability came into the Cabinet.

He is survived by his wife, a son and three daughters.

LORD BROOKEBOROUGH

20 AUGUST 1973

LORD BROOKEBOROUGH, KG, PC, CBE, MC, who was Prime Minister of Northern Ireland from 1943 to 1963, died on Saturday at the age of 85. A staunch representative of the Anglo-Irish aristocracy and an unyielding believer in the Protestant ascendancy, he had a far-reaching effect on the province's political leadership.

Brookeborough was a man of courage, conviction and great charm. But his political sense was seriously found wanting by the intransigence with which he excluded the Roman Catholic minority from responsibility and participation. He believed that, being basically republicans, they were not in a constitutional sense to be trusted.

He laid the foundation of his reputation in his early years as Prime Minister. With Dublin neutral, Belfast was a base for the Allies: a back door firmly shut on the enemy. The union with England was his abiding concern and he would allow nothing to compromise it. While Northern Ireland MPs at Westminster took the Conservative whip, his government at Stormont reenacted most of the Attlee Government's social measures.

When he resigned the Premiership of Northern Ireland in March, 1963, he was Ulster's longest serving Prime Minister, having held office for two months short of 20 years. He had also established a United Kingdom record by holding government office continuously for 33 years.

The Right Hon Sir Basil Stanlake Brooke, first Viscount Brookeborough, of Colebrooke, Co Fermanagh, and a baronet, both in the Peerage of the United Kingdom, was born on June 9, 1888, of a family which was one of the oldest to settle in Northern Ireland from England. He was eldest son of Arthur Douglas Brooke, and he traced his ancestry back to Sir Basil Brooke, knighted by Queen Elizabeth I. For many generations since, they have been known as "The Fighting Brookes".

Some of his later ancestors did battle for William of Orange on the Boyne, and they supplied a long and distinguished line of sailors, soldiers, statesmen and administrators through the centuries.

Basil Brooke went to Winchester, and afterwards passed through the Royal Military College, Sandhurst, before he was commissioned to the Royal Fusiliers. Later he transferred to the 10th Hussars, fought with them throughout the First World War, taking part in the Dardanelles campaign, was awarded the MC, the Croix de Guerre with Palm, and mentioned in dispatches.

He had in 1907 succeeded to the family baronetcy, and the Colebrooke Park Estates, before returning to Ulster after the war ended. In 1921 he became a Senator in the first Northern Ireland Parliament, but retired a year later to resume full-time duties as a Commandant of the Special Constabulary in his own county. He was then 33. He had been out of Ireland for most of his young manhood, and he was now brought for the first time into close touch with the welter of problems with which both South and North were bemused following upon the state of virtual civil war in the South and the creation of Ulster as a separate province. Brooke's post in Co Fermanagh was near enough to the Free State border to be a dangerous one, and both he and the men whom he commanded were often in peril.

For seven years after resigning from the Senate he remained out of the active political scene at Stormont, but in many other ways served the Province, and his party's relentless campaign to preserve the Union. But in 1929, under strong pressure from his friends, he agreed to stand for the Northern Ireland Parliament, and was elected for Lisnaskea. His impact upon practical politics was immediate. In 1933 the Premier, Sir James Craig, as he then was, made him Minister of Agriculture, a post which he retained until 1941. Under his direction as a practical agriculturist himself, the farming and allied industries in Ulster were transformed. Large and far-reaching schemes for the marketing of milk, eggs and meat were introduced, the farmers were encouraged and aided to increase proficiency in cultivation, and within the space of these seven or eight years the Ulster countryside assumed a prosperity which it had never known before.

With the outbreak of war in 1939, the Irish Free State remained stubbornly neutral. Lord Craigavon had died while still Premier, a post in which he was succeeded by that other veteran Ulsterman John M. Andrews, who counted Brooke among the ablest members of his cabinet, and as the strain of the war developed he transferred him from agriculture to the Ministry of Commerce and Production. It was the ideal choice and under his guidance the Ulster contribution to the war effort developed enormously.

He made frequent journeys to London for consultation and to counter the suggestion to the British Premier and his ministers that those workers in Ulster still unemployed should be moved to English factories by demanding that the raw materials and the instruments of output should be supplied to Northern Ireland, so that Ulster's men and women could work at home. In particular, he arranged for the lifting of the Limitation of Supplies Order so that the Province might receive additional quantities of many materials as, for example, textiles and metals, so that Ulster was able still more enormously to increase its war output.

In May, 1943, John Andrews, then 72, and feeling the burden of his years and office, resigned as Premier. Sir Basil Brooke was the inevitable successor. It was a period of intense strain because from time to time his concentration upon the war effort was deflected by events in Eire, and he suffered deep personal losses in the fighting. But he maintained all his many sided activities and in particular made and maintained wide contacts with officers of all ranks in the American and other Allied Forces in Northern Ireland.

With the end of the war he was able to turn his attention to those other issues which his country, like others, had to face in the process of transformation. It was here again that his experience, energy, and force of character were so manifest. He was particularly active in his efforts to consolidate and extend the industrial developments in Ulster.

Otherwise he constantly countered the attempts from Dublin to end partition, declaring that he was a unionist first and a Conservative second, always making it clear that both his Government and himself sought no interference in the affairs of Eire and proclaiming Ulster's desire to live in friendly neighbourliness with the south. He led the Unionist Party at the polls at five general elections, 1945, 1949, 1953, 1958, and 1962. Only once was he opposed in his constituency, Lisnaskea, and he then defeated a Nationalist opponent.

His leadership came under criticism early in 1963 from a group of Unionist backbenchers who were mainly concerned about directorships held by other members of the Government. The split was healed and Lord Brookeborough was given a unanimous vote of confidence. But a serious operation which coincided with this affair forced him to retire from office. He declined an earldom.

Although it attracted little criticism in Great Britain at the time, his refusal to bring the Roman Catholic minority into active participation in public affairs stands out in retrospect as a serious blemish on his political record. In that respect his mind was prejudiced to an extent that damaged the political development of the province. He was also by modern standards casual in his approach to political duties. Lord O'Neill of the Maine, who succeeded him as Prime Minister, wrote of him that he was good company and a good raconteur, and those that met him imagined that he was relaxing away from his desk. But, O'Neill said they did not realize that there was no desk.

In the last three years of his life, years in which the Stormont institution came under its greatest strain and eventually crumbled, Brookeborough made only occasional forays into political life. Last year he appeared next to Mr William Craig on the balcony of the Stormont Parliament building, a diminuitive figure beside the leader of the Vanguard movement who was rallying Right-wing Unionists against the Government.

He opposed the Westminster White Paper on the future of Northern Ireland and caused some embarrassment to his son, Captain John Brooke – the Unionist chief whip and a Faulkner man – by speaking against the Government's proposals on the night before the Assembly elections.

In his private life, he as a man of the simplest and most modest tastes and habits. His greatest recreation was farming, and he won many awards. But he also liked shooting, fishing and golf.

He was created CBE in 1921, and made a Privy Councillor of Northern Ireland in 1933. He was created a Viscount in 1952.

He married, in 1919, a kinswoman, Cynthia, daughter of Captain and the Hon Mrs Sergison, of Cuckfield Park, Sussex, and they had three sons, two of whom were killed in action during the Second World War. The surviving son, John Warden Brooke, now succeeds to the viscountcy. His wife died in 1970 and in 1971 he married Sarah Eileen Bell Calvert, widow of Cecil Armstrong Calvert, FRCS.

* * *

GEORGE O'BRIEN

Brilliant Dublin personality

4 JANUARY 1974

PROFESSOR GEORGE O'BRIEN, Professor of Economics, University College Dublin, 1926–61, died on Monday. His contribution to the study of Irish economic history is of the highest importance and his three-volume work on the subject has by no means been superseded. Born in Dublin in 1892, he was called to the Irish Bar in 1913.

John Vaizey writes:

Professor George O'Brien had not left Dublin since before the First World War and finding himself with a travel phobia and an adequate income, he brought the world to Dublin. He dined out almost every night with friends, usually at a club, and his conversation was as brilliant and well-informed as any in the days of the Irish literary revival of the later part of which he had a detailed and wry memory. His taste and brilliance were both masked and revealed by a manner at once diffident and courteously ruthless. His loyalty to his friends (many of whom had been his students) was complete. His interest in the world – "so hard to keep up, the 7 o'clock news, then all the papers, so much in them" – never diminished. His conversation was interspersed with his memories of Yeats ("a thoroughly inaccurate man"), of Keynes, for whom he had a high regard, which was warmly returned, of Sir Theodore Gregory (an epic dinner on Ash Wednesday when all the Catholics demanded beef, the Protestants fish, and the Jews ham), of people like Maud Gonne and her evidence to the Banking Commission, which made him endlessly fascinating.

He was superbly unselfconscious, whether pouring Burgundy from his tea pot at high tea in the Dail, where he was a Senator, eager not to lose the country vote by parading his bourgeois tastes, or putting down a guest who asked where he kept his books – "in the garage, of course; would you expect to see joints of meat hanging in the dining room if you dined with the butcher?" His scholarship was as remarkable for its depth as for its breadth, and his modest attitude to it was a mark of another and more civilized age. Brilliant young businessmen like Dermot Ryan welcomed his advice as did the Minister for External Affairs. Though he never travelled, George knew the world. Seeing a battered hat in the hall of the Kildare Street Club, a man back from the war said "Well, at least George is still here." George, his kindness, courtesy, wit and zest, is alas not.

KATE O'BRIEN

Novelist and playwright

14 AUGUST 1974

MISS KATE O'BRIEN, the novelist and playwright, died yesterday at the age of 76.

She was Irish and her own people and their land inspired her most remarkable work. In regard to them her touch was unfaltering and her pen incisive. She saw deeply into the psychology of the Irish middle-class and was able to recreate an historical period with unusual conviction. Knowing Spain intimately she could write of it almost as confidently as of Ireland. Her taste was impeccable and she had subtlety, beauty and imagination at her command.

Kate O'Brien was born in 1897 the fourth daughter of Thomas O'Brien of Boru House, Limerick. She was educated at Laurel Hill Convent in that city and went on to University College, Dublin. Then, moving to England, she entered journalism and was for some time in Manchester on the staff of the then *Manchester Guardian*. Also as a young woman she found employment for a year at Bilbao in Spain, a country which she loved and came to know extremely well.

In 1926 her first attempt at drama, *Distinguished Villa*, was produced at the Little Theatre. It was a drab and distressing play; but it was saved by the patience and accuracy of its observation and by the deep sympathy with which several of its persons were treated. It proved that the strength of its authoress lay not in her hatreds but in her affections. The next year The Arts Club Theatre put on *The Bridge*. It too displayed her keen appreciation of character – but it also indicated that she had a deep sense of the sadness of human lives in their varied entanglements. It had, however, some defects of laboriousness which tended to conceal its qualities.

It was not until 1931 that she published *Without My Cloak*. It showed her to be a writer of fine originality who could exert and sustain an unusual power. Her scene was laid in a provincial town in Victorian Ireland and her characters were middle-class Irish people. It was a world which had lasted into her own time and the fidelity and feeling of her presentation made it an exceptional first novel. It won the Hawthornden Prize and the James Tait Black Memorial Prize. J. B. Priestley described it as a "peculiarly beautiful and arresting piece of fiction".

In 1934 *The Ante-Room* returned to the large Victorian family whose saga had occupied its predecessor, though in this case the action was limited to three days. While a mother – worrying to the last about her children, lay dying, Miss O'Brien gathered them together, as it were in the ante-room, in an atmosphere of suspense and hidden conflict. Collaborating with Geoffrey Gomer and W. A. Carot she turned it into a play. Staged at the Queens Theatre in 1936 it was a skilful piece of work, for out of the quietude of a remote Ireland a sense of tension grew; but the difficulty of compressing a subtle and slowly-moving study of temperaments within the compass of the stage proved at times too great. There was, a reviewer wrote, nothing to shout about, but much to admire.

Mary Lavelle which appeared in the same year was the idyll of an Irish governess in Spain. Deep understanding was again combined with a sharp power of characterization. *The School-room Window* was a play produced in 1937 at the Manuscript Theatre Club, a well written, slightly sentimental study of a cultivated family in an emotional crisis. *Farewell Spain*, a travel book, was timely in so far as the country she made her subject was, when she published it, a centre of world attention. Much of her description possessed high merit; but it was a difficult moment to have chosen for a book of great reflective quality. In *Pray for the Wanderer* in 1938 Miss O'Brien returned to her familiar Ireland. It had desultory charm, but the theme was slender and conventional. The time was the present, and though there was plenty of politics in it, she avoided rancour.

After an interval of two years, *The Last of Summer* was County Clare just before the outbreak of the war. It was high romance; another of her assured and fine-edged pieces of work. Her later books included *My Ireland* in 1962 and *Presentation Parlour* in 1963.

* * *

EAMON DE VALERA

The embodiment of Irish nationalism

30 AUGUST 1975

MR EAMON DE VALERA, the Irish nationalist leader and President of the Republic of Ireland from 1959 to 1973, died yesterday at the age of 92.

About a man who has been in turn a guerrilla commander, a political prisoner, a successful revolutionary, a partisan in civil war, a founder and leader of a political party, an elder statesman, and a head of state there will be found no consensus in the estimation of his contemporaries. By outsiders de Valera was thought of as a protoliberator from the bonds of empire, as an austere statesman of grave utterance with an honoured memory at the League of Nations, as the embodiment of whatever is consistent in the aspirations of the Irish nation. To part of his own people he was a hero of 1916, the last of the commandants to surrender, the one leader to survive the national struggle who never flinched in his purpose, the one man of his time with a pre-eminent claim to govern the Irish people. To another part he was a danger to the state, a politician of tricks and turns who was capable of disastrously wrong decisions, to whose actions most of the misfortunes of the country since 1921 were attributed, and that most dangerous of power-seekers, a man with an invincible sense of his own righteousness.

The complexity of his character adds to the difficulty of judgment. Gentle and courteous in private, he was often withering and autocratic in his public dealings. To know what the Irish people wanted, he once said, "I have only to examine my own heart". It was a way of short-circuiting democratic consultation to which he frequently resorted. There was a bleak integrity and refusal to count the cost about many of his actions that was in apparent contradiction to the transparent opportunism of others. The dialectical refinement and argumentative stamina with which he vindicated the settled principles of his policies were used with equal effect to justify his occasional tergiversation. Yet this much even his detractors must concede: he possessed unshakable courage and resolution, his patriotism was unalloyed and passionate, and in the flat years of post-revolutionary politics he was the only figure in Irish public life with magic to his name.

The most fateful moment of his career, and that by which all that followed must be judged, was when Griffith and Collins returned from London with the treaty of December, 1921. It afforded neither political integrity for the island nor republican status for the 26 counties. It was, said de Valera, "neither this nor that". Certainly it compromised the full demands of Sinn Fein. Yet it gave the Free State effective and evolving independence, it was approved by a majority of the Dail and it was assuredly acceptable to most of the Irish people. Was de Valera justified in these circumstances in repudiating the treaty and allying his unrivalled prestige and command of loyalty with the fanatics of armed resistance? There is no need to impugn his motives in order to conclude that he was wrong; for from that grave decision flowed an atrocious period of civil war, animosities that bedevilled Irish politics for four decades and retarded the development of the country, and the continuance of the Irish Republican Army as a threat to civil order.

His subsequent conduct of the affairs of the state, creditable as it was in many ways, could not efface that disservice. He was Prime Minister for 16 years and then off and on for another five. He accomplished much: yet the two objectives of his later political career which seemed to be nearest to his heart, and on which he certainly expended most rhetoric – the end of partition and the restoration of the Irish language – were as far as ever from accomplishment when at last in 1959 he sailed into the placid waters of the presidency.

There was a grandeur about his public career and a simple dignity in his bearing that eminently suited him for presidential office; for he held a place of honour in the history as well as in the contemporary affairs of his country. Tall; austere in his habits and his dress; grave and firm of countenance; soft, dry, and labyrinthine in speech; he dominated his countrymen, uniting and then dividing their loyalties as no man other than Parnell had done before him.

Eamon (it is the Irish form of Edward) de Valera was born in New York on October 14, 1882. His father Vivion de Valera, a music teacher of poor health, was a native of Spain; his mother, Catherine Coll, had come to America from Co Limerick in 1879. Vivion de Valera died when his son was two years old, and the child was sent to his mother's people in Limerick. He attended successively a national school, the Christian Brothers' School at Charleville, and Blackrock College, in Co Dublin. Later he took good degrees in arts and science at the Royal University of Ireland, taught mathematics in Rockwell College, Carysfort Training College and Holy Cross College, and became a mathematical lecturer in St Patrick's College, Maynooth.

De Valera was imbued with nationalist ideas from an early age. During his period of schoolmastering he adopted and studied the doctrines of Sinn Fein, and attended constantly at the meetings of the Gaelic League, where he obtained a sound acquaintance with the Irish language. He joined the Irish Volunteers at their inauguration in 1913, and rose to officer's rank in the separatist section of that movement after the schism occurred with the Redmondite section. In 1914 he played an active part in the Howth gun-running, and he became adjutant of the Dublin Brigade of the Volunteers in 1915.

For all practical purposes de Valera's public career began with the Rising of 1916, when he commanded the force of insurgents stationed in Boland's Mill, Dublin. Militarily he was the most successful of the Irish leaders; Boland's Mill was the last post to be surrendered and it was surrendered only on the orders of the insurgent Commandant-General. De Valera was tried and sentenced to death. The sentence was commuted to one of penal servitude for life, and he was imprisoned in Lewes gaol. There is no evidence that he was reprieved because of his American birth. It is more likely that he and another commandant, Thomas Ashe, were reprieved because by that time the unfavourable public effect of the executions was beginning to appear.

Early in 1917 the seat for East Clare fell vacant, and Sinn Fein nominated de Valera, whose part in the rising had made him a national hero. During the election the general amnesty of Irish political prisoners was proclaimed, and de Valera returned to Ireland. Immediately he found himself not only the parliamentary representative of East Clare, having polled more than twice as many votes as his opponent, but, as one of the few insurrectionists to escape execution, the acknowledged leader of the republican element in the country. In accordance with Sinn Fein's political strategy, he abstained from taking his seat at Westminster and devoted himself, instead, to the reorganization of the Volunteers. His personal influence helped greatly to rally the dissipated elements of the movement, and his election to the presidency of Sinn Fein in the autumn of 1917 marked a significant step – the assimilation of Sinn Fein to the Volunteers.

Under the presidency of Arthur Griffith Sinn Fein had not been a republican organization; its objects had been cultural and in politics more or less constitutional. At the same time its branches permeated the country, providing an effective means for the dissemination of nationalist views. The Castle authorities sought to ridicule the insurrection by identifying it with Sinn Fein, an outlandish-sounding organization which in fact had had nothing to do with the rising. The trick had the opposite effect; for once the British, by executing the leaders of the rising, had invested a forlorn and mismanaged enterprise with the glory of martyrdom, Sinn Fein became the beneficiary of the new national sentiment. When under de Valera's presidency the republican and previously constitutional elements of nationalism were fused, an instrument was created more powerful even than that which Parnell had brought into being.

During the winter of 1917–18 de Valera toured, preaching the duty and organizing the means of armed rebellion against England. In April, 1918, his campaign reached its height on the rumour that conscription would be applied to Ireland. He was arrested on a charge of treason and confined in Lincoln prison. In December, while he was still a prisoner, a general election, in which Sinn Fein swept the country, was held. In January the 73 Sinn Fein members constituted the first Dail Eireann in Dublin, reaffirmed their allegiance to the Republic proclaimed in 1916, and selected de Valera as their first President.

In February, through the agency of Michael Collins, he escaped from Lincoln and made his return to Ireland. For the next four months he was occupied in vain attempts to induce the Peace Conference to include Ireland in the scope of its deliberations. Meanwhile, the Volunteers and British troops were in daily conflict, and Ireland knew all the horrors of internal war. De Valera, constantly on the run, was at the heart of the Irish resistance. In June, however, leaving Griffith as Acting-President of the Republic, he went to the United States in search of money. The 17 months which he spent there were a medley of success and disappointment; but although he could not induce Washington to recognize the Irish Republic, he succeeded in his main object. When he returned to Ireland in December, 1920, he had raised a loan of $6m for the Republican Government.

Guerrilla warfare raged all through 1920 and the first half of 1921, and the Dail functioned amid extreme difficulties and dangers. In May, 1921, the second Dail Eireann was constituted, and in July the Truce was signed. De Valera went to London to meet Lloyd George, but the two reached no agreement on the matters at issue. De Valera invented and advanced the idea of "external association", an Irish republic in association with the British Commonwealth. But British constitutional thinking had not at that time advanced so far.

In October, on the invitation of Lloyd George, de Valera sent plenipotentiaries to London to conclude an acceptable treaty. A treaty was signed in December establishing the Irish Free State with Dominion status, and incorporating an oath of allegiance to the King. It was instantly denounced by de Valera, and approved by a majority of the Dail after prolonged and bitter debate. About the honours of that debate controversy continues to this day.

De Valera resigned his office as President of Dail Eireann, and he and his followers left the Dail, and did not appear in it again until 1927. Although he had ceased to be President of the Dail, de Valera was still President both of Sinn Fein and of the nominal Republic. All the enmity which he had borne against the British Government in Ireland was transferred after the Treaty to his fellows who had fallen so far from their faith as to accept Dominion status in a partitioned Ireland. For nearly a year he conducted, though at first equivocally, a campaign against the new Government which for horror matched anything in the previous three years. The Treaty party, in spite of the deaths of Griffith and Collins, showed unexpected competence and resolution, and early in 1923 the Republicans had been driven out of all save a few strongholds, and the leader instructed his followers to dump their arms and abandon the fight for the time being. In August he came out of hiding to contest an election in Clare. He was arrested on his political platform in Ennis, and did not regain his liberty until the following July.

De Valera's life during the next three years was quiet. His party, refusing to take the Oath of Allegiance, continued to abstain from the Dail. In 1926, however, the Government made nomination for the Dail conditional on an affidavit to take the Oath. De Valera changed his tactics, and proposed at the annual Ard Fheis, or general convention, of Sinn Fein that the Republicans should take their seats. The proposal split Sinn Fein. The irreconcilables, who still refused to acknowledge the existing Dail, retained the title of Sinn Fein; de Valera's partisans, pledged now to legislative action, formed a new organization under the name of Fianna Fail.

While in opposition, Fianna Fail was organizing its programme for the next general election. Its principal points were the abolition of the Oath, the retention of the land annuities which had been pledged to Britain by Cosgrave's financial agreements of 1923 and 1926, and the development of the Free State's resources towards a condition of self-sufficiency. The Government had improved the country's commerce with England, and there was virtually free trade between the two nations. In 1930–31 the world depression began to affect Ireland, cattle prices on the English market declined and the farmers began to experience vague doubts concerning the wisdom of free trade with England. Furthermore, those two years witnessed a revival of terrorist tactics by the Irish Republican Army, which had cast itself loose from de Valera's control as soon as he consented to take the Oath (as an empty formality).

In 1931 the Government approved an Amendment to the Constitution which outlawed the IRA and kindred Republican bodies, and established a military tribunal for the trial of political offences. This action helped to alienate the people from the Government. Furthermore, de Valera was now in control of a daily newspaper, *The Irish Press*: the funds for it he had collected by a visit to the United States in 1930, and for the first time the Cosgrave Government was opposed by a serious daily paper. In February, 1932, Cosgrave appealed to the country, and the general election gave the Fianna Fail-Labour coalition a majority of five over all other parties.

De Valera formed a Government – a Government which, for all intents and purposes, consisted of himself. Virtually an autocrat within his Cabinet and party, he put his policies into immediate practice. He released the Republicans who had been gaoled by the military tribunal and without officially notifying the British Government of his intention, introduced a Bill to abolish the Oath. The Bill was carried in the Dail, but eventually was held up by the Senate which in turn de Valera abolished. When he defaulted on the current instalment of the land annuities and demanded that the British claim to them should be tested by law, the British Government stipulated that the case in accordance with a decision of the 1930 Imperial Conference should be tried by an Empire tribunal. De Valera refused to negotiate on these terms. Thereupon England, in an attempt to recoup herself for the loss of the land annuities, imposed heavy import duties on Free State agricultural produce. De Valera retaliated with severe tariffs on British goods, and an economic war developed which was to cause almost untold trouble to the Free State and bring its agriculture to the verge of ruin.

He continued his campaign against the imperial connexion by studied disregard of the Governor-General. He then recommended his recall, and the nomination of a country shop-keeper as the next incumbent revealed his intention of degrading the dignity of the office and eventually abolishing it.

In spite of the dire results of his experiment in economic nationalism de Valera was returned to power, though not always with an absolute majority for his party in the Dail, at successive elections in 1933, 1937, and 1938. In this he was helped by his unrivalled political acumen, by the disorganized state of the opposition parties, and by the disastrous eruption into politics of General O'Duffy and his Blue Shirts. All the same, his redistributive social policies and his steady progress towards the next best thing to a republic were sufficiently in tune with the sentiments of a large enough part of the electorate.

He seized the occasion of the Abdication of King Edward VIII to slip through two Bills eliminating all the functions of the Governor-General from the Constitution and introducing a form of "external association" with the Crown and Commonwealth; and in 1937 he brought in a new Constitution in which the Irish Free State became Eire (which is the Irish for Ireland), with a president and a reformed senate. The Constitution laid juridical claim to the whole of the province of Ulster and accorded a "special position" to the Roman Catholic Church.

These unilateral moves, which in earlier days would have been highly provocative of the British, were accepted with equanimity on this side of the Irish Sea, where the Irish question had fallen out of politics, where the conception of the Commonwealth had lost much of its formality, and where de Valera's moves were recognized as making little practical difference.

De Valera's stature was quickly recognized on the international stage at Geneva, where he was chairman of the Council of the League of Nations in 1932 and President of the Assembly in 1938. His speeches on behalf of collective security were straight and firm, and he was an advocate of action by the League against Japan in Manchuria and Italy in Abyssinia.

In the spring of 1938 the ruinous economic war between Britain and Ireland was at last called off. In London de Valera negotiated an agreement in three parts which secured generous terms for his country. First the British Government gave up the naval bases at Queenstown, Berehaven, and Lough Swilly and renounced its right to further naval facilities in Irish ports in time of war ("a more feckless act can hardly be imagined", was Sir Winston Churchill's comment); next Ireland paid £10m to compound for the land annuities and other suspended payments, and as a corollary the penal duties imposed by both sides were abolished; next a trade agreement was reached of great benefit to Irish agricultural production.

Two matters which de Valera kept in the forefront of domestic policies were the Irish language and partition. Irish as an official language in state affairs, its compulsory introduction into the school curriculum, some knowledge of it as a qualification for public office, these were ideas common to all the founders of the new state. De Valera alone among politicians never seemed to lose his enthusiasm in the face of overwhelming evidence of the policy's failure as a means of resuscitating the language. For him language was a badge of nationhood: "I believe that as long as the language remains you have a distinguishing characteristic of nationality which will enable the nation to persist. If you lose the language the danger is that there would be absorption."

Nor did the hopes of a united Ireland prosper any better. In fact every step in de Valera's progress to abolish links with the Crown drove that distant prospect farther into the distance. Partition was the ostensible reason for his policy of neutrality in the war – a policy which received the general endorsement of his countrymen, whose opportunities to become individual belligerents were unlimited.

In October, 1939, at the instance of Churchill who was then First Lord of the Admiralty and apprehensive about defence of the Western Approaches, strong representations were made to de Valera to grant naval facilities at Berehaven. He was inflexibly opposed. The British Cabinet briefly considered coercion before dismissing it. The following summer a different approach was tried. Malcolm MacDonald was sent to Dublin with proposals under which a declaration by the British Government accepting the principle of a united Ireland together with a joint North-South working party for that purpose would be exchanged for Eire's entering the war on the side of the United Kingdom. De Valera, spotting that Belfast would still retain a practical veto and knowing that belligerency would disunite his people, did not warm to the proposal.

In the wake of Pearl Harbor Churchill had one more try. "Following from Mr Churchill to Mr de Valera. Personal. Private and Secret. Begins. Now is your chance. Now or never. 'A Nation once again'. Am ready to meet you at any time. Ends." De Valera's characteristically dry reply was, "Perhaps a visit from Lord Cranborne would be the best way towards a fuller understanding of our position here."

In some ways de Valera interpreted the obligations of neutrality in a sense convenient for Britain and its allies, in other ways he was unbendingly pedantic: he protested against the arrival of American troops in Northern Ireland, he declined the request of the United States, backed by Britain, to remove Axis consular and diplomatic representatives who were believed to be endangering allied security, and he made himself somewhat ridiculous by the nicety of calling on the German Minister in Dublin on May 2, 1945, to express his condolence on the death of Adolf Hitler.

De Valera was returned to power at two elections during the course of the war, but his unbroken period of office of 16 years came to an end in 1948, when an uneasy coalition of opposition parties secured a majority against him. He formed two more governments, in 1951–54 and 1957–59, but he had nothing new to offer his countrymen. His presence at the centre of the stage prolonged the political division of

Ireland along lines drawn in the 1920s, and kept a younger generation of politicians from their full inheritance.

In the summer of 1959, at the age of 78, and with his sight badly impaired, he allowed his name to go forward as a candidate for the presidency. His manner of going was characteristic of the turbulence of his long career. He was never one to scruple at altering the Constitution if he thought he could improve it. His last attempt was to substitute for proportional representation the British system of simple majorities in single-member constituencies, more favourable, it was felt, to his own party; and he so arranged things that the plebiscite on this issue should fall on the same day as the presidential election, hoping, his critics alleged, to confuse the constitutional issue with a test of his own undoubted prestige. Their stratagem, if it was one, failed. He was duly elected President but proportional representation remained.

When his term of office expired in 1966, he stood for re-election. He was opposed by Mr T. F. O'Higgins, a much younger man belonging to the Fine Gael Party. De Valera was returned by a bare 10,000 majority in contrast to his majority of 120,000 in 1959. The cities turned against him, where the modernity of his opponent rang more true than de Valera's appeal to the visionary values of a united Gaelic Ireland.

As President he scrupulously refrained from political partisanship. His public visits abroad were few. He was in Italy on St Patrick's Day, 1962, and received from the hands of the Pope the insignia of the Supreme Order of Christ, the Vatican's highest decoration. In the summer of 1964 he visited the United States, whither he had been invited by President Kennedy when the latter made his triumphal tour of Ireland shortly before his assassination. De Valera addressed a joint session of Congress to whom he expressed the hope that one day another representative of Ireland would be able to stand before them and announce that "our severed country has been reunited and the last source of enmity between the British people and the Irish people has been removed and at last we can be truly friends".

His second term of office expired in 1973, and the de Valeras retired to the modest seclusion of a convalescent home at Blackrock, Co

Dublin, there to continue the regular observance of the religious duties which they had long practised. He had married in 1910 Miss Sinead ni Fhlannagain. She died at the beginning of this year. There were five sons (one of whom is dead) and two daughters of the marriage.

* * *

JOHN A. COSTELLO

Former Prime Minister of Irish Republic

7 JANUARY 1976

MR JOHN A. COSTELLO, who was Prime Minister of the Republic of Ireland from 1948 to 1951 and again from 1954 to 1957, died on Monday at the age of 84. His government took Ireland out of the Commonwealth in 1949.

John Aloysius Costello was born in Dublin on June 20, 1891, the son of an official in the Registry of Deeds. From the Christian Brothers' School in North Richmond Street, he went on to read languages at University College, Dublin, and was called to the Irish Bar by Sir Ignatius O'Brien, the Lord Chancellor, in 1914. At University College, Dublin, he was unsuccessful as a student politician, being twice defeated for the coveted office of Auditor of the Literary and Historical Society. To the end of his days, he maintained, not wholly without rancour, that his opponents had triumphed through bribery and corruption.

Costello's family background was fervently Catholic and staunchly nationalist. He was fond of recalling the disadvantages under which an ordinary Irish Catholic laboured at the Irish Bar when he was a young man. But he did not allow any such resentments to divert him into active politics. He applied himself diligently to the mundane task of learning the barrister's craft under the able guidance of his master, Hugh Kennedy, the future Chief Justice of the Irish Free State. In 1921, both Kennedy and Costello were retained as counsel in the *habeas corpus* case of Egan v Macready, in which the Master of the Rolls in Ireland defied precedent to hold that there was no proper legal basis for executions by the Crown Forces. The verdict was a bodyblow for the so-called law and order policy of the Lloyd George government in Ireland. It was Costello's effective initiation in Irish politics.

When the Irish Free State was set up in 1922, Costello was appointed assistant to the Attorney General, his former master Hugh Kennedy. He himself eventually succeeded as Attorney General in 1926. As such he participated in the Imperial Conferences leading up to the recognition of the sovereignty of the Dominions by the Statute of Westminster in 1931. Had any judgeship fallen vacant in these years he would have succeeded to it. Such was not the event, and when Mr de Valera replaced Mr Cosgrave as Premier after the General Election of 1932, Costello returned to full-time practice at the Bar. In the following year he was elected to Dail Eireann and was prominent as an Opposition spokesman during the following fifteen years.

In 1948 Mr de Valera was at last ousted from office by an inter-party government formed out of an unlikely alliance between the pro-Commonwealth socially conservative Fine Gael (of which Costello was a member), the ultra-Republican Clann na Poblachta led by Sean MacBride, and the Labour Party. Costello was the Fine Gael frontbencher most acceptable to the other parties and he was, as a consequence, selected as Taoiseach (Prime Minister) over the heads of more eminent members of his own party. One of his first acts was the declaration in Canada that it was his intention to take Eire out of the Commonwealth. It was assumed, in fact wrongly, that MacBride had forced his hand. Costello had his own reasons for the action. He argued that the link with the Commonwealth that remained under Mr de Valera's 1937 Constitution was a sham and served only to provoke violence among Republican extremists. In fact, the secession from the Commonwealth turned out to be of little practical importance. In matters of trade and citizenship the British and Irish Governments agreed to retain their mutually preferential arrangements. Costello's sanguine hope that his action would take the gun out of Irish politics was not realized. Partition remained as a target for violence. The British Government responded to the Republic's secession from the Common-wealth by passing the Ireland Act, 1949, which copper-fastened the position of Northern Ireland within the United Kingdom. The futile anti-partition campaign supported by Costello's government did nothing to alter that.

In social and economic matters, Costello's government was more successful. The Anglo-Irish Trade Agreement (1948) provided more favourable terms for Irish agricultural exports to Britain while land reclamation and improvement schemes helped productivity. Housing and hospital services were improved. However, in 1951, when some members of the Catholic hierarchy opposed the provision of a free non means-tested maternity service, Costello preferred to accept the resig-nation of his excitable and combative Minister of Health, Dr Browne, rather than persevere with the original proposals accepted by the Government. This episode resulted in the fall of his government and Mr de Valera returned to office. Costello was offered a supreme court judgeship by the new Government – an unusual gesture in a country where judgeships are part of the spoils of political office. He declined it.

In 1954, following a general election, a second inter-party government was formed under Costello's leadership. It was committed to economic expansion but the emergence of a large balance of payments deficit forced it to take deflationary measures. Before it was able to reap the benefit of these and of measures designed to attract capital to Ireland it was swept out of office. Renewed violence on the border had led to the prosecution of IRA suspects. This prompted Sean MacBride to withdraw his party's support from the Government. Although it might yet have been able to survive, Costello, whose determination had been temporarily undermined by his wife's death, gave up the ghost and resigned. In the subsequent election Mr de Valera was returned with his largest-ever majority. Two years later Costello retired to the back-benches and concentrated on his practice at the Bar.

Although he attained the highest political office, Costello always seemed to remain first and foremost a lawyer. Politics was his second string and he sometimes gave the impression of treating it as a sort of relaxation. Yet, in it, he played a useful role. By his tact and genuine concern for the needy, he maintained an unlikely coalition which breathed new life into Irish democracy by providing a credible alternative to Mr de Valera's Fianna Fail. Yet he never achieved political greatness. He was without the aura of those who had been nurtured in the heroic politics of the Irish revolution. His most commendable personal qualities proved political weaknesses. He lacked the ruthlessness and hunger for office of the really ambitious; he was too loyal and kindly to deal toughly with colleagues; his religious piety led him to succumb to clerical pressure. His public remarks could be remarkably inapt to an occasion and in the manner of the advocate he was, he often over-stated his case; as an antidote to pretension he tended to adopt "plain man" attitudes and make rabble-rousing speeches that belied the cultured, highly intelligent man his closer associates knew.

At the Irish Bar, "Jack" Costello was an immense and much loved figure. He carried on a large practice well into his eighties, a purposeful figure bustling busily around the Law Library in Dublin's Four Courts or poring intently over papers at his desk, flicking his propelling pencil in the air as he read. In the closely knit, not uncritical, community that is the Irish Bar his qualities of kindness and compassion as well as his transparent honesty were universally recognized. In his later days he had the aura of a survivor from a bygone golden age. Every honour was paid to him. His colleagues recognized in him the supreme all-round craftsman of the profession. He was equally at home haranguing a jury or cross-examining a recalcitrant witness as unwinding a complex set of facts, or arguing a difficult legal point. The latter he tended to do with an informality and gruffness, almost amounting to irreverence, which belied the erudition and complexities involved. His experience as a chancery junior and later as a law officer gave him a wider knowledge of Irish law than most practitioners. He did not hesitate to tell judges that he knew what a statute meant as he had drafted it. He threw himself into a case with immense zest, utterly unable to conceive that his client might be in the wrong. He was a master of the tactics of litigation and possessed an originality of approach, generally the fruit of painstaking investigation, which was an invaluable asset in a difficult situation. His most memorable performance was his cross-examination of Patrick Kavanagh, the Monaghan poet, when the latter sued an Irish paper for libel in the early 1950s. Costello seemed to know the poet's work better than the author himself. It was wholly characteristic that when Kavanagh found himself in financial difficulties as a result of losing this action, Costello went to great pains to find him a lecturing post in University College, Dublin.

Costello is survived by three sons and one daughter. One son, Declan, is currently Attorney General of Ireland.

BRIAN FAULKNER

Former Prime Minister of Northern Ireland

11 MARCH 1977

LORD FAULKNER OF DOWNPATRICK, PC, Prime Minister of Northern Ireland from 1971 to 1972, died on March 3 in a riding accident. He was 56.

Brian Faulkner was the last Prime Minister of Northern Ireland in the Stormont regime and the one and only Chief Executive under the devolved constitution which a Conservative Government handed to Ulster in its place. They were years of seismic disturbance in the political life of the province. No one could have remained at the centre of affairs in such a period unless he possessed exceptional political tenacity and flair, as Faulkner unquestionably did. Nor could anyone have remained there, in the heated atmosphere of Ulster politics, without attracting accusations of inconsistency and bad faith, and many such accusations were levelled at Faulkner. They were the more difficult to dispel because his outstanding political qualities did not include the ability to inspire personal loyalty or generalized public trust in any high degree. Nevertheless, in respect of three fundamental matters at least he displayed a strong consistency from the start of his premiership onwards. He was unshakably committed to the Union. He knew, and acted on the knowledge, that the exclusive tenure by unionists of all political offices of consequence could not endure and was an obstacle to stability in the peculiar conditions of Northern Ireland. And he knew that a political settlement was not to be had so long as subversive violence was not being effectively repressed.

To fall from office twice within three years and each time to have the structure supporting the office fall with you, may seem proof enough of political failure. But on both occasions Faulkner was more the victim of others' miscalculations than of his own. It is arguable that the politicians of superior status in Westminster and Dublin, by frustrating the talents and exhausting the credit of the most effective politician in Belfast, fumbled with a possible key to the pacification of the province and lost it.

Arthur Brian Deane Faulkner was born on February 18, 1921, and was educated at Elm Park preparatory school in County Armagh and at the College of St Columba, Rathfarnham. The latter is a Protestant school near Dublin and he went there in 1933 when his father, a Belfast textile merchant, gave him the choice of schooling in Ireland or England. The 12-year-old Brian Faulkner chose Ireland and always declared himself an Irishman while defending to the end the North's connexion with Britain.

Northern Ireland was exempted from conscription in the Second World War and Faulkner went to work in his father's factory soon after he left school. His interest in politics began soon after the war and in 1949 he became Unionist member for the East Down constituency.

He succeeded Colonel Topping as Chief Whip in 1956 and was appointed Minister of Home Affairs in December, 1959. In March, 1963, he was appointed Minister of Commerce and at that stage what was probably the most satisfying period of his life began. He travelled the world "selling" his country to industrialists looking for new factory sites and prised out of the Government the most generous incentive terms offered anywhere in the United Kingdom.

When violence broke out on the streets of Londonderry and other Northern Ireland towns in 1968 and 1969 the Stormont Government and Unionist party became divided over the question of what concessions, if any, were to be made in the face of the civil rights agitation. Faulkner's position appeared to be equivocal, and he resigned office in the dying days of Captain Terence O'Neill's administration, in readiness, or so it seemed, to make his own bid for the leadership. When the time came however on May 1, 1969, the Unionist Party preferred the more orthodox choice of Major James Chichester-Clark (now Lord Moyola). Faulkner joined his administration as Minister for Development, and later had the task of reorganizing local government.

His doubts and misgivings about a programme of civil reform under pressure of disorders were almost certainly genuine, and they were resolved in favour of reform largely because Faulkner became persuaded that the economic development of the province, which he had so successfully stimulated and in which he took pride, was dependent on a policy of conciliation. From then onwards he was dependably on the side of civil reform.

Almost two years later in 1971 Major Chichester-Clark resigned in deteriorating conditions of violence and political intransigence and the Unionist Party elected Brian Faulkner as its leader. He was then 50.

His powers of political management and his talent for fluent and trenchant public communication gave the Stormont Government an air of renewed competence. He also made good his words of conciliation towards the Roman Catholic community by making an offer to their political representatives which was large by the measure of that time. He proposed, to go with the reform of local government, a system of functional Parliamentary committees to oversee administration with at least two of the four salaried chairmanships going to the opposition. The first response of the opposition was favourable, but party pressures, mistrust, and the exacerbation of terrorism and counter-terrorism, caused the Catholic politicians to decline cooperation, and a little later to remove themselves temporarily from Stormont.

In that summer the level of bombing, especially in the centre of Belfast, increased alarmingly and Faulkner came under the lash of hard Unionists just as his predecessors had done. In August he did what had long been contemplated and ordered the internment of suspected subversives. The decision was his, although he took it after advice from the security chiefs and consultation with the Home Secretary.

Mr Heath and his colleagues in London began to doubt the capacity of Stormont to govern. Faulkner was called to London in March, 1972, to hear the Cabinet's proposals for the province. They included the appointment of a Secretary of State and the transfer to Westminster of statutory and executive responsibility for law and order. That he would not yield, believing that it would be seen by the IRA and others as a first and major step on the road to a terrorist victory, and that it would leave the Government of Northern Ireland bereft of any real authority. Faulkner and his colleagues offered their resignation. It was accepted and the Stormont Parliament and Government were suspended.

In the immediate aftermath of the prorogation of Stormont, Faulkner identified himself with the public expressions of unionist outrage. But he was soon counselling moderation, first by refusing to countenance any campaign of civil disobedience and then by a readiness to inspect the ideas for a reconstituted provincial government which Mr Whitelaw, the Secretary of State, was beginning to float.

When the proposal for a new form of provincial government, reduced in status and including as the centre-piece an executive in which representatives of both communities in Ulster would be seated, had been enacted, Faulkner led a diminished Unionist Party into the elections for the new Assembly. There had been prominent defections from the party and the consolidation of a block of unionist opinion which would have no compromise with Mr Whitelaw's power-sharing ideas. Just before the election Faulkner's Unionists were constrained to issue a statement saying that they would not be prepared to participate in government "with any whose primary object is to break the union with Great Britain". That assurance led afterwards to accusations of broken faith, when the Faulkner Unionists showed readiness to join with the Social Democratic and Labour Party in the new executive. Faulkner's reply was that the SDLP had given adequate assurances that it would work within the new constitution so long as it was endorsed by a majority in the province.

The Assembly elections of May, 1973, returned a majority in favour of reaching an accommodation within the terms of the new constitution. But there was an ominously large block of irreconcilable "loyalist" members. It required a further round table conference to get an agreed executive. This took place at Sunningdale in December, 1973, and was attended by the British and Irish Prime Ministers as well as leaders of the participating politicians from Belfast. In the end it was on Faulkner that most pressure was put to make concessions – a serious misjudgment on the part of Mr Cosgrave and Mr Heath since Faulkner, who was the pivot of the new construction, was also the least securely supported in his own political constituency. In particular the insistence on a Council of Ireland for which growing executive powers were envisaged proved fatal to the new Executive's chances of survival.

No sooner had the Executive opened shop in January than Faulkner lost his party in the country, when the council of the Unionist party left him no option but to resign its leadership. He set about putting together a party of his own, in which he had as little success as might be expected. In spite of that the Executive got off to a good start with colleagues from across the sectarian divide working well together.

In May a unionist organization springing from the Belfast working class threatened a strike in protest against the form being given to the Council of Ireland, which was seen as a first step on the road to Irish unification. Late – too late – changes were agreed removing the most offensive features of the Council, but the strike went ahead, accompanied by some intimidation and strong-arm menaces in the streets. It spread with remarkable rapidity, embracing key workers in the public utilities. The Army, which judged the task unachievable, was not ordered to break the strike or service the city. The Executive was beleaguered and impotent. Mr Merlyn Rees, the Secretary of State, felt unable to reinforce it, and on May 28 Faulkner and his party colleagues resigned and the Executive collapsed.

That was the end of Faulkner's effective political career. He retained, however, an admirable consistency of view in his eclipse, and when he spoke on the affairs of Ulster he spoke in his familiar tones of moderation and firmness. In August of last year he bowed out of Ulster's political life. He was made a life peer in the New Year honours.

Horsemanship was an abiding interest with Faulkner. He hunted regularly in the countryside of Co Down, where he lived, and was an MFH. He married in 1951 Lucy Barbara Ethel, daughter of William Forsythe. They had two sons and a daughter.

PROFESSOR FRANCES MORAN

16 NOVEMBER 1977

PROFESSOR FRANCES ELIZABETH MORAN, who for 30 years was Professor and then Regius Professor of Laws at Trinity College, Dublin, died on October 7 at the age of 83. She was a woman of dominant and attractive personality who achieved success in a country which still has rather old-fashioned ideas about the place of women in society.

Born on December 6, 1893, the second daughter of Senator James Moran, she was educated at Dominican College and Trinity before being called to the Irish Bar in 1924, at which she took silk in 1941. In 1925 she was appointed to the first of a succession of posts in the Law School at Trinity. In 1932 she became Professor of Equity at the King's Inns and in 1934 was appointed Professor of Laws at Trinity. From these two positions she dominated Irish legal education, and won a place of peculiar respect and affection in the hearts not only of lawyers but of Trinity graduates in general. In 1944 she was made Regius Professor at Trinity, holding the chair until 1963. She retired from the King's Inns professorship in 1968.

Fran Moran's lectures were rigorous affairs. She liked to begin at 9 am, and on the stroke of the hour her petite figure, beautifully groomed, and clad in a rather formidable black silk garment, mounted the rostrum. A few well-directed questions on such topics as the Rule in Shelley's Case and the Contingent Remainders Act, 1887, exposed the ignorance of the class, whose members were then quite content to accept an account of the law of property dictated at paralyzing speed. These lectures were not marked by slavish adherence to the latest research, but rather taught the virtues of accuracy and precision. Sloppiness in law or in the use of English was not tolerated. As she took a keen, if somewhat selective, interest in the lives of her pupils, and was always well-informed, the future lawyer might also find that any deviation from the high standards of behaviour to be expected of a member of a learned profession was rebuked in some scorching phrase of the kind which comes easily to citizens of Dublin assessing each other's conduct.

Acquaintance revealed the mellow side of her character. Like all Irish people, she loved a social occasion, and was an indefatigable attender at Trinity Week parties – always adorned in a very gay, but never unsuitable hat. To a favoured few she would dispense sherry, cigarettes, and legal gossip with a lavish hand in her own college rooms. She was always receptive to new ideas, and surprisingly tolerant of the changes suggested to her by the junior members of her staff. Most suitably, she became the first woman to sit on the Board of the College. Her taste for adventure led her to attend the Nuremberg Trials (her comments on judges, counsel, and prisoners would have been an addition to international law and history if anyone had collected them), and also to undertake some world tours for the International Federation of University Women, of which she became President.

MICHEÁL Mac LIAMMÓIR

Doyen of the Dublin stage

8 MARCH 1978

MICHEÁL MAC LIAMMÓIR, the Irish actor, author, director and designer, died on March 6. He was 78.

No one on the Dublin stage of the past half century had been more conspicuous. Creatively volatile and relishing talk – there the Irish counterpart of Compton Mackenzie – he spent his life in the service of the theatre. Once he remembered how a Galway landlady, expressing it to the last, silky vowel, had told him of a piano tuner's "gorgeous shower of fingers". Mac Liammóir's life was a gorgeous shower of surprises; ready for stage adventure, he acted classical parts by the score – Hamlet, Romeo, Othello and Iago, Goethe's Faust, Ibsen's Brand – travelled the world, described in Gaelic and English his work and his journeys, and to the end, even when his eyesight had failed, was actively engaged. His last book, *Enter A Goldfish* (1977), mixed autobiography and fiction.

In Dublin where he was a loved figure – in 1973 he became a Freeman of the City and received an honorary degree from Trinity College – he leaves his memorial in the Gate Theatre, established in 1928 with Hilton Edwards, his lifelong companion; there he was involved with 300 productions. He was familiar, too, on the London stage, especially in one-man performances where he talked through the evening in a voice like fine claret. He never quite lost, in tone or aspect, his early romantic fervour. The autobiographical books, particularly *All For Hecuba*, do more justice to him than his plays (such as *Ill Met By Moonlight*) which could be blurred.

Born at Cork, on October 25, 1899, he was a child actor making a London debut, as Alfred Willmore, in 1911 in a play called *The Goldfish*.* Noel Coward, aged 10, was Prince Mussel. Thence he went to Sir Herbert

* His Irish birth was a myth fostered by himself. Alfred Wilmore was his real name and he was wholly English. ed.

237

Tree at His Majesty's (Young MacDuff, Oliver Twist) and also to revivals of *Peter Pan*. Wanting to be a painter, he studied at the Slade, and lived abroad. Returning to Ireland, he joined (1927) the touring Shakespeare company of his brother-in-law, Anew McMaster; directed at the Galway Gaelic Theatre (1928); and then began his Dublin half century.

From the record of a life of myriad parts we can select a Hamlet (London, 1935), a suavely chill Brack in the Hammersmith *Hedda Gabler* of 1954; the superb de Moura in *The Hidden King* (Edinburgh, 1957); and the renowned one-man entertainments. The best were *The Importance of Being Oscar* (1960), taking Wilde from Bunthorne days to the last dying crackle of wit; and *I Must Be Talking To My Friends* (1963), a biography of Ireland from the Saints and Scholars to the modern world. He was Iago in the Orson Welles film of *Othello* (1949).

* * *

PROFESSOR F. S. L. LYONS

Perceptive Irish historian

24 SEPTEMBER 1983

PROFESSOR F. S. L. LYONS, who died in Dublin on September 21 at the age of 59 after a short illness, was formerly Provost of Trinity College, Dublin and the foremost Irish historian of his generation. At the time of his death he had not completed the official biography of William Butler Yeats on which he had been working since 1974. In this and other respects Irish historical scholarship has been greatly diminished by his death.

Francis Stewart Leland ("Lee") Lyons was of Irish Protestant stock, part Church of Ireland, part Presbyterian. He was born in London-derry where his father was a bank manager; was sent to school at Dover College in England and then at the High School in Dublin; and read History at Trinity College, Dublin, where he subsequently became a Fellow and lecturer.

In 1964 he was appointed first Professor of Modern History in the University of Kent at Canterbury and was subsequently master of Eliot College at that university. In 1974, after a keen contest, he was elected Provost of Trinity College, Dublin. He was a Fellow of the British Academy and of the Royal Society of Literature.

Lyons was a prolific writer. In his early work he studied the old Irish Nationalist Party and his life of John Dillon, the party's last leader, was a splendid sustained portrait of a melancholy, dedicated patriot. Even if there is an excess of detail in places, this work has a quality of sympathy for the subject which makes it an even finer biography than his more acclaimed work on Charles Stewart Parnell.

Through his work on Dillon and the Irish Parliamentary Party Lyons gained an insight into, and a respect for, Catholic Nationalist Ireland to which he was alien by background and upbringing. This aided his book *Ireland since the Famine* which is the definitive work of modern Irish history. It is authoritative, dispassionate, impartial and always lucid.

But behind the cool professional historian there lurked the Protestant Irishman in search of an identity. This found some expression in Lyons's Ford lectures delivered in Oxford in 1978 and published under the title: *Culture and Anarchy in Ireland*. In them he spoke of the anarchy of the mind and heart that had beset Ireland, an anarchy which sprang from the collision of seemingly irreconcilable cultures, unable to live together or to live apart, caught inextricably in the web of their tragic history.

This theme of cultural identity, especially of the Anglo-Irish, was of course central to the study of William Butler Yeats which Lyons undertook in 1974. So keen was he to complete this task that he resigned as Provost in 1981, three years before his term had run, so as to devote himself exclusively to it.

Lyons brought the same competence that characterized his historical work to his other activities. He was a fine squash player, a capable public speaker and a sound administrator. He was unlucky in becoming Provost at a time when the college was more beset with problems than opportunities but he applied himself dutifully to the task and even undertook fund-raising tours abroad which cannot have been congenial to him.

But those who expected that he would make a dramatic impact as Provost misjudged the man and perhaps the potential of the office. In manner Lyons, though always pleasant, was reserved and correct, not revealing much about his deeper feelings. This precluded intimacy, and it may also have contributed to the fact that he did not make much impression outside the university world.

There were none, however, who came in contact with Lyons who did not admire this shy, honest, dedicated man, accomplishing so much so well in a relatively short life, and remaining unspoilt by the honours his work brought him.

Lyons married in 1964 Jennifer McAllister. He is survived by her and by their two sons.

ANITA LESLIE

8 NOVEMBER 1985

ANITA LESLIE, the writer, who died at Oranmore Castle, Co Galway, on November 5, aged 72, represented all that was most captivating and individual about the Anglo-Irish aristocracy.

The only daughter of Sir Shane Leslie, she was related to the Churchill family and her many books included best-selling biographies of Winston Churchill's mother, Jennie, and of her cousin, Randolph Churchill. An *Irish Times* reviewer caught the atmosphere of her life well in writing, "... if Somerville and Ross, J. P. Donleavy and Caroline Blackwood all sat down together to write the Great Irish Novel, they might evoke something like the world of Anita Leslie." Her childhood was spent at her ancestral home, Castle Leslie, at Glaslough, Co Monaghan, and she was educated by 14 governesses and seven schools. A brief career on the stage, as a "Cochran Young Lady", was succeeded by an even briefer one training horses, an abiding love of her life: she was later Joint Master of the Galway Blazers. Her wartime service was spent first with the MTC in South Africa and Egypt, and then as Editor of a forces newspaper in the Middle East where (in between cajoling non-English-speaking compositors and hectic chases from Turkey to the Euphrates) she met her future husband, the submarine commander and later lone round-the-world sailor, Bill King. Determined to see active service, in 1944 she took the only step possible for this and volunteered for the French Army as an ambulance-driver. For her bravery in the advance on Germany she was twice awarded the Croix de Guerre. Anita Leslie always wrote from the inside, both as a member of the vanishing aristocratic world she so affectionately chronicled, and as a deeply intuitive judge of character. Many of her books were about members of her own family: apart from *Jennie* and *Cousin Randolph*, she wrote *The Fabulous Leonard Jerome*, *Cousin Clare* (a biography of Clare Sheridan), and *Mr Frewen of England*. Among her best known books were *Edwardians in Love*, a brilliant portrait of the Prince of Wales's set, the official biography of Francis Chichester, and two fascinating auto-biographies, *The Guilt and the Gingerbread* and *A Story Half Told*. All her books were characteristic of her generous spirit: anecdotal, shrewd, funny, and so full of life that they were sometimes – in manuscript at least – somewhat disorganized. She described how, after a day spent hunting, she would "hanker for that silent corner in my turret where I left all those papers weighted with stones, and crave to get back to that carefully documented chaos which I alone understand and which everyone is begged not to touch." Anita Leslie had a rare gift for friendship, and those lucky enough to share it would be bombarded with superb letters, sometimes three in the same post, full of stories, asides and exclamation marks, and written at all angles on the paper in spidery long-hand. She was extraordinarily sympathetic to, and always fascinated by, generations younger than her own, and she took great delight in her family and grandchildren.

FREDERICK H. BOLAND

Irish voice at the UN

8 DECEMBER 1985

DR FREDERICK BOLAND, who died on December 4, aged 81, was Irish Ambassador in London from 1950 to 1956.

The outstanding Irish diplomat of his time, he was a former President of the General Assembly of the United Nations, and Chancellor of the University of Dublin (Trinity College), from 1964 to 1982.

Born in 1904, Boland was the son of H. P. Boland a civil servant. He had an outstanding career first at Merchant Taylor's School, at Clongowes Wood and finally at Trinity College, Dublin, where he took his BA and in 1925 his LLB. He held the coveted office of Auditor of the College Historical Society.

Unlike many of his generation in the still very unionist Trinity of the 1920s, he decided to make his life in Ireland. After two years as a Rockefeller Scholar at American universities he joined the newly fledged Irish Diplomatic Service. He served at the League of Nations and helped to draft some of de Valera's memorable pre-war speeches.

He was Assistant Secretary of the Department during the difficult war years when Ireland remained neutral despite considerable external pressure. Except for a brief period after Dunkirk, he advocated that neutral Ireland should go as far as possible to accommodate Britain and her allies and so helped to counteract the Anglophobia of Joseph Walshe, the Head of the Department.

In 1946 Boland succeeded Walshe. In this role he had a formative influence on the development of the Irish Foreign Service. He resisted pressure for outside appointments, preferring to find recruits among existing civil servants, and so created the sound if unspectacular corps that has served the Republic up to the present day.

In 1950 Boland replaced Winston Churchill's friend, John Dulanty, as Ambassador to the Court of St James. His term was set in difficult circumstances, with the aftermath of the Irish withdrawal from the Commonwealth in 1949, and the incessant anti-partition campaign inaugurated by politicians at home.

However, Boland's pragmatic and practical approach struck a definite chord of sympathy among the official classes in Britain and served to counteract the antipathy built up as a result of political utterances. His high standard of professional expertise helped to create a more sensible image of the country he represented.

One of the triumphs of his term was de Valera's visit to Downing Street to dine with his old adversary, Winston Churchill, whom he had never met before. The two men parted friends.

In 1955, Ireland was admitted to the United Nations and in the following year Boland left London to become his country's first Permanent Representative. Once again he found himself resisting doctrinaire attitudes. A junior colleague in the Irish delegation, Conor Cruise O'Brien, wanted Ireland to pursue a neutralist foreign policy as between East and West. This approach found favour for a time with Frank Aiken, the Irish Foreign Minister, and was manifested in Ireland's support for discussion of the candidature of Communist China. Boland was, characteristically, more cautious. With some justice O'Brien likened him to the eighteenth-century Duke of Newcastle in his horror of enthusiasm.

As became the professional diplomat he was more concerned with his country's interests than her role and he had the bureaucrat's healthy respect for the realities of power. While realizing that Ireland's anti-colonial past made her sympathetic to the emerging nations, the close ties – and potential pressures – between Ireland and certain western countries, notably Britain and the United States, should not be disregarded. Significantly when Ireland was offered the presidency of the General Assembly in 1960 as the nominee of the western group, this offer was made contingent on Boland being the man to fill the office.

In style Boland was closer to Whitehall than to the new Ireland. While this may have accounted for his tendency to pay excessive lip-service to the nationalist enthusiasms of his political masters, it was also true that he often helped to dissuade them from the excesses to which those enthusiasms might have led them.

Technically he was superb: he combined – as so few do – common sense and immense intellectual ability and was an urbane speaker with a delightful sense of the apposite phrase. The firm and polished manner in which he filled the presidency of the United Nations in a session made difficult by Khrushchev's visit in the aftermath of the U-2 incident was a source of pride to an Ireland just beginning to find its feet internationally after the isolation that followed the Second World War. On one occasion he broke his gavel when he restored order after Khrushchev had banged the table with his shoe.

On his retirement from the diplomatic service in 1964, Boland was appointed a director of many Irish companies. His international reputation and sound judgment were valued assets, especially to the export-conscious.

Boland married in 1935 Frances Kelly. They had one son and four daughters. His wife, who had been an artist, was as outspoken as her husband was discreet. Their youngest daughter Eavan is one of Ireland's outstanding younger poets.

SIOBHAN McKENNA

17 NOVEMBER 1986

MISS SIOBHAN McKENNA, actress and scholar, died in Dublin yesterday at the age of 63. Her most famous role was as Shaw's St Joan, though she was also memorable in Synge, Sean O'Casey and Chekhov.

Born in Belfast on May 24, 1923, she was educated at St Louis Convent, Monaghan, and University College, Galway, where her father held the chair in mathematics. She herself took a First in English, French and Irish literature.

Gaelic was the only language she spoke at home, and as she grew up she became involved in the Gaelic theatre. Her first stage appearances were in Irish-language versions of European classics at Galway's An Taibhdhearc. She played a Gaelic Lady Macbeth and roles in O'Casey and Eugene O'Neill, as well as translating Shaw's *St Joan* – to create for herself the title role in Gaelic – and J. M. Barrie's *Mary Rose*.

In 1943 she went to Dublin and for the next few years appeared at the Abbey Theatre. There she played English-language parts, but also got the chance to tour in a number of Gaelic ones. In 1947 she made her first appearance on the London stage as Nora Fintry in *The White Steed* at the Embassy and Whitehall theatres.

From then onwards she was busy for a while in Britain. In London her roles included Regina in *Ghosts* at the Embassy (1951) and the title role in Heloise at the Duke of York's in the same year. She was Pegeen Mike in *The Playboy of the Western World* at the 1951 Edinburgh Festival, and in 1952 she had nine months at Stratford.

These performances were all well received but she came to a greater prominence with her performance of the title role in *St Joan*, at the Arts Theatre, in 1954. From the moment she made her entrance, barefoot, in a tattered red flannel dress, she held the audience spellbound.

An Irish girl was, anyway, an inspired piece of casting for the Maid of Lorraine. But in addition she brought to the part both the necessary peasant qualities, earthy and humorous, and the lofty vision of Shaw's anachronistically Protestant saint. She herself said that Joan's character was merely a reflection of her own, and it was always her favourite role. Contemporary opinion was that her performance equalled – even surpassed – that of Sybil Thorndike.

In 1955 she went to America where she made her debut at the Ethel Barrymore Theatre as Miss Madrigal in *The Chalk Garden.* The following year she played St Joan at the Sanders Theatre, Cambridge, Mass., and later came back to New York with the role. At the Phoenix Theatre it got the same awed reception as in London two years before. She did a good deal of work in North America over the next five years, appearing, among other roles, as Viola, directed by Tyrone Guthrie at Stratford, Ontario, and as Lady Macbeth, at the Cambridge, Mass., Shakespeare Festival.

She was back in Europe in 1960, touring *The Playboy of the Western World* to the Dublin, Edinburgh, Paris and Florence festivals. Pegeen Mike was another of her great roles, and her enthralling voice seemed utterly fitting for Synge's purposes. The only possible criticism was that her sheer intensity threatened to relegate whoever played Christy Mahon to oblivion. Synge's play made one of her few significant film roles.

Though she could get parts wherever she liked, she never really tore herself away from Ireland to achieve international stardom. In the opinion of some, she was not – curiously, given her undoubted literary intelligence – a good chooser of a role for herself at first reading, and found herself in too many inappropriate parts.

Certainly, Ireland remained her theatrical as well as domestic home, and Dublin was the scene of her third great role, Juno in O'Casey's play, at the Gaiety, in 1966. Appearing with Peter O'Toole and Jack McGowran, she turned in a performance that, somehow, avoided all histrionics, to produce a Juno who was unpretentious and universal.

Among landmarks in her later career were her solo shows, *Here Are Ladies* (1970), an anthology of women as seen by Irish writers from Yeats to Joyce and James Stephens; and her portrayal of Sarah Bernhardt (1977), who had been an early inspiration. This was also filmed. Her Agrippina in *Britannicus* (Lyric, Hammersmith, 1971) was also memorable.

Though passionately Irish – in youth she was the classic red-haired beauty – Siobhan McKenna was not given to political utterance. She got herself into hot water in 1959 with some remarks on the status of Northern Ireland. These drew from the then Prime Minister of the province, Lord Brookeborough, the opinion that she needed spanking, and she never again involved herself in political controversy.

She was appointed to the Council of State of the Republic of Ireland in 1975. She married, in 1946, the film actor, Denis O'Dea. He died in 1978, and she is survived by a son.

* * *

EAMONN ANDREWS

6 NOVEMBER 1987

MR EAMONN ANDREWS, hon. CBE, who died yesterday, at the age of 64, was completely a man of the television age. As sports commentator, quiz chairman, interviewer, and "host" to show business personalities, he became a national celebrity, not from the exercise of any acquired or traditional expertise but simply by virtue of being himself: charming and apparently unflappable.

He was born on December 19, 1922, the son of a Dublin carpenter. He was educated by the Christian Brothers at Synge Street, Dublin. He was a prize-winning choirboy; and, while still a schoolboy, became All Ireland juvenile boxing champion (middleweight). At the age of 16 he offered himself to Radio Eireann as a boxing commentator, and he was accepted. He continued as such, giving also commentaries on rugby and soccer, while a clerk in a Dublin insurance company. In addition, he studied acting under Ria Mooney at the Abbey, took part in plays on Radio Eireann, and had his own play, a solemn (and unsuccessful) work entitled *The Moon is Black*, produced at the Peacock.

English audiences first met him in 1949, when he toured England with the Joe Loss Band Show as chairman of a "Double or Nothing" quiz. In the following year, he took over from Stewart MacPherson as the presenter of the successful BBC quiz programme, *Ignorance is Bliss*.

It was in July 1951 that his television career proper began, as chairman of the panel game *What's My Line?* Four years later he began to run his own programme *This is Your Life* – "the unofficial honours list" – which, perhaps because of its kind-hearted, sentimental approach to its subjects, their lives and achievements, became enormously popular.

The family and friends were in on the secret; it was the "victim" and the audience who were in the dark until the last minute when Eamonn, clutching the big red book with the gold embossed inscription THIS IS YOUR LIFE, would pounce and utter to so-and-so, brogue in cheek, those immortal words; "dis is yur loife". The life, a naked biography compressed into half-an-hour, was embellished by anecdotes from all manner of acquaintance, with Aunt Ada flown in from the other side of the world for the finale, copious tears tearing down her cheeks. Early on, Eamonn himself had the red book turned on him.

When he was not pouncing he was also doing for the BBC, among other things, the children's programmes *Crackerjack!* and *Playbox*. He four times won awards as "TV Personality of the Year".

In 1960 he became chairman of Radio Eireann and helped to set up Irish television; but this did not interrupt his work on the other side of the Irish Sea.

In 1964 his contract with the BBC expired, and the Corporation took it upon itself to terminate *This is Your Life*. A disapproving Andrews moved to Independent Television as "link man" for Saturday afternoon's *The World of Sport* and as host to show business and other celebrities in *The Eamonn Andrews Show*, which, in the course of four years, slowly discovered that a Sunday evening audience was ready to accept some serious conversation as well as professional flippancy and show business gossip. The show ran throughout the 1970s and was the forerunner of similar "chat shows".

The re-organization of Independent Television in 1968 took Andrews away from sport to become the presenter of a regular week-night current affairs programme, *Today* – a job which he did for ten years. *This Is Your Life* was then resuscitated, and it ran and ran, attracting huge audiences without fail.

In 1984 Andrews' career came full circle with the revival, under his chairmanship, of the show that first made his name, *What's My Line?*

It was possible to watch Eamonn Andrews carefully for a long time without noticing the professional skill with which he worked, guiding a conversation, drawing none of the limelight to himself. It is not to do him justice simply to say that he had "the gift of the gab"; what he did was to imbue his guests with a confidence which allowed them to shine through. In this he showed an unobtrusive professionalism.

The remarkable affection which television viewers felt for Eamonn Andrews was based, however, not only on the skill of his work. It grew, too, from his genuine interest in, and friendliness for, people. These qualities made it easy for his audience to identify with him and to feel that he had taken them with him to meet and share the world of gorgeous actresses, brilliant comedians and cheerfully ebullient politicians.

Andrews was a man of considerable business interests. He was also a devout Roman Catholic, and received a Papal knighthood in 1964 for his charitable works. He never relinquished his Irish citizenship.

He married, in 1951, Grainne Bourke, who survives him with their adopted children; a son and two daughters.

SEAN MacBRIDE

Irreconcilable Irish Republican

16 JANUARY 1988

MR SEAN MACBRIDE, who died yesterday in Dublin, at the age of
83, was, in later life, a prominent international advocate of human
rights and disarmament. Before that, he had a notable career in the
Republican Movement in Ireland and was Foreign Minister in the
government which established the Republic of Ireland and which took
that country out of the Commonwealth, in 1949.

MacBride was born on January 26, 1904, the only child of the beautiful
and graceful Maud Gonne, daughter of an Englishman stationed as an
Army officer in Ireland. She had rejected the privileged Anglo-Irish
world and espoused the popular nationalist cause.

Yeats had loved her for "her pilgrim soul", but had been rebuffed.
Instead, she married Major John MacBride – "drunken, vainglorious
lout" the forlorn Yeats called him – an Irish soldier of fortune who had
fought against the British in the Boer War and who was executed for
his part in the Irish rebellion of 1916. Sean MacBride, an only child, was
always greatly influenced by his mother.

Soon after his birth, Maud left his father and took the child with
her to Paris. His first language was French, and he spoke English with
a foreign accent. After his father's execution, however, he returned to
Ireland, and went to school at Mount St Benedict, Gorey.

But he soon took up arms himself in the rebel cause, and was first
thrown in gaol in 1918, when he was only 14. He opposed the Anglo-
Irish Treaty of 1921 and took part in the subsequent civil war.

When the Republican side was defeated, he moved to London for
a time and found employment as a journalist on the High Tory *Morning
Post*. But he was back in Ireland in 1926 when Mr de Valera, followed by
the majority of former Republicans, decided to espouse constitutional

politics. MacBride opposed him, and remained active in the IRA. He was widely regarded as a sinister ruthless extremist, and he was charged with complicity in the murder, in 1927, of Kevin O'Higgins, Minister for Justice, but the charge was later dropped. He had, in fact, a perfect alibi. For a time he was chief-of-staff of the IRA.

In the late 1930s, following the adoption of a new constitution, MacBride severed his IRA connections, and turned to practise at the Irish Bar. During the Second World War, when the IRA took the German side, he achieved eminence as a defender of Republican prisoners.

After the war, he entered constitutional politics as leader of the new Clann na Poblachta Party, with a following composed of "incorrigible Celts", disgruntled IRA, and political adventurers. With the defeat of de Valera's party in the 1948 general election, MacBride became Minister for External Affairs in a coalition government. He seemed to be the coming man of Irish politics.

The new Government severed all remaining links with the Commonwealth and declared a Republic. A vigorous but rather futile propaganda campaign was launched abroad aimed at the removal of Partition, which the Attlee government had consolidated by the Ireland Act 1949.

MacBride announced that the Republic would not join NATO as long as Partition remained. What was not known at the time was that he attempted to negotiate a bilateral defence pact with the United States.

As a Foreign Minister his demeanour was suave and sophisticated. He made an important contribution to the European movement, especially in the Council of Europe. He interested himself in many subjects outside his department. The repatriation of external financial assets and the development of forestry were two of his pet themes. On the whole, his colleagues were agreeably surprised by his moderation.

In 1951, however, MacBride's position was undermined by a split within his own party. A Bill for a free State maternity service, which had been introduced by the Minister of Health, fell foul of the ubiquitous Roman hierarchy. The Minister, for whose resignation MacBride then called, resigned with several of his followers, and the Government fell.

At the subsequent general election Clann na Poblachta polled less than one-fifth of its earlier vote, and MacBride found himself a member of a party of two in the Dail. He lost his own seat in the 1957 general election – an election which he had precipitated when the Government moved against the IRA following the renewal of armed raids into Northern Ireland. This brought to an end his career in Irish politics.

He continued to practise full-time at the Bar until 1963. He was a shrewd tactician and a tireless worker, but he was neither an outstanding advocate nor an especially acute lawyer.

After he lost his seat in the Dail, he turned his attention to the international human rights movement. As Irish Foreign Minister he had helped to draw up the European Convention on Human Rights, and he was a founder member of Amnesty International, for which he did much work. In 1963 he moved to Geneva to become Secretary-General of the International Commission of Jurists, which monitored the observance of human rights world-wide.

He was appointed United Nations High Commissioner for Namibia to oversee the implementation of UN resolutions to end South African rule there. He also interested himself in disarmament and was President of the International Peace Bureau in Geneva. He received the Nobel peace prize in 1974, and the Lenin peace prize three years later – a first-time, albeit incongruous, "double".

In the last two decades of his life MacBride came to occupy a neutral position as between East and West. His one-time enthusiasm for European integration evaporated and he displayed a marked disenchantment with the United States with whom, as Foreign Minister, he had been prepared to commit Ireland to an anti-Communist military alliance. He was criticized for being more vocal in his condemnation of human rights violations when they occurred in the West or under regimes friendly to the West.

On disarmament, he indulged in the luxury of advocating ideal solutions without having to accept responsibility for the risks involved in dismantling Western defences. On Northern Ireland, while putting on record his opposition to violence, he concentrated his criticism on the alleged malpractices of the United Kingdom administration and opposed any compromise on the Republic's claim to sovereignty over the North. In 1986, he surprised many by opposing a referendum which sought to delete the prohibition of divorce from the Irish constitution. Since making his peace with the Roman Church in the 1940s he had ever after been a devout Catholic.

In all that he touched, MacBride showed extraordinary dedication and tenacity. He seemed oblivious to positions other than his own, and in argument he showed little understanding of opposing viewpoints. In his pursuit of his own ideals and objectives he did not allow himself to be diverted by personal considerations or feelings. Although he had considerable charm, this made him appear somewhat cold. If he did not spare others, he did not spare himself. He worked tirelessly without thought for any tangible reward and never hesitated to commit his own money to causes which he supported.

He married, in 1926, Catalina Bulfin, who died before him. There was one son and one daughter of the marriage.

SAMUEL BECKETT

Unassuming genius who probed the quandary of human existence

27 DECEMBER 1989

SAMUEL BECKETT, WHO died in Paris on December 22, aged 83, was one of the truly great literary figures of this century and his writings for the theatre in particular brought him universal acclaim. His plays, especially *Waiting for Godot, Endgame* and *Krapp's Last Tape*, are part of the standard repertoire in theatres round the world.

These and his novels are considered classics of modern literature as naturally a part of an educated person's experience as the works of Ibsen, Kafka or James Joyce.

Although he once declared that "the artist who gambles his being is from nowhere, and has no brothers," Samuel Barclay Beckett did possess a biography which he was characteristically modest and discreet about. His Schopenhauerian pessimism caused him to consider his birth (at Foxrock, near Dublin, on Good Friday, April 13, 1906) a calamity, and yet his early years were happy enough. His father, William Frank Beckett, a respected and well-to-do quantity surveyor, and his mother, Mary (nee Roe), were very fond of their second son, and he of them: their deaths, in 1933 and 1950 respectively, grieved him deeply.

"Willie" Beckett was a cheerful, plump man, who much enjoyed taking long walks and sharing jokes with his son, whose outstanding sporting and academic record at school and university made him, an early school-leaver himself, immensely proud. Though like all the family a practising Protestant, Beckett senior was less passionate in his belief than his wife or his elder son Frank, who succeeded him at the head of the family firm. As for Samuel's faith, this did not survive his student years, but Christian mythology was to remain a haunting motif behind his writing until the end.

255

He was sent first to Miss Ida Elsner's Academy, a Stillorgan kindergarten, and then commuted on the old "Dublin Slow and Easy" to Earlsfort House prep school. After that he went to Portora Royal School in Ulster, and Trinity College, Dublin, first as pensioner and then as Foundation Scholar.

He had an active extracurricular life, notably in the Modern Languages Society and in the chess, golf and cricket clubs. He is, in fact, one of the very few great writers to have played in first-class cricket: Wisden records his participation in the Northamptonshire versus Dublin University match in July, 1927. His first visit to France, a cycle tour of the Loire chateaux, took place in the summer of 1926.

In the BA finals examinations in Modern Literature (French and Italian) held at the end of 1927 he was placed first in the first class, winning, like Oscar Wilde before him, the distinction of a medal. He was chosen to represent Trinity in the regular scheme for exchanging Lecteurs with the Ecole Normale Superieure in Paris; he filled the two term interval by accepting a temporary teaching post at Campbell College, Belfast, and then took up his French appointment in October, 1928.

Jean-Paul Sartre was a near-contemporary at the Ecole Normale, but the two men had little contact. On the other hand, Beckett formed a close friendship with Alfred Peron, who had been Lecteur at Trinity and whose death later at the hands of the Germans affected him deeply. The major event of these years was the meeting with James Joyce. In spite of the fact that the two Irishmen differed in background (Joyce's of course was Catholic and lower-class) as well as in temperament, Joyce having an exuberance his more sombre junior lacked, their acquaintance grew into friendship based on mutual admiration and respect. Although never his secretary, Beckett helped Joyce in many ways and was at first influenced by him. He was particularly impressed by Joyce's dedication to his art, and came to share it, although his path as a writer soon diverged from his friend's.

On the expiration of his Paris contract in 1930 he returned to Dublin to take up a post as assistant in French to Professor Thomas

B. Rudmose-Brown, a cultivated and widely read man who had had a decisive role in forming his literary tastes as an undergraduate. When the short critical study of Proust (commissioned by Chatto and Windus on Richard Aldington's recommendation) appeared in 1931, Beckett seemed well-launched on the academic career which his ability naturally destined him for, and which his father very much hoped he would make a success of.

But he soon found he had no vocation for, and little skill at, university teaching. The crisis came during the Christmas vacation of 1931 when he was visiting friends in Germany, and he telegraphed his resignation. Irresponsible as the act appeared at the time, it was decisive in cutting the umbilical cord with Trinity and the Dublin circles in which a lesser man might have been content to accept the pre-eminent place his talents granted him. Not that Beckett ever denied his Irishness, or lost his respect for those Irish painters and poets, such as Jack B. Yeats, Denis Devlin and Thomas McGreevy, whose work he praised in print whenever he was given the opportunity.

The years that followed were lonely and unhappy, but they were not wasted. Beckett travelled widely in Europe, making himself an expert in the visual arts (he later used his connoisseurship to champion neglected artists like Henri Hayden and Bram van Velde), and in the major European languages and literatures. He even lived for a time in Chelsea, but Paris was the only place where he felt truly at home, and in 1937 he settled permanently in Montparnasse.

In the following year the novel *Murphy* was published in London. Although he tried subsequently to repudiate most of his early work, Beckett still considered this book the foundation stone of his oeuvre. Its publication was hardly a triumph, but a few were affected by it, notably Iris Murdoch, who read it as an undergraduate at Oxford, and who later paid homage to it in *Under the Net*.

Throughout these years Beckett eked out the annuity which his father had left him by doing literary translations, his skill in this art being highly valued by editors. The outbreak of war found him vacationing with his family in Dublin; he got back to France just in time, preferring, as he later put it, "France in war to Ireland at peace". His Eire citizenship would have protected him from molestation in occupied Paris, but influenced by Peron and his own distaste for Nazism he chose to join the Resistance. When the group was betrayed to the Gestapo, Beckett narrowly missed arrest and eventually found his way to Roussillon (Vaucluse), where he wrote his last novel in English, *Watt*. He went into hiding, bravely taking on the job of agent de liaison, classifying information about German troop movements and translating it into English for transmission across the Channel; traces of this dangerous occupation survive in the anxiety his heroes feel about "writing their report".

The liberation of France enabled Beckett to continue his annual summer visits to his family (ended only by his mother's death). It was, incidentally, a very musical family, the harpsichordist John Beckett being a younger cousin. After a harrowing spell as interpreter and store-keeper at the Irish Red Cross hospital in Saint-Lo (Normandy), Beckett resumed his Paris existence. There, he wrote, almost in an inspired trance, those works in French (later self-translated into English) on which his reputation will permanently rest: the trilogy of novels *Molloy*, *Malone Dies* and *The Unnamable*, and the play *Waiting for Godot*. Nothing he composed later, not even *Endgame* or the BBC play *All that Fall* (1957), nor the novel *How It Is* (1961), was quite to equal these earlier works in profundity, originality and imaginative power. In profundity, because the trilogy and *Waiting for Godot* probe the big questions of human existence: who are we and why are we here? In originality, because Beckett evolved a style which succeeds in balancing comedy and tragedy, the grotesque and the sublime; in fiction it made him the greatest experimenter since Joyce, in drama an innovator more radical even than Pirandello. Imaginative power, finally, because his finest work, like Kafka's, attains almost effortlessly the status of universal myth: the outcast heroes of his novels, like his two clowns waiting by a country roadside for Godot, the elusive benefactor who never arrives, are to the literature of the post-war period what Joseph K was to the world which emerged from Passchendaele and Verdun.

His masterpiece is probably *Molloy*, written in 1947, a complex novel in two parts about the psychological odyssey of a man sent to look for another and undergoing in the process a painful transformation into the social reject whom he seeks but fails to unearth anywhere except in the depths of his own soul.

In later years, while still continuing to write new drama and prose, Beckett took an increasing interest in the direction of his own plays. His productions of *Krapp's Last Tape* and *Waiting for Godot* at the Schiller-Theater in Berlin and of *Happy Days* at the Royal Court in London, were the first of many which offered fresh, authoritative readings of works which he simplified and stylized in ways other directors would not have dared.

He "loosened up" in other ways, too: his prose became increasingly autobiographical and even nostalgic in tone. In *Company*, published in 1980, he probed with candour his own complex motivations in creating so many "wearish" old men "for company", and wrote affectionately about his childhood and especially of his father, walking the hills armed with a packet of his favourite sandwiches and a flask of Scotch whisky as he waited for Mary Beckett's protracted labour to end and young Samuel to be born.

The Paris creation of *Godot* by Roger Blin in January, 1953, made Beckett world famous. The influence he exerted over the theatre, in terms both of writing and direction, was particularly important. Figures as pre-eminent as Harold Pinter and Peter Hall (director of the first British *Godot* in 1955) owe him an immense debt.

But, though universally admired and much written about (Beckett studies quickly became an academic growth industry), he accepted surprisingly few honours and then (the 1969 Nobel Prize especially) only with reluctance. A modest and unassuming man, he was courteous and generous with people he trusted and intransigent only about standards of production and translation of his writings. He refused steadfastly to don the mantle of the "great man of letters" that he undoubtedly was, and, at least as far as the press was concerned, remained a recluse to the end, because in his view literature was too serious a matter to be trifled with: he felt it grotesque to receive personal attention for giving expression to what he called "the issueless predicament of existence".

For "who may tell the tale," he wondered in his finest poem, "of the old man?/weigh absence in a scale?/mete want with a span?/the sum assess/of the world's woes?/nothingness/in words enclose?"

The answer is that Samuel Beckett did, with a wit, a humility and a compassion which will ensure his immortality.

He married Suzanne Dumesnil, a musician and teacher; they had no children. She died earlier this year.

* * *

CARDINAL O FIAICH

10 MAY 1990

CARDINAL TOMAS O FIAICH, Archbishop of Armagh, died aged 66 on May 8. He was born on November 23, 1923.

Tomas O Fiaich was the right man in the right place at tragically the wrong time. His sense of identity with the Catholic people of South Armagh, from whom he sprang and whose spiritual leader he became, could be doubted by none who knew him. It showed itself in simple habits of speech, behaviour, and leisure interests. While a Professor at the national seminary in Maynooth he spent as many weekends as he could on visits to his home parish of Crossmaglen. There he liked to assist in the work of the local clergy and to turn out in support of the county Gaelic football team. At a deeper level, his consciousness of origin stimulated much of his research as a professional historian.

Both in personality and achievement Monsignor O Fiaich seemed well fitted to undertake the pastoral care of a community among whom he was literally at home, especially at a time when Border atrocities and consequent army actions were causing severe distress in the area. What met the needs of Armagh Catholics did not necessarily serve the wider interests of the Irish Church. The very attributes which endeared him to his own people made him appear narrow-minded and one-sided on the broader stage. As Archbishop of Armagh, he was ex officio Primate of All Ireland with a national as well as a diocesan function. The Northern crisis prevented an easy merging of the two roles. Unionists, who at first welcomed the appointment of an Ulsterman with whose temperament they felt in tune, began to judge him guilty by association: they translated his concern for friends and neighbours under harassment into a half-condonation of violence. In the overheated atmosphere of suspicion permeating so much of Northern life, even the Cardinal's interest in Irish and his use of the Irish version of his name struck some unionists as blatant allegiance to an ethos not only alien but hostile as well. Catholics in the South and West of the country naturally felt no antagonism of this kind, but the Cardinal was not well-known to them and they tended to see him sometimes as a spokesman for the Northern minority rather than as the Church leader charged with speaking in the name of all Irish Catholics.

These assessments were simplistic and unjust, as also was the English inclination to write him off as an "impossible" Irishman. The Cardinal's *curriculum vitae* helps to redress the balance. He was born at Crossmaglen, County Armagh, the second son of Annie and Patrick Fee (who used the anglicized form of the surname). His father was principal of the nearby Cregganduff elementary school and here Tomas received his early education before going on to Saint Patrick's College, Armagh, and ultimately in 1940 to Maynooth, where he took a First in Celtic Studies.

He was ordained in Wexford in 1948. His potential as a scholar had already been identified. Instead of assigning him to a parish, the Armagh diocesan authorities sent him to University College, Dublin, to study early and medieval Irish history. Father O Fiaich took his MA in 1950, again gaining First Class honours, and then went on to Louvain to acquire a licentiate in historical science summa cum laude and a thorough competence in French and German. After serving briefly as a curate in Moy, County Tyrone, he became Lecturer in Modern History at Maynooth in 1953 and Professor of Modern History in 1959.

From this base he took part in a number of extracurricular activities. He perfected his knowledge of the Irish language on successive holidays in Donegal and was chosen to be president of the association for Irish-speaking priests, Cumann na Sagart. He launched the competition Glor na nGael to promote the use of Irish in towns and villages throughout the country. State recognition came when the government invited him to chair the Commission on the Restoration of Irish and later to be chairman of Comhairle na Gaeilge, the advisory council to oversee implementation of the Commission's findings. For many years he maintained a prolific output of lectures and articles on medieval Irish history.

In 1964 his fellow-graduates elected Father O Fiaich to the Senate of the National University of Ireland. He became President of Maynooth in 1974 at a difficult time for the old institution, now part seminary-cum-papal university and part secular university within the Irish state system.

On August 23, 1977, Pope Paul VI nominated him to be the 113th Comharba Phadraig or successor of Saint Patrick in the See of Armagh. It was the first time in 110 years that a priest not already a bishop was elevated to the Primacy. At the consistory of June 1979 Pope John Paul II conferred the Cardinal's hat on Archbishop O Fiaich.

His episcopacy began on a fresh note, and indeed on an unusual platform, for an Irish Catholic Bishop. In a lengthy interview published by the *Belfast Telegraph* he suggested that the time had come for the Republic to consider adopting a new constitution. His reasoning was ecumenical: "a very short basic document", he said, would serve as a constitution acceptable to Catholics and Protestants alike.

Under his chairmanship, the Irish Bishops were to make a number of progressive statements on international questions such as nuclear disarmament and the exploitation of the Third World. Economic measures at home, leading to unemployment and other social ills, were also criticized and the problems posed by sexual relationships in the modern world were spoken of at least in a caring tone.

As President of the Irish episcopal conference, however, Cardinal O Fiaich conspicuously lacked the skill of his predecessor, Cardinal William Conway, in anticipating events. No agreed position had been formulated by the Bishops in advance of the campaign in 1983 to write a prohibition of abortion into the Republic's constitution. The Bishops were similarly left floundering in 1985 when the government introduced a measure to remove anomalies in the law regulating the sale of contraceptives. On each occasion a late intervention by Cardinal O Fiaich struck a moderately liberal note. He pointed out on behalf of the episcopal conference that Catholics could, in good faith, oppose constitutional change without incurring the charge of approving abortion.

However, in 1986, when the government proposed a further constitutional change which would have removed the ban on divorce in the Republic, the Cardinal, in the name of all the Bishops, advised against it while still allowing for Catholics within limits to adopt, in conscience, views different from those of their Church leaders.

The commitment to practical ecumenism continued. At the annual Glenstal conference and elsewhere the Cardinal used to acknowledge the obligation on Catholics, as the largest body of Irish Christians, to make the greatest effort and if need be, the greatest concession in pursuit of the ecumenical ideal. Sadly, the Cardinal failed to carry this commitment very far in inter-church dialogue, in theological discussion or in the pastoral practice of the Roman Catholic Church in Ireland.

It would be wrong to suppose that foot dragging on ecumenism in Ireland has been confined to the Roman Catholic Church. The reformed churches, especially elements among mainstream Northern Presbyterians (i.e. not merely the Paisleyites), remain slow to move. Protestant caution, in turn, was in some degree stimulated by the Primate's public appeals on behalf of Northern Catholics when he felt they were meeting less than just treatment from the authorities. In August 1980, he spoke in outraged terms about conditions in the Maze prison. A number of prisoners were involved in the so-called "dirty protest" at the time. The Northern Ireland Office, unionist opinion and the governing committee of the Presbyterian Church in Ireland rejected the Catholic Primate's criticism on the ground that the prisoners were the authors of their own misfortune and were in any event convicted criminals.

O Fiaich did not retract. His basic position remained that special court procedures raised a doubt concerning convictions and that an argument over what clothes a prisoner should wear did not merit exacerbation of this condition by the withdrawal of all privileges. The vigorous plea, so typical of Tomas O Fiaich's loyalty to his own community, may have been overstated. It did not, however, justify the suggestion, widely heard among British as well as Northern Ireland commentators, that he was somehow equivocal in his attitude towards the IRA and other perpetrators of violence. He condemned violence time and again. This continued to be the case when he tried to explain why some people voted for Sinn Fein and when he campaigned for the release of persons who, he believed, had been convicted wrongly of IRA bombing outrages in Britain.

Tomas O Fiaich's tragedy was to be so patently himself, a warm-hearted Irishman, anxious to be fair to all but especially conscious of the ties of culture and history binding together his own Catholic people. His humane instincts would in calmer times have made him a lovable, fatherly figure. In an age of trouble and division, these qualities situated him inevitably on one side of the fence, so that his honest aspiration for a united Ireland was assumed by some to render him untrustworthy.

ERNEST WALTON

29 JUNE 1995

ERNEST WALTON, NUCLEAR PHYSICIST and winner of the Nobel Prize for Physics, died in Belfast on June 25 aged 91. He was born on October 6, 1903.

In the role of Erasmus Smith's Professor of Natural and Experimental Science from 1947 to 1974 at Trinity College, Dublin, Ernest Walton devoted his exceptional gifts largely to the teaching of science to undergraduates. But in the history of science he will always be associated with the achievement of nuclear transmutation which, in the early 1930s, ushered in a new era of physics.

It was in the spring of 1932 that Walton, together with his colleague John Cockcroft, managed to split the atom artificially, using accelerated atomic particles. Working from the Cavendish Laboratory in Cambridge, the two had constructed a 12ft high apparatus, consisting of electricity transformers, thick glass cylinders, vacuum pumps and car batteries.

The machine could convert mains electricity into a high voltage capable of accelerating a beam of protons inside an evacuated glass tube. One morning, when Walton had managed to crank the power of the machine up to 600,000 volts, the highest voltage he had yet achieved, he directed the particle beam onto a target containing lithium, also inside a vacuum tube. This was the moment when an atomic nucleus was first artificially split; the protons smashed into the lithium nuclei which then split into two nuclei of helium, the resulting helium nuclei producing tiny sparks on a detecting screen behind the target. Walton and Cockcroft published their findings several days later in a short letter in *Nature* under the unassuming title "Disintegration of Lithium by Swift Protons". The announcement generated huge excitement among the scientific community.

Ernest Thomas Sinton Walton was born in Dungarvan, Co Waterford, the son of a Methodist minister from Northern Ireland, and

Walton himself remained unmistakably an Ulsterman. He went to the Methodist College, Belfast, and in 1922 gained a mathematical sizarship at Trinity College, Dublin. A contemporary of Walton, A. J. McConnell, was to be a future Provost of Trinity College, and both were elected to scholarships in 1924. In his finals, Walton gained the gold medal in experimental science and took the Brooke prize. The award of the FitzGerald Scholarship at the same time enabled him to turn to research.

When his postgraduate work brought him a travelling scholarship, Walton was attracted to Cambridge by Lord Rutherford's research at the Cavendish Laboratory. Rutherford formed the highest opinion of him and when they were joined by John Cockcroft, Rutherford set the two younger men to work together, with momentous results.

Rutherford had achieved in 1919 the conversion of the nuclei of nitrogen atoms into oxygen by bombarding them with alpha particles. It was an epoch-making experiment, the first in which, by human agency, one kind of atom had been changed into another: the realization of the alchemist's dream. The high energy particles used in these experiments were of natural origin.

Walton then turned to the production of an intense stream of bombarding particles. With Cockcroft he devised the apparatus now in the Science Museum at South Kensington by which the first transformation, in 1932, by entirely artificial means of one kind of matter into another was effected: lithium and hydrogen were converted into helium. It was an astonishing feat with the resources then available and, in spite of later technical advances, the "Cockcroft-Walton accelerator" is still used today.

Walton was now overwhelmed with opportunities to pursue his experimental work on a larger scale. But he was a modest man who disliked publicity, and when he was asked to return to a fellowship at Trinity he did not hesitate to take up the work of a university teacher. His decision surprised other scientists, and the appearance from time to time of his important but infrequent papers revived the impression that he had turned his back on great opportunities.

But if Walton felt any regrets he never expressed them. He wanted to teach and he was quite prepared for the administrative routine into which a college fellow is inevitably drawn. Indeed, because of his overriding loyalty and commitment to his college, he did not take up an invitation to participate in the Manhattan Project.

He was an exceptional teacher, whose lectures were models of lucid exegesis, brilliantly illustrated by demonstration experiments. Entirely free from affectation or conceit, he was courteous, patient and in every way helpful with his students, whose complete respect he commanded.

Apart from university administration, Walton was drawn increasingly into public service, partly because of Eamon de Valera's high regard for him. To his work with the Dublin Institute of Cosmic Physics and learned societies was added membership of many public commissions and committees. Appointed to his chair in 1947, he directed the work of the School of Experimental Science towards nuclear physics.

The prohibitive cost of nuclear projects limited his range in research, but Walton, who was to become president of the Irish Pugwash Group, believed profoundly that peaceful applications of nuclear energy, could procure immeasurable benefits for humanity.

Not long after becoming a fellow of Trinity, Walton was awarded the Hughes medal of the Royal Society. In 1951 his colleagues learnt with great satisfaction that he and Cockcroft were to share the Nobel Prize for Physics. This belated recognition of his work pleased him enormously, and when he returned with the prize and dined with his colleagues in Dublin, he spoke with unusual animation about his work and experiences. But the natural modesty remained and no man did less to seek the limelight or to court popular applause.

Walton retired in 1974 and went to live in Belfast, but he remained a frequent visitor to the physics department and college to which he dedicated most of his life.

In 1934 he married Winifred Isabel Wilson who predeceased him in 1983. He is survived by his two sons and two daughters, three of whom followed their father into careers in physics.

MOLLY KEANE

23 APRIL 1996

MOLLY KEANE, AUTHOR, died yesterday aged 91. Born on July 20, 1904, a lingering representative of a bygone age, she captured in her novels the lost world of the Anglo-Irish gentry. Marooned in their crumbling Georgian houses, overlooking their ever-shrinking demesnes, they lived a life of decaying splendour of horses and hunting, cocktails and couture curiously insulated from the growing political turbulence of their times. If "the Troubles" pricked at the edges of their consciousness at all, they certainly never became troublesome enough to put off a tennis party.

But this burnished reflection of a fading past was not the real subject of Molly Keane's novels. Her memories had a lacerating edge, and beneath the glittering surfaces of a carefree world lay the shadows of tribulation and despair, the hopelessness and disappointment of human life. Handsome heroes grow gradually mad, plain heroines love with dull desperation, middle-aged governesses decay, lonely and unloved.

Molly Keane wrote her first 12 novels under the pseudonym M. J. Farrell. She proved herself an acerbic mistress of her form before lapsing into a nearly thirty-year silence in which she neither published nor wrote. When she took up her pen again she was in her late seventies. *Good Behaviour* was published under her real name in 1981 and was nominated for the Booker Prize, but beaten by what she called "that awful Indian book", *Midnight's Children*. It was televised by the BBC the next year. She followed it with two more novels, both, as she put it, scavenging on her past experience, *Time After Time* (1983) and *Loving and Giving* (1988).

Mary Nesta Skrine, always known as Molly, grew up in Co Wexford. In many ways, hers was the idyllic youth typical of the Ascendancy society of 1920s Ireland. Her father was a classic Anglo-Irish squire:

a horseman to whom a hard day's hunting meant a hard day's work. Like Papa in *Good Behaviour*, he conversed almost entirely in variants of "Whoa, steady", Keane would later recall. Her mother, by contrast, was something of an intellectual. She wrote reviews for *Blackwood's Magazine*, studied Italian and was "almost a good poet". Yet despite their differences in character, her parents were completely caught up in one another and abandoned their children to their own devices and the hired ministrations of a small army of servants.

The young Molly was described as "a wild red rip". She did not manage life at all, she said, she flung herself at it, and as a result was an extremely unlikeable child. She argued incessantly with her older sister, Susan, who was a better horsewoman at an earlier age, and thus a favourite of their father's, but she craved the affection of her brother Charlie, and would follow beside his pony from an early age, precariously astraddle an old grey donkey. Between them the children got through seven governesses, one of whom was sacked for divulging the facts of life. But, in the sporting field, where things mattered most, they were kept more sternly in control. A girl's upbringing was hardly less rigorous than a boy's and they were expected to set themselves unflinchingly at the toughest fences and never to cry when they were thrown.

Molly went to school for the first time when she was 14. It was a prim institution for young ladies and she was horribly homesick for her country life. The other girls detested her, she later said, and so she began to write, completing more than half of her first novel before she left, although it was not published until eight years later, when she was 26.

It was while she was at school that the angry reality of Irish politics finally impinged on their blinkered lives. Members of the Irish Republican Army came to burn down her parents' house. Her father got hold of an old bayonet and tried to attack them, but the men politely requested him to desist, protesting that they did not want to have to shoot him. They then proceeded to set fire to their home, though, with a sort of clumsy courtesy they approached her mother as she watched from a haycock, bringing her an antique wine cooler. They did not know what it was, but thought it might contain her jewels.

Molly kept her writing a secret as long as she could. "Young men would have been afraid of you if they thought you could read, let alone write," she said. Her first novel, *The Knight of Cheerful Countenance*, a gauche romance, was accepted by Mills and Boon, and published under the pseudonym of M. J. Farrell, a name which she chose after seeing it over an Irish pub while she was returning from hunting.

Molly carried on writing mainly because she wanted money to boost her clothing allowance. "I was mad for gaiety," she said. "Glamour was what I went in for, in clothes and in people." She met her future husband, a gentleman farmer called Bobby Keane, at a hunt ball. He was four years her junior and they waited some time until they got married in 1938, although they would regularly sleep together at friends' houses or on holidays abroad. He had a slight stammer, so they married in London to avoid the long speech-making of an Irish affair.

Moving to a house in the Blackwater Valley, Molly Keane at first lived very much the sort of life her parents had before her. They hunted and played poker, and hired a starchy nanny to look after the children though she was in the end traded in for a lovely Irish cow. All this while Keane continued to write under her pseudonym, in the space of 20 years turning out 12 novels. She also wrote plays. In her teens she would spend months at a time with a couple named Perry in Co Tipperary. It was with their son Perry that she wrote a play, *Spring Meeting*, produced in 1938 by "Binkie" Beaumont and directed, like all her subsequent plays, by John Gielgud. It gave Margaret Rutherford her first major West End role, and was highly successful.

However, in 1946 Keane's husband died after undergoing heart surgery. He was only 37. Her writing dwindled. "I stopped", she said, "because writing makes you think and I didn't want to think." Besides, her brand of elegant wit was going out of fashion. When John Osborne's *Look Back in Anger* was staged at the same time as one of her plays she reaped scalding reviews and her last two plays flopped. On top of this she had been left with the upbringing of two daughters as well as a large country house to run. Keane moved to England for five years while her daughters were at school but later returned to Ireland, where she bought a smaller house overlooking Ardmore Bay in Waterford.

Keane's decision to start writing again in the late 1970s was typically pragmatic: she needed to make money and she finished *Good Behaviour* in 1978. Sir William Collins, who had published all her previous work, was distinctly unimpressed: it was far too black a comedy, he said. It was Peggy Ashcroft, who had come to stay with her old friend, who persuaded Keane to persist with it.

Keane was renowned for her lingering descriptions of food, whether the snipe toasted over the nursery fire, with blood seeping onto buttered toast, or the rabbit mousse which chokes "Mummie" to death in *Good Behaviour*. In 1985 she published a cookbook, *Nursery Cooking*.

Right into old age she remained a picture of bright-eyed sweetness with the smile of a bashful girl at a party and a taste for simple country clothes. She never lost her intelligent but mischievous sense of humour or her sound good sense. She often smiled over the fuss made of her in her old age, and firmly refused to write her autobiography.

The Irish Government named her one of "Ireland's Treasures" for her past work which brought her a useful stipend.

Molly Keane is survived by her two daughters.

MICHAEL O'HEHIR

30 NOVEMBER 1996

MICHAEL O'HEHIR, Irish sports broadcaster, died in Dublin on November 24 aged 76. He was born in the same city on June 2, 1920.

Michael O'Hehir was best known in Britain for his broadcasts of the Grand National. For nearly 40 years, beginning in 1946, he took up the commentary at the approach to Becher's Brook and continued until the horses had cleared Valentines. He was, in the words of his colleague Peter O'Sullevan, a charismatic commentator. His most memorable performance was at the 1967 race when what he called "a right pile-up" occurred at the fence after Becher's, from which Foinavon emerged to win at 100–1.

O'Hehir also covered other big races for the BBC, notably the Cheltenham Festival, where Irish steeplechasers have enjoyed much success down the years. Towards the end of his career Queen Elizabeth the Queen Mother sought him out and in conversation impressed him with her knowledge of the breeding of the great Irish horse Arkle. He recalled that he was the object of some criticism from his more republican-minded friends for hobnobbing with a member of the Royal Family, but he was glad to have met her.

O'Hehir was responsible for bringing into Irish and then British racing the American practice of on-course commentaries. He was the leading racing commentator on Irish radio and television and also did commentaries for the American broadcasting network NBC. In the 1950s he provided racing tips on a radio programme sponsored by the Irish hospital sweepstake, which ran the greatest racing lottery of the day and for which tickets were bought widely, although illegally, in Britain and the United States. The wags called him "Mick the Liar". "Jack the Liar" was the man who provided the weather forecast on the Irish radio.

Although he attained international renown as a racing commentator,

O'Hehir's first loves were the games of hurling and Gaelic football. He was taken on by Radio Eireann to do commentaries in 1938 when he was only 18. Through the succeeding years in pre-electrification rural Ireland, whole communities congregated on Sunday afternoons at the houses of the few who had battery wirelesses to hear his commentaries on matches with their vivid word pictures. It provided much-needed entertainment.

It helped that, despite his Dublin upbringing, O'Hehir's voice was as much rural as urban. In the 1950s the broadcasts were beamed through Radio Brazzaville to distant corners of the world where Irish exiles lived and were embellished by evocative personal greetings to some of them. O'Hehir had an ability to switch into resonant, melodious tones full of sentiment and nostalgia for this purpose.

Michael O'Hehir was born in Glasnevin, a northern suburb of Dublin. He was the only child of a Co Clare man who was a junior civil servant and a hurling enthusiast. The young Michael was educated by the Christian Brothers at the O'Connell Schools, where he was on the hurling team. He later went to University College, Dublin.

In 1944 he became racing correspondent of the *Irish Independent*. From 1961 to 1972 he was head of sport in the newly founded Irish television station, *Telefís Eireann*. His talents as a journalist and administrator were rather less than those he possessed as a broadcaster.

But even in the latter role his greatest days were before television became established. He never quite succeeded in adapting to the demands of the screen, where word pictures are often superfluous and analysis more important.

O'Hehir was a small, plump, jolly man with a winning smile. Although universally popular, he was never what is called "one of the lads". He was a teetotaller and always sported on his jacket the pin of a Roman Catholic temperance organization called the Pioneers. He treasured the old certainties of the religion in which he had been brought up. He was a member of Family Solidarity, an organization opposed to abortion or divorce. He described himself as a workaholic.

In 1985 he suffered a stroke which impaired his speech and he was confined to a wheelchair thereafter. He was still able to attend sporting events and enjoyed listening to his son Tony, who had followed him as a sports commentator. With assistance he recorded his memoirs and was present when they were launched just a fortnight before his death. Among the 800 people who attended the launch was the President of Ireland, Mary Robinson, who had written a gracious foreword, and his old friend Lester Piggott, whom he counted the most accomplished jockey he had ever seen.

He is survived by his wife Molly and by three sons and two daughters.

* * *

DERMOT MORGAN

2 MARCH 1998

DERMOT MORGAN, ACTOR, comedian and writer, died yesterday aged 45 after collapsing at home. He was born on March 3, 1952.

The part of the blundering Father Ted made Dermot Morgan famous throughout the British Isles, but his comic talent had long been appreciated – and feared – in his native Ireland. For two decades he had been sending up everyone in Ireland whom he considered pompous, and causing regular scandals. Although *Father Ted* was filmed in Co Clare, it was made for Channel 4 – and for Morgan as for many others, it was success in Britain that finally forced open all doors at home.

Father Ted is the head priest on Craggy Island, off the west coast of Ireland, where he lives in the zany confinement of Parochial House with two other eccentric priests, Dougal and the unhinged Jack, and their housekeeper, Mrs Doyle. Their surreal adventures became a cult. As well as meddling around the island, betting, and chasing local wildlife, Ted was also revealed to have an illegitimate son.

Naturally, the show was condemned by some Catholic bishops, who complained that it made the clergy look like idiots. No doubt that piece of idiocy – with 200,000 earnest leaflets being sent to homes around Dublin – helped to boost it further.

Playing the well-intentioned but ineffectual Father Ted was but the last round in Dermot Morgan's struggle with the Roman Catholic Church. As what he called "a severely lapsed Catholic", he remembered and resented the influence the Church had had in his youth. He was educated at a Christian Brothers college, which he later described as "good paramilitary training", and for a while he intended to become a priest. Compulsory religion in adolescence, however, inoculated him against the idea, and behind his adult lampoons stood a conviction that the Church was systematically hypocritical.

After University College, Dublin, he became a teacher in 1974, but always knew that he wanted to write and perform, and appeared as a stand-up comic in small clubs. He left teaching in 1978, and broke into television with a four-year stint on Mike Murphy's popular comedy show *The Live Mike*.

As well as sending up politicians, Morgan played the young and eager priest Father Trendy, who was hooked on modern communications and given to elaborate metaphors. His book *Trendy Sermons*, published in 1982, took many well-aimed potshots at the Church. Some of his targets condemned him as blasphemous (though others thought him hilarious), and he found himself dropped by every Irish radio and television station. He was forced to return to the small-time comedy circuit, and briefly faced bankruptcy.

Three years later, however, he topped the Irish charts with *Thank you very much, Mr Eastwood*, a record mocking the boxer Barry McGuigan's habit of thanking his manager, Barney Eastwood, for everything after his fights. Morgan was also renowned for his mimicry of politicians such as Charles Haughey, and in 1992 he greeted Albert Reynolds's entry into office with another record, *A Country and Western Taoiseach*, with fine impressions of Reynolds and the Justice Minister Padraig Flynn.

In 1990, with Gerry Stembridge, Morgan began writing, directing and performing in *Scrap Saturday*, a sharp satirical radio show akin to *Spitting Image.* It tore into Irish politicians, making many distinctly uncomfortable. Morgan won a Jacob's radio award in 1991, when he was also voted Ireland's National Entertainer of the Year.

However, despite its popularity, *Scrap Saturday* was abruptly cancelled in 1992, apparently because the originating broadcasting service, RTE, with its dependence on the Government, considered it too risky. RTE, however, claimed that the programme had simply "run out of steam". Morgan later said of Irish politics that "it was getting harder and harder to outstrip reality", and last year his demotic and unwitty abuse of Irish MPs made front-page news in Ireland.

When *Father Ted* began in April 1995, RTE declined to screen it, though some parts of the Republic were able to receive it on Channel 4. Later, however, with the series winning plaudits in Britain, RTE caved in and quickly found it had a popular hit. The humour, after all, was not only at the expense of the Church and the Pope, or even the Irish, but attacked every kind of taboo. Although considered too incorrect for American audiences, it was screened in many other countries.

"Before Ted, my fame ended at Howth," Morgan said, but after Ted he was to be seen as a personality on high-profile shows such as *Have I Got News for You* and *The Late Late Show*, and chatting with Clive James and Russell Harty. He continued to give one-man performances, although a tour of Ireland last year, with a show called *Addressing the Nation*, drew mixed reviews.

In 1996 Morgan won an award for Top TV Comedy Actor for his part as Ted, and *Father Ted*, produced by the production company Hat Trick, which specializes in comedy, also won a Bafta award for Best Comedy and several others. It was also successful on video.

A third eight-part series of the madcap half-hour comedies, written by Graham Linehan and Arthur Mathews, begins on Channel 4 next Friday. As one of the station's great successes of recent years, it is being promoted by an extensive advertising campaign.

A clever and fluent wit, Dermot Morgan was always on the lookout for a gag. His writing was remorselessly mischievous and derisive, and his success could be measured by the controversy that he continued to excite. He had recently been working on a drama series and developing two further sitcoms, as well as a novel. He was passionate about football, and also wrote a film about the Archbishop of Dublin in the 1950s who condemned a football match in the Republic against players from communist Yugoslavia.

Dermot Morgan was separated from his wife, Suzanne, for several years before their recent divorce. He is survived by two sons from his marriage, and by his long-term partner, Fiona, and their son.

* * *

JACK LYNCH

21 OCTOBER 1999

JACK LYNCH, former Taoiseach of the Republic of Ireland, died in hospital in Dublin yesterday aged 82. He was born on August 15, 1917.

Jack Lynch was twice Taoiseach, from 1966 to 1973 and, again, from 1977 to 1979. By his firmness in the cause of moderation he ensured that Ireland was not engulfed in a bloody civil war as a result of violence in Northern Ireland from 1969 onwards.

At first this violence was directed at the Catholic population and was a response by Protestant mobs and the police to a peaceful civil rights movement. In August 1969 Lynch was forced by bellicose ministers in his Fianna Fail Government to state bluntly that it would not stand by if there were further attacks on Roman Catholics. Irish troops were moved to border areas and orders given to provide military training for civilians from the Catholic community in Northern Ireland. However,

Lynch countermanded these orders and the Catholic areas of Belfast were protected by bringing in soldiers from Britain. Despite this, some members of the Dublin Government went ahead with secret preparations for an armed intervention in Northern Ireland if the occasion arose.

In April 1970 Lynch dismissed two ministers, Charles Haughey and Neil Blaney. They were charged, in company with some others, with conspiracy to import arms illegally, but they were all acquitted. It was part of the case for the defence that the importation was authorized by the Government. It was not clear whether Lynch was completely ignorant of the importation, as he claimed, or whether he had acquiesced out of weakness or for tactical reasons in the activities of the ministers involved until these were unmasked by British Intelligence and leaked to Liam Cosgrave, the Opposition leader.

On the day of his acquittal Charles Haughey made a statement which was generally taken as a call for Lynch's resignation. In this tight corner Lynch reacted with a decisiveness and toughness that he had not hitherto revealed. He faced down Haughey and Blaney and got the overwhelming backing of the Fianna Fail Party. He demanded acceptance of his position that the border could be removed only by peaceful means and he took strong action against the IRA by setting up a non-jury court in which its members could be prosecuted.

It was not easy to maintain this policy as leader of the traditional Republican Party at a time when the Stormont Government was pursuing a partisan security policy which culminated in the clumsy introduction of internment without trial in August 1971. Blaney, his friend Kevin Boland and some others left Fianna Fail in protest. Haughey ate humble pie and bided his time. Lynch appeased the more republican elements in his own party by calling on the British Government to declare in favour of the unification of Ireland in the long term.

In the wake of the shooting of 13 civilians by the British Army in Londonderry in January 1972, Lynch recalled the Irish Ambassador in London and declared a day of national mourning. On that same day the British Embassy in Dublin was burnt to the ground by an angry mob. While British public opinion was affronted that the police had not prevented this outrage, Lynch was unwilling to run the risk of loss of life and probably calculated that this symbolic act of revenge would help to defuse popular indignation.

The next month the British Prime Minister, Edward Heath, acceded to Lynch's demand that the Northern Ireland Parliament and its Government at Stormont should both be abolished. Direct rule from Westminster followed. Negotiations were initiated with the Dublin Government that were to lead to the Sunningdale agreement of 1973 and the establishment of the short-lived power-sharing Executive in Northern Ireland representative of nationalists as well as of unionists. Lynch had left office by the time the agreement was concluded. But by committing his party in the negotiations to the position that the status of Northern Ireland within the United Kingdom could not be changed without the consent of a majority of its inhabitants, and working within that context to improve the position of the nationalist population, Lynch set a new agenda for politics on the island of Ireland which provided a basis for a modus vivendi in the short term and a structure within which a settlement was to be pursued for the rest of the century.

John Lynch, as he was baptized, was born within earshot of the Shandon Bells in the city of Cork. He was one of seven children. His father was a tailor. He received his schooling from the Christian Brothers at the North Monastery in his native city. At the age of 17 he joined the Civil Service as an assistant to the registrar in the Cork Probate Office. It was a taxing job as the registrar was deaf.

Lynch read for the Bar at the same time and was called to the Irish Bar in 1945. He practised in Cork. Meanwhile, he had acquired fame as a sportsman and was a member of the Cork teams that won the All-Ireland County Championships in hurling and Gaelic football. On the field he never initiated foul play but ... opponents who fouled him frequently found that it made him play even better. It was a pattern that was to reassert itself in his political career.

Lynch had no family background in politics, but shortly after he began to practise at the Bar he was invited to join Fianna Fail and to stand for the party in the Cork constituency ... In the general election of 1948 he was duly elected to the Dail, where he contributed thoughtfully in Opposition, especially on legal issues.

In 1951 Eamon de Valera returned to power and appointed Lynch Parliamentary Secretary to the Government. Six years later, after another spell in Opposition, he became Minister for Education. When, in 1959, de Valera was succeeded as Taoiseach by Sean Lemass, Lynch took over the latter's portfolio at the Department of Industry and Commerce. He was content to be guided by his civil servants and his public utterances were generally unspectacular – often almost banal. In comparison with some of his more thrusting younger colleagues he seemed dull and un-ambitious. But Lemass valued his contribution and made him Minister for Finance in 1965.

When Sean Lemass announced his imminent resignation in 1966 several of these younger ministers, including Charles Haughey, prepared to contest the succession. Lynch made no move and eventually had to be persuaded by Lemass to allow his name to go forward as a candidate. When he did so, Haughey withdrew and Lynch was elected party leader by a large majority.

As Taoiseach Lynch's style remained unspectacular. Unlike his predecessors, he acted as a chairman rather than a leader. He seemed to exert little authority over members of his Government, some of whom became restless and issued veiled challenges to his leadership. At the same time Lynch displayed firmness in standing up to farmers' demonstrations. He made a very good impression in television interviews and gained popularity. His soothing and honest demeanour appealed to the uncommitted voter and Fianna Fail was returned for the fourth successive time at the general election of June 1969.

Apart from the management of the situation in Northern Ireland, the major achievement of Lynch's Government was to lead the Irish Republic into the European Economic Community in 1973. But this was not a matter of great controversy since the move had the backing of Fine Gael, the main opposition party, and secured a majority of over 80 per cent in the necessary referendum. In other respects the Government's performance was less than satisfactory. Many of the ministers were inexperienced or of low calibre. A sluggishness and inefficiency invaded the public sector generally, which reflected Lynch's passive approach to the processes of government. A policy of budget deficits was introduced in 1972 that had damaging long-term effects on the economy.

Encouraged by dissensions within the main opposition party, Lynch called a general election early in 1973. However, Fine Gael and Labour formed an alliance for the first time since a previous coalition had left office in 1957. Although Fianna Fail held its percentage of first preference votes, this coalition was returned to power. Lynch conceded defeat with characteristic good grace and it seemed that he was ready to retire. However, he was persuaded not to do so.

He did not make a very forceful impression in opposition. In 1975 a groundswell of opinion at local level in the party forced him to restore Charles Haughey to the front bench. Pundits predicted defeat for Fianna Fail in the 1977 general election. Lynch may well have shared their view as he felt compelled to put forward a programme lavish in extravagant promises. But, in the event, Fianna Fail was returned with the largest electoral majority in the history of the state.

The increased expenditure and reductions in taxation that Fianna Fail introduced on its return to power fuelled an economic boom. This created the confidence to break the link with sterling in 1978 and enter the European monetary mechanism. However, in 1979 the boom ran out of steam amid labour and farm unrest. Lynch was clearly weary.

Fianna Fail suffered a massive loss of votes in the elections for the European Parliament held that year. Its deputies in the Dail became restless as their electoral prospects were threatened. Lynch's policy on the North alienated the more republican elements in the party. He had quietly shelved the policy forced on him in opposition of calling for a British statement of intent to withdraw from Northern Ireland and seemed willing to settle for internal power-sharing without the addition of a Council of Ireland. Some backbenchers made an issue of an agreement for cross-border air surveillance secretly introduced in the wake of the murder of Lord Mountbatten in Sligo in 1979. Lynch's efforts to discipline them were resisted by the parliamentary party. It was a sore blow for him that Fianna Fail lost two by-elections in his native Cork. He brought forward his intended date of resignation by a couple of months and went in November 1979. He was confident that his deputy, the Finance Minister George Colley, could defeat Charles Haughey for the succession. In fact, Lynch's resignation had come too late for Colley, and Haughey was elected by a narrow majority.

Lynch did not seek re-election to the Dail at the general election of 1981 and played no further part in politics. He never attended party meetings and made no secret in private of his distaste for his successor. For a time he was chairman of Irish Distillers, the company that produced the Cork whiskey called Paddy, a drink that he enjoyed greatly (albeit always in moderation). He made it clear that he had no interest in becoming President of Ireland and made few pronouncements on public issues. He lived quietly in retirement, dividing his time between his house in Dublin and a country cottage in West Cork. He had been in poor health since he suffered a severe stroke in 1995.

Although he was the leader of a party born of militant Irish republicanism, Jack Lynch never shared the extreme nationalism and atavistic resentment towards things British that was the stock-in-trade of so many of his colleagues. He was genuine in seeking the conciliation rather than the coercion of unionists in the North. Those in Northern Ireland and Britain who criticized his failure to deliver fully on the security front did not make due allowance for his domestic political difficulties, which were exacerbated by the behaviour of the security forces in Northern Ireland. However, it must also be said that he had an elusive quality and an ambiguity of expression that may have precluded total trust. This certainly accounted for the total lack of rapport that existed between Edward Heath and himself.

In domestic politics Lynch was shrewd and adroit, if somewhat lacking in vision and in mastery of economic issues. He had a deep distrust of the flamboyant, invariably opting for the obvious solution rather than the bold stroke. He was generous to opponents and there was, in turn, no acrimony towards him in the other political parties. With his doleful blue eyes he had the disconcerting quality of exciting sympathy if he was attacked. He attracted a type of vote to Fianna Fail that was lost to it after his departure. His was the last Fianna Fail Government that had an overall majority in the Dail.

As a person Jack Lynch had many attractive qualities. He was soft-spoken and unassuming, even if he was not quite as bereft of ambition as he liked to appear. He had a warmth and charm that made even the most casual encounter with him a most pleasant experience. He was always dignified and was possessed of a gentleness and simple courtesy that could be very winning. He was also loyal to old friends (especially Cork ones) and was quite prepared to disregard party affiliations in order to reward them. Nor were all his benefactions to old friends in the public domain. He was an entertaining raconteur. He enjoyed social gatherings, especially if they ended with a sing-song at which he would sing *The Banks of my own Lovely Lee*.

Lynch married in 1946 Maureen O'Connor, who survives him. A lively outgoing person, she supported him in his political career, although she would have much preferred it if he had remained in private life. There were no children of the marriage.

REV. F. X. MARTIN

Scholar who debunked the Easter Rising and
defended Viking Dublin

28 FEBRUARY 2000

THE REV. F. X. MARTIN, Professor of Medieval History, University College Dublin, 1962–88, was born in Ballylongford, Co Kerry, on October 2, 1922. He died in Ballyboden, Co Dublin, on February 13, aged 77.

"Every city needs a permanent monument to ugliness as a grim reminder of what has to be avoided," remarked the Rev. Professor F. X. Martin after he had failed to prevent the building of such a monstrosity in Dublin. In 1978 he had led a demonstration of 20,000 people to protest against the proposed erection of civic offices on the site of the Viking settlement at Wood Quay. He carried the battle to the courts, where he obtained a temporary injunction from the High Court, halting the development on the ground that the site was a national monument. But the action ultimately failed in the Supreme Court and the new civic offices went ahead.

All was not lost, however, because the time bought by Martin's action enabled archaeological work to be carried out on what became the largest excavated Viking settlement in Western Europe. As a mendicant friar Martin pleaded inability to pay the costs and damages awarded against him, and in a curious twist the Dublin Corporation later awarded him the Dublin Millennium Medal for his defence of Viking Dublin.

Francis Xavier Martin was one of four sons of a medical practitioner in Ballylongford, Co Kerry, to enter the religious life. He was born when the Irish Civil War was raging; his mother gave birth prematurely after a raid on the family home by government troops. Martin subsequently moved his practice to Dublin, and young Frank was sent to school with the Jesuits in Belvedere. At school he displayed a turbulence which even the rule of the monastic life never succeeded in curbing. He entered the Augustinian order in 1941 and was ordained priest in 1952.

He studied history at University College Dublin (UCD) and won a travelling studentship with a thesis on Francis Nugent, an unorthodox Capuchin friar who was one of the main agents of the counter-reformation in Ireland. Martin then went to Peterhouse, Cambridge. He was the first Roman Catholic priest to be admitted to the student body of Cambridge's oldest college since the Reformation, and went on to row in the Peterhouse boat.

In 1959 Martin was appointed an assistant lecturer in history at UCD. Three years later the chair of medieval history fell vacant on the retirement of the celebrated Jesuit scholar Aubrey Gwynn. Martin, who was really an early modernist rather than a medievalist, won support as the person most likely to defeat another clerical candidate, favoured by the Roman Catholic Archbishop of Dublin.

Martin proved an excellent appointment. He inspired his students with his enthusiasm for the Renaissance and did not allow his Catholic allegiance to influence his treatment of history unduly. He was selfless with his time, supervising students and helping them with their future careers. He relished the intrigues of academic life, contending with some bizarre senior colleagues, and could be rough in imposing his will.

As a scholar Martin soon yielded to the lure of the limelight when he diverted his attentions from his own period to the Easter Rebellion of 1916, the 50th anniversary of which was nigh. His contribution was valuable and courageous, in many respects pioneering the "revisionist" trend in Irish scholarship: he established the fact that the rebels had come out in treacherous defiance of their commanding officer, Professor Eoin MacNeill. Until then the 1916 leaders had been accorded sacrosanct status in nationalist Ireland.

Martin had a fine writing style and was meticulous in his research. His output was formidable even if it remained insufficiently focused for academic purists. His subjects ranged from Dermot McMurrough, the cuckolded King of Leinster who invited in the Normans to Ireland, to denominational education in colonial Australia (he had two terms as a visiting professor at Australian universities).

He joined Theo Moody of Trinity College Dublin in editing a series of television lectures entitled *A Course of Irish History*, which in its published version (now in its fifteenth impression) is the most read outline of Irish history. He was also one of the editors and a sizeable contributor to *The New History of Ireland* published by the Royal Irish Academy between 1976 and 1989.

He was active in promoting medieval inter-disciplinary studies, and his essay "Crowning the King", based on a lecture given in Dublin's Christchurch Cathedral in 1989, provides an interesting revised version of the crowning there in 1487 of pretender Lambert Simnel as King of England. His last work, completed in collaboration with Dr Clare O'Reilly, was on the history of the Augustinian order.

FX, as Martin was known, was an ebullient, genial and charismatic man with a sense of fun and generous instincts. He devoted much of his time to assisting other scholars and was almost reckless in his readiness to share the results of his research. He was something of a bon viveur, moved in smart society, loved a song and was counted a snappy dresser.

Yet, within the monastery, he drove himself very hard, rising to pray and meditate while his confreres slept, and working far into the night when they had retired. He had a rugged appearance and a raw vigour and vitality that made him seem indestructible. It was especially poignant that not long after his retirement, which he had fought the college authorities hard to delay, his memory became impaired. He was confined within his community for much of his last five years.

SISTER GENEVIEVE
O'FARRELL

1 JANUARY 2002

SISTER GENEVIEVE O'FARRELL, OBE, Principal of St Louise's Comprehensive College in the Falls Road, West Belfast, from 1963 to 1988 died in Belfast on December 29, 2001, aged 78. For those 25 years this remarkable yet little-known heroine dedicated her life to the under-privileged girls in one of the most deprived areas of Western Europe; for most of these years she was also trying to run a normal school in a war zone as the Falls Road was the theatre for a guerrilla war between the IRA and the British Army. A woman of great courage and spirituality, she defied the Roman Catholic Church, the IRA, and the Army in her tenacious determination to give her girls the best possible start in life, never hesitating to take on all those who stood in her way.

Pride of place in education in the Catholic and Protestant communities in Northern Ireland had long been given to the Province's grammar schools; the children who failed to qualify at the age of 11 were second-class citizens. Challenging this system and fighting for the rights of the "rejects" became the focus of Sister Genevieve's vocation. She believed that separating children at the age of 11 was not only educationally unsound, but contrary to Christ's teaching.

Her chance to put her beliefs into practice came in 1963. The Catholic Church had opened a new secondary school for girls on the Falls Road in 1958 with Sister Genevieve as vice-principal and her close friend, Sister Ita Polley, as Principal. Five years later, when Sister Ita fell ill, Sister Genevieve took over.

Initially a school for 800 girls, St Louise's became the largest single-sex school in Western Europe, with 2,400 girls aged 11 to 18. It was never intended that girls who had failed to qualify for the grammar school should stay on after the school leaving age, but Sister Genevieve created the conditions that encouraged 80 per cent of them to do so. Girls who in the past would have left school to "stitch hankies" or serve behind the counter in a shop were passing A levels and going to university. In 1988 Mary O'Hara, who had failed the 11-plus, won a scholarship to Cambridge – much to Sister Genevieve's delight.

It was one of Sister Genevieve's achievements that girls who were not going to take A levels or progress to university felt equally valued by the school. The "parity of esteem" that has eluded so much of the British education system existed and flourished at St Louise's.

Sister Genevieve had her critics, not least when the Troubles started in 1969. She was determined that the violence and tensions in the Falls Road should not undermine her girls' chances of a first-class education and a good job or career. The difficulties she faced were formidable. Burning buses and army roadblocks frequently disrupted journeys to and from school. Girls were sometimes picked up by the Army for questioning; their homes were turned over by soldiers or taken over by gunmen; their fathers and brothers were killed or sentenced to long terms of imprisonment.

Through all these years, St Louise's remained a haven of peace and normality. Republicans who were critical of what they perceived as Sister Genevieve's pro-British stance, particularly when she accepted a British honour in 1978, nevertheless respected her for her courage and her devotion to the girls. She did her best to prevent her girls becoming actively involved in the republican movement, but if they did and were imprisoned, she visited them regularly. They were still her girls. Two of her former pupils are known to have been killed on "active service".

The keys to Sister Genevieve's success as a school principal were her profound religious conviction, her emphasis on good discipline, her unfailing sense of humour and her inspiring leadership of both teaching staff and pupils. When she retired as Principal in 1988, the then Secretary of State, Brian Mawhinney, flew in to present her with flowers and to meet "the woman who had his entire department terrified".

Mary O'Farrell was born on March 22, 1923 in Tullamore, Co Offaly, a small town 50 miles west of Dublin. The youngest child and only daughter of a devoted Catholic family, this quiet and shy child attended the Convent School run by the Sisters of Mercy but was under no pressure to enter the religious life. When, at the age of 18, she was sure that God was calling her to His service, it was not to a cloistered life of a nun that she turned but to the Daughters of Charity of St Vincent de Paul, "a tough army of charity" whose members lived and worked in the world. Her family were uneasy about joining "that hard order", but having decided to follow the example of St Vincent and St Louise de Marillac, Mary O'Farrell never looked back.

She entered St Catherine's Seminary at Blackrock on February 26, 1942, where she came under the influence of Sister Philomena Rickard, whose job it was to train the seminary sisters in what, pre-Vatican Two, was a tough regime and to inspire them with the practical idealism of the founders. On leaving the seminary, the sisters were expected to accept their first placement with holy indifference to their own wishes. Mary did not want to be a teacher, but to serve the poorest of the poor in the slums of a great city as the earliest sisters had done. The Sister Provincial had other ideas. Mary was sent to Manchester University and then to Sedgley Park College of Education and did not shine at either institution. She was given the religious name of Sister Joseph and then of Sister Genevieve. She made her vows on June 29, 1947, but she cannot have been altogether happy about the direction her religious life was taking. It was only nine years later, in 1956, when she was sent to West Belfast, that she was convinced that teaching was after all what God had called her to do.

In her retirement Sister Genevieve's vocation continued in her devotion to the welfare of former republican and loyalist paramilitaries, many of whom she encouraged to pursue educational goals in prison. It was typical of her that she won the gratitude and affection of men from both sides of the sectarian divide. She was also a member of the Standing Commission of Human Rights in Northern Ireland and a member of the BBC's governing body in the Province.

In 1994 the pressure of her work and of the many public roles she had undertaken took its toll. She suffered a severe stroke and was unable to look after herself for the rest of her life. Her closest friends in the community, Sister Ita and Sister Declan Kelly, and her own Catholic faith helped her to come to terms with terrible misfortune.

* * *

MAUREEN POTTER

8 APRIL 2004

MAUREEN POTTER, COMEDIENNE AND ACTRESS, was born in 1925. She died on April 7, 2004, aged 79.

Maureen Potter was Ireland's best-loved woman comedian, a unique performer whose long career stretched back from the heydays of music hall and variety to television and film and whose annual appearances in Dublin pantomime became something of a national institution. A gawky figure with wide eyes, she was a classic clown who was as much at home with slapstick as she was with stand-up comedy. As an actress she excelled in the works of James Joyce and Sean O'Casey and could more than hold her own against such native talents as Siobhan McKenna and Cyril Cusack.

Potter was born in Dublin and educated at St Mary's School, Fairview. She began performing from an early age, singing and dancing in local clubs and halls and at 14 made her debut at the Gaiety Theatre, Dublin, in the pantomime *Jimmy and the Leprechaun*, which starred Jimmy O'Dea.

Potter was to be associated with both the star and the theatre for most of her working life ... Maureen – known affectionately as "Mo" in

Ireland – proved a perfect foil to him and they toured in variety both in Ireland and England.

Their partnership in the annual Gaiety Theatre pantomimes became a much-loved staple of the Dublin theatrical calendar with O'Dea usually playing "Mrs Mulligan", his special characterization of the Dame figure, and Potter as his daughter. Around them they built a formidable crew of comedy actors (Milo O'Shea and Danny Cummins were regulars) and many of the sketches became classics. She worked with O'Dea in variety and later in television until his death in 1965.

After his death she worked on television in partnership with Danny Cummins and they were noted for their famous dance routines. In 1965 she headlined in *Gaels of Laughter*, a revue at the Gaiety Theatre, which ran every summer for a record-breaking 15 years. The shows, often produced under the banner of the Eamonn Andrews Studios, were lavish spectaculars with singing, dancing and many topical sketches. Potter dominated the show throughout. She was asked on many occasions to take the show abroad but firmly refused to travel outside her native city, even declining an offer to appear at the Royal Albert Hall in London.

She periodically appeared in straight film and theatre roles. She made her screen debut in *The Rising of the Moon* (1957), John Ford's portmanteau with the Abbey Players, and in 1967 she was cast as Josie Breen in the Joseph Strick adaptation of Joyce's *Ulysses*, which was banned in Ireland for 33 years. Ten years later she starred opposite Sir John Gielgud in another Joyce film, *A Portrait of the Artist as a Young Man*, appearing as Dante. On stage in Dublin she was hilarious as one of the homicidal old ladies in the black farce *Arsenic and Old Lace* opposite Siobhan McKenna and in 1988 she appeared at the Gate Theatre in *Juno and the Paycock*.

Although she claimed to have retired from the stage at the beginning of the Nineties she began performing a one-woman show at Clontarf Castle, which became a sellout annual event. The show, billed as "The Queen of Irish Comedy" attracted an audience that was largely too young to have seen her in her heyday at the Gaiety. Holding the stage for more than an hour, she sent up Irish dancing and impersonated Ian Paisley and various nuns and saints as well as hoofing with more energy than performers half her age. Many younger Irish comics acknowledged her influence, including the late Dermot Morgan of *Father Ted* fame.

In later years frequent tributes to her appeared on Irish television and in 1984 she was given the freedom of the City of Dublin although she regarded her greatest honour as being asked to place her hand-prints outside the Gaiety Theatre. "I'm delighted to get my hands on the Gaiety," she quipped, "because I worked here for 60 years. The Gaiety is the most aptly named place I know." The director John McColgan made a documentary, *Supertrooper*, about her and several videos were released of her performing live at Clontarf Castle. She had suffered ill health in recent years but found time to write a series of charming children's books, the best-known of which is *Tommy the Theatre Cat*.

MARY HOLLAND

9 JUNE 2004

MARY HOLLAND, JOURNALIST, was born on June 19, 1936. She died after a long illness on June 7, 2004, aged 67.

The journalist Mary Holland campaigned for 30 years for a new order in Ireland, thought that she had seen it achieved at the end of the 1990s, but was then disappointed by the outcome. All along, she had been one of the bravest, best known and most humane of reporters of the Troubles and their aftermath.

An Irish Catholic by birth, and a fashion writer by trade, she had been sent to Northern Ireland in 1968 to report for *The Observer* by its legendary editor David Astor, and was appalled by what she found.

Northern Ireland was on the brink of collapse. The civil rights movement had highlighted the second-class status of the Catholic minority, and the violent response of the unionist majority made Westminster's intervention, after decades of neglect, almost inevitable.

Catholic agitation was brutally put down by the Royal Ulster Constabulary and its vicious reserve force, the B Specials. Loyalist mobs were allowed to run free. The government at Stormont denounced Catholic protesters as revolutionaries and enacted legislation designed to increase police powers and appease Protestants.

Returning "home" to Ireland, Holland was surprised to discover that she was at heart a liberal Irish nationalist, anxious for reconciliation between Catholics and Protestants in the context of an "agreed" Ireland. But in the sense of supporting the "armed struggle" she was never a republican. When she chanced upon one of two British soldiers being dragged to their deaths by a mob in West Belfast in 1988, she was horrified.

"How did we let it happen?" she wrote. "He passed within a few feet of myself and dozens of other journalists. He didn't cry out, just looked at us with terrified eyes as though we were all enemies in a foreign country who wouldn't have understood what language he was speaking if he called out for help."

Yet she was stalwart in defence of the principle that a journalist has the right to protect her sources. In 2002, giving evidence to the Saville tribunal investigating the shooting, on "Bloody Sunday", of 13 civilians by British paratroopers in Derry 30 years before, she refused to name a man whom she had seen that day opening fire on soldiers. The man had subsequently been shot and wounded, and she had interviewed him, but he had spoken with her in confidence and she would not betray his name.

She came to recognize that her wholehearted endorsement of the Good Friday accords was, at best, premature. She had seen the apparent commitment by unionists and republicans, including Sinn Fein, as the key to everything, little realizing that most of those taking part would swiftly change the locks.

Mary Holland was born in London in 1936. Her father, though part of a long established Irish Catholic family, was employed by the British foreign service, so, with her parents abroad most of the time, Mary and her two brothers boarded at schools in England and Ireland – an experience which to some extent, she said, "cauterized" her emotions.

After reading English at London University, she found work first on a local paper, but soon switched to *Vogue*. She proved a surprise hit writing about couture, but yearned to be a Fleet Street reporter.

Thanks to David Astor's denunciation of the Eden government for its "crooked" prosecution of the Suez crisis, *The Observer* was then the trendiest title in town, in which style and substance were briefly in perfect equilibrium. Holland squeezed in via the fashion pages, but made it clear that her role model was Katherine Whitehorn, the politically engaged columnist.

Rising, in spite of herself, to the position of fashion editor, she pestered Astor to let her do some "real" reporting, and she was sent to Ireland. It was 1968, and Astor was curious about the state of affairs revealed in Ulster by the civil rights movement and the peculiar determination of the Unionist government at Stormont to keep Catholics in their place.

The situation soon deteriorated, leading to the arrival of British troops and the beginning of the long war between the Provisional IRA and all those perceived to represent British imperialism.

In the midst of the chaos, Holland found time to marry Ronald Higgins, a rising young diplomat. But this proved little more than an interruption. Her husband was posted to Jakarta, which she found highly uncongenial, and after a few months of frustration, she bolted back to London, and thence to her beloved Ulster.

She reported fearlessly from Belfast, alerting the British public to the horrors of their Ulster slum while refusing to accept republican terror as the appropriate nationalist response. She saw the collapse of the Stormont Parliament and Bloody Sunday, the Ulster workers' strike, the rise of loyalist murder gangs, the IRA's relentless bombing campaign.

She also worked in television, and during the 1970s was one of the presenters of *Weekend World*, produced by LWT, where Peter Mandelson was among her colleagues. Her documentary *Creggan* won the Prix Italien in 1980.

Professionally, her greatest crisis came in 1979 with the arrival at *The Observer* of its new editor-in-chief, the Irish nationalist turned Ulster Unionist, Conor Cruise O'Brien. His first act in charge was to dismiss Holland, whom he regarded as a republican fellow-traveller. Dismayed, she switched to The *Irish Times*, which was happy to have her, and found a continuing platform in England in the *New Statesman*.

She had, in the meantime, married one of the most romantic revolutionaries in modern Ireland: Eamonn McCann, a veteran of street protests in Derry. They had a daughter and a son before the marriage ended.

Over the years, Mary Holland won numerous awards for her journalism, including a share of the 1994 UK Scoop of the Year for her reporting of John Major's secret dealings with the IRA and, in 2003, a Special Judges presentation at the Irish Press Awards for her "outstanding contribution to Irish journalism over three decades".

She is survived by her son and daughter.

JOE CAHILL

26 JULY 2004

JOE CAHILL, IRISH REPUBLICAN activist, was born in Belfast on May 19, 1920. He died there on July 23, 2004, aged 84.

If, as one senior unionist politician once remarked, Martin McGuinness is the "Godfather of Godfathers" of the Republican movement, then Joe Cahill had claims to be Grandfather of Grandfathers of the IRA. In an association with the Republican movement that predated the Second World War, Cahill was one of its most ruthless and effective operators, responsible for much of the IRA's military successes of the early 1970s, and most notoriously, the man believed to have ordered the Warrington bombing of 1993.

Joe Cahill was born into a large, Mass-going Republican family in Divis Street in West Belfast. Like many hardened Republicans he was educated by the Christian Brothers and at the age of 16 joined the illegal Republican Boy Scout movement, eventually becoming a full-fledged member of the Irish Republican Army in 1938.

He was one of six men convicted of the murder of Patrick Murphy, a Catholic policeman, in 1942. Only one of the gang of six was hanged for this crime when the British Government – after a plea from Pope Pius XII – chose to exercise clemency. Cahill was but 21 years old, and three days from the gallows.

Cahill eventually served 7 years in prison, only to be rearrested in 1957 during the IRA's border campaign of 1956–62, spending another 4 years behind bars. He subsequently became disillusioned with the ineptitude of the Republican movement, and not least its godless flirtation with Marxist doctrine in the wake of the campaign, and he left the movement in 1964 to become a building foreman. He returned to the fold in 1969 as the more nationalist and Catholic wing, the Provisionals, was beginning to engage in confrontation with Loyalist gangs in Belfast.

Cahill's role was to patrol the Catholic areas of Belfast and to man the barricades. In April 1971 he replaced Billy McKee as Officer Commanding the Belfast Brigade, a position he held until shortly after his internment in August of that year. By this time his aptitude for eluding the security forces had earned him the moniker of the "Emerald Pimpernel". He foiled the British Army that month when child lookouts alerted him to soldiers about to storm a classroom where Provos were staging a secret press conference. Cahill rushed out through a back door, surrounded by armed guards.

Obfuscation and calculated ambiguity were not Joe Cahill's forte. "Our aim is to kill as many British soldiers as possible," he told those assembled in Dublin, before making an abortive fundraising trip to America in 1971. The United States Government arrested him when he landed, and he was prevented from remaining in the country.

The Belfast Brigade's campaign of terror, including "Bloody Friday" and the bombing of the Abercorn restaurant, where nine and two were slaughtered respectively, was to no small degree down to Cahill's merciless proficiency. But the IRA's campaign convinced many British politicians that a resort to dialogue was inevitable. So later in 1972, Harold Wilson met an IRA delegation in Dublin. Cahill remembered the meeting as a "waffling session" and "complete waste of time", also noting that Wilson was "disappointed that none of us took a drink".

Cahill was eventually arrested by the Irish Gardai in May 1972 and charged with being a member of an unlawful organization. He immediately embarked on a hunger strike in Mountjoy prison and was freed in late June, owing to a lack of evidence.

He was re-arrested by the Irish police in 1973 and sentenced to three years in prison for being a member of the IRA and illegally importing arms on board the German ship *Claudia*. After suffering a heart attack in 1973 he was released on health grounds two years later. He then returned to the IRA, replacing the fanatical Seamus Twomey as leader, in an effort to curb an internecine feud with the Official IRA.

However, Cahill became uncomfortable about another leftwards turn in the movement, and in the shake-up of 1977, Cahill lost his post as "Adjutant General" in charge of the IRA's "Army Council". Nevertheless he continued his association with the Republican movement, and was arrested once again in 1984 for illegally trying to enter the United States. Three years later he was arrested for trying to smuggle 150 tons of arms into the Irish Republic on the trawler *Eksund*. In his final act of terrorism, he is understood – according to security sources – to have masterminded the Warrington bombing of 1993. A three-year-old and a boy of 12 were killed in the attack. Cahill was aged 73 at the time.

Cahill went on to contribute to the current Peace Process. His backing for the Provisional IRA's ceasefires of 1994 and 1997 were critical in securing a cessation of violence. He stood unsuccessfully as a Sinn Fein candidate in Antrim North in the 1998 Northern Ireland Assembly against the Rev. Ian Paisley.

Cahill's connections with Sinn Fein president Gerry Adams were steeped in family history. Adams had escorted Cahill through the streets of Belfast when he was the IRA's commander in the city; and Adams's father, had been part of Cahill's IRA gang of the 1940s.

In his heyday, Joe Cahill was recognizable for his cloth-capped, bespectacled demeanour and for his simple and stubborn disposition. He was not a man for euphemism or compromise. "We are going to stop at nothing to end British rule," he once said. He later remarked: "I was born in a united Ireland. I want to die in a united Ireland."

He is survived by his wife Annie, and seven children.

BOB TISDALL

2 AUGUST 2004

BOB TISDALL WHO died in Queensland on July 28, 2004 was the last surviving gold medallist of the Los Angeles Olympics of 1932. At those games, running for Ireland, he won the 400 metres hurdles in a field that included the Olympic gold medallists of 1924, 1928 and 1936. 68 years later, aged 93, he jogged with the Olympic torch for 500 yards near his home in Nambour, Queensland, as it made its journey in 2000 from Mount Olympus to the Sydney games.

Robert Morton Newburgh Tisdall was born on May 16, 1907 in Hatton, a small town in upcountry Ceylon (now Sri Lanka), where his father, the younger son of an Irish landed family, was a tea planter. Young Bob returned to Ireland when he was 5 and was brought up by relatives in Tipperary until his parents returned some years later.

He received his schooling at the local Nenagh Primary School and then at Mourne Grange, Co Down, and Shrewsbury. Inheriting athletic ability from both sides of his family (his mother was an Irish hockey international) he early displayed promise as an athlete.

On leaving Shrewsbury he took up employment in a tea and rubber company in London and played rugby for Harlequins. But the London air affected him badly, and he returned to Nenagh, where his parents had re-established themselves, having been forced to leave Ireland by the local IRA during the war of independence. After a period boating around his beloved Lough Derg and up the Shannon, he was persuaded by his old housemaster Freddy Prior that he should try for a place at Gonville and Caius College, Cambridge. Caius looked favourably on athletes and numbered among its graduates the 1924 Olympic champion Harold Abrahams. Tisdall got his place and read agriculture and forestry.

He quickly made his mark in university athletics. He toured South Africa with the Achilles Club, a combined Oxford and Cambridge team. On the ship going there he met Jo Guttridge, who lived in Natal and whom he was to marry when he graduated in 1931. On the return journey he met General Smuts, who became his political hero.

Tisdall achieved national prominence at the intervarsity games in March 1931 when, in an unprecedented performance, he won the 120 metres hurdles, the long jump, the shot put and the quarter-mile. Asked how he had done it, he remarked: "Tell Lady Astor I trained on beer." Lady Astor was a formidable temperance campaigner and MP.

When Tisdall left Cambridge in 1931 the world was in the throes of the Great Depression. He congregated with his fellows in the Amateurs Club for unemployed Oxford and Cambridge graduates, situated near Piccadilly. He delivered peeled potatoes to hotels to make ends meet. Then he spent six months as ADC to the Maharajah of Baroda travelling on the Continent with his entourage. In 1932 Tisdall was persuaded by some Cambridge friends to try for the Olympic Games that were to be held in Los Angeles that summer. He took a disused railway carriage in an orchard near the Sussex Downs and trained on the hills and occasionally in the grounds of Lancing College before joining the Irish team in Ballybunion, Kerry. The event he chose, the 400 metres hurdles, was one that he had run only once previously.

The ten-day overland journey to Los Angeles was so exhausting that he had to rest in bed for four days to restore his weight. Having qualified for the finals he suffered an attack of the jitters while he waited in the tunnel for the race, but he was sportingly calmed down by Lord Burghley, the defending champion. Tisdall led all the way to win comfortably in a world record time of 51.7 seconds. But because he knocked the last hurdle he was, under the prevailing rule, denied the record. No sooner had he won than he had to come to the assistance of the Irish hammer thrower Pat O'Callaghan, who was being inhibited by the spikes on his shoes from getting his full length. Tisdall filed them down and O'Callaghan, the defending champion, won the event with his last throw, making it the greatest day Ireland has ever known at the Olympics. After three days of celebrations Tisdall was offered a last-minute chance to compete in the decathlon and, although he could not do justice to himself, he finished first in two events and came eighth overall.

Tisdall was feted in Hollywood, especially by Douglas Fairbanks, who had won a wager of $1,000 on his race. He received such a hero's welcome in Ireland that he determined to settle there. At a lunch given in the Guinness brewery in Dublin he was offered £1,000 if he would allow them to use his statement after the Olympics that he had won on Guinness. But he was unwilling to sacrifice his amateur status by doing so. He did voluntary work setting up a youth movement with the President of the Irish Olympic Council, General Eoin O'Duffy; it later became the Irish quasi-Fascist blueshirt movement. But he was offered no paid employment.

Declining offers to enter Irish politics, he returned to England empty-handed apart from a gift of £200 from O'Duffy. He tried his hand unsuccessfully selling works of art. He then got a job at 30 shillings a week making a golf course, on a promise never fulfilled from Sir Warden Chillcott of a post as secretary of the club when the course was built. Decent and honourable himself, Tisdall was trusting to the point of gullibility and was often taken in. He also wrote a book, *The Young Athlete*. It was dedicated to Lord Burghley.

At the end of 1933 Tisdall emigrated to South Africa, where he worked as a schoolmaster before setting up a gymnasium in Johannesburg. When war broke out in 1939 he helped to raise a regiment of the South African Irish and was part of the force that chased the fleeing Italians out of Ethiopia. He reached Egypt but was recalled to South Africa in 1941 before the major military engagements in those parts. He served out the war looking after a prisoner-of-war camp.

After the war he was a salesman for a mining house. However, in 1948, saddened by the defeat of Smuts in the general election, he decided to leave South Africa. He prospected for mica near Lusaka in Northern Rhodesia before becoming a farm manager in Kenya. His wife left him. He subsequently met and married a Leicester girl, Peggy Fellowes. They settled on a coffee farm formerly owned by Germans near Oldeani in Tanzania and he enjoyed some financial security for the first time in his life. He became a friend of Julius Nyerere, the President, and promoted sport in his spare time. The East Africa Olympic Committee sent him as its representative to the Rome Olympics of 1960.

In the mid-1960s he returned to live in Co Cork, but he found the cold and damp intolerable. So, after a few years, he emigrated to Queensland, where he bought a farm. He was an honoured guest at the Los Angeles Olympics in 1984. He was also feted on his occasional return visits to his beloved Tipperary, all the more so as Ireland has won only one gold medal in a track event since his victory in 1932. In 2002 a statue of him racing over hurdles was erected in Nenagh.

Tisdall retained his charm and handsome appearance into advanced old age. He also kept himself fit, playing tennis, golfing and swimming. At 86 years of age he did his first parachute jump from 12,000 feet. At 90 years of age he missed "shooting his age" over 18 holes of golf by one shot. With characteristic sensitivity and modesty he declined to present the medals for the 400 metres hurdles at the Sydney Olympics in 2000 because he thought it might distract from the winner's moment of glory. But he was delighted to carry the Olympic torch through Nambour and to be present at the Games. He had unquenchable faith in the ideal of sport as a vehicle for bringing about peace and human brotherhood.

He is survived by his second wife, Peggy, and their three children, as well as by one daughter of his first marriage.

GEORGE BEST

26 NOVEMBER 2005

GEORGE BEST, FOOTBALLER, was born on May 22, 1946. He died on November 25, 2005, aged 59.

George Best was the most talented British football player of his and arguably of any generation. He appeared to play and read the game at a different pace from those around him. He possessed dribbling skills which, in the words of his team-mate Pat Crerand, could leave opposing defenders with "twisted blood", and a balance which enabled him to ride or avert the most ruthless tackles, which his reputation and ability to humiliate the hard men of the game inevitably attracted.

His goal-scoring record was phenomenal for a winger. Best was quick, brave, and a sublime passer of the ball when he could curb his natural inclination to hold on to it for as long as possible. At his best, he gave the impression that thought and execution were a seamless whole, and at all times he approached the game with the passion and excitement of a young boy. Even the incomparable Pele once called him "the greatest footballer in the world".

Best secured his status as a footballing legend in the great Manchester United team of the 1960s, outshining even Bobby Charlton and Denis Law in a side which won league titles in 1965 and 1967 and which in 1968 became the first English club to win the European Cup.

He made 464 appearances for the club, scoring 178 goals, and also won 37 caps for his native Northern Ireland.

Yet at the age of only 26, driven to distraction by the media hysteria that surrounded his every move, and frustrated beyond the point of return by the decline of his team, he walked out of Manchester United for the last time, effectively ending his career in top-flight football.

The conventional wisdom is that Best's early departure from the game was the result of the weaknesses in his personality, which became abundantly apparent as he sought to fill the gap his retirement left in his life with alcohol and womanizing. He was seen as the paradigm of the flawed genius, impelled towards self-destruction by the same forces from which he derived his greatness. But although there was truth in this, Best's decline did not happen in a vacuum. He and every aspect of his life were simply subjected to a level of scrutiny from the press which was unprecedented in that era, familiar though such intrusion into the private lives of sportsmen has become since.

Best very much reflected the era of social, industrial and technical revolution that was the 1960s. The abolition of the maximum wage for footballers slowly, and greatly, transformed the game. The increasingly well-rewarded players had more autonomy and more money to spend, and in liberalizing times, more opportunity to live raucous lifestyles. Although he was an extreme example, George Best epitomized the transformation of footballers into good-time boys, semi-pop stars.

Best's long hair and good looks led to him being dubbed "the fifth Beatle", a reputation enhanced by the novel sound of screaming adolescent girls wherever he played. Treated like a pop star, he began in time to live like one. He opened a boutique, drove a series of E-type Jaguars, advertised every imaginable product and had to employ three full-time secretaries to field the 10,000 items of fan mail he received per week.

Something eventually had to give, but it was to Best's credit that he held his game together for as long as he did. Decline when it came was mercilessly chronicled in the press. Although he was to make comeback attempts (notably at Fulham, Hibernian and in the United States), it was for an increasingly rudderless playboy lifestyle rather than for his sporadic footballing exploits that Best became renowned.

The column inches that had once eulogized his performances on the pitch began to chronicle a seemingly endless succession of drunken binges, women and episodes of gambling and brawling. The nadir came in 1984 when Best was imprisoned for two months for drink-driving and evading arrest. But no amount of infamy could undo the truth of the observation made by his friend and fellow-player, Rodney Marsh, that "everyone, deep down, wanted to be George Best".

The skills that were to make Best the most exhilarating player of his era were learnt on the sprawling Cregagh estate in Belfast, on which he was raised. He was the eldest child of a Protestant shipyard iron-turner, Dickie, and his wife, Anne, a quick and skilful amateur hockey player from whom Best believed he inherited not only his athleticism but also his tendency to alcohol abuse (his insistence on the genetic provenance of the latter trait sat rather uneasily with his considerable guilt about the contribution the notoriety that came to surround him made to his mother's early death).

Best was obsessed with football from infancy. At 14 months – an age when most children can barely walk – he was photographed with a ball at his feet, and for years he insisted on taking a ball to bed with him. Every year he received exactly the same Christmas present – a new ball, kit and boots.

He was an able pupil, the only one in his year to pass the 11-plus examination, but he gave up his place at the Grosvenor High Grammar School when, marked out by his uniform as a Protestant, the daily ordeal of passing through sectarian Roman Catholic areas became unbearable. He rejoined his former classmates at the local secondary modern, and put his hopes for the future on being spotted by one of the talent scouts who frequented local matches.

This dream began to fade as he was continually rejected on the grounds that he was too small and thin ever to make it in the professional game, however dazzling his performances. Best resigned himself to finding a manual career and, at 15, left school and passed an examination to be taken on as a printing apprentice. One week later, he was approached by Bob Bishop, the local scout for Manchester United, with the offer that every young player dreamed of. Bishop sent a telegram to Manchester which simply said: "I have found a genius."

Within 24 hours of his arrival, overawed by the experience of meeting the players and riddled with self-doubt about his size, Best staged his first walkout. On finding that his son regretted this impulsive decision, Best's father telephoned Matt Busby, the United manager, and persuaded him to give him another chance.

Busby nurtured his shy new charge, and was to find his faith amply repaid long before the turmoil of Best's later years at United. His first match was a home tie against West Bromwich Albion in September 1963.

In the early days Best applied himself to honing his natural talent with a dedication that flatly contradicted his later reputation for skimping on training.

As a child, he practised kicking a tennis ball against doorknobs until he had mastered striking them dead-centre, the precondition for the ball returning to him rather than flying off at an angle. Later on, he would aim to hit the crossbar at least nine times out of ten from the penalty spot, then from 20 yards, then 30 and then 40 before repeating the process with his weaker left foot until it became as reliable as his right.

Such dedication soon paid great dividends, and the world first noticed Best at his best in Manchester United's 5–1 defeat of the European giants Benfica in 1966. The Belfast boy scored twice in the opening ten minutes in what was the Portuguese side's first home defeat in the European Cup. One supporter ran on the pitch with a knife, wanting a lock of Best's hair. The press dubbed him "El Beatle".

Having helped United to the league championship in 1967, Best starred again in Europe when the Reds became the first English side to lift the European Cup, beating Benfica at Wembley in 1968. In extra time, with the score level at 1–1, Best walked the ball into the net to put United on their way to a 4–1 triumph.

Other outstanding performances included his double hat-trick against Northampton Town in an FA Cup fifth-round tie in 1970, and what may be considered his parting shot, a 1980 strike for San Jose Earthquakes, in which he tormented and worked his way around four defenders before placing the ball beyond the reach of the goalkeeper.

On the international field too, there were memorable moments:

in 1971 he scored a hat-trick against Cyprus in Belfast and in a home tie against England had an audacious goal against England disallowed. The goalkeeper Gordon Banks had the ball in his hands, preparing to take a kick, when Best nipped in, got the ball, and headed a shot into the net. The referee, however, was not impressed.

There was controversy too. In 1970 he was sent off against Scotland in Belfast for throwing mud at the referee. More seriously, the following year, he briefly withdrew from the squad after threats from the IRA.

Because of Manchester United's foreign commitments in the European Cup, Best's time spent in the United States and his general errant behaviour, he appeared for Northern Ireland only 37 times. Understandably, he may have lacked incentive. A team which drew from such a comparatively tiny pool of players could never be potential world champions. When his friend, the journalist Brian Madley, said in front of a press conference that he thought Best only the world's second-best footballer, the mercurial Ulsterman later remonstrated with him: "Do you think if I had played for Brazil and Pele played for Northern Ireland, you'd still be saying the same thing?"

Opinion was divided between those who saw Best's career as a shameful waste of talent and those who were simply grateful to have had the opportunity to see him grace the game. Best himself insisted that he alone had the right to be disappointed that his career did not last longer, and that he was not. He was particularly fond of relating in that context the tale of the night porter who brought a bottle of champagne to his Bloomsbury hotel room soon after Best had quit Manchester United.

Confronted by the sight of the former Miss World, Mary Stavin (one of four winners of that accolade to share Best's bed), spilling out of her negligee and by piles of cash Best had won in a casino that evening scattered on the bed, the porter pocketed a £50 tip and asked if Best would mind him asking a question: "Where did it all go wrong, George?"

Just as he played football in defiance of the constraints faced by ordinary players, Best felt no obligation to live his life according to the conventional rules of society. For him, it was enough to be George Best.

He was comfortable to spend the latter part of his career playing for lesser clubs because he found it enjoyable. Thanks to his partnership with the equally unpredictable Rodney Marsh, Best particularly seemed to enjoy his two seasons at second division Fulham. The two thought English football had become dreary, and they managed to inject an element of theatre back into the game.

He left a string of women in his wake, but his charm led most to forgive him. He drank away much of his adult life, but was loved enough to have an entire evening of BBC television devoted to his 50th birthday celebrations. He was always a favourite television guest, and in 1998 he joined Sky Sports as a regular football pundit.

In 2001 he published an autobiography, *Blessed*, followed by *Scoring at Half Time*, a collection of the anecdotes which had accrued to his flamboyant life. This year he published another memoir, *Hard Tackles and Dirty Baths*, which he described as the inside story of football's – and his own – golden era, the 1960s and early 1970s.

However, the years of heavy drinking had taken their toll. In 1999 he was found to have severe cirrhosis of the liver. Despite intensive treatment, his health worsened, and in 2002 he had a liver transplant. Within a year he was reported to be drinking again, his second marriage collapsed and in 2004 he was banned for 20 months for drink-driving.

Best's bedrock was a stubborn nonconformity, a certainty that he was special, which was the wellspring of his genius, and the source of the adulation, the envy, and the censure which dominated his life. It was the anchor which enabled him to survive the chaos into which his life degenerated for so long, and the reason why he was unwilling or unable to prevent that process.

Best was twice married; in 1978 to Angela MacDonald James (divorced 1986), by whom he had a son, and in 1995 to Alex Pursey (dissolved 2004), 25 years his junior.

JOHN McGAHERN

30 MARCH 2006

JOHN MCGAHERN WAS ARGUABLY the finest Irish prose writer of his generation. His novel *Amongst Women* was short-listed for the Booker Prize in 1990 and made into a much admired television series. His *Memoir* published last year also won high acclaim and was read melodiously by the author himself on the BBC's *Book at Bedtime*.

Although born in Dublin, he spent the first nine years of his life in Leitrim in north-east Connacht where his mother was a primary school teacher. His father, who had been an IRA gunman in the War of Independence, was a police officer stationed twenty miles away. John was close to his rather gentle mother and was traumatized by her death from cancer when he was only nine. He and his six siblings were moved to live in the police barracks with their father who was a sadistic bully and beat them unmercifully.

Young John had promised his mother that he would become a priest. Clinging on to her memory through his teenage years, he resisted with steely determination his father's plan to apprentice him to a shopkeeper and cycled seven miles each day to complete his schooling with the Presentation Brothers in Carrick-on-Shannon. He was befriended by a prosperous Protestant neighbour who lent him books and he became an avid reader. "There are no days more full in childhood," he recalled, "than those days that are not lived at all, the days lost in a book."

The dream of becoming a priest was replaced by that of becoming a writer. "I would no longer have to die in life in order to circumvent death and the judgment and to keep the promise to her I loved," he wrote; "instead of being a priest of God I would be a god of a small vivid world."

At the end of his schooldays he won a scholarship that would have enabled him to follow his late mother to university. Instead, attracted by the prospect of a secure job and long holidays, he opted to train as a primary teacher. In the summers he worked on building sites in England. As soon as he arrived in England, he thought of all the great English writers he had read and had the awesome feeling that he was stepping on to sacred ground. It was wholly in character that the republican dream never attracted him, representing for him an even greater delusion than the religious one.

After he qualified McGahern taught in Dublin. He was able to attend evening classes at University College Dublin and took a degree. He tried his hand as a writer while steering clear of the bohemian pubs where the Dublin literati assembled. As a result of an extract from an unpublished novel in a literary journal he was spotted by Faber and Faber for whom he wrote *The Barracks*, published in 1963. It won a literary prize and he was able to take a year off from his teaching. He went to London where he met and married in a register office a Finnish theatre producer. His second novel *The Dark* appeared. Its depiction of adolescent sexuality mentioning the dreaded masturbation offended Ireland's puritanical censors and the book joined the list of notable Irish literary works to be banned.

Dublin's austere authoritarian Archbishop McQuaid was not best pleased and instructed a reluctant parish priest, who was the school manager, to dismiss McGahern. The Teacher's Union, usually so militant, was pusillanimous about taking up McGahern's case. "If it was just the auld book maybe we might have been able to do something for you," their general secretary told him, "but with marrying this foreign woman you have turned yourself into a hopeless case entirely; and what anyhow entered into your head to marry her when there are hundreds and thousands of Irish girls going around with their tongues out for a husband."

McGahern found work as a supply teacher in London. But he was not prepared to move to Finland when his wife got an offer of a television post there. They parted. He then met and lived with an American photographer, Madeline Green, whom he married in 1973. He had a research fellowship at the University of Reading for a time and a visiting professorship at Colegate University in upstate New York.

Although his next, not altogether satisfactory, novel *The Leavetaking* published in 1975 may have been inspired by the events of his dismissal in Dublin, he never lined up with Joyce or other Irish writers who made a thing of rejecting their Irish Catholic background. True, he had ceased to be a believer and thought that repressive sexual teaching had done harm in Ireland. But he remained grateful that he had been brought up in the Church; he said that it taught him a great deal about ceremony and mystery and sacrament and the equality of all men and women under the sun.

Nor, unlike Joyce, was he disposed to separate himself forever from his homeland and was gratified when his wife agreed to settle there with him in 1974. He acquired a small farm near where he had been brought up and wrote. Two collections of short stories and a novel entitled *The Pornographer* appeared before *Amongst Women* established his reputation. The main character, the tyrannical father Michael Moran, an unpredictable severe man obsessed with appearances and lacking any self-awareness, was based largely on his recently deceased father and is drawn memorably with feeling and some understanding. But almost equally compelling is the picture it gives of the cohesiveness of the family in rural Ireland. One critic felt able to disregard the yawning gap between ragged Leitrim of the time and Paris of the belle époque and compare McGahern's treatment to Proust.

After the triumph of *Amongst Women* it took the meticulous, painstaking McGahern over a decade to produce his next novel *That They May Face the Rising Sun*. Unusually, it was without a plot and depicted the cycle of the year in a rural community where nothing happens. As always, his evocation of the countryside down to the smallest detail in his lucid, economical, carefully honed prose was masterly. His sense of where he belonged, the centre of his world and the inspiration of his writing, is plain. Depicting as it does with some regret the vanishing rural communities of small farms where life had remained unchanged for so long it cemented his position not just as a great Irish writer but also as a sociologist of twentieth century Ireland.

If *Amongst Women* exorcized the ghost of his feared father it was left to his *Memoir* written after he was diagnosed with cancer to give voice at last to his pent-up deep feeling for his long-departed, gentle and much beloved mother. Recalling their walks to school along the lanes when she named the flowers for him and occasionally picked them, he remarked, "I must have been extraordinarily happy walking that lane to school. There are many such lanes all around where I live and in certain rare moments over the years while walking in these lanes I have come into an extraordinary sense of security, a deep peace, in which I feel that I can live for ever."

McGahern was a reticent, modest, shy, serious, apparently benign man but not so totally benevolent that he was incapable of occasional sharpness or did not enjoy some sly humour about his fellows or an item of scurrilous gossip.

He is survived by his wife.

* * *

CHARLES HAUGHEY

14 JUNE 2006

CHARLES HAUGHEY, who died on June 13, 2006, aged 80, served three separate terms as Prime Minister (Taoiseach) of the Republic of Ireland between 1979 and 1992. For almost 30 years he was arguably the central and certainly the most controversial and glamorous figure in Irish public life.

To many he epitomized the new Irish capitalist class, dynamic, ruthless and brash, just like their Irish-American prototype. After his dismissal from Jack Lynch's government in 1970 and subsequent acquittal on charges of conspiring to import arms illegally, presumably for use in Northern Ireland, he became the focus within the Fianna Fail party of hardline Irish republicanism. The legacy of this dogged his periods as Taoiseach in that he was deeply distrusted by Ulster Unionists and never realized his ambition to achieve a historic breakthrough on Northern Ireland.

When he became Taoiseach for the third time in 1987 he presided over the necessary cutbacks that provided the essential basis for the dramatic expansion of the Irish economy since the mid-1990s. But prosperity bred corruption, and his final period in office was marred by a series of scandals that pursued him in retirement and culminated in his disgrace and humiliation.

Haughey's parents came from Swatragh in the Sperrin mountains of East Tyrone and were both active in the guerrilla war preceding the creation in 1921 of the Irish Free State. His father, Sean Haughey, was the officer commanding the South Derry IRA and became a commissioned officer in the Free State Army that defeated the republicans in the civil war. He was stationed in the West of Ireland when Charles, the second of seven children, was born at Castlebar, Co Mayo, September 16, 1925.

Sean Haughey's career did not thrive after he left the Army in 1928. He was dogged by ill-health and died in his forties. The family of four boys and three girls were brought up in fairly straitened circumstances on the north side of Dublin.

Charlie (as he was generally known) went to school with the Christian Brothers in St Joseph's Fairview where he was a clever student and a good hurler and footballer, if somewhat truculent and hot-tempered on the field of play. He won a scholarship to University College Dublin, where he studied commerce. While there, he was one of the leaders of a crowd of its students who on VE-Day in 1945 burnt the Union Jack outside Trinity College. It was, it should be added, a response to some Trinity hearties who had burnt the Irish tricolour on the roof of the college.

Having taken his degree Haughey went on to qualify as a chartered accountant and practised for a time. Despite his family background on the Free State side he joined the republican Fianna Fail party. In 1951 he married the daughter of its deputy leader, Sean Lemass.

After several unsuccessful bids he was elected to the Dail in 1957. When Lemass became Taoiseach in 1959, Haughey was one of a group of thrusting young men whom he brought into government to replace the veteran republicans who had served under de Valera since 1932. Haughey held the portfolios of Justice, Agriculture and Finance in turn. Incisive and highly intelligent, he rapidly mastered his brief in each department and was not afraid to make bold innovations even in the teeth of advice from his civil servants. He had enviable qualities of clarity and imagination. Succession rights for widows, free travel for pensioners and tax exemption for the earnings of stallions and artists were measures long remembered to his credit.

However, Haughey seemed to disdain the priest-like image of impeccable respectability cultivated by previous Irish political leaders. Although far from handsome, he had a way with women that was legendary. There was about him a whiff of scandal. Rumours abounded of high living and sharp property deals, encouraged by his apparent but unexplained affluence. Small in stature, he bore himself with ceremony and dressed immaculately. He bought a large Georgian house situated in several hundred acres, became a patron of the arts, rode to hounds with the gentry and flirted with their womenfolk.

Yet he remained a man of the people, accepted as one of their own by his North Dublin constituents who were to support him mightily through thick and thin. They recognized in him a kindly, open-handed man capable of genuine compassion for those in need and always as good as his word. But others derided him as abrasive, intimidating, arrogant and crooked.

Within his party, Haughey was distrusted by old-guard republicans who could not forget that his father was a "Free Stater" and suspected that Haughey himself was an opportunist with little commitment to their austere ideals. This was one factor in the failure of his bid to succeed Lemass in 1966 when he was forced to yield gracefully to Jack Lynch. He was apprehensive that in a future leadership contest he would be upstaged by Neil Blaney, a hardline republican from Donegal.

This may provide an explanation for Haughey's involvement in the plan to import arms for use in Northern Ireland in 1970. It surprised observers who had never seen him as a hardliner on the issue of partition and recalled that in 1962 he had put down a previous IRA campaign by the establishment of a non-jury military court to try those involved.

The attempted importation led to his dismissal as Finance Minister by the Taoiseach Jack Lynch. At the time Haughey was in hospital as a result of injuries said to have been incurred in some kind of riding accident. He, Blaney and several others were charged with conspiracy to import arms illegally but all were acquitted. It was an unsatisfactory episode for all concerned. There were indications that the whole Government had connived in the operation until it was discovered by the police and leaked to the Leader of the Opposition.

In the wake of the attacks on the Catholic areas of Belfast in 1969, the Irish Government was under pressure to be ready to give aid to the Catholic population in Northern Ireland to defend themselves if they were attacked by Orange mobs and once again not protected by the police. But Haughey's own denial in evidence that he had sanctioned the importation was contradicted by several witnesses as well as one of his co-accused. When, following his acquittal by the jury after a sensational trial, he called on those responsible for the prosecution to "take the honourable course", he was faced down by Lynch and forced to eat humble pie on the back benches.

But Haughey was nothing if not resilient. He travelled the length and breadth of the country addressing party meetings, consolidating his position with the rank and file and uttering the odd bit of Anglophobia. There were soon to be found in every neck of the woods self-styled patriots, wheeler-dealers and sharp operators proud to proclaim themselves "Charlie men".

In 1975 Lynch was constrained to recall Haughey to the front bench and he was appointed Minister for Health and Social Welfare when Fianna Fail won a landslide victory at the 1977 general election. As a minister, despite a restricted budget, he once again displayed that spectacular flair that made his colleagues seem flat-footed. He even squared the circle in the controversy about legalizing the sale of contraceptives (including condoms) by making them available to married couples on a prescription from a doctor. It was, he announced brazenly, an Irish solution to an Irish problem.

When Lynch retired late in 1979, Haughey seemed to be the best man to revive his party's flagging fortunes and he was elected, albeit by a narrow majority that included few of his Cabinet colleagues. But, in his first term as Taoiseach, Haughey proved a disappointment. Although he began well by demanding more action from his ministers and promising a correction in public finances, he showed a lack of toughness that belied his public image in not cutting back expenditure and not sacking inefficient or dissident ministers.

He struck up an amiable relationship with Margaret Thatcher whom he presented with a Georgian silver teapot at their first meeting. He persuaded her to make the first official visit by a British prime minister to Dublin and won acceptance for the idea of joint action by the two governments on Northern Ireland rather than awaiting an internal settlement among the parties there.

He and some ministers hinted that the agreement to examine the totality of relationships between the two islands would enable the issue of partition to be reopened. For a period the British Government, although irked, seemed content to allow him to make political mileage out of these claims, influenced perhaps by the fact that the policing of the border was more efficient than under Jack Lynch. But Thatcher's inflexibility in face of the hunger strikes in Northern Ireland soured relations. The electoral boost it gave to republican hunger-striker candidates in border constituencies precipitated Haughey's narrow defeat in the 1981 general election.

He was, however, back in office after a further general election in February 1982. This term was even less successful than his first. He was dependent for his majority on a left-wing Independent and could not make the necessary cutbacks. His relationship with Thatcher collapsed when the Irish Government backtracked to adopt a neutral position in the EEC and at the United Nations at the time of the Falklands invasion.

In November 1982 he was forced from office after the death of one of his backbenchers and was defeated in the subsequent general election. On polling day his election agent was caught presenting himself to cast his vote in two different places. It was revealed by the incoming government that Haughey's Justice Minister, who was one of his chief henchmen, had had the telephone lines of several critical journalists tapped to listen to conversations with disloyal members of his government. Haughey was pilloried by the media. As it seemed inevitable that he would be replaced as leader of Fianna Fail, journalists vied with one another in writing his political obituary. However, Houdini-like, he held on where a less doughty fighter would have resigned, and rivalries among possible successors helped to ensure his survival. He was then able to rid the party of his most hostile opponents within it, including Desmond O'Malley, who left to form a new party.

In opposition between 1982 and 1987, Haughey marked time while his successor, Garret FitzGerald, who had promised to rectify the public finances, failed to have this done and lost credibility. Somewhat irresponsibly, Haughey castigated any feeble cutbacks as Thatcherite or monetarist. He emerged as a champion of traditional family values when he supported an anti-abortion amendment to the Constitution and opposed the introduction of divorce.

He also opposed the Hillsborough agreement giving the Irish Government a permanent advisory role in the government of Northern Ireland, saying that he was opposed to its accepting that Northern Ireland had a right to choose to remain part of the UK. However, when his stance proved unpopular, he changed tack and announced that he regarded the agreement as binding and would work it if returned to office. But when FitzGerald's government moved to legislate for the extradition of political offenders, which was the price of the agreement, Haughey opposed them tooth and nail.

Haughey was returned once more as Taoiseach after the general election in February 1987. He chose a government that excluded the "wild men" of his 1982 administration. He did a deal with the unions on pay restraint. His tough Finance Minister, Ray McSharry, introduced

317

the cuts that FitzGerald's Fine Gael party had advocated but failed to implement. This revived business confidence.

Haughey showed his old flair for the spectacular initiative when he sponsored a low-tax Financial Services Centre in Dublin's docklands that attracted many foreign institutions to set up there. He worked the Hillsborough agreement, albeit with a lack of enthusiasm, and relied on his genial Foreign Minister, Brian Lenihan, to smooth out differences with the British. In the aftermath of the carnage caused by an IRA bomb at the Remembrance Day Service at Enniskillen in November 1987, he agreed to enact legislation to allow for the extradition of political offenders to Britain although he insisted on inserting the safeguard that each application would have to be examined and approved by the Irish Attorney General.

Thatcher always felt that she understood the incisive, short-spoken Haughey better than FitzGerald, whose talkativeness and obsession with trivia irritated her. But that did not stop her from giving Haughey several unmerciful dressings-down when the Irish Government failed to deliver on the security front. While often unyielding, he was restrained and statesmanlike in his responses even when the behaviour of the security forces in Northern Ireland gave cause for complaint.

New political initiatives were ruled out because unionist leaders were loath to have direct contact with Haughey despite his benign assurances that they would be surprised at his generosity when they got to negotiations. Peace was impossible as long as the IRA was not prepared for a ceasefire without a prior commitment from the British to withdraw from Northern Ireland. However, through some Belfast priests and Martin Mansergh, an Oxford-educated Anglo-Irishman who was his devoted political adviser, Haughey opened lines to the leadership of Sinn Fein that were to bear fruit some years after he had left office.

Haughey cut an impressive figure during the Irish presidency of the European Union in 1990 when his mastery of the issues and urbanity were much admired. He had the government buildings splendidly restored for the occasion; the Dublin wits called it "the Chas Mahal".

Abandoning his previous scepticism about the effects of European integration on Irish neutrality, he now emerged as a full-blooded advocate of political union on the road to Maastricht. He struck up a singularly good rapport with the French President François Mitterrand, whom he liked to regard as a kindred spirit. Chancellor Helmut Kohl was grateful for his prompt support for German unification. Ireland was to be rewarded with the generous allocations of structural funds that fuelled the unprecedented economic boom of the 1990s.

By then, however, Haughey's days in power were numbered. After he had called an unnecessary general election in 1989, he was forced to enter into a coalition government with the Progressive Democrat Party under his old adversary Desmond O'Malley. It offended a core value of Fianna Fail to join in a coalition government. The manner in which Haughey went over the heads of his ministers to arrange it was deeply resented, as was the dismissive and foul-mouthed way in which he dealt with colleagues who dared to disagree with him.

In 1991 he was forced to set up an inquiry into the beef industry in response to allegations of questionable links between his government and a leading beef exporter. There were other scandals involving people with whom Haughey had close associations.

Then, in early 1992, a disgruntled Sean Doherty, who had been his Justice Minister when the telephones of journalists had been tapped in 1982, announced that Haughey had known all about it at the time. Although Haughey denied the charge, and Doherty could not be counted as a reliable witness, having previously denied that he had told Haughey, the Progressive Democrat Party decided that it had had enough and could no longer support a government led by Haughey. He went quietly rather than fight another election.

Haughey left office to a chorus of acclamation, especially in the Dail which he had dominated imperiously since he became Taoiseach. He made no further political pronouncements. He rode his horse on Portmarnock Strand most mornings. He sailed his yacht *Celtic Mist* around the coast and made visits to an island off Kerry that he had bought in the 1970s. His horse, *Flashing Steel*, won the Irish Grand National in 1995. He opened his house and gardens for charitable causes and received visitors like one to the manor born. His enduring hold on popular affections was evident whenever he made a public appearance.

Then, in 1997, in the course of an inquiry into gifts made to a government minister by a Dublin businessman called Ben Dunne, it emerged that Dunne had also made gifts of more than £1 million to Haughey in 1987. Haughey at first denied the gifts in correspondence with a judicial tribunal of inquiry before which he then had to appear in a blaze of publicity to admit that he had lied.

Instead of enjoying an honoured retirement, he was embattled, defending himself against prosecutions and tax claims, and had to endure examination by a special tribunal of inquiry set up to examine government decisions affecting those from whom he had received donations. His explanation that he knew nothing about any donations because he had left all his financial affairs in the hands of a trusted accountant, now deceased, was characteristically brazen.

The public indulgence long accorded to him as a likeable rogue evaporated, especially when it seemed that he might have diverted to his own use funds collected for the treatment in America of his ailing long-time friend and ministerial colleague Brian Lenihan.

His domestic tranquillity and that of his loyal wife and family was upset when Terry Keane, a judge's wife and Haughey's long-time mistress, went public with graphic details of their affair in the columns of *The Sunday Times*. Tales of clandestine trips to Paris and Haughey's extravagances (notably on Charvet shirts) titillated the Irish public.

Still, he did not falter, remaining apparently oblivious to any wrongdoing on his part, treating critics and interrogators alike with the lofty disdain of which he was a past master. His prosecution on charges of obstructing the tribunal by his lies was aborted when a long-standing adversary, the Deputy Prime Minister Mary Harney, remarked in an interview that he should be sent to prison.

Finally, in October 2000, before his cross-examination at the tribunal of inquiry had reached the most interesting questions, his doctors said that his prostate cancer made it impossible for him to go on. The presiding judge decided to continue the questioning in private and at a slower pace. So far the tribunal has not completed its deliberations so the question whether Haughey granted favours in return for donations remains unanswered. He had, however, to make large payments to the Revenue for unpaid tax arising mainly out of gifts he received.

Haughey is survived by his wife Maureen, by three sons and one daughter. One son, Sean, a former Lord Mayor of Dublin, remains a member of the Dail for the North Dublin constituency long represented by Haughey himself.

* * *

SAM STEPHENSON

22 NOVEMBER 2006

SAM STEPHENSON, ARCHITECT, who died on November 9, 2006, aged 72, was arguably the most outstanding architect based in Ireland of his generation; he was certainly the most controversial.

In 1962 he and his partner Arthur Gibney won a competition to design the headquarters in Dublin of Ireland's Electricity Supply Board. This involved the demolition of a dozen or so 18th-century houses that were in the middle of a quarter-mile streetscape with mountains in the background; it was one of the glories of the Georgian city. All hell broke loose as the Irish Georgian Society and kindred preservationists flexed their muscles for the first time. Princess Grace of Monaco was among the thousands who signed a petition to halt the destruction. Sir Albert Richardson came from London to lend support. *The Sunday Times* correspondent wrote that no London vandal had done worse.

Stephenson entered the fray, calling down a bubonic plague on preservationists and asserting boldly that Georgian buildings were not worth keeping. He voiced a crude nationalist resentment towards Dublin's colonial heritage as well as the self-interest of a new class of native entrepreneur who wished to make a killing out of redevelopment.

Born on 15 December 1933 Stephenson was one of five sons of a librarian who had taken part in the Easter rebellion of 1916. His uncle was a Jesuit so Stephenson went to Belvedere, the Jesuit school and played for its rugby team.

Stephenson was fortunate to enter practice in the late fifties when the Irish economy was emerging from stagnation and there were pickings to be had from friends in the Fianna Fail Government. He canvassed for the future Taoiseach Charles Haughey, helped to raise funds from developers and ran unsuccessfully for the Senate.

When, in 1965, the Central Bank decided that to signal its new importance it needed a building that towered over the financial district in Dublin, it retained Stephenson. He designed a building 30ft higher than the level permitted by the planning authority, hoping it would not be noticed. It was. The row that resulted deprived him of the kudos that he deserved for a remarkable hanging design that had been inspired by the great Irish-American architect Kevin Roche. Stephenson joked that it was his "biggest erection".

The rich of the brave new Ireland, like Stephenson's close friend Haughey, preferred to live in old gentry houses so, apart from a commission to build an Irish house for the broadcaster Eamonn Andrews, Stephenson was denied the opportunity to make a mark in domestic architecture. However, buildings for the Irish Turf Board and the Currency Centre of the Central Bank in the 1970s are acknowledged masterpieces.

More controversial were the new civic offices on the old Viking site in Wood Quay, consisting of four bunker-like towers, a design that owed something to Stephenson's admiration for Hitler's architect, Albert Speer. The city fathers took fright at the outcry after two of them were built and brought in other architects to complete the job. Stephenson comforted himself by proclaiming that the great architects of the past had not been appreciated by contemporaries.

Stephenson dabbled in property speculation with developer associates and lived extravagantly. In the lean years of the 1980s this led to financial disaster. As there was little work for architects in Ireland, he dissolved his fruitful relationship with the talented Gibney and set up in London with Stone Toms. Irish developers were pleased to employ him and through his friendship with one of them, the Tipperaryman Ned Ryan, he joined the circle around Princess Margaret.

Stephenson's marriage was a casualty of the changed direction of his life. Only in 1991, when he married a much younger woman, did he regain domestic stability. He set up home in a Georgian house at Leixlip, near Dublin, and had a second family. He kept up his architecture, albeit in lower key than in his palmy days, and exhibited his well-crafted watercolours and drawings at the Royal Hibernian Academy.

Although short in stature, the bearded Stephenson with his white linen suits and lime-green shirts was always a presence. He was self-assured without being arrogant and was possessed of a delightful ease of manner and ready wit. His instincts were generous. He made friends easily, even with those who had been his sternest critics. A hot-tempered man in need of some forgiveness himself, he bore no grudges.

In later life he expressed regrets for his former abrasive disregard for the great architecture of the past and claimed that he now went to bed with Palladio and woke with Lutyens. But if he abandoned the Modernist faith in architecture he rediscovered his faith in religion and became a daily Mass-goer in recent years.

He is survived by his wife and by six children.

DAVID ERVINE

9 JANUARY 2007

DAVID ERVINE, ULSTER Volunteer Force terrorist and spokesman of the Progressive Unionist Party, was born on July 21, 1953. He died following a heart attack on January 8, 2007, aged 53.

As the IRA started to achieve electoral success through Sinn Fein in the 1980s, loyalist terrorist groups sought to create political machines of their own. One of the organizations to emerge was the Progressive Unionist Party, which represented the illegal Ulster Volunteer Force and was headed by the charismatic figure of David Ervine. Conforming to none of the malign caricatures of Ulster Protestant politicians, Ervine was neither a colourless bank manager, a belligerent preacher nor a tattooed thug. Articulate, persuasive and apparently repentant, he was widely touted as the alternative voice of loyalism.

A convicted member of the UVF, Ervine became an outspoken critic of terrorism. He was also among those trying to foster cross-community relations in Northern Ireland, insisting that he was "trying to move away from tribalism" and "sectarian politics". Unlike mainstream unionist parties, he talked openly to Sinn Fein, and played a key role in the Good Friday agreement of 1998.

David Walter Ervine, the youngest of two brothers and two sisters, grew up in Protestant East Belfast, the heart of working-class loyalism. He was educated at Orangefield Boys' Secondary School. His father was an iron-turner who served in the Royal Navy during the Second World War and became a member of the Northern Ireland Labour Party; his father's socialist leanings were to have a lasting effect on him.

As a teenager, however, Ervine was drawn to terrorism. Like many other Protestants of his generation, he was spurred to "join up" after Bloody Friday, July 21, 1972, when the IRA exploded 22 bombs in Belfast, killing nine people. He became a member of the UVF that year and at the age of 21 he was stopped in a car with five and a half pounds of commercial gelignite. The Army bomb disposal unit tied a rope around his ankle, pointed a pistol at him and sent him back into the vehicle to retrieve the device. He was sentenced to 11 years' imprisonment, of which he would serve more than five.

At Long Kesh, Ervine joined the UVF prisoners' wing under the UVF commander Gusty Spence, a dominant figure in militant loyalism and, like Ervine's father, a socialist by inclination. Ervine credited Spence with "unlocking the door". Whereas imprisonment tends to strengthen the political resolve of republican terrorists, it often has the reverse effect on loyalists, something Ervine recognized. "It made me think about the police, the Army and judge who put me there because they were defending their country – which was exactly what I thought I'd been doing."

Ervine talked about being "peculiarly Irish" in Long Kesh, learning enough Gaelic to cause havoc among the republican prisoners. During their drill practice he would shout "about turn" in Irish through the wire, reducing their ranks to chaos.

When released from prison he developed an interest in politics, though financial necessity dictated that he set himself up initially as a newsagent and milkman. Owing to IRA attention he had to give up the business and move house three times.

Being incarcerated with Spence opened Ervine's eyes to the often complex relationship between being working class and being a loyalist. Central to Ervine's emerging political vision was the belief that in the past, while working-class Catholics had been abused for their disloyalty, working-class Protestants had been manipulated for their loyalty by the Ascendency and by London. The PUP's ideal was of an inclusive, socialist United Kingdom (the party's constitution was based on that of the British Labour Party) that would forge working-class links between Protestants and Catholics: "We are saying that you can be a citizen of the UK irrespective of your religion." Ervine often quoted John Hume's father, who in warning him of the limitations of pursuing a nationalist agenda, had once said to him: "You can't eat a flag."

As a spokesman for the PUP, Ervine attended the 1994 Labour conference in Blackpool with Spence. Ervine pursued pragmatism: "I don't want to wake up every morning and ask myself am I British or Irish? I want to think 'Am I late for work?'."

The PUP's electoral mandate was minimal. Its principal role was to ensure that the UVF did not return to violence, Ervine describing himself as having "an insight into the thinking of the paramilitaries".

The UVF declared a ceasefire in 1994, and despite the breakdown of the concurrent IRA ceasefire in 1996, Ervine continued to urge his men not to go back to violence. In a historic move he visited John Major at 10 Downing Street in July 1996. Two years later, on the promise of prisoner remission, the PUP was one of the unionist parties most keen to sign up to the Good Friday agreement. Nevertheless the UVF continued and continues to be involved in punishment beatings, drug trafficking and other crime, not to mention an internecine war with the splinter group, the LVF, by whom Ervine was loathed.

He was elected to the Northern Ireland Assembly as MLA for East Belfast in 1998, and re-elected five years later. Last year, despite the PUP's paramilitary links, Ervine was invited to join the Ulster Unionist Assembly Group. The move was ruled invalid.

Like his counterpart Gerry Adams, David Ervine was an accomplished orator, comfortable in front of the cameras and willing to take his message to London, Dublin and Washington.

He liked to quote Bernard Shaw, and will be remembered for his trademark moustache and knitted jumpers; like his hero Spence, he would often be seen smoking a pipe.

He is survived by his wife, Jeanette, and by two sons.

TOMMY MAKEM

3 AUGUST 2007

TOMMY MAKEM, IRISH FOLK SINGER, was born on November 4, 1932. He died on August 1, 2007, aged 74.

The godfather of modern Irish music who left a huge mark on the 1960s US folk music scene Tommy Makem was voted, along with Joan Baez, as one of the two "most promising" acts at the Newport Folk Festival in 1961. Within little more than a year he had been usurped and it was Bob Dylan who was playing king to Baez's queen in the burgeoning Sixties American folk movement. But the assessment of the festival judging panel was perceptive, for Makem was a seminal figure who was still a popular and much loved performer 40 years on.

He was born into a family of singers in Co Armagh, and his mother Sarah Makem was reputed to have a repertoire of more than 500 songs. She never performed outside her own rural locality, but her evocative voice and extensive song catalogue attracted the attention of the BBC, which recorded her singing the title song of its influential 1950s folk series, *As I Roved Out*. Such a background meant, as Tommy Makem later put it, that he learnt to sing before he could talk. When the American collector Diane Hamilton recorded his mother in the early 1950s, she also recorded his rich baritone and he made his first appearance on disc on the 1955 compilation, *The Lark in the Morning*. During her visit, Hamilton also introduced Makem to Liam Clancy, a young singer from Co Tipperary. It was the start of a fruitful musical partnership that would endure for another four decades.

Seeing more future for Irish traditional music in America than at home, both Makem and Clancy emigrated in 1956. By this time, Clancy's elder brothers Tom and Paddy were already living in New York, where Paddy was running the Tradition record label. Makem and the three brothers began to perform as a quartet, first at parties and then, as their fame spread by word of mouth, in New York's Irish clubs and bars.

Tommy Makem

The Rising of the Moon, the first Clancy Brothers and Tommy Makem album, was released in 1959. The set comprised mostly Irish rebel songs and was followed swiftly by *Come Fill Your Glass With Us – Irish Songs of Drinking and Blackguarding.*

Dressed in the trademark Aran sweaters that would become the stereotypical sartorial standard for other Irish performers from Val Doonican to the Dubliners, they had a vigorous and earthy approach that made them favourites on the emerging American folk scene. The centre of musical activity at the time was Greenwich Village, New York, and the quartet sang and hung out regularly in its bars and coffee houses, where they met and befriended young American singers such as Phil Ochs and Bob Dylan. National prominence followed when they appeared on Ed Sullivan's television show in late 1961 and they graduated from pass-the-hat appearances at folk cellars to the concert stage at Carnegie Hall. In 1963 they performed at the White House for President Kennedy, who was ever eager to cultivate the Irish constituency.

They were also serious musical innovators and without their early influence it is doubtful whether the Celtic cultural tiger would have gone on to roar in the way that it later did. Until the arrival of Makem and the Clancys, Irish traditional song had been sung mostly unaccompanied in a dated style that was dying on its feet. Influenced by such American folk acts as the Weavers and the Kingston Trio, the quartet reinvigorated the tradition by backing their hearty harmonies with guitar, whistle, harmonica, drums and banjo.

Makem was an accomplished whistle player and is also credited as the first to introduce the five-string Appalachian banjo into Irish music when he used the instrument on his 1961 solo debut album, *The Songs of Tommy Makem*. The set included such, then little-known, traditional songs as *The Foggy Dew* and *The Irish Rover*, which would soon become standards and the subject of hundreds of cover versions. It also led to his award-winning performance that year at the Newport Folk Festival.

With America conquered, in 1963 the quartet returned to Ireland for their first concert on home soil. Their international acclaim was crucial in restoring Ireland's pride in its own musical traditions and led the way for the success of such groups as the Dubliners.

But their influence was considerable, not only in reviving and transforming Irish music, but also on American folk performers. Dylan adapted their version of Dominic Behan's *The Patriot Game* to become *With God on Our Side*, one of his most potent early protest songs. Decades later, Dylan acknowledged the debt when he invited Makem to appear at his star-studded 30th anniversary gala concert at Madison Square Garden, New York, in 1992.

In 1961 they moved from the tiny specialist Tradition label to Columbia and averaged at least an album a year throughout the rest of the decade. Makem, who had also developed as a songwriter with compositions such as *The Winds are Singing Freedom*, *Gentle Annie* and the much covered *Four Green Fields*, eventually left for a solo career in 1969.

He thrived touring as a solo act and hosted a number of television shows. But in 1975 he found himself sharing a bill with Liam Clancy again at a festival in Cleveland, Ohio. They did a short set together and the euphoric reception persuaded them to resume their partnership. They continued to work as a duo until 1978, making six albums, including *Liam Clancy and Tommy Makem* in 1976. This included their famous cover version of Eric Bogle's *And the Band Played Waltzing Matilda*.

After they went their separate ways once more in 1988, Makem continued to perform on the international Irish circuit. He also ran a club, called Tommy Makem's Irish Pavilion, on the corner of 57th Street and Lexington Avenue in New York. The club was used as the venue for the after-show party after Dylan's 30th anniversary concert, and Makem loved to tell the story of how he turned up after the concert and was initially refused entrance to his own pub by Dylan's security as he had mislaid his ticket.

In 1997 he published the book *Tommy Makem's Secret Ireland*, which indulged his interest in Celtic mythology. Two years later, he began a similarly themed one-man theatrical show, *Invasions and Legacies*, which explored themes from Irish history and legend. He continued to record, and his 1998 album, *The Song Tradition*, was regarded as his best work in many years. In 2000 he started the Tommy Makem International Festival of Song in South Armagh. His sons, Shane, Conor and Rory, continue the family tradition and are a popular fixture on the Irish-American folk scene, where they tour as the Makem Brothers.

Dylan acknowledged the influence of Makem and the Clancy Brothers in his 2004 autobiography *Chronicles Volume One*. Recalling time spent with them in the early 1960s in the White Horse Tavern in Greenwich Village, he described them as "musketeers" and wrote how he had been moved by their "rebellion songs".

Leading the tributes Clancy said that Makem, who had lung cancer, was a fighter until the end, adding: "He just would not give up."

He is survived by his three sons.

* * *

CONOR CRUISE O'BRIEN

20 DECEMBER 2008

CONOR CRUISE O'BRIEN's life straddled diplomacy, politics, historical scholarship, literature and journalism. He was a diplomat at the United Nations, a professor in the United States, a government minister in Ireland, the editor-in-chief of *The Observer* in Britain and a writer whose work commanded attention throughout the English-speaking world. He was an inveterate controversialist the quality of whose judgment and the wisdom of whose actions were often questioned, especially in his homeland. But none could deny the force of his intellect, the skill of his exposition and the courage with which he clung to his convictions.

He was born on November 4, 1917 into a family caught up in the heady political and literary life of Dublin. His mother Katherine, daughter of the Irish Party MP David Sheehy, was probably the original of Miss Ivors, a strident nationalist girl depicted in James Joyce's short story *The Dead*. His father, Francis Cruise O'Brien, was a waspish journalist who disconcerted his associates by abandoning his religion and speaking with an Oxford accent. He died suddenly in Conor's presence on Christmas Day 1927 when the boy, his only child, was ten.

Conor's mother carried out her agnostic husband's wish that their son should not be sent to a Catholic school. From the non-denominational Sandford Park he went on to the predominantly Protestant Trinity College Dublin. Having been educated in a minority culture apart from the mainstream of Catholic Ireland, he was to remain an outsider in Irish life, widely perceived as having the accent and superior attitude to his compatriots associated in many of their minds with Trinity and the Protestant Ascendancy.

At Trinity O'Brien read Irish and French before turning to history and made a clean sweep of all available prizes. However, contemporaries thought him arrogant and denied him election to the highest office in the college debating society. He married, before he left Trinity, Christine Foster, a fellow-student who belonged to a noted liberal Protestant family in Ulster.

In 1944 he entered the Department of External Affairs, having served briefly in the Department of Finance whose work he found uncongenial – he was never numerate and had little interest in economics. He worked on a virulent campaign for Irish unification launched by Foreign Minister Sean MacBride in 1949, running the Irish News Agency which spewed out propaganda on the subject. For all his later protestations there is no contemporary evidence that he was other than enthusiastic about the policies he helped to forward.

If O'Brien subscribed fully at this stage to the irredentist national aims of the Irish State, he remained apart from the strong Catholic ethos of its people. Yet, the influence of the Catholic Church on literature remained a constant preoccupation. In 1952 he published under the pen-name Donat O'Donnell a book entitled *Maria Cross*, a collection of essays on Catholic writers including Albert Camus, Graham Greene and Evelyn Waugh. His book *Parnell and his Party*, published in 1956, established him at one stroke in the front rank of Irish historians.

In 1956 O'Brien was appointed head of the United Nations section of the Department of External Affairs. Ireland upset the United States and her allies by its decision to vote in favour of a resolution to discuss the admission of Communist China to the United Nations. As Foreign Minister Frank Aiken was a man of limited intellect it was widely assumed, although it was not the case, that he was led astray by O'Brien. O'Brien believed that Ireland should make neutral Sweden its model and did not hide his conviction that imperialism was a greater evil than local communist movements in the developing world.

Dag Hammerskjold, the Swede who was Secretary General of the United Nations, had observed O'Brien and read *Maria Cross*. He requested the Irish Government to second O'Brien to serve with the United Nations in the Congo, where civil war had broken out after it became independent of Belgium. Although a UN resolution had stated that force was to be used in the last resort to remove foreign mercenaries who were assisting the secessionist regime of Moise Tshombe in Katanga, O'Brien was reviled as unnecessarily pugnacious when he actually ordered the use of force. Belgium and Britain had an interest in maintaining a compliant regime in mineral-rich Katanga. Under pressure from the Western powers, Hammerskjold was on his way to negotiate with Tshombe when he was killed in an aeroplane crash. After Hammerskjold's death, it was impossible for O'Brien to establish definitively that he had acted within his remit. He was recalled to New York and relieved of his post.

Feeling bitter that colleagues in Ireland's UN delegation had undermined him and aching to tell his story, O'Brien resigned from the Irish diplomatic service. In interviews and in the columns of *The Observer* he accused Harold Macmillan and his government of duplicity in supporting a UN resolution to end the secession of Katanga while working secretly to prevent its implementation. He then wrote a superb but rather sharp book *To Katanga and Back* in which he blamed Hammerskjold for allowing him to be made a scapegoat. His account has been essentially vindicated by historians but its tone and content were such as to leave him with few friends in high places.

By this time O'Brien's marriage had broken down, his wife complaining that it was impossible to go on living with a man who thought he was God. He had formed an attachment to a colleague Máire MacEntee, whose father was Tanaiste (Deputy Prime Minister). The affair was made public by British newspapers when Miss MacEntee appeared in the Congo at the height of the crisis. It was used as a stick to beat O'Brien in the United Nations and it embarrassed the Irish Government. Following O'Brien's divorce in Mexico, they were married in a Catholic church in New York. This was possible because O'Brien had been baptised a Catholic and his first marriage in a registry office was, therefore, invalid in the eyes of the Church.

Leaders of the emerging African nations admired O'Brien's stand against the colonial powers. In 1962 Kwame Nkrumah, President of Ghana, invited him to become Vice-Chancellor of the University of Ghana. Relations went sour little over a year later when O'Brien protested publicly against the dismissal of the Chief Justice who had acquitted some of the President's political opponents. There were also disputes about academic freedom, one of which culminated in several lecturers being deported. Courageous as ever, O'Brien stood his ground and Nkrumah knew he would lose face in Africa if he dismissed O'Brien. They parted by mutual consent at the end of the three year term. The O'Briens' connection with Ghana was maintained when they adopted a boy of mixed Irish-Ghanian parentage. They also adopted a daughter who is half African.

From 1965 to 1969 O'Brien was Albert Schweitzer Professor of Humanities at New York University. He shocked the academic world by branding William Butler Yeats as a fascist. He took part in the agitation against the war in Vietnam and was arrested and man-handled together with other demonstrators during Stop the Draft Week in 1967. Never a man to flinch from a row, he was involved in a bitter confrontation with

Encounter magazine whom he exposed as the recipient of money from the C.I.A.

In these years O'Brien was still very much a figure of the Left. But he had become interested in Edmund Burke whose reflections on the revolution in France he edited and who was to influence him profoundly. The death in 1970 of his cousin the Trinity lecturer and socialist Senator Owen Sheehy-Skeffington removed a major left-wing influence on him.

O'Brien had returned to Ireland in 1969 when the Labour Party invited him to run for the Dail. He was successful and became that party's spokesman on Northern Ireland. At first, he identified with the movement for civil rights among the Catholic population that was directed against discrimination in housing and employment. However, when the IRA began their campaign of violence, he came to see that the root of the problem lay in the Republic's claim to Northern Ireland irrespective of the wishes of its inhabitants. In his book *States of Ireland* published in 1972 he challenged the nationalist dogma that Ireland was one nation. Ultimately it re-shaped Irish attitudes but at the time it caused people to doubt O'Brien's nationalist credentials.

As a minister in Liam Cosgrave's coalition government formed in 1973, O'Brien urged his colleagues to settle for power-sharing in Northern Ireland and not to press for a Council of Ireland that was anathema to unionists. His wise advice was not heeded and provision was made for a potentially powerful Council in the Sunningdale Agreement. This undermined support among the Protestant community for the unionists who had joined with moderate nationalists in a power-sharing executive and led to its collapse.

But like many prophets of doom, O'Brien was not held in any esteem for his prescience by those to whom his warnings were directed. He irritated nationalists by concentrating all his criticism on the IRA and overlooking the misdeeds of the security forces. Even less acceptable was his challenge to the glorification of the 1916 Rebellion. He fell foul of the media when in his capacity as Minister for Posts and Telegraphs, he forbade interviews with supporters of Sinn Fein, the political wing of the IRA.

O'Brien's manner, which was sometimes supercilious and pugnacious, did not help. Rather than search for common ground with others, he preferred to focus on points of disagreement. It was always an imperative to spell out his views to the full, however impolitic that might be. His uproarious wit, which could be cutting, his compulsive irreverence and tendency to indiscretion made enemies. He was also prone to fail in the simple politenesses of life, such as honouring appointments.

In the 1977 general election the Government of which O'Brien was a member was heavily defeated and he himself lost his Dublin seat. 'I was sore in my head for about six months', he wrote later, 'and then I was very glad.'

But he would not be silenced. He railed against the IRA and their fellow-travellers within the Fianna Fail party. He continued to expose the ambivalence, even among constitutional nationalists, about according Northern Ireland a right to self-determination. The honeyed words and what he saw as the essential intransigence of the persuasive Ulster nationalist leader John Hume advocating 'an agreed Ireland' was a favourite target. O'Brien warned that a withdrawal of British troops would lead to mass slaughter. Direct rule, he concluded, was the least bad solution and the defeat of terrorism the most important objective.

In truth, Ireland, for all the largely unrequited love he bore it, was too restricted a stage for the man the Irish nicknamed 'the Cruiser'. He was fortunate when he was recommended to the new American owners of *The Observer* as an editor-in-chief by David Astor and also by his old adversary Harold Macmillan who said the paper needed another J. L. Garvin. At his best O'Brien was a brilliant columnist, concise in analysis, witty, and always easy to read. In 1980 he was named columnist of the year in the Granada press awards. He blotted his copybook, however, by giving evidence at the Monopolies Commission against Tiny Rowland's takeover of the paper. He was retired as editor-in-chief in 1981, although he continued to write a full-time column until 1984.

For the rest of his life O'Brien worked unabated from his seaside home in Howth near Dublin, apart from occasional terms at American universities. He managed a punishing schedule of journalism and more profound scholarship. Although he rarely finished a day fully sober, he was always at his desk by six o'clock the next morning with his sharp mind fuelling an even sharper pen.

O'Brien had a life-long affection for Jews. He had been delivered by the renowned Jewish doctor Bethel Solomons. He had enjoyed the friendship of Jewish boys at school and in Trinity and shared their horror of fascism. His sympathy found expression in *The Seige*, a book about Israel and Zionism published in 1986. He was faulted for not presenting the Arab case fairly. He had declined an offer to talk to Yassir Arafat, the Palestinian leader.

O'Brien's indifference to the fate of the Palestinians was also symptomatic of a declining sympathy for the Third World and its aspirations and grievances. In international politics, as in Ireland, he came to be perceived as a figure of the Right. He focussed more on the evils of terrorism than the political conditions that had nurtured it. Even on apartheid, of which he had been such a relentless critic, he broke ranks with former friends by taking a post at the University of Capetown in 1986, only to be forced to quit after a student demonstration against him. Economic exploitation of poorer countries did not engage his attention in the way that had once made him such a determined opponent of political imperialism and racial discrimination.

He continued to be a scourge of republicans and their fellow-travellers at home whether in his weekly column in the *Irish Independent* or in *The Times* to which he became a regular contributor. His favourite target was Charles Haughey who was Taoiseach in 1979–81, for part of 1982 and 1987–9. Haughey's unexplained wealth, his arrogance and associations with the illegal importation of arms in 1970 made him a good target. But O'Brien did not know when to stop and, in the absence of proof, the campaign deteriorated into a vendetta; Haughey, who did not deign to reply, sailed on regardless to serve for seven years as Taoiseach and was exposed only after he had retired.

O'Brien also broke with his old colleagues in the Labour Party when they helped to negotiate the Anglo-Irish Agreement in 1985, on which the Ulster Unionists were not consulted and which gave the Irish

Government an institutionalised consultative role in the government of Northern Ireland. He advocated the reintroduction of internment without trial. As he continued to challenge the sacred cows of nationalist Ireland, it seemed that in his defiant way he relished being a kind of itching powder of his own people.

All the time he was working away on his hero and fellow Trinity man Edmund Burke from whose speeeches and other writings he could quote long passages. What was termed a thematic biography was published in 1992 under the title *The Great Melody*. It was not so much a biography as a brilliant polemical vindication of his subject and a refutation of all those – from Tom Paine to Sir Lewis Namier – who had written Burke off as a time-serving toady of mighty aristocrats.

O'Brien put Burke back into the context of his background among the Irish Catholic gentry of the eighteenth century who were deprived of civil and political rights by the Penal Laws. Burke, O'Brien maintained, was conditioned by that background to resent the abuse of power whether by tyrranical governments or by revolutionaries. O'Brien empathised with Burke as a fellow Trinity man and an intellectual involved in politics dominating party leaders by sheer intellectual power – he even unearthed a possible family connection. The identification between author and subject throughout the book was such that some felt O'Brien had recreated Burke in his own image.

Much as O'Brien admired the religious convictions of Burke, whom he believed may have wished to die a Catholic, neither this nor his own wife's strong religious faith led him back to the Catholic Church. He could never forgive the hurt inflicted on his mother as a result of some of its harsher rules. His book, *On the Eve of the Millenium*, published in 1996, was highly critical of Pope John Paul II's Church, which he grouped with Muslim fundamentalists as forces leading the world away from the values of his beloved Enlightenment. His vision of the future was pessimistic.

He was especially pessimistic about his own country. With what he may have thought was Burkean prescience he foresaw that the IRA ceasefire of 1994 would not hold and he insisted that communal warfare would be the inevitable outcome of any effort under the Downing Street Declaration of the previous year to foist all-Ireland institutions on Ulster unionists. This led him to join Bob McCartney's UK Unionist Party, which was free from the sectarian overtones of other unionist parties and favoured closer integration with mainland Britain. As such he served on the Northern Ireland Forum in 1996 that was to lay the groundwork for the Good Friday Agreement of 1998.

O'Brien felt that the Good Friday Agreement, which brought Sinn Fein into government, was disastrous and, in a curious twist, argued that Northern unionists would be better off moving of their own accord to join with the Republic on terms that protected them rather than soldier on in a state where concessions to Republicans under threat of force were the order of the day. This accorded with his own long-term dream of an Ireland dominated by moderate unionists and moderate nationalists working in harmony to repress extremists on both sides. But it was too clever by half for unionist rank and file and he was forced to take leave of the UK Unionist Party while continuing to support its policy of non-participation in the new power-sharing government.

O'Brien published a book of memoirs in 1999. While there was an amount of special pleading and much repetition of old themes it afforded an insight into the roots of the personal insecurity and vulnerability that underlay a self-assurance that so often came over as arrogance. It also revealed a man of quite narrow focus without any real interests outside politics and literature.

O'Brien continued to contribute a regular column to the *Irish Independent* until early 2007. To the end he predicted that Ian Paisley and his party would never enter a power-sharing executive with the former terrorists of the IRA whose conversion to constitutional politics O'Brien did not credit. Although he believed that Israel should retreat to its 1967 boundaries, his abhorrence of terrorism led him to take an understanding view of the stances and international adventures of the Bush presidency even in the Middle East.

O'Brien is survived by his wife Maire, a poet in the Irish language, their two adopted children and also a son and daughter of his first marriage. Kate, a writer who was a daughter of his first marriage, died in 1998.

* * *

VINCENT O'BRIEN

2 JUNE 2009

NO TRAINER IN MODERN TIMES has matched the achievements of Vincent O'Brien, acclaimed as at once an alchemist of his art and a colossus of the Turf.

Over jumps he won three Grand Nationals in succession beginning in 1953, with *Early Mist, Royal Tan* and *Quare Times*. He saddled four Cheltenham Gold Cup winners within six seasons with *Cottage Rake* three times, (beginning in 1948) then *Knock Hard* in 1953; and he won three consecutive Champion Hurdles with *Hatton's Grace*, starting in 1949.

On the Flat he saddled six Derby winners at Epsom beginning with *Larkspur* in 1962 and including, in 1970, *Nijinsky*, the last horse to win the triple crown of Derby, 2,000 Guineas and St Leger. He also trained the Prix de l'Arc de Triomphe winner, on three occasions, with *Ballymoss* (1958) and *Alleged* (1977 and 1978).

O'Brien's skills encompassed every racing distance, from *Gladness*, who outstayed her rivals in the 1958 Ascot Gold Cup and Goodwood Cup, to a host of sprinters right up to *College Chapel* who was his 25th and final Royal Ascot winner in the 1993 Cork and Orrery Stakes.

In Britain he topped the trainers' list in 1966 and again in 1977 with a record £439,124 in prize money.

Michael Vincent O'Brien was born on April 9, 1917, son of Dan O'Brien, a farmer who trained horses on a small scale at Churchtown, Co Cork. When his father died, his eldest half-brother inherited the farm but had no interest in horses, so, in 1944, O'Brien was able to rent the yard and gallops.

He had taken out a licence to train the previous year. His first owner was Frank Vickerman, who was instrumental, through his spectacular gambling, in setting O'Brien on the road to success. Vickerman was persuaded to provide financial support for *Cottage Rake* who, as a six-year-old, had one amateur riders' race to his credit. The animal had been discovered originally running wild in a bog.

Cottage Rake soon proved to be the first example of O'Brien's uncanny instinct for picking champions. In a run of five Irish Cesarewitch successes which had begun with *Good Days*, *Cottage Rake* won for him in 1947 and the following year began his series of three Cheltenham Gold Cup victories.

On the Flat in Ireland, and at the highest level of National Hunt racing in England, O'Brien gave striking early notice of his talent and versatility. But he abruptly quit the National Hunt scene in 1954, never to return. However, he had already begun to illuminate the Flat in spectacular fashion, his first star horse being *Ballymoss*, who narrowly went down to *Crepello* in the 1957 Derby. *Ballymoss* won the Irish equivalent, however, then the St Leger. The following season, when *Gladness* was also scoring brilliantly, *Ballymoss* ignited the headlines by capturing, in succession, the Coronation Cup, Eclipse Stakes, King George and Queen Elizabeth Stakes and Prix de l'Arc de Triomphe. O'Brien was on his way to becoming a living legend.

The springboard for his success was at Ballydoyle in Cashel, Co Tipperary. O'Brien had moved there in 1950, the year before he married Jacqueline Wittenoom of Perth, Australia. Ballydoyle was just an ordinary farm when he took over but it was to become one of the finest training establishments in the world.

O'Brien was the ultimate perfectionist who influenced fellow trainers. He was one of the first to weigh horses after races, and also pioneered the deployment of air transport for them. He tried to leave nothing to chance. There was always a stand-by horsebox in case of a breakdown.

Success brought just rewards, but it was not all plain sailing. In 1960 he lost his licence for 18 months (a term later reduced to a year) after the doping of a horse called *Chamour*. However, in a libel action brought by O'Brien, the stewards acknowledged that he bore no personal responsibility for the drugging offence.

Over the years, O'Brien turned more and more to American blood, and, with his partners, who included Stavros Niarchos, Robert Sangster and John Magnier, he invested heavily at the Keeneland sales in Kentucky, particularly in the descendants of that great American sire, *Northern Dancer*. For some years, the syndicate was rich enough to outbid all opposition and helped to create an inflationary spiral in bloodstock values.

O'Brien's extraordinary eye for a yearling gave his partners the confidence to spend vast sums, and he built up what amounted to a new industry in Europe, the business of stallion promotion.

In 1987, the business aspect of O'Brien's life was taken further with the flotation of Classic Thoroughbreds, a company formed with Sangster, Magnier and others to buy, race and sell bloodstock. In the same year he became champion trainer in Ireland for the twelfth time.

He was revered as a uniquely talented trainer of race horses, respected and loved by associates and competitors alike.

He is survived by his wife, Jacqueline, two sons and three daughters.

ALEX "HURRICANE" HIGGINS

26 JULY 2010

ALEX "HURRICANE" HIGGINS, who died on 24 July, aged 61, was a precocious snooker talent who established himself as the most innately gifted player of his generation. He had the capacity to create a riveting spectacle in almost every frame he played. Through television, his magnetic qualities came to be savoured by a clientele outside that of the game's captive audience, lifting it in a very short time out of smoky backrooms and into the international arena and setting it before mass audiences.

Higgins came into the spotlight in 1972 when, a month short of his 23rd birthday, he became the world professional champion by defeating John Spencer 37-32 in a room at Selly Park British Legion Club, Birmingham, where beer crates were used by the audience as vantage points.

His reward was a first prize of £480. Ten years later, in 1982, when he regained the game's most coveted title by completing a memorable 18-15 victory over the six-times champion Ray Reardon with a 135 total clearance, he collected a cheque for £25,000. That figure reflected the extent of snooker's boom in the late 1970s and early 1980s. For this, Higgins could justifiably claim much of the responsibility.

Higgins played almost as important a role in putting snooker on the sporting map as did the decision of the BBC – vindicated by more than 20 years of outstanding viewing figures – to cover the game and its major tournaments. Following the 1982 final, Higgins proclaimed himself the "people's champion". It was hard to disagree with this accurate, if immodest, verdict and until the end of his career he retained the ability to draw large crowds.

In tandem with abundant, instinctive talent, Higgins also had courage and resolve. In the eyes of many observers, the 69 clearance fashioned to take the penultimate frame of his semi-final against Jimmy White in the 1982 World Championship remains the finest such break under pressure.

His unpredictability, both in his choice of shots on the table and in his moods off it; the publicity which constantly surrounded him; and the instinctive, lightning speed with which he potted balls at the height of his powers, attracted an enormous and loyal following. When he was on form, his ability to pot the most awkwardly placed of balls was legendary.

Higgins was not always faithful to his fans, and frequently dodged out of a back entrance rather than sign autographs. This often boorish behaviour and his brushes with authority were, for the most part, forgiven by his adoring public.

But his mercurial temperament was often likely to let him down when he came up against less spectacular, more consistent players. And his unruly, often drink-fuelled behaviour – first seen outside the tournament halls, but as time went on frequently spilling over into the competition venue itself in the form of abuse to match referees and his fellow players – made him simply a commodity impossible to handle by the game's administrative bodies. A career bright with promise and brilliant in achievement ended with Higgins homeless and virtually penniless after having won and lost a fortune of several millions of pounds.

Alexander Gordon Higgins was born in Belfast on March 18, 1949. At 11 he began playing snooker at the Jampot club, close to the council house in the Sandy Row area of South Belfast where he lived with his parents and three sisters. At 16 he compiled his first century break at the snooker table. Three years later he won both the Northern Ireland and All Ireland amateur championships.

Given his phenomenal capacities and the invaluable ability to deliver his best in tight corners, Higgins should have lifted more trophies. He was runner-up in the 1976 World Championship, soundly beaten 27-16 by Ray Reardon, and suffered a not dissimilar fate in 1980. On that occasion his self-destructive tendency of playing to the crowd when ahead 9-4 in the final threw a lifeline to Cliff Thorburn of Canada, who recovered to win 18-16.

Higgins revelled in being the centre of attention, a fact which might explain why he invariably played well at Wembley Conference Centre, the largest auditorium on the circuit, where he always enjoyed vociferous support.

He won the Benson and Hedges Masters there in 1978 and 1981, the British Gold Cup in 1980, the World Championship again in 1982, the Irish Professional Championship in 1983 and 1989, and, having rallied from a seemingly hopeless 7-0 deficit to edge Steve Davis 16-15 in the final, the 1983 United Kingdom Championship.

A carousing, undisciplined lifestyle inevitably took its toll as the years passed. It did not help that the wiry Higgins rarely ate a square meal, the odd banana often meeting his nutritional needs.

His most turbulent spell ran from February 1989 to April 1990. Having reportedly fallen head first out of an upstairs window of the flat he shared with his girlfriend Siobhan Kidd, after a heated argument, he arrived at the European Open in Deauville, France, on crutches. Hopping around the table, and sweating profusely, he astoundingly negotiated his first match. A month or so later, with a broken ankle anything but fully healed, he demonstrated remarkable stamina to win the Irish Championship and edge Stephen Hendry 9-8 in the final of the Benson and Hedges Masters.

By now twice divorced, Higgins continued to stage public displays that suggested increasing emotional and mental instability. In 1990 he threatened to have Dennis Taylor, his Northern Ireland teammate at the World Cup, "shot" and, the worse for drink, physically assaulted a press officer after losing in the first round of the World Championship. The World Professional Billiards and Snooker Association (WPBSA) banned Higgins for the entire 1990-91 season and stripped him of all ranking points, which meant he tumbled from 14th to 120th on the world list, a demotion from which he was unable to recover.

It was a crippling punishment, even when placed alongside the then record £12,000 fine imposed by the WPBSA when he headbutted the tournament director, Paul Hatherell, during the 1986 United Kingdom Championship. With the glory days behind him, Higgins became increasingly bitter, using press conferences as vehicles to criticize the referee, his opponent, the WPBSA or playing conditions.

Playing in the qualifying competition of the 1995 World Championship in Blackpool, Higgins was on the verge of an eventual defeat by Tai Pichit, of Thailand. As always, he stubbornly fought on and had compiled a 110 break when he turned to John Williams, a senior referee, and asked him to move before the next shot was played. Williams, standing behind Higgins, was bemused. "But I'm not in your line of sight," he said, to which Higgins retorted, "No, you're in my line of thought." Williams refused to budge and Higgins, sobbing ever more loudly, cleared the colours for a run of 137, ironically his highest break in the event with which he will always be associated.

An increasingly unruly lifestyle continued to undermine his career and for several years from 1997 he was not seen in professional competitions. In 1999 throat cancer was first diagnosed, though, remarkably, Higgins fought the disease for the next ten and more years. After a long break from professional snooker, Higgins was seen at the Irish Professional Snooker Championships in 2005 and the two following years but was defeated in the first round on each occcasion.

In 2007 he published his autobiography, *From the Eye of the Hurricane.*

Latterly he had lived in sheltered housing in Belfast. Higgins had a daughter with his first wife, Cara, and a son and a daughter from his second marriage, to Lynn Avison.

DR GARRET FITZGERALD

20 MAY 2011

GARRET FITZGERALD, WHO DIED yesterday in Dublin, aged 85, was a highly successful Irish Foreign Minister between 1973 and 1977 but a less successful Taoiseach during two terms in the 1980s. Although he held these high offices it may be that his most lasting contribution to Irish life was not as a politician but in the manner in which, as lecturer and writer, he helped to mould Irish opinion to accept membership of a closely knit European Community, the right of Northern Ireland to determine its own future and a more pluralist society in the Republic itself.

Born in Dublin on February 9, 1926, he was the youngest of four sons of Desmond FitzGerald, a literary Londoner of Irish parentage who became involved in the Irish revolution and was a government minister in the Irish Free State between 1922 and 1932. Garret FitzGerald was at school with the Jesuits at Belvedere and studied modern languages at University College Dublin. He worked for Aer Lingus, the Irish national airline, until 1958 when he became a lecturer in economics at his old university.

He developed an interest in journalism and became Irish correspondent of British and overseas newspapers. In his weekly economic column in the *Irish Times* he struck a buoyant note and helped to create the optimistic mood of the 1960s when the Republic of Ireland experienced growth following a long period of stagnation. He had boundless mental energy and an insatiable appetite for statistics. He talked a lot and at immense speed. He was never a ready listener.

FitzGerald was especially enthusiastic in spelling out the advantages of membership of the European Economic Community, high among which he rated detachment from dependence on Britain, which he dubbed the sick man of Europe. This was more than an economic calculation; he longed for an Ireland that reached beyond the narrow confines of the Anglo-Saxon world. In this he may have been influenced by his Francophile father.

Garret FitzGerald's affability, lack of self-importance, generosity and enthusiasm made him popular with the students he lectured at University College Dublin, but, in the wake of his behaviour during the student disturbances of 1968, elder statesmen of the college came to distrust him as unreliable and lacking in judgment.

In 1965, he had entered politics as a member of Fine Gael, his father's old party. He turned his vast intellectual energy to good account as their front bench spokesman on education and then on finance. But he was distrusted by more conservative colleagues, including the party leader, Liam Cosgrave, for whose replacement he intrigued incessantly.

In 1973 Jack Lynch's Fianna Fail government was defeated after sixteen years in office and Cosgrave led Fine Gael into a coalition government with Labour. Perhaps because he distrusted FitzGerald's judgment and thought him too socialist, Cosgrave did not offer him the finance portfolio that he had held in opposition. Instead, FitzGerald followed in his own father's footsteps and became Minister for Foreign Affairs. He was later to describe his four years in that office as the happiest of his life.

As Foreign Minister FitzGerald did not suffer the same unpopularity as ministers directly involved in harsh economic measures forced on the government in the wake of the oil crisis of 1973. He evaded responsibility for an unpopular wealth tax of which he was the real progenitor. He got credit for the 1973 Sunningdale Agreement on Northern Ireland that he helped to negotiate. He was to the fore persuading the British Government to accept a Council of Ireland that seemed to have the potential to evolve into an all-island government. This, as he later accepted, undermined the Unionist leader Brian Faulkner and ensured that the power-sharing administration that emerged under the agreement was short-lived.

A fluent French speaker, FitzGerald was a highly creditable spokesman for his country in the European Economic Community that Ireland had joined in 1973 and from which it was receiving generous subventions. By contributing valuably at the Council of Ministers on general issues and displaying a commitment to the ethos of the Community, FitzGerald counteracted what was unkindly described as the stereotype of "Paddy the amiable pickpocket".

FitzGerald was not popular with cabinet colleagues of his own party, because of his interference in their portfolios, his leaking to the press and what they perceived as a general lack of loyalty. However, his public standing was high. When the Government suffered a heavy defeat at the general election of 1977, and Cosgrave resigned the leadership of Fine Gael, FitzGerald succeeded without opposition.

As leader, he refashioned his party. The organisation was streamlined. It became less overtly conservative on social and moral issues. FitzGerald's enthusiasm and idealism appealed greatly to the younger elements in the electorate, especially feminist women, who desired a more modern society free from the shibboleths and restrictions of the past. Oozing rectitude, he made a contrast with the sinister rugged figure of Charles Haughey, who succeeded Jack Lynch as Taoiseach in 1979. The best that FitzGerald's detractors could do was to deride him as an absent-minded academic – an image he rather confirmed when he appeared in public wearing odd shoes.

FitzGerald had a brief sojourn as Taoiseach following the 1981 general election and a more extended term between 1982 and 1987. He inherited an economy whose public finances had fallen into disarray. Cutbacks in public expenditure were imperative and Fine Gael had campaigned on the need for such measures. But, in government, FitzGerald sided with the Labour ministers in resisting the necessary cutbacks. The public finances deteriorated further, the economy stagnated and there were no jobs for the young.

In the area of British-Irish relations, FitzGerald repaired the damage done by Charles Haughey's withdrawal of support during the Falklands' war and won Mrs Thatcher's approval for a plan, hatched up largely by senior officials on both sides of the Irish Sea, by which the Dublin Government was given an institutionalized advisory role in the governance of Northern Ireland. This concept found expression in the Hillsborough Agreement of 1985 establishing a secretariat near Belfast where representatives of the British and Irish Governments liaised. It was the one really popular achievement of FitzGerald's term as Taoiseach. Although the actual agreement fell far short of what had been proposed by the Irish Government, the negative reaction of the Ulster Unionists made it appear a diplomatic triumph.

FitzGerald later boasted that his good relationship with Mrs Thatcher was a major factor in winning her consent to the agreement. However, when her memoirs were published, it emerged that she was much less impressed by FitzGerald, whom she found garrulous and woolly, than by the short-spoken, incisive and flirtatious Haughey. FitzGerald's response was characteristic: Mrs Thatcher, he said, had denigrated him because she had not forgiven him for persuading her to do something she later regretted.

It was true that the improvement in security that Mrs Thatcher had hoped for consequent upon the Hillsborough agreement did not materialize. Nor did hopes that greater sensitivity to the concerns of the Catholic population on the part of the administration would woo voters away from the IRA and their political arm, Sinn Fein. But by making direct rule less attractive to unionists it may have sapped the unionist will to resist power-sharing with nationalists and so made a new settlement possible following the IRA ceasefire in the 1990s.

FitzGerald's stated attitude towards Ulster unionists had always been more benign than that of most Irish nationalist politicians. His mother, although a committed republican, was of Ulster Presbyterian stock and he had long harboured an ambition to forge a genuine union of the two Irish traditions. His views on this were set out in his book *Towards a New Ireland* published in 1972. He was one of the first politicians in the Republic to accept the right of Northern Ireland to self-determination.

Although a committed and theologically informed Catholic, FitzGerald yearned to make the Republic a pluralist society that would be more acceptable to Ulster Protestants. However, by negotiating the Hillsborough Agreement secretly behind the backs of the Ulster Unionists he belied his respect for their right to a say in their own governance and so lost their trust irreparably.

As a step towards creating a more pluralist society in the Republic FitzGerald decided to hold a referendum in 1986 to remove the ban on divorce contained in the Constitution. However, the proposal was not thought through in sufficient detail and was roundly defeated. Those who were sceptical of FitzGerald's political judgment found confirmation for their view in the result.

Even more damaging may have been a loss of trust among those who had close dealings with him. Conor Cruise O'Brien, a disillusioned former colleague, remarked later that FitzGerald was unaware of the darker side of his own character and lived in the sunny confidence that he was invariably acting for the common good which, by a happy coincidence, often coincided with his own good. FitzGerald was not always as good as his word and had a way of recollecting events and conversations as he would have wished them. He took too much on himself and was a poor manager. Cabinets rambled on inconclusively discussing minor matters; critics derided it as government by seminar.

FitzGerald's government finally broke up when, at the beginning of 1987, the Labour ministers refused to accept cuts in social services. These were cuts of a kind that, in previous years, had been avoided in response to Labour pressure. This fact was not lost on former Fine Gael voters and at the subsequent general election there was a massive defection to the newly formed low taxation Progressive Democrat Party. Fianna Fail returned to government under Mr Haughey.

FitzGerald resigned the leadership immediately, leaving the party that he had brought to an all-time high, at as low an ebb as it had been when he became its leader. In his bid to broaden its appeal he had alienated many of its staunchest supporters. At heart he was never really a party man.

After he had left office, FitzGerald became a director of an aeroplane leasing company called Guinness Peat and borrowed heavily from his bank to buy shares on the eve of a public floatation. This was aborted at the eleventh hour and he was left with a substantial loss. He had to surrender all his assets to the bank, which then wrote off the outstanding debt.

One beneficial effect of FitzGerald's financial misfortunes, which were accentuated by expenses necessitated by his wife's chronic illness, was that he had to return to regular journalism as a weekly contributor to the *Irish Times*. He remained a constructive and independent contributor to national debate on many issues. His enthusiasm for closer European integration and his faith in the Commission as the guardian of smaller countries was undiminished. At times, however, he indulged himself somewhat stressing his own high-mindedness and attempting to justify his failures in government. This was a weakness of his rather wordy memoirs *All in a Life* (1991). He also published two fine collections of stimulating essays entitled *Reflections on the Irish State* (2002) and *Ireland in the World* (2005). A further volume of memoirs appeared last year. He was at work to the end.

FitzGerald married, when he was only 21, Joan O'Farrell who was, unlike her husband, a descendant of the Geraldine FitzGerald family that had once virtually ruled Ireland. She was an assertive, outspoken woman, who was credited with exercising immense influence over her husband, especially in his assessments of people. She was bed-ridden for many years before her death in 1999. FitzGerald's devoted care of her was much admired. There were two sons and one daughter of the marriage by whom he is survived.

DECLAN COSTELLO

10 JUNE 2011

DECLAN COSTELLO WHO DIED ON 6 JUNE was Attorney General in the Republic of Ireland from 1973 to 1977. As such, he led for the Irish Government in the case taken against the British Government under the European Convention of Human Rights alleging the torture of men detained by the security forces in Northern Ireland. Subsequently he became a judge and ultimately president of the High Court, the second most senior office in the Irish judiciary.

David Declan Costello was born in Dublin on August 1, 1926 the third of five children of the future Taoiseach John Costello, who was shortly to become Attorney General. Declan attended a small private day school near his home called Xavier's before going on to University College Dublin, where he took a first in economics and law and starred as a debater. His call to the Bar was delayed until 1949 because he was struck down with tuberculosis and had to recuperate in a sanatorium in Switzerland.

On his return to Dublin to commence practice he was drawn into politics, his father having been elected Taoiseach in a coalition government that had ousted Eamon de Valera after 16 years in office. Costello was adopted as a candidate for his father's party, Fine Gael, in the general election of 1951 and topped the poll in a largely working class constituency in north Dublin.

Moved by the poverty he saw in his constituency Costello tried to nudge his party leftwards. In 1965 his proposals for more planning and intervention by government in the economy as well as increased investment in housing and social services were adopted as the 'Just Society' programme for the forthcoming general election.

The election was lost. It was not long before Costello grew restless again, sceptical of the commitment of the leadership to his 'Just Society' programme and feeling marginalised on the front bench. In

1967, shortly after his party leader Liam Cosgrave had moved him from the social welfare portfolio, he announced that for reasons of health he had decided to retire from politics.

Costello, who had taken silk in 1965, now devoted himself full-time to his practice at the Bar. While he was never to achieve the pre-eminent position once occupied by his father, he was highly rated and built up specialities in trademark law and defamation. As in politics, his purposefulness and dedication commanded respect but his chilly (but always polite) manner could be forbidding.

Costello made a political comeback at the 1973 general election at which a Fine Gael-Labour national coalition was returned with Liam Cosgrave as Taoiseach. Cosgrave, unimpressed by Costello's political gyrations, disappointed him by denying him a ministry that would enable him to implement his progressive social ideals. He was appointed Attorney General.

As Attorney General Costello was involved in the negotiation of the Sunningdale agreement providing for power-sharing in Northern Ireland and a Council of Ireland. The British Government hoped that with this new beginning, the Cosgrave government would drop the case under the European Convention of Human Rights taken by their predecessors alleging torture of detained persons by the security forces in the province.

These hopes were not realised. Costello pursued the case in such a combative manner that his British counterpart Sir Peter Rawlinson remarked in his memoirs that he was not sure whether he was dealing with a litigant or a lawyer. Costello, for his part, complained that there was no basis for a friendly settlement when those responsible for ordering illegal techniques of interrogation had not been identified and no prosecutions taken against those who had committed criminal assaults. The ill-tempered litigation ground on through lengthy hearings to an eventual finding by the European Court of Human Rights that the British Government was guilty of inhuman and degrading treatment – but not torture.

Costello was also central to the refusal of the Irish Government to extradite political offenders, having put forward at Sunningdale the argument that it would be contrary to international law and so inconsistent with the Irish Constitution to do so. The British Government was unimpressed by this far-fetched argument or by legislation enacted on Costello's advice allowing prosecutions in the Republic for offences committed in Northern Ireland.

Domestically Costello was an active and reforming Attorney General. Cosgrave came to repose considerable trust in him. Untroubled by doubts and a relentless worker he was quick to reach definite conclusions even in areas of the law with which he was previously unfamiliar.

He had legislation enacted transferring responsibility for criminal prosecutions from the Attorney General to a Director of Public Prosecutions (DPP), who was made totally independent of government. The government had cause to regret this total independence when the newly appointed Director insisted, irrespective of their wishes, on prosecuting British soldiers who had wandered across the border accidentally.

A law reform commission was established in relation to whose work the Attorney General was given a central role. A devout catholic, Costello asked the commission to examine the law relating to the annulment of marriages, the expansion of which at civil law in line with the teaching of the Roman Catholic Church he canvassed as a desirable alternative to the introduction of divorce.

In 1977, shortly before the general election that resulted in the defeat of the Cosgrave government, Costello accepted appointment as a judge of the High Court. He was assigned to hear commercial or chancery cases. His dispatch was rapid and his judgments on law outstanding. He was counted less good at assessing the veracity of witnesses. Some barristers found him exacting and some felt that he made up his mind too early and did not pay attention to their submissions. He did not hesitate to mould the law and procedures to produce what he saw as a just result.

In 1980 Costello was charged to hold an enquiry into an explosion on a ship at the Whiddy Island oil terminal in Co Cork where over fifty people perished. In the report, which was remarkable for its grasp of technical issues, he distributed blame between the Total company, which owned the ship, and Gulf Oil, which owned the terminal. Instinctively repressive towards wrongdoers, he did not mince his words accusing some witnesses of trying to mislead him.

Costello's conservatism on family law, rooted in his religion, disappointed those who misunderstood the limits of his radicalism. He punished erring husbands by crippling maintenance awards. He rejected an appeal by a teacher in a Roman Catholic school who had been dismissed because she was living with a man to whom she was not married.

In 1992, he divided the nation when he acceded to an application that a 14 year old girl, who was pregnant, should be prohibited from going to Britain because she intended to seek an abortion there. The constitutional ban on abortion had to be reworded so that it could not be invoked to prevent persons leaving the country.

Costello had to endure the promotion over his head to the Supreme Court of judges much less distinguished as jurists. Finally, in 1995, he was appointed President of the High Court. He made several bold innovations in matters of procedure before he retired in 1997.

In retirement Costello remained active pursuing a wide range of intellectual and artistic interests as well as playing tennis. He advocated that social and economic rights of the underprivileged, including the disabled, should be given constitutional protection. In 2006 he published a powerfully argued article in a legal journal demonstrating the illegality under international law of the invasion of Iraq by the United States and Britain.

Costello had an elder brother who suffered from mental illness and a handicapped son, to whose care he devoted much of his time. He was to the forefront throughout his life in charities for the care of the mentally ill and helped to organise the Special Olympics in Dublin in 1985.

He is survived by his wife Joan, four sons and two daughters. His eldest son, a solicitor, is president of the Law Society of Ireland while one daughter is a barrister.

THE KNIGHT OF GLIN

17 SEPTEMBER 2011

DESMOND JOHN VILLIERS FITZGERALD, 29th Knight of Glin, was president of the Irish Georgian Society and an art historian who produced ground-breaking books on the history of Irish paintings and furniture.

The exact origin of the title accorded to the head of the FitzGerald family of Glin in Limerick is obscure but it was well established in usage by Elizabethan times when the family were one of few among the old Irish aristocracy in Munster to survive the conquest by the new English torch-bearers of the Reformed faith.

Disadvantaged by the Anti-Popery laws, the FitzGeralds of Glin became Protestant in the middle of the eighteenth century. Successive generations married English wives and the family were clearly identified with the Anglo-Irish Protestant Ascendancy long before Desmond was born on July 13, 1937. With the independent Irish state hell-bent on breaking the British connection, his English mother Veronica Villiers hurried to London for the birth to ensure that her child would be British. It was only fourteen years since the Irish civil war when her father-in-law, the 27th knight had, from his wheelchair, repelled republicans who came to burn Glin Castle telling them that they would have to burn him with the house as he was not moving.

Through his mother, young Desmond was descended from what Maynard Keynes famously described in his Essays in Biography as "the most remarkable family of all – the great Villiers connection from whom are descended all the ambitious fascinators, with so much charm of countenance and voice and so hard a little nut somewhere inside who were the favourites and mistresses of our monarchs in the seventeenth century and of the parliamentary democracy ever since."

His early life was unsettled by tensions between his parents followed by his father's tuberculosis and early death in 1949. Younger than his two sisters, Desmond grew up a solitary child uninterested in sport of any kind. He failed common entrance to Eton, despite the coaching of his mother's admirer, Sir Shane Leslie, and went to Stowe.

That was not a success and he ended his schooling in Canada, all arranged by his mother's second husband Ray Millner, a Canadian businessman who was a devoted stepfather. The Knight then spent three carefree years at the University of British Columbia before going on to Harvard where he took a Masters in art history.

This opened the way to his appointment in 1964 to the department of furniture in the Victoria and Albert Museum. While his years there may have been blighted by an imperfect sympathy with the director Roy Strong, he did acquire a formidable expertise in his field. He cut a figure in London society, becoming a member of White's and persuading the editor of *Burke's Peerage* to include his pedigree. The Knight's marriage in 1967 to Louise de la Falaise was a Society event featured in the press. It proved short-lived and he married again in 1970 Olda Willes who shared his artistic interests producing a book on historic Irish gardens and, more vitally, provided the warmth that enabled him to cope with the depressions that were a recurring feature of his life.

He made regular visits to Ireland where Glin Castle was being kept in readiness by his mother and generous stepfather. He formed a close friendship with Desmond and Mariga Guinness, the founders of the Irish Georgian Society and became chairman of its London chapter.

In 1975 Ray Millner died and the Knight moved with his wife and young children to live between Glin and Dublin where he acted as representative of Christies, organising mainly sales of the contents of the houses of the aristocracy and gentry who were forced to sell up. "The hard little nut somewhere inside" and the charm that were part of his Villiers inheritance made him an effective sales representative. He was well organised, efficient and good at press relations.

His short fuse and intolerance of philistines made him enemies and they were not slow to pinpoint a contradiction between the Knight's commitment to the preservation of old houses and the promotion of the sales of their contents. He defended himself saying that he did not urge owners to sell but merely saw that they got the best deal if they did so. He himself was a tireless collector of old Irish paintings and furniture, much of it repatriated from abroad.

Concurrently he pursued his own scholarship joining forces in a fruitful if often argumentative partnership with the redoubtable Trinity professor Anne Crookshank to produce several volumes on the history of Irish paintings. Unearthing forgotten works and artists, they proved, without making extravagant claims, that Irish painting was more than a tiny off-shoot of English art and had been influenced by the Italians, the French and the Dutch.

In 1991 he succeeded Desmond Guinness as president of the Irish Georgian Society and injected a new professionalism into the organisation. They made regular fund-raising trips to the United States which were remarkably successful. Suzy Knickerbocker the New York columnist proclaimed the Knight of Glin her favourite title.

In the 1990s, as the Celtic Tiger began to roar and peace in Northern Ireland beckoned, the old official suspicion of those who were seen as champions of the preservation of an essentially British heritage receded. The Knight pointed out that what was being preserved had been the work of Irish craftsmen. He cultivated those in power and helped to secure tax advantages for the owners of historic houses and the funding of a heritage trust along the lines of the National Trust in Britain. There was an irony that in government the sons and grandsons of those who had been burning the houses of the Ascendancy were now subsidising the survivors of that class to remain in them. The Knight was appointed to the board of the Heritage Trust and also to the board of governors of the National Gallery of Ireland.

In 2007 he published in collaboration with James Peill a definitive history of Irish furniture which had been the area of his greatest expertise and interest since his London days. His status as a scholar was recognised by an honorary doctorate from Trinity College Dublin and election to membership of the Royal Irish Academy. Even more touching was the production by the local Glin historical society of a beautifully illustrated scholarly book on the history of the Knights of

Glin. He was proud of his warm relationship with the people of his ancestral territory whose endeavours he was ever keen to encourage.

He was diagnosed with cancer of the throat in 2010. He remained remarkably cheerful braving his illness, keen to see friends, hear the latest gossip and deliver, albeit hoarsely, forthright comments on events and their participants.

He is survived by his wife Olda and three daughters. There are no traceable legitimate heirs on the male line which means that he is in all probability the last Knight of Glin.

* * *

MARY RAFTERY

25 JANUARY 2012

IN 1999 JOURNALIST Mary Raftery, who died in Dublin on January 10, aged 54, produced on Irish television a documentary entitled *States of Fear*, which exposed the sexual and physical abuse that had been suffered by children committed to industrial schools run by Roman Catholic religious orders on behalf of the State.

It made clear that the responsible government department had failed to make the kind of inspections that might have exposed the abuse, a failure she ascribed to indifference to the underclass of Irish society who made up the inmates and deference to clergy who ran the schools.

It was not the first exposé of Irish industrial schools but it made a greater impact, perhaps because it tapped into a growing disillusionment with the Church among those reared as Catholics. The Taoiseach Bertie Ahern, ever sensitive to the public mood, responded immediately with an apology to victims promising a thorough inquiry and compensation.

A Residential Institutions Redress Board was established and some 14,000 victims, many of whom were resident in Britain, were compensated; the average of awards was in excess of €60,000.

The revelations of sexual abuse fuelled charges of hypocrisy against a church that had been obsessed with sexual sin yet failed to police it among its own clergy. This hypocrisy was further evidenced by a cover-up of clerical child abuse that formed the subject of a further devastating documentary produced by Raftery in 2002 entitled *Cardinal Secrets* – the Archbishop of Dublin was a cardinal. A subsequent enquiry eventually led to the resignation of several bishops.

Mary Frances Thérèse Raftery was born in Dublin on December 21, 1957, the daughter of an Irish diplomat whose career ran into the sands, the result of which was that the family returned permanently to Dublin when she was twelve. She was moved to the lay Pembroke School from a convent school after she had written an essay critical of the Papacy. She was among a small number of female students who chose engineering as a subject at University College Dublin but she abandoned her course, yielding to the attractions of agitation in student politics and journalism.

After college, she continued in journalism writing for *In Dublin* and *Magill* magazines before joining RTE, Ireland's chief television network, in 1984 to work on current affairs. Her interest in industrial schools was ignited by investigations into crime revealing how many members of criminal gangs had spent their childhood in these schools.

A doughty campaigner determined to achieve maximum exposure of any malpractice, she talked down in her calm unyielding tones cautious elements in RTE who stood in her way. She was, however, punctilious in not taking advantage of victims, taking care to show them extracts from interviews she proposed to use so that they could confirm that they were happy with them.

Some of the detail of her stories was disputed and she was criticized for lack of balance in failing to pay tribute to the philanthropic work of the clergy and to their right to be protected from unproven allegations.

But the gravamen of her charges was established and led to widespread disillusionment among Catholics with their church and especially its leadership. It earned for her the right to be acclaimed as among the most influential Irish journalists of her time.

She herself departed from RTE in 2004 to work freelance and wrote for the *Irish Times* on the follow-up to the abuses she had exposed. She produced a further documentary highlighting the State's responsibility for excessive committals to mental institutions; the Republic of Ireland, she ascertained, had had a higher proportion of its citizens in such institutions than any other country. Her play about abused children *No Escape* was produced in Dublin's Peacock Theatre in 2010

She faced her fatal cancer with matter-of-fact realism and prepared the humanist service she desired after her death. "The most important thing a journalist can do," she remarked looking back, "is to give a voice to people who have been silenced".

Outside her work Raftery's main enthusiasms were rugby football and music – she was a talented cellist in her student days.

She is survived by her husband and one son.

* * *

AENGUS FANNING

27 JANUARY 2012

AENGUS FANNING WHO DIED in Dublin on January 17 at the age of 69, was for almost thirty years the charismatic, fearless editor of Ireland's *Sunday Independent*, the country's most read and most controversial newspaper. As such he orchestrated debate on the fierce arguments and unedifying scandals that have accompanied the transformation of a traditional Catholic nationalistic, insular and rather narrow-minded society into something very different and less well-defined. It was a measure of his stature that he survived, bloodied but unbowed, through incidents and mistakes that would have brought down most editors.

He was bred to journalism in that his family had, since the 1880s, run a paper in Birr in what was once called the King's County. But his father was a teacher who had settled in Kerry having married a fellow teacher who was an Ulster Presbyterian up to the time of her marriage.

This background made the young Fanning feel something of an outsider among his fellow pupils at the Christian Brothers School in Tralee, where he had been born on April 22, 1942. But prowess at Gaelic football, where Kerry reigns supreme, leading to a place on the county team put that to rights, albeit that he kept up his cricket refusing to comply with the rule of the Gaelic Athletic Association prohibiting participation in English games. He played the clarinet for long hours daily and had to be diverted from making music his career; it remained a lifelong passion.

At University College Cork, where he studied economics, Fanning forsook Gaelic football for rugby but his interest in Kerry's football remained as an anomalous exception to his general rejection of narrow Irish nationalism.

He entered journalism through the family's newspaper, the *Midland Tribune*, before moving to Dublin in 1969 as a reporter on the daily *Irish Independent*. As that paper's agricultural correspondent he covered the tense negotiations in Brussels on farm prices and fishing quotas that were of such moment to the underdeveloped Irish economy. He was often first with the news, having charmed politicians and officials into giving him the story. He was a surprise choice when translated at a young age to become editor of the group's Sunday paper in 1984.

At the time Tony (now Sir Anthony) O'Reilly, the majority shareholder in Independent Newspapers, was using its original Irish newspapers as a base to expand and become a worldwide media group. The profitability of the Irish titles, including the *Sunday Independent*, was crucial to that strategy. It was threatened not only by other Irish papers but also by the well-funded Irish editions of British papers.

Fanning delivered handsomely increasing the circulation of the *Sunday Independent* by 50% in a fairly stagnant market and making it the cash cow of the group. He did so by transforming what had been a staid conservative paper into one that was exciting and provocative with pungent opinion columns, salacious gossip and fashion; a strange mixture of the tabloid and the highbrow. It became, in his own words, a kind of Sunday brunch, something for everybody.

A restless soul with a low boredom threshold, Fanning was determined that his paper would never bore. The iconoclast in him rejoiced in features that challenged or shocked the pillars of Irish society. Circulation was his polestar and entertainment his mantra. He had an uncanny instinctive feel for what would make people in middle Ireland buy the paper even if they did not approve of everything in it. He bubbled with ideas fuelled by his insatiable curiosity, multifarious interests and personal contacts.

Fanning was faulted for allowing free rein to some writers who conducted personalised campaigns. Critics charged him with pro-British bias in his hostility not only to the IRA but to more strident nationalist politicians. The severe criticism voiced in his columns of John Hume for talking to Sinn Fein leader Gerry Adams in an effort to achieve an IRA ceasefire was especially resented. Fanning insisted that he gave a platform to all viewpoints except those who espoused violence.

His editorship had many fraught moments. There were record libel awards and settlements. In 1996 the paper's crime correspondent Veronica Guerin was shot dead by criminals she was investigating. He was blamed by some, rather unfairly, for not restraining her. In 2000 he found himself in the eye of the storm when the controversial former London journalist Mary-Ellen Synon cast obloquy in her column on the Paralympic games at Sydney. Directors of the paper joined in the public outrage and the paper had to apologize. But Fanning was obdurate in his refusal to sack Synon whose feisty writing he valued; he was rather hurt when she resigned rather than rest her column until the storm blew over. He was famously loyal to his staff.

This loyalty was reciprocated by them, albeit that they felt severely tested at times by his unorthodox methods. Generally rather hands-off in approach, he could make occasional disconcerting interventions into their areas of responsibility. High words and rows abounded; on one occasion fisticuffs with one of his staff were reported in another paper and he apologized publicly. The two men were soon friends again. Fanning lived for the next edition and bore no grudges.

The master stroke of his editorship was the recruitment early on of Anne Harris whom he was later to marry. She gave the paper the magazine-like character that captured the female market and was one of several loyal lieutenants who anchored the whole operation, neutralising Fanning's unpredictability yet allowing scope for the inspiration and flair he provided. He, for his part, had as little respect for normal methods of management as he had for schools of journalism or political correctness. David Palmer, a group chief executive recruited from the *Financial Times* early in the new century, departed quite bewildered by how the whole thing worked.

With his great mane of long fair hair, his handsome ever-youthful appearance, his soft-topped BMW (often driven in bus lanes or parked on footpaths), his singular charm and slightly raffish lifestyle, Fanning cut a spectacular figure. He was a man happy and determined to be himself. He swam daily, participated in jazz concerts and promoted an annual music festival in his ancestral Birr. He seldom missed a Test match at Lord's.

He was predeceased by his first wife. He is survived by his wife and by three sons of his first marriage, two of whom are journalists while one plays in a jazz band.

LOUIS LE BROCQUY

27 APRIL 2012

ALTHOUGH LOUIS LE BROCQUY, who died in Dublin on 25 April at the age of 95, would develop into one of the foremost Irish artists of the 20th century, his early painting activities were clandestine. He frequented the city's art galleries and painted furtively in his spare time while he dutifully studied chemistry at Trinity College Dublin as his grandfather sought to steer him into the family oil refinery business.

Later in life he recalled: "I made illicit experiments with paints hidden in laboratory cupboards. One day these were discovered by my grandfather with a silence I still remember. I believe he then knew that I had abandoned ship."

So it was that le Brocquy made the switch from oil to oils. That pained moment, which happened when he was 22, led on to more than 70 years of artistic creativity. He received no formal training, instead learning intuitively by studying artists such as Velasquez, Rembrandt, Vermeer, Goya and Manet. With the support of his mother he travelled to view art collections in London, Paris, Venice and Geneva.

In 1946 he moved to London where his early paintings attracted attention and he became prominent in the contemporary art scene. He began to exhibit internationally, winning a major prize in 1956 at the Venice Biennale. In 1958 he was included in the landmark exhibition Fifty Years of Modern Art at the Brussels World Fair. In the same year he married his second wife, the Irish painter Anne Madden, and left London for the French Midi.

In the years that followed he showed striking versatility in producing paintings, book illustrations, tapestries and stage settings. However, he had one disastrous year, 1963. He said of it: "I completely lost my way. I lost my vision. I continued painting of course but my efforts had no meaning. I was in despair and eventually destroyed some 40 works, large and small."

To break this cycle his wife Anne suggested a visit to Paris and it was there, in the Musée de L'Homme that he chanced upon one of the great inspirations of his life. This took the form of Polynesian "ancestral heads", skulls remodelled with clay and decoratively painted. Le Brocquy was to produce, over more than three decades, the extraordinary series of heads which is regarded as one of his greatest themes. Described as psychologically incisive portraits, they have a spectral quality, being deliberately deprived of context. The heads are seen as hovering in time and space, conveying a sense of detachment.

One critic said: "They are disturbing, like seeing the face of a ghost peering out of the canvas. Many have a pared-down quality reminiscent of a death mask or a corpse on a mortuary slab hidden behind a thin white sheet." Among his most sought-after works were the heads of Irish authors. Ireland's writers are more celebrated than its painters, and le Brocquy made a productive connection with them in various ways, including book illustrations and stage designs. Most of all he painted the heads of writers such as Samuel Beckett, James Joyce, W. B. Yeats and Seamus Heaney.

According to le Brocquy: "James Joyce I never knew other than through his writing, but Samuel Beckett was a dear friend. I chose Yeats as my subject having known him when I was a boy and because of his vast and mysterious personality."

He said of his various studies: "I have sought to bring their spirits back from the place into which they have faded, not exactly as an archaeologist searching for traces of them, but more as an alchemist rebuilding those ancient glittering eyes."

Over the decades he produced more and more versions: Picasso, whom he knew, was among his subjects, while one of the more recent was that of his friend Bono, the Irish rock star. Much has been written about the heads. One comment, from his friend the painter Francis Bacon, was: "Le Brocquy belongs to a category of artists – obsessed by figuration outside and on the other side of illustration – who are aware of the vast and potent possibilities of inventing ways by which fact and appearance can be reconjugated."

Among his other celebrated works were drawings for a book called *The Tain*, Thomas Kinsella's 1969 translation of an 8th-century Ulster epic. The illustrations, which he described as "shadows thrown by the text", made such an impact that le Brocquy recreated some as full-scale tapestries.

His themes at various times in his long and productive life included travelling people, who he said impressed him by their "vitality, mystery and wildness, their insistence on freedom from every external regulation".

His work usually met with acclaim in Ireland, but an exception was *A Family*, a Cubist painting which portrayed a family in a stark and severe fashion, reflecting some of the fears and worries of the Cold War period. This proved ahead of its time in the conservative Ireland of the day, being denounced in 1950s Dublin as "a diabolical caricature" and an "unwholesome and satanic distortion". Years later it sold for over £1 million and was eventually housed in the National Gallery of Ireland.

In 2000 le Brocquy returned to live in Dublin, where celebrations and exhibitions accompanied his 90th birthday.

Born in Dublin on November 10, 1916, he married Jean Stoney in 1938. They had a daughter. They were divorced in 1948. There were two sons of his second marriage to Anne Madden.

MAIRE MACSWINEY BRUGHA

8 JUNE 2012

MAIRE MACSWINEY BRUGHA, who died on 20 May aged 93, was little over two years old in August 1920 when her father Terence MacSwiney, the 40-year-old Lord Mayor of Cork, was imprisoned for presiding at a court established by the revolutionary Sinn Fein government and embarked upon a 74-day hunger strike to death in Brixton prison. It evoked such sympathy in Britain and further afield that support for the law and order policy of the Lloyd George government was seriously undermined. Even King George V expressed disquiet.

The independence within the Empire negotiated by the Sinn Fein leaders a year later did not satisfy MacSwiney's widow Muriel or his militant sister Mary, who was a member of the revolutionary Dail. They joined the republicans who took up arms against the settlement, leaving young Maire in the care of friends.

At the end of the Irish civil war in 1923 Muriel, the English-educated daughter of the Catholic unionist Murphy family that distilled 'Paddy' whiskey, took Maire, then her only child, with her to Germany. The child was installed in a boarding school for five years and then handed over to a German family, seeing her mother only for short holidays or occasional visits. All ties with Ireland were cut and Maire spoke only German.

Meanwhile Muriel, who had left the Catholic Church, fraternised with revolutionaries in Paris and had a further daughter by a communist journalist she met there. In 1932 when Maire was fourteen, her father's sister Mary, who had been appointed co-guardian in Terence MacSwiney's will, located her and brought her back to Ireland.

Muriel sued for custody in the Irish courts alleging that her daughter had been kidnapped. However, when interviewed by the judge, Maire said she would prefer to remain with her aunt. An order was made to that effect with the rider that the child, who was made a ward of court, was not to be involved in republican activities. Muriel, who was to live to be 90, refused ever to see her daughter again.

Educated at a school run by her aunt Mary and Mary's younger sister, Annie, who were known by the wags of Cork as the republican ladies with the Oxford accents, Maire proved a brilliant student. She went on to University College Cork where she took a first in French and Irish before teaching in her aunt's school.

She married in 1945 Ruairi Brugha whose father Cathal Brugha (formerly Burgess) had been a minister in the underground Sinn Fein government and had then been killed fighting on the republican side in the civil war. Before marrying, Maire secured from her husband a willing assurance that he would take no further part in the republican movement into which he had been drafted as a boy by his family.

On marriage she abandoned her doctorate thesis and concentrated on rearing her Irish-speaking family of one girl and three boys while her husband managed the thriving drapery business his widowed mother had built up in central Dublin. He joined Fianna Fail in the 1960s and lent valuable support to his party leader Jack Lynch's moderate policy attempting to defuse the conflict in Northern Ireland.

Both Brughas became active in organisations promoting dialogue with unionists in the North hoping this would lead in time to a united Ireland. Whereas Ruairi was instinctively conciliatory seeing all points of view, his determined wife was less so, especially when it came to laying blame for the Troubles.

She also maintained strong contacts with France and Germany, confessing to feeling partly German and was active in an organisation that raised funds for the Third World.

In 2005 she published an evocative memoir entitled *History's Daughter* telling the story of her strange early life and paying homage to the memory of her aunt Mary, the first person who had given her true love. A devout Catholic, having known no religion until she was fourteen, she believed that her deceased father had kept her safe in life.

She was predeceased by her husband and is survived by one daughter and three sons.

MAEVE BINCHY

1 AUGUST 2012

MAEVE BINCHY WAS, according to one recent review, the Queen Mum of literature. Nobody had a bad word to say about her, or if they did, they had the sense to keep it to themselves. Her heart-warming stories of small-town life in a changing Ireland sold more than 40 million copies worldwide.

Her death on 30 July after a short illness at the age of 72 was a national event in Ireland, where she had presided over the world of popular fiction, particularly women's fiction, for more than 25 years. But her loss will be felt in every country where insight into the depth of feeling of ordinary people and a genius for story-telling are appreciated. She raised the everyday to the status of a once-in-a-lifetime experience.

There were those who claimed too much for her, most obviously those who saw in her an Irish reincarnation of Jane Austen. Binchy herself was quick to dismiss such nonsense. Told once that she had easily outsold the combined works of James Joyce, Samuel Beckett, Brendan Behan and W. B. Yeats, she commented: "I was very pleased, obviously, to have outsold such great writers. But I'm not insane. I do realise that I am a popular writer who people buy to take on vacation. I'm an escapist kind of writer. I didn't think for a moment that I was better than any of these people. I was just lucky I lived in this time of the mass-market paperback."

In the pantheon of middlebrow, middle-class, mid-market women writers, Binchy's place was assured. Barbara Taylor Bradford was more earthy and accorded greater significance to money and ambition; Joanna Trollope was at once darker and steamier; the younger generation, typified by Cecelia Ahern, are more open about sex, more cynical about relationships and yet, perversely, more cloyingly romantic. Binchy's unique, populist quality, analogous perhaps to Austen scripting an episode of *Coronation Street*, was her ability to open up small, enclosed worlds in which hope, disappointment, despair and banality were embodied in the usually suburban lives of characters whose deepest wish was only to be happy and to find love in an imperfect world.

Maeve Binchy was born on May 28, 1940 in the south Dublin suburb of Dalkey. She was the eldest child of William Binchy, a successful barrister, and Maureen, a former nurse.

Growing up in a small community, some miles from the city centre, Binchy's upbringing had a provincial quality to it at odds with its location. Her father had to work hard for his success, managing to buy his first house only when his children were already at school. Her mother, meanwhile, was more interested in gardening than housework. The young Maeve went through school at the fashionable Holy Child convent in nearby Killiney, developing in her teens, alongside her natural academic bent, a passion for romance that for many years was destined to remain unconsummated. Even when she won a place to study history at University College Dublin she was obliged to return home each night before midnight, where her father would be waiting up for her.

In 1961 she began teaching Latin, French and history at Pembroke School, in leafy Dublin 4, known to its pupils as Miss Meredith's. There she remained, apparently content, until 1968. It was during one of the long summer breaks that she visited Israel and worked briefly on a kibbutz, losing her faith as a result but discovering her vocation as a writer. Her father passed on her letters home to the *Irish Independent*, which published them, leading to a job offer from the *Irish Times*.

Binchy was never a reporter, always a commentator, and her column in the *Irish Times* remained a much-loved feature for the next 32 years. On a visit to London in the mid-1970s, she met Gordon Snell, a children's writer and occasional broadcaster. The two began to see one another, and Douglas Gageby, her editor, not wishing to lose her talents, agreed that she should write for the paper from London.

Marriage in 1977 was followed three years later by a move back to Dublin, where the couple bought a period cottage in Dalkey just up the road from Binchy's childhood home.

Light a Penny Candle, Binchy's first novel, was published by Century in 1983, securing a UK record advance of £52,000. The story was deceptively simple. Elizabeth, a young English girl of Irish origin, is evacuated to Ireland during the war, where she becomes the lifelong friend of Aisling O'Connor. The two girls' paths cross and re-cross over the next 20 years as they each undergo the joys and disappointments of adult life.

It sold in millions around the world and was followed by a succession of novels, most notably *Echoes*, *Circle of Friends* and *Tara Road*, as well as several collections of short stories, including *Dublin 4*, *Victoria Line* and *Central Line*, the latter featuring the lives of London commuters.

Tara Road (1998) is typical of the Binchy oeuvre. "Ria and Marilyn have never met – they live thousands of miles apart, separated by the Atlantic Ocean: one in a big, warm, Victorian house in Tara Road, Dublin, the other in a modern, open-plan house in New England. Two more unlikely friends would be hard to find: Ria's life revolves around her family and friends, while Marilyn's reserve is born of grief. But when each needs a place to escape to, a house exchange seems the ideal solution. Along with the borrowed houses come neighbours and friends, gossip and speculation as Ria and Marilyn swap lives for the summer . . ."

Across the world, women realised that they had found the narrator of their own imagined lives. In Dublin the money began to pour in. Binchy and Snell were able to gut their Dalkey home and rebuild it from the inside out, adding a second home to the rear of the original for their guests.

Otherwise, life continued much as usual. Binchy, increasingly troubled by osteoarthritis and too old to have children, wrote on a production-line basis, maintaining her *Irish Times* column alongside her fiction until the year 2000, when she announced – inaccurately – that she intended to retire.

Generous to a fault, yet no slouch with money, she continued to turn out books, including *Aches and Pains* (1999), a wry look at illness and the realities of modern medicine, and *The Return Journey* (1998), a collection of stories written over the previous 20 years. She was still producing a novel every two years in her last decade, culminating with *Minding Frankie* (2010), her last novel.

A reviewer for the *San Francisco Chronicle* was unstinting in her praise. "Binchy makes you laugh, cry, and care. Her warmth and sympathy render the daily struggles of ordinary people heroic and turn storytelling into art."

She died in the evening of her fame, popular with her neighbours (and the staff of Finnegan's, her pub), adored by her public and respected by her peers. Her husband, Gordon, survives her.

SEAMUS HEANEY

31 AUGUST 2013

GENIUS LIBERATES. It also intimidates. Long after his death in 1939, W. B. Yeats continued to cast a shadow over the development of poetry in Ireland. He was to Irish poets of the postwar era what Shakespeare has always been to English playwrights – nonpareil.

The shadow finally lifted one day in May 1966 with the publication by Faber & Faber of *Death of a Naturalist*, the first collection by Seamus Heaney, who died yesterday aged 74. It was a literary sensation. The Ulsterman's deceptively simple pastoral verse proved both a counterpoint to the strident immediacy of pop music and an inspiration to his fellow poets, drawing thousands of young people back to the written word.

From the outset, Heaney's poems were rooted, earthbound, tactile, crafty, respectful of ritual and of manual skills. *Digging* described his father and grandfather's adeptness at turning the turf, and struck a typical note of self-deprecation – and a pride in his own implement:

> *Between my finger and my thumb*
> *The squat pen rests.*
> *I'll dig with it.*

The impact of the collection was felt not only in Belfast, where Heaney was teaching, and in London, where Faber & Faber presented its new signing as a new-found 'master', but throughout the literary world. Post-Yeats but pre-Heaney, Ireland was a middle-ranking poetic power. With Heaney, it dominated the landscape.

Many have commented on the fact that as his native Northern Ireland was increasingly convulsed by political and religious violence, Heaney, a Catholic, remained true to his calling, refusing to become a poster boy for the nationalist cause or a Republican pamphleteer. This should not suggest that he was unmoved by the death and destruction through which he was living. For years, it seemed, he had lived in dread of what was coming. In the title poem of his first collection, he recalled how as a child he loved the frogs that gathered around the flax ponds near his home. But then one day the mood changed. The angry frogs invaded the flax dam.

> *I ducked through hedges*
> *To a coarse croaking that I had not heard*
> *Before. The air was thick with a bass chorus.*
> *Right down the dam gross-bellied frogs were cocked*
> *On sods; their loose necks pulsed like sails. Some hopped:*
> *The slap and plop were obscene threats. Some sat*
> *Poised like mud grenades, their blunt heads farting.*
> *I sickened, turned and ran. The great slime kings*
> *Were gathered there for vengeance and I knew*
> *That if I dipped my hand the spawn would clutch it.*

Heaney did not dip his hand. Instead, he left Belfast and fled to Wicklow to perfect his art. But he could not escape his inheritance entirely. *Requiem for the Croppies*, from *Door Into the Dark* (1969), recalls the bloody defeat by the British of a band of insurrectionists in Wicklow in 1798. Lyrically, in full awareness of the power of his message, the poet confronts the resilience and romanticism of the Irish struggle. The 'Croppies' – poor sharecroppers risen in support of the United Irishmen – had embarked on their doomed campaign with barley in the pockets of their greatcoats with which to feed themselves on the run. Then, as the Redcoats responded, came the 'final conclave'.

> *Terraced thousands died, shaking scythes at cannon.*
> *The hillside blushed, soaked in our broken wave.*
> *They buried us without shroud or coffin*
> *And in August ... the barley grew up out of our grave.*

The many collections that he published after *Death of a Naturalist* were acclaimed by critics and the general public alike. Poems such as *Mid-Term Break, Punishment, Mossbawn Sunlight, The Tollund Man* and *Poet's Chair* became classics, anthologised in a dozen languages, admired by critics, on school curriculums from Belfast to Boston and from Liverpool to Lyons.

Soft-spoken, with famously twinkling eyes, Heaney was a formidable critic and scholar, whose translation of *Beowulf* became a worldwide bestseller. He was also a teacher, for five years Professor of Poetry at Oxford and over several decades a visiting professor at Berkeley and Harvard. The award of the 1995 Nobel Prize for Literature conferred formal recognition of what had been apparent for years. Academicians praised the Derry man for creating "works of lyrical beauty and ethical depth, which exalt everyday miracles and the living past". Heaney – Famous Seamus – had become quite simply the best known poet in the world. In Ireland he was regarded as a national treasure.

Seamus Justin Heaney was born on April 13, 1939, less than three months after the death of Yeats (who had won Nobel Prize for Literature in 1923). He was the eldest of nine children born to Patrick Heaney, a small farmer and cattle dealer, and his wife, Margaret, *née* McCann. Heaney's father was hard-working and laconic; his mother outgoing and opinionated. Out of their qualities, their son would recall, came the quarrel with himself that fed his poetry.

Mossbawn itself is a marshy townland halfway between Belfast and Londonderry. More to the point, it sits halfway between the nationalist village of Toome, famous in song as the place where the rebel Roddy McCorley was hanged, and Castledawson, dominated by the Big House of the Chichester-Clarks, one of the last Ascendancy families to wield real power in Ireland. Growing up in this microcosm of the Northern divide, Heaney was well aware of the faultlines of Irish society. His own large family was nationalist-inclined but not involved politically. The future poet, like his parents, did not have a bitter disposition, and he grew up largely without enemies.

What changed everything – beyond the fact that his aunt Sarah had instilled in him a love of reading – was the award in 1951, when he was 12, of a scholarship to St Columb's College, a Catholic boarding school in Derry City. At St Columb's the young Heaney found himself studying Latin, modern languages, Irish history, Gaelic, religion and English, as well as mathematics and the sciences.

From St Columb's Heaney progressed to Queen's University Belfast, a majority of whose students were then Protestant and unionist. Professor John Braidwood, a Scot, introduced him to Anglo-Saxon and Old Norse, joining him to a train of thought that linked the bogs of Ireland to the bogs of Denmark – the source material for his celebrated *Tollund Man* sequence of poems – and ultimately to *Beowulf*.

He started to write poetry seriously after graduating with first-class honours in 1961, and within a year, while pursuing a teaching qualification at St Joseph's College, he began to be published in local journals, most obviously *The Honest Ulsterman*, edited by James Simmons. Switching to the English department at Queen's in 1966, he was persuaded by the English poet Philip Hobsbaum to join what became known as "The Group", a gathering of young poets that included Derek Mahon and Michael Longley.

Belfast, though, was no place for a poet whose mandate clearly transcended provincial squabbles, especially as the political violence began to intensify. In 1970 Heaney accepted an invitation from Berkeley to be a visiting professor and enjoyed the experience. Not long after his return to Queen's he resigned his lectureship and embarked on a peripatetic academic career that would be crowned by his appointment in 1984 as Boylston Professor of Rhetoric and Oratory at Harvard.

Heaney moved easily between teaching, research and writing, winning numerous awards along the way. He even found time to compile, with Ted Hughes, two anthologies, *The Rattle Bag* and *The School Bag*, that probably introduced more young people to poetry than any collection since the *Oxford Book of English Verse*, edited by Sir Arthur Quiller-Couch in 1900.

Seamus Heaney

Thematically, Heaney in the 1980s drifted away from Mossbawn, becoming markedly more abstruse and classically referential, putting at risk his gift of the common touch. Yet, in this mature phase, affected by his growing awareness of civilisations and literatures across time and space, he was still capable of producing masterpieces. *Poet's Chair*, from his 1996 collection *The Spirit Level*, was universally acclaimed, reaching back to his earliest influences while acknowledging his inevitable transformation.

> *My father's ploughing one, two, three, four sides*
> *Of the lea ground where I sit all-seeing*
> *At centre field, my back to the thorn tree*
> *They never cut. The horses are all hoof*
> *And burnished flank, I am all foreknowledge.*
> *Of the poem as a ploughshare that turns time*
> *Up and over. Of the chair in leaf*
> *The fairy thorn is entering for the future.*
> *Of being here for good in every sense.*

Heaney, like Yeats, had a keen appreciation of himself as a public man, ready to give a speech, lead a discourse, or simply adorn a grand occasion. He was not stuffy or pompous, however, and never took himself more seriously than the situation demanded. He told the story of when he was staying at the home in Ludlow of one of his dearest friends, the academic Bernard McCabe. A taxi driver turned up to take Heaney to Shrewsbury, where he was due to deliver a lecture. The driver, a local man, looked at the shaggy-haired Irishman. "Who are you, anyway," he asked. "Some sort of poet?" "That's right," Heaney answered, "some sort of poet."

The singer and documentary film-maker David Hammond, whose favourite retreat was a house overlooking the sea in Co Donegal, was another close friend. His refusal to play his guitar after news came through of a particularly brutal political murder yielded *The Singer's House*, one of Heaney's most enduringly popular poems.

People here used to believe
that drowned souls lived in the seals.
At spring tides they might change shape.
They loved music and swam in for a singer
who might stand at the end of summer
in the mouth of a whitewashed turf-shed,
his shoulder to the jamb, his song
a rowboat far out in evening.
When I came here first you were always singing,
a hint of the clip of the pick
in your winnowing climb and attack.
Raise it again, man. We still believe what we hear.

Heaney's life was greatly blessed by his long marriage to Marie Devlin, the sister of the author and broadcaster Polly Devlin. A native of Ardboe, Co Tyrone, Devlin was a young schoolteacher and an authority on Irish myth and legend. They married in 1965 and had two sons and a daughter. If any one person kept Heaney's feet on the ground, it was his wife – as he regularly acknowledged. She was also his constant inspiration and most valued critic.

In later life, having survived a stroke, Heaney found himself ever more in demand from academics and 'Heaneyboppers'. There was still time though for academic projects, including *The Burial at Thebes*, a version of Sophocles's *Antigone*, later turned into an opera directed by his fellow Nobel laureate and poet Derek Walcott. The gala performance at Shakespeare's Globe Theatre in London turned out to be only the seventh opera Heaney had ever attended. It was nice, Walcott confessed, to have arias that contained more than, 'I love you, I love you ... never leave me.'

There are critics who argue that Heaney's best work was behind him as the hands of the millennium clock advanced towards the new century. While the American poet Robert Lowell dubbed him "the greatest Irish poet since Yeats' and John Carey said he was 'the one undoubtedly major poet in the English-speaking world", back home the begrudgers were moving out of the woodwork. In one clamorous pamphlet, the Irish essayist and critic Desmond Fennell condemned what he called Heaney's "Anglo-American" turn of mind. The poet was good, said Fennell, but not that good, and he drowned out other voices.

If the criticism stung, Heaney did not complain. He let his poems speak for him, written either in his house near Sandymount, south Dublin, or else in his second home in the Wicklow Hills, where for years he was unreachable by any means other than fax. The only time he publicly bridled at the assumption of others was in 1982 when Blake Morrison and Andrew Motion included him in the *Penguin Book of Contemporary British Verse*. "Be advised!" came the retort. "My passport's green. No glass of ours was ever raised to toast the Queen."

In 1995, during a visit to Londonderry, President Clinton chose a stanza from Heaney's play *The Cure at Troy* in support of his Irish peace initiative:

> *History says, don't hope*
> *On this side of the grave.*
> *But then, once in a lifetime*
> *The longed-for tidal wave*
> *Of justice can rise up,*
> *And hope and history rhyme.*

Heaney's health had been failing for some years. His 2010 collection *Human Chain* was written after he suffered a stroke. Its central poem, *Miracle*, was directly inspired by his illness and his faltering recovery.

He is survived by his wife, Marie, and his two sons and one daughter.

ALBERT REYNOLDS

22 AUGUST 2014

ALBERT REYNOLDS, WHO DIED yesterday in Dublin, aged 81, was a much-maligned and derided politician in the bear pit of domestic Irish politics. However, when he was Taoiseach he won acclaim as a peacemaker for conducting the negotiations that led to the IRA ceasefire in Northern Ireland in August 1994.

First, he convinced a sceptical British prime minister, John Major, to join in making the Downing Street Declaration of December 1993. This stated that the British Government had no selfish economic or strategic interest in retaining Northern Ireland and accepted the right of Ireland as a whole to self-determination, albeit subject to the right of a majority in Northern Ireland to decide whether or not to join the Republic. He then used the declaration to persuade the Sinn Fein leader Gerry Adams to get the IRA to drop as a precondition for a ceasefire that the British Government should announce its intention to withdraw from Northern Ireland.

Major found Reynolds's "take it or leave it" approach a rugged experience; on one occasion an exasperated British prime minister snapped his pencil in half. Reynolds recalled: "He chewed the bollocks off me, but I took a few lumps out of him." Major was to write later: "The great thing about my relationship with Albert Reynolds was that we liked one another and could have a row without giving up on one another."

In negotiating with the Sinn Fein leaders, Reynolds reversed the practice of successive Irish Governments, which was to refuse to have any communication, direct or indirect, with Sinn Fein as long as it supported IRA violence. He removed the ban on Sinn Fein representatives appearing on radio or television and, despite strong British opposition, he persuaded President Clinton to give Adams a visa to enter the US. By August 1994 Adams felt strong enough to persuade the IRA to call a complete ceasefire. It was observed more strictly than most people had expected, so enhancing Adams's credibility. Reynolds justified his actions by saying: "These people must be shown the benefits of going down the constitutional road. The IRA have nowhere to go. I've stripped away all their excuses, one by one."

The peace process was to be fraught with difficulty because of the refusal of the British Government or the unionists to negotiate a settlement for the future governance of Northern Ireland unless and until the IRA disarmed. The gap was not bridged and there was a brief renewal of IRA violence in 1996 and 1997 (for which Reynolds criticized John Major) followed by a further ceasefire leading to the negotiation of the Good Friday Agreement in 1998.

By then Reynolds was long out of office as Taoiseach. He had resigned in December 1994 after his Labour colleagues in the coalition pulled out of government over the appointment of his Attorney General Harry Whelehan as President of the High Court. A last-ditch effort to mend fences collapsed when it emerged that Reynolds had failed to reveal some relevant facts in a speech on the performance of the Attorney General's office in a case concerning the failed extradition to Northern Ireland of a paedophile priest, Father Brendan Smyth.

A report of this incident in *The Sunday Times* charged Reynolds with lying. Reynolds, a prickly character with a track record of litigation (his home was nicknamed "Litigation Lodge" in the Irish press), sued in the High Court in London. It came to a hearing in 1997. No credible evidence was produced to contradict Reynolds's assertion that he had not been made aware of the facts he had failed to disclose. But the paper argued that even if it could not prove that Reynolds lied deliberately, its journalist had reasonable grounds for believing that Reynolds had done so and, as it was a matter of public interest, it was entitled to rely on the defence of qualified privilege.

This argument was rejected by the judge and the jury then found for Reynolds but refused to award him damages (the judge eventually awarded him one penny). Reynolds was ordered to pay most of the costs.

Having saved face in Ireland by attributing the jury verdict to anti-Irish prejudice, Reynolds appealed and a retrial was ordered; *The*

Sunday Times appealed further to the House of Lords and, although it was unsuccessful on the ground that it had not published Reynolds's explanation of his comments to the Dail, a wider principle of public interest defence was established. The "Reynolds defence" in Lord Nicholls's ruling cemented for the first time a "public interest defence" that newspapers have relied on ever since. The case itself was settled before the retrial on terms as to costs more acceptable to Reynolds.

Albert Reynolds was born in the village of Roskey in Co Roscommon on November 3, 1932. He won a bursary to Summerhill College in Sligo but had to become a railway clerk on leaving because his parents could not afford to send him to university.

In 1955 he organised a dance to raise money for the parish church in his native Roskey. It was so successful that he reinvented himself as a musical impresario in partnership with his brother. The pair started a showband and operated a chain of dance halls. But Reynolds walked away in 1966 after falling out with his brother. He opened a bacon factory in Dublin. Noticing that the bacon offal was being thrown away, he had an idea of converting it into pet food and established a successful pet food business in Longford. He joined Fianna Fail there and was elected to the Dail for the local constituency in 1977.

Reynolds was to the fore in the campaign to install Charles Haughey as Taoiseach in 1979 and was rewarded with a succession of ministerial posts. Horse racing was his passion and he loved a bet; he said that he approached politics in the same way and most of his gambles paid off.

One that failed was his decision to provide export insurance to a favoured beef exporter trading with Iraq in 1987. Saddam Hussein failed to pay and Irish taxpayers were left with a huge bill. A tribunal of inquiry that reported in 1994 criticized Reynolds but stopped short of finding that he had acted from improper motives.

He became the leader of a group of disenchanted rural ministers who were described derisively in a reference to Reynolds's crooning days as the "country and western alliance". From this base he challenged Haughey, whom he replaced as Taoiseach early in 1992.

The coalition government with the small Progressive Democrat party that Reynolds inherited did not survive charges of dishonesty he unleashed against its leader. At the subsequent general election Fianna Fail suffered heavy losses but Reynolds held on to office by forming a surprising coalition with the Labour Party.

A born dealmaker, he negotiated an IR£8 billion subvention for Ireland from the European Union at the Edinburgh summit in 1992. This fuelled the boom that began before he left office in 1994.

In 1997 Reynolds sought nomination to be president of Ireland. He felt betrayed when a clear majority of the Fianna Fail parliamentary party chose Mary McAleese as their candidate. He devoted himself to business thereafter as a director of companies.

Alzheimer's prevented him from attending the 20th anniversary of the Downing St Declaration in Dublin, but Sir John Major turned up at his home to pay his respects.

Reynolds married in 1962 Kathleen Coen by whom he is survived. There were two sons and five daughters of the marriage. Philip, the eldest son, followed his father in the pet food business.

THE REV. IAN PAISLEY

22 AUGUST 2014

LORD BANNSIDE, more commonly known as the Rev. Ian Paisley, died an enigma, a puzzle to both his supporters and detractors.

No public figure did more in his lifetime to inflame sectarian hatred in Northern Ireland, widen the province's divisions or wreck successive efforts to achieve peace through compromise. He was a man of thunderous, apocalyptic rhetoric whose battle cries were "No surrender", "Not an Inch" and "Never, Never, Never". He was ejected from the European Parliament in Strasbourg after telling Pope John Paul II: "I denounce you, Antichrist". He said of Roman Catholics: "They breed like rabbits and multiply like vermin."

In 2003 every last shred of hope inspired by the 1998 Good Friday Agreement appeared to have been dashed when Paisley's Democratic Unionist Party (DUP) finally overtook the Ulster Unionist Party (UUP) to become the largest party in the Northern Ireland Assembly. On the nationalist side, Sinn Fein had likewise overtaken the Social Democrat and Labour Party (SDLP), leaving the two hardline parties to confront each other.

"I am not going to sit down with the bloodthirsty monsters who have been killing and terrifying my people," Paisley had once declared, but he underwent a breathtaking conversion. In May 2007 he and the DUP agreed to share power with Sinn Fein, a party of whom he had said only the previous year: "They are not fit to be in partnership with decent people."

At his inauguration as First Minister he declared: "I believe that Northern Ireland has come to a time of peace, a time when hate will no longer rule. How good it will be to be part of a wonderful healing in our province." He then astonished both his supporters and detractors by working so happily with his deputy, the former IRA chief-of-staff Martin McGuinness, that they were dubbed the "Chuckle Brothers".

McGuinness said: "It wasn't a show, it wasn't an act – we had, I think, a real friendship and a real understanding of our role in history, our place in history and the need to provide good leadership."

The "Big Man", as Paisley was known, was certainly a complex man. Reviled for much of his life as a sectarian bigot and preacher of hatred, he was also in private a man of considerable charm and humour with a nice line in self-deprecation. He condemned Catholicism vehemently, but as an MP he had a reputation for helping Catholic and Protestant constituents equally assiduously, once campaigning against the demolition of a convent. He was a man of enormous energy who, in his mid-seventies, was simultaneously an MP, MEP, member of Northern Ireland's Assembly, leader of the DUP and Moderator of the Free Presbyterian Church of Ulster.

Ian Richard Kyle Paisley was born on April 6, 1926, the second son of a Baptist pastor. He was raised and educated in Ballymena, a deeply conservative town that later became his political power base, and at the age of 16 delivered his first sermon in Sixmilecross in Co Tyrone. "It lasted two-and-three-quarter minutes," he later recalled. "I sat down in total confusion. I needed to be taught a good lesson not to be proud."

He attended the Barry School of Evangelism in South Wales and the Reformed Presbyterian Theological Hall in Belfast. He was ordained by his father and became pastor of the Ravenhill Evangelical Mission Church in East Belfast, which consisted chiefly of defectors from the local Presbyterian church. His mother marked the occasion by giving him a text from Isaiah: "No weapon that is formed against thee shall prosper; and every tongue that shall rise against thee in judgment thou shalt condemn." He took it to heart and repeated it whenever occasion demanded.

The Ravenhill congregation rapidly became the stronghold of the Free Presbyterian Church of Ulster, which Paisley and a group of kindred spirits established at Crossgar, Co Down, in March 1951. In the 1960s it was rebuilt as the Martyrs' Memorial Church with seating for 2,000, and the faithful (and the curious) from Ulster and abroad flocked to hear Paisley fulminate against his opponents.

The Rev. Ian Paisley

He ruthlessly exploited the acute personal rivalries and arcane doctrinal disputes of Irish presbyterianism to swell the ranks of the Free Presbyterians. They proselytised, spread and multiplied until the church boasted more than 100 branches as far afield as Africa, Australia and Canada. Paisley was elected Moderator every year for 57 years until January 2008 when his position as Northern Ireland's First Minister obliged him to protect gay rights and other social doctrines abhorrent to his church. Paisley had routinely denounced homosexuality, once launching a campaign called "Save Ulster from Sodomy".

A merciless scourge of the Presbyterian establishment, Paisley once fomented serious disorder outside the Presbyterian General Assembly in Belfast and went to prison for three months. He occupied himself by writing a 191-page commentary on the Epistle to the Romans, which earned him a doctorate from the Christian fundamentalist Bob Jones University in South Carolina.

Paisley was convinced from the outset that the defence of Protestant Ulster required him to be as active in the political arena as well as the religious one. Within weeks of his ordination in 1946, he helped to organise an Irish base for the National Union of Protestants, which denounced any political development containing the slightest hint of advantage for the Catholic Church.

He first achieved notoriety during the 1964 election when his demand that the police remove a small Irish tricolor in West Belfast precipitated the worst rioting for 30 years. As tension mounted, Paisley steadily increased his political strength, assisted by the growth of militant Protestant organisations such as the revived Ulster Volunteer Force (UVF) though he always denied any links with those who resorted to violence. He was accused of inciting violence with his biblical hyperbole and then denouncing loyalists when they carried out atrocities.

While forging his early extremist reputation, he produced and mocked a Roman Catholic Eucharist wafer during a televised speech to the Oxford Union, denouncing those who believed it sacred, and he famously threw snowballs at Jack Lynch, the Irish prime minister, when he visited Northern Ireland in 1967.

What sealed Paisley's rise to prominence was his hostility to the nationalist Civil Rights Movement in the late 1960s. In 1968 he was jailed for a second time, serving six weeks for organizing an illegal counter-demonstration against a civil rights march in Armagh.

Paisley stood for Bannside in the Stormont elections of February 1969 and very nearly beat Captain Terence O'Neill, the Northern Ireland prime minister. The following May he won that seat, and proceeded to excoriate political reforms embarked on by government to address the nationalist minority's grievances.

Paisley's wife, Eileen, a shopkeeper's daughter whom he had married in 1956, was never far from his side. His favourite election slogan was, "Vote for my wife's husband." She always called him "Honeybunch".

He was elected to the House of Commons in 1970 with a comfortable victory over the official Unionist candidate in North Antrim, one of Northern Ireland's safest unionist seats. In the two general elections held in 1974, however, he made common cause with the official UUP, which had joined him in repudiating the Sunningdale Agreement, a comprehensive constitutional settlement proposed by Edward Heath's government that proposed a power-sharing executive and a Council of Ireland to establish closer co-operation between the North and the South.

A province-wide Loyalist strike in May 1974 brought down the new power-sharing government. Paisley was involved in preparations for the strike though, with an unfailing instinct for self-preservation, he cautiously withheld unqualified support until it became apparent that it had massive backing. The executive's collapse represented a total victory for Paisley.

Paisley consistently topped the polls in Northern Ireland's European elections after 1979; but in 1981 he attracted criticism, and some ridicule, when he declared that he would mobilise, and if necessary arm, Northern Ireland's loyalists in the manner of Sir Edward Carson during the controversy over Home Rule before the First World War.

Later that year he vowed to make the Province "ungovernable" and raise a "third force" of armed men, 50,000 strong, to tackle the IRA. Only 5,000 appeared at a rally he addressed that November.

The Anglo-Irish Agreement of November 1985, which gave the Dublin Government a consultative role in Ulster's affairs, brought Paisley back on to the political stage, bellowing defiance at British ministers and denouncing "the lying, treachery and betrayal to which unionists had been subjected".

The campaign of opposition produced serious disorder in 1986 after several thousand of his supporters had drilled in the streets of Hillsborough, Co Down, one July night. Thereafter, however, he was increasingly restrained by the leader of the UUP, Jim Molyneaux, with whom he had an uneasy alliance.

When serious inter-party talks resumed after 1991, he felt deeply uncomfortable about Dublin's involvement, but was unable to prevent his unionist allies from pursuing discussions. Similarly, as John Major advanced the search for a comprehensive political settlement, Paisley's threats of obstruction were largely ignored. When he accused Major of lying, Paisley was ejected from Downing Street in 1994.

The DUP boycotted the negotiations that produced the Good Friday Agreement of 1998, and campaigned vigorously against an outcome that Paisley and many unionists regarded as a surrender to the IRA. Unionist disillusionment grew in the years that followed. When, in the assembly elections of November 2003 the DUP overtook the UUP as the largest party in the province, Paisley, once denounced as a political dinosaur, had, in the 21st century, become more powerful than ever.

Paisley followed his appointment as First Minister in May 2007 with an official visit to the formerly reviled "Free State" where he and Bertie Ahern, the Irish prime minister, met and shook hands at the site of the Battle of the Boyne, where William of Orange had secured the Protestant ascendancy.

In May 2008, Paisley suddenly announced his intention to step down as First Minister. The previous month he had been embroiled in a small scandal when it emerged that his son, Ian, was on his parliamentary payroll as a researcher in spite of being a member of the Stormont Assembly and a junior minister. In 2010 Paisley's North Antrim seat in the House of Commons was won by Ian, continuing a political dynasty.

Paisley's wife was elected to the Belfast City Council in 1967 and sat in the Northern Ireland Assembly. She was made a life peer, Baroness Paisley of St George's, in 2006. One of his three daughters, Rhonda, an artist who had a canary called Matisse, represented the DUP on the Belfast Council and served as Lady Mayoress in the mid-1980s; Cherith at one stage edited her father's magazine, *Protestant Blueprint*, while Sharon married a Belfast engineer. Their second son, Kyle, is a Free Presbyterian church minister.

Paisley himself was made a life peer in 2010. Even in ailing health he never lost his feistiness. During one of his sermons in which he ruminated on death, he said: "If you hear in the press that Ian Paisley is dead, don't believe a word of it. I'll be more alive than ever... I'll be singing as I sang never before."

He is survived by his wife, his two sons and three daughters.

JACK KYLE

29 NOVEMBER 2014

JACK KYLE, WHO DIED yesterday, aged 88, was one of Ireland's greatest rugby players. As out-half on their international team he was the main architect of their winning the triple crown in 1948 and 1951 and the Five Nations championship outright in 1948 and 1951. On the British Lions tour to New Zealand and Australia in 1950 he was acclaimed as the best out-half they had seen; a view widely shared in the northern hemisphere.

Nicknamed "The Ghost", the stocky Kyle was quick on the break and an elusive runner, rarely caught in possession. After one game, when he ran rings around France, the *Irish Independent* wrote:

> *They seek him here, they seek him there,*
> *Those Frenchies seek him everywhere.*
> *That paragon of pace and guile,*
> *That damned elusive Jackie Kyle.*

However, to thousands of people living in Africa, he was simply "Dr Kyle". When his playing career ended, having struggled to get his fellowship in surgery, he answered the call for medical personnel in the Third World, working for 2 years in Indonesia and eventually settling in Chingola, a mining town in Zambia. His house was on the edge of a golf course, where he played regularly, doing battle with monkeys who would dart out of the trees to pinch his golf balls.

He was the only surgeon in the area and became a household name. On one occasion he was presented with a man who had a stab wound to his heart – an operation he had never performed before. At the weekends he flew up into the bush to treat broken bones or other problems in remote clinics. All the children from the villages would line up on the landing strip when they heard his plane.

By the 1990s 80 per cent of his patients had AIDS, still a relatively new condition. Despite his protestations, he was regularly pressed into service as a GP. He used to refer to a huge medical encyclopaedia on his desk and could be found asleep in front of it late at night. A deeply modest man, Kyle said: "I was only the second opinion. They always saw the witch doctor before they saw me."

His care of all patients irrespective of colour and his opposition to segregation in sports clubs earned him the title of the white man with the black heart.

Kyle's modesty meant that few people in Zambia realised they were being treated by a famous sportsman. When Kyle's daughter, Justine, who was born in Zambia, returned to Ireland to boarding school and was taken to watch a rugby match, she recalled: "All these men came over and they were going on and on and on about dad. He always felt that rugby was a gift which just came naturally to him because he played on instinct and that the surgery was much more difficult to achieve."

Of his rugby, Kyle agreed. "These things are done on a subconscious level. The ball goes into your arms, and suddenly an opening appears and away you go."

He was born John Wilson Kyle in Belfast on February 10, 1926, the youngest of four children of a business executive. Sport ran in his family – his father was a football enthusiast, his elder brother Eric got a final trial for the Irish rugby team, and one of his sisters became a hockey international while the other played at interprovincial level. At Belfast Royal Academy Kyle starred at boxing and cricket as well as rugby. The headmaster Alex Foster, a former rugby international, was an early mentor.

Kyle studied medicine at Queen's University, Belfast and quickly established himself as out-half on their team. He played for an Irish XV against the British Army at Ravenhill in Belfast in December 1945 and in the unofficial internationals against France and England the following year. When official internationals resumed in 1947, Kyle was in undisputed possession of the out-half position. His immense potential was revealed when Ireland defeated England by a record margin of 22 points to nil in Dublin.

1948 saw him in full bloom as Ireland swept all before them. He sent Barney Mullen, the Ireland wing, in to score one of the two tries that defeated Wales at Ravenhill giving Ireland its first triple crown since 1899 and a first grand slam. The following season it was a well placed cross kick by Kyle, taken by his regular henchman wing forward Jim McCarthy, that overcame Wales at Swansea to secure another triple crown.

On tour with the Lions in the summer of 1950, Kyle scored a try and made another to enable the touring team to hold the New Zealanders to a draw in the first Test. Although the All Blacks won the next three matches, Kyle was proclaimed one of the stars of the series. He also played in the two matches when the Lions defeated Australia. "There would have been no tour without Jack Kyle," said his captain Karl Mullen. One person not so impressed was Kyle's father who grumbled to his other son: "Does that brother of yours ever intend to graduate in medicine?"

Kyle returned to complete his medical course and to enjoy another vintage year on the rugby field in 1951 with victories – albeit narrow – for Ireland over France, England and Scotland but, in the final game, they were denied the triple crown when, under the rules then in force, a Welsh penalty was enough to equal a try by Kyle, which was one of the most brilliant solo runs of his career and is happily fully recorded.

Kyle succeeded Mullen as Ireland captain in 1953. However, a torn thigh muscle knocked him out for most of the following season and deprived him of the extraordinary acceleration that had been such a key part of his game. His tackling and ability to get his three quarters moving were sometimes faulted. But there were still moments of rare genius displaying extraordinary anticipation in defence to save hopeless situations. In 1956 his only international dropped goal deprived Wales of the triple crown. In 1958 he played on the team that defeated Australia in Dublin – the first Ireland victory over a touring team – and went on to surpass the previous record of 42 caps for any international player. He was appointed OBE the next year.

Kyle was always the perfect sportsman, modest in victory, gracious in defeat, eschewing confrontation of any kind on the field or off it. He loved the game for itself and it was wholly in character that he went on playing club rugby at a junior level for several years. He was also active in youth organisations.

In exile Kyle maintained a keen interest in Irish affairs and made regular visits home. In July 1966 he wrote to the Irish newspapers from Zambia condemning Ian Paisley's provocative behavior towards the Catholic population in Northern Ireland. A man of deep religious commitment, Kyle preached on the need for tolerance in Dublin's St Patrick's Cathedral in 1982.

Both his children settled in Ireland and, finally, in his mid-70s he followed them, retiring to a house in Co Down near a golf course where he played regularly. He was honoured by medical schools and fêted as a guest at rugby occasions throughout the island. He expressed pleasure that it was for the whole of Ireland that he had played rugby.

He had broader interests, notably as a lover of music and a student of literature – he could recite extensively from the poetry of William Butler Yeats.

Surviving cancer of the bone marrow diagnosed in 2008, Kyle was at Cardiff's Millennium stadium in March 2009 when, in a thrilling finish, Ireland defeated Wales to win the Grand Slam for the first time since 1948. He was the only survivor present from the 1948 team. The next month he gave the address at the funeral of his "dear dear friend" Karl Mullen, who had captained the Irish team in 1948. He continued to live an active life until this year.

Kyle married in 1957 Shirley Anderson, a librarian whom he had met when studying at Queen's University. When, ten years later, they divorced in Zambia Kyle was awarded custody of their two children Caleb and Justine. Caleb is in business in Dublin while Justine is a language teacher. Her book *Conversations with my Father: Jack Kyle* was published earlier this year.

BRIAN FRIEL

3 OCTOBER 2015

BRIAN FRIEL, WHO DIED yesterday, aged 86, may have been Ireland's greatest living playwright, but he was an intensely private, self-effacing man who lived almost his entire adult life in rural Co Donegal, looking across Lough Foyle to his native Northern Ireland, and hated giving interviews.

Friel let his plays speak for him. Over six decades he wrote more than 30, the most celebrated of which were *Philadelphia, Here I Come!*, *Translations* and *Dancing at Lughnasa*. They were peopled by colourful, sympathetic characters – sometimes comic, sometimes tragic. Many were set in a small, fictional community in Co Donegal called Ballybeg (Baile Beag is Irish for "small town"), but they explored universal themes – love, identity, memory, family relationships, emigration, conflict, dislocation, the clash of cultures. His work earned him the sobriquet "Ireland's Chekhov".

Though an Irish nationalist by temperament and upbringing, Friel seldom wrote explicitly about politics but he made an exception in *The Freedom of the City*. He wrote that play in 1973, a year after he joined the march against internment in Londonderry that ended with British soldiers killing 13 protesters on what became known as "Bloody Sunday".

Friel later expressed reservations about it. "One of the problems with the play was that the experience of Bloody Sunday wasn't adequately distilled in me," he said later. "I wrote it out of some kind of heat and some kind of immediate passion that I would have wanted to quiet a bit before I did it. It was really . . . a very emotive time. It was really a shattering experience that the British Army, this disciplined instrument, would go in as they did that time and shoot 13 people. To be there on that occasion, and to have to throw yourself to the ground because people are firing at you is a very terrifying experience. Then the whole cover-up afterwards was shattering too."

Friel's great friend was Seamus Heaney, the poet and Nobel laureate who was a fellow Catholic from Northern Ireland. They sat together on the board of Field Day, a travelling theatre company Friel set up in Londonderry with Stephen Rea in 1980 to encourage original, independent Irish theatre.

Bernard Patrick Friel was born on January 9, 1929 in the village of Killyclogher, near Omagh, the son of a schoolmaster and a postmistress. He was also, he recalled in "Self Portrait", "the grandson of peasants who could neither read nor write".

His family moved to Londonderry when he was ten. He was educated at St Columb's College, the alma mater of Heaney and John Hume, the nationalist politician, who also became a friend in later life. Friel then went to St Patrick's College Maynooth, a seminary in the Republic, to study for the priesthood, but left and followed his father into education instead. After training in Belfast, he returned to Londonderry and spent ten years teaching maths.

Friel's literary career began with short stories, many for *The New Yorker* magazine, which paid handsomely. In 1960, he gave up teaching to become a full-time writer, supplementing his income with articles for *The Irish Press*, a now defunct Dublin newspaper. Like his father before him, he joined the Nationalist Party – also now defunct – but found it intolerably dreary. "We used to meet once a month wherever it was, in a grotty wee room, and there'd be four or five old men who'd sit there and mull things over. It was really hopeless."

He stopped writing short stories "at the point I recognised how difficult they were" and began writing plays. Initially he had little success, but in the summer of 1963 he visited Sir Tyrone Guthrie, the former director of the Old Vic, at his theatre in Minneapolis. There he gained the "courage and daring to attempt things", he said. He learnt "that people at the theatre are moved by their stomachs and their hearts. You can never move people intellectually in the theatre."

On his return, he wrote *Philadelphia, Here I Come!* – the play that made his name. It thrived on Broadway and was later made into a film. Set in Ballybeg, it portrayed an Irish emigrant on the eve of his move to the US, and used two actors to play the central character – Gar Private and Gar Public.

Friel used the proceeds to move across the border in 1968 to a new house overlooking the River Foyle that he had built in the village of Muff in Co Donegal. That was the year before the Troubles erupted in Northern Ireland. "I would much prefer to be under the jurisdiction of the Irish Government," he said. However, he was back in Londonderry on Bloody Sunday. After *The Freedom of the City*, he wrote another "political" play, *Volunteers*, about IRA prisoners excavating an archaeological site in a contemporary Irish city and the political, historical and personal forces that entrap them.

Thereafter, he wrote several plays that examined family dynamics and were reminiscent of Chekhov. They included the acclaimed *Aristocrats*, staged in the West End and on Broadway, which portrayed the collapse of a once-proud family of Irish Catholic gentry.

His next great success was *Translations*, the first play staged by Field Day with Rea, Neeson and Ray McAnally in the cast. Set in 1833, it tells of English soldiers arriving in Ballybeg and anglicising Irish place names for the first Ordnance Survey map of Ireland – and of a love affair between a soldier and a local girl who do not speak each other's tongues. The play uses both English and Gaelic and was acclaimed. Friel insisted that "it was treated much too respectfully".

In the early 1980s, Friel moved his family from Muff to the older house in Greencastle, deeper in Co Donegal, where he remained for the rest of his life. His output diminished during that decade because the management of Field Day was so time consuming, but he returned to international prominence in 1990 with *Dancing at Lughnasa*.

Set once again in Ballybeg it is loosely based on Friel's mother and four aunts and portrays the collapse of their traditional way of life in 1936. It won three Tony Awards and was turned into a rather less successful film starring Meryl Streep. Friel never achieved quite such success again, though he continued to produce challenging works such as *The Home Place* (2005) – about the Protestant experience in Ballybeg as the Ascendancy wanes in 1878. He also adapted several Turgenev and Chekhov plays.

By that stage his place in the pantheon of great Irish writers was long cemented. He was appointed to the Irish Senate in 1987, though he never attended and resigned in 1989. BBC Radio broadcast six of his plays in a "Brian Friel Season" in 1989, the first living playwright to receive that honour. In 2006, Mary McAleese, the Irish president, presented Friel with a gold torc, a Celtic neck ornament, to mark his election as a Saoi ("wise one") by the Irish association of artists called Aosdana. It is an honour only seven living members can hold at one time. "Being made a Saoi . . . is extreme unction," he quipped. "It is a final anointment – Aosdana's last rites." At an 80th birthday party for Friel at Dublin's Abbey Theatre in 2009 Seamus Heaney read four poems about "the work and worker we celebrate here."

Friel's final years were, however, to be blighted by the death from cancer in 2012 of a daughter. He is survived by his wife Anne Morrison, whom he married in 1954, his three other daughters and a son. One daughter Judy followed her father into the theatre as a director.

MAUREEN O'HARA

26 OCTOBER 2015

MAUREEN O'HARA, WHO DIED in Idaho on October 24, 2015, was the ultimate Hollywood "Colleen", a fiery Irish actress dubbed the "Queen of Technicolour" for her flame-red hair, flashing emerald eyes and peaches and cream complexion. Frustrated at being typecast for her looks – she once wrote that "Hollywood would never allow my talent to triumph over my face" – O'Hara judged, with some truth, many of her films to be "stinkeroos".

The handful she rated more highly included *How Green Was My Valley* (1941) and *The Quiet Man* (1952), in which she and her co-star John Wayne displayed a sizzling on-screen chemistry.

O'Hara is perhaps best remembered for her role in *The Miracle of 34th Street* (1947). She played the mother of Natalie Woods, the budding child star. Later she said "I have been mother to almost 40 children in movies ... but I always had a special place in my heart for little Natalie." In later years, she was often stopped by children asking "Are you the lady who knows Santa Claus?" to which she would reply, "Yes I am. What would you like me to tell him?"

Highly athletic, able to fence and to box, she often performed her own stunts and held swashbuckling roles, knocking Tyrone Power to the ground for stealing a kiss in *The Black Swan* (1942).

Later she became the first woman president of a US-based scheduled airline.

The daughter of an opera singer and the owner of a clothes company, she was born Maureen Fitzsimons in South Dublin on August 17, 1920. A tomboy, she begged her father, part-owner of the Dublin football club Shamrock Rovers, to create a women's football team. At six, she began acting, and having scooped up prizes including the All-Ireland Cup for her portrayal of Portia in *The Merchant Of Venice*, was accepted at 14 for the acting school of the Abbey Theatre, Dublin.

Her father insisted she learn bookkeeping and secretarial skills lest the acting fail. By 17, she had a lead role at the Abbey, and was dining after the play one night in a Dublin hotel when she was introduced to the American actor and singer, Harry Richman. Appalled that he was drunk – "absolutely crocked" – O'Hara was surprised to receive a call to say that on Richman's say-so Elstree Film Studios in London were offering her a screen test. She did not rate the "movies", later writing, "I was the biggest theatre snob imaginable". A family friend told her she should seize the chance.

Within days, she and "mammy" were on the mail boat to England. Elstree plastered her in Mata Hari-style make up, made her wear a gold-lamé gown and sweep across a set to slam down a telephone and storm off. She looked, said O'Hara, "ridiculous, like a ten-dollar hooker". She later said to her mother, "if that's the movie business then I want nothing to do with it". Plans to return to Ireland were dashed, however, when she was introduced to the actor and film producer, Charles Laughton. He cast her as Mary Yellen in *Jamaica Inn*, changing her screen name to "O'Hara" on the grounds that Fitzsimons was too long to fit the credits.

During filming, as a "favour" to Laughton's lawyer, she went on reluctant dates with a production manager on set, George Hambley Brown, who subsequently became a film director and the father of the journalist Tina Brown. As filming drew to a close, Laughton told O'Hara they were going to America to film *The Hunchback of Notre Dame*. She was to be Esmeralda. Two hours before the boat was due to leave, Brown telephoned O'Hara, declaring his love and begging her to marry him. She dashed to meet him only to discover he had invited her to a registry office. In a panic, she agreed to wed him. The following day her mother chanced upon the wedding ring at the bottom of O'Hara's purse and in 1941 the marriage was annulled. She later married the film director Will Price, by whom she had a daughter, Bronwyn. They divorced in 1953.

By then, O'Hara was the unwilling star of numerous Hollywood swashbucklers. The outbreak of the Second World War, while she was filming *The Hunchback of Notre Dame*, confined her to America. This enforced exile was to blame, O'Hara later wrote, for the lack of "serious, character-driven" roles offered to her. "After I got to Hollywood, I resented that I didn't get a crack at more dramatic roles because I photographed so beautifully." She made good use of her flashing green eyes to express what she deemed her most compelling quality – "inner strength".

A clash in filming schedules meant she could not, to her great dismay, accept Alfred Hitchcock's offer of the lead role in *Rebecca*. They first met when Hitchcock directed *Jamaica Inn* (1939) and O'Hara said that she never "felt the strange feeling of detachment with Hitchcock that many other actors claimed to have felt when working with him".

In her breakthrough film, *How Green Was My Valley*, she played the daughter of a Welsh mining family mired in the Depression. It won five Oscars. This was the first chapter in a 20-year collaboration with the Irish-American director, John Ford, for whom she later acted in *The Wings of Eagles* (1957). Ford, on first meeting O'Hara, said, "I'm an Irish rebel, a freedom fighter. Bet you didn't know that." Judging that "no one would ever announce such a thing at a party, for everyone to hear" O'Hara assumed he was testing her reaction, coolly replying, "I didn't know. What part of Ireland are you from?"

In 1944, Ford asked her to star in *The Quiet Man*, which tells of an Irish-American returning to Ireland seeking land and true love. Written off as a "silly little Irish story" by the studios, it took Ford six years to raise the necessary money. O'Hara played Mary Kate Danaher, the love interest for Sean Thornton (Wayne) the Irish-American boxer. Their courtship on screen was by turns turbulent and tender and, when the lovers are caught in a downpour, discreetly erotic. Ford asked O'Hara to say a sentence that would trigger a shocked look from Wayne at the film's end. She agreed on condition that neither she, Ford nor Wayne would ever disclose the sentence.

"I was the only leading lady big enough and tough enough for John Wayne," declared O'Hara. Gearing up for the film's fight scene, Wayne thought she was aiming to break his jaw and raised a hand to stop her. "My hand snapped off the top of his fingers and I broke a bone in my wrist," she said later. "Big lusty, absolutely marvellous – definitely my kind of woman" was Wayne's verdict. He added: "I've had many friends, and I prefer the company of men. Except for Maureen O'Hara."

In 1961, she starred in the comedy *The Parent Trap*. She retired in the 1970s after finding marital happiness with her third husband, Charles F. Blair. The first pilot to fly solo over the North Pole in a single-engine aircraft in 1968, he was also a US airforce general and the couple met as he piloted the plane taking O'Hara to Ireland for the first time after the war. The airline he founded in the Caribbean was the world's largest seaplane operator. After marrying in 1968, they moved to the Virgin Islands and Blair made O'Hara the publisher of the *Virgin Islander*, a monthly magazine. In 1978, he died in a seaplane accident. O'Hara thought he had been monitoring Cuba for the CIA. After his death, she ran the airline and magazine, then sold both for £1.5 million, saying that the key lesson she learnt from Hollywood was to hold on to her money.

In 1991, she had a powerful comeback in *Only the Lonely*, stealing the show as the domineering Rose Muldoon, mother of a single policeman (played by John Candy) based in Chicago.

O'Hara, a naturalised American citizen, returned to live in Ireland in 2005. She later went back to America to live in Idaho near her grandson Conor Fitzsimons, a hairdresser who launched a hair product line called The Red Collection named in honour of O'Hara. She is survived by his mother her daughter Bronwyn, who was briefly an actress before becoming a mother.

SIR TERRY WOGAN

1 FEBRUARY 2016

TERRY WOGAN, WHO DIED yesterday aged 77, had a strong claim to being Britain's favourite broadcaster. For the vast swathes of Middle England who tuned into his breakfast show on Radio 2, that was certainly the case. Ironically as an Irishman, Wogan was lauded for his ability to make Britons feel good about themselves with his masterful use of gentle self-mockery that was laced with great personal warmth.

In a 50-year broadcasting career he exuded a whimsical Irish charm. His seemingly effortless drollery, delivered in soft, slightly croaky, world-weary tones, won him both lasting friendship with millions of viewers and listeners and the admiration of his broadcasting peers.

The Queen once told Wogan that she listened to him every morning and on espying him at a Buckingham Palace reception she once cried "flab" in reference to his "fight the flab" campaign on the *Wake Up to Wogan* radio show in the Seventies. When she asked, "How long have you worked at the BBC?" he replied, "Your Majesty, I've never worked here", meaning that he was simply doing what he loved.

His retirement in 2009 was national news. Gordon Brown led the tributes and *The Times* published an ode: "Stop all the clocks, cut off the telephone, Terry Wogan is abandoning his microphone."

Wogan, who took British citizenship in 2005 and was knighted the same year, never rose to accusations from his countrymen that he had somehow betrayed the land of his birth. Indeed, he said he always regarded himself as a "West Brit from the start"; among his earliest memories were listening to the BBC on the wireless. "I'm a kind of child of the Pale," he said. "I'm an effete, urban Irishman. I think I was born to succeed here."

He would become as well known, if not quite as well loved, as a television presenter for the BBC – a cuddly doyen of light entertainment in his well-tailored pastel suits with handkerchief in breast pocket. His mobile eyebrows would arch ironically and his turquoise eyes would twinkle beneath a generous mop of hair that in latter years was reputedly replaced by a toupee.

Presenting his own primetime chat show, *Wogan*, he provided some of the most memorable and notorious television moments of the Eighties, including an interview with the sports presenter David Icke, who had metamorphised into a religious prophet in a garish shell suit. When Icke revealed that he was the "son of the godhead", Wogan told him that the audience was "laughing at him, not with him". Vanessa Redgrave once simply got up and left. Through it all, Wogan was assuredly composed, though he gave the impression of managing a shambles with haphazard bonhomie. The only time he was clearly lost for words was in 1990 when an inebriated George Best said: "Terry, I like screwing," and all Wogan could say in return was: "Ladies and Gentlemen, George Best," before rapidly bringing the interview to a close.

The show ran for a decade from 1982 and at its peak drew a thrice-weekly audience of eight million. It was ignominiously pulled from the schedules in 1992 to be replaced by the Spanish-set soap opera Eldorado. In a rare moment when he allowed his guard to drop, he admitted that the programme's peremptory end was the low point of his career and that he had also been deeply hurt by the "envious and vitriolic" knocking by TV critics in the broadsheets.

Licking his wounds, Wogan returned triumphantly to his greatest professional love, and started presenting *Wake Up to Wogan* again on Radio 2 in 1993 after a nine-year gap. He based the show on reading through the 500-plus letters and emails he received every morning and the result would be a stream of consciousness that he would "make up as I go along". His listeners, whom he dubbed Togs (Terry's old geezers and gals) happily connived in running gags, double entendres and dreadful poems, while Wogan delighted in reading out the "banter" which came his way. "I'm looking for a keen eye for the ridiculous, lateral thinking, a laugh at life," he said.

Wogan professed in serious moments that the BBC was the "greatest broadcasting company in the world". So much so, that he rejected a lucrative opportunity to present a chat show for Disney Corporation in 1988. Attending meetings in Beverly Hills, he recalled "feeling the stultifying weight of boredom drag me beneath the table".

In any case, Wogan felt that he was fulfilling an important role as a bridge between Britain and the Irish Republic. Having joined the BBC in 1969 as the Troubles in Northern Ireland were beginning, he said it was "very difficult to come up with a cheery morning voice after a horrific bombing incident" but that many Irish people would approach him "grateful to me for being an Irish voice without apology".

He was determined to retire from his daily breakfast show before people started saying "clear off, you old fool". When he hung up his microphone in 2009, he said that his gentler presenting style had become outdated and that the "in yer face" style of his successor Chris Evan was more in tune with the times.

He continued to present a weekend show on Radio 2, describing the medium as his favourite. "Radio stimulates the brain, the imagination, it provokes reaction," he said. "Television, by providing the picture to go with the thought, stunts the imagination, makes it redundant."

One of his longest stints, just short of 30 years, was on the *Eurovision Song Contest* on which he would drily comment on the increasingly kitsch entries. He said that he loved the show, "for its grandiose awfulness and manifest foolishness". His own suitably silly excursion into song, *The Floral Dance*, resulted in an unexpected Top 30 hit in 1978.

Beginning in 1980 Wogan hosted the annual *Children in Need* appeal, an annual telethon which has raised more than £300 million for children's charities. He sat on the board of trustees and regarded it as one of the best things the BBC had done and the thing in his career that he was most proud of.

When being interviewed about his life, Wogan was rarely serious. To charges that he short-changed his listeners by being lightweight and middle of the road, he said: "They're only half listening anyway. It's a mistake to think that everyone is clinging to your every word."

Michael Terence Wogan was born on August 3, 1938 into a lower-middle-class Catholic family in Limerick. His father, Michael, had worked his way up to manage of the Limerick branch of Leverett and Frye, grocers and wine merchants. Terry Wogan later admitted that his broadcasting career was a reaction against his "hard-working, diligent and meticulous father". "Anything which doesn't come freely and easily to me is something from which I will stride away, with a spring in my step and a light laugh."

Limerick was a town where, in Wogan's own words, there was "not a lot of Christianity but plenty of religion". At his schools, a primary in Limerick and the Jesuit Belvedere College in Dublin, he felt the full force of an austere atmosphere. "The Jesuits were very clever men," he recalled. "My mother said it was Jesuits' fault I didn't believe [in God] because they made me think."

The often brutal Jesuit regime was softened by the affection that was showered upon him by his maiden aunts, one of whom owned a bookstore in Dublin and fostered in Wogan a lifelong love of reading.

On leaving school he became a clerk with the Royal Bank in Dublin. The boredom was leavened with practical jokes that included wet sponges flying across the counter when he was serving customers. "There was one old farmer who really stank," he said. "When he came in, it was heads down, and we all disappeared behind the counter until he walked out again."

After four years in the bank he spotted a newspaper advertisement for Radio Eireann, which was looking for announcers and newsreaders. He smooth-talked his way through the interview and was offered a place. His favourite assignment was a *Hospitals' Requests* programme, in which he had to sort through hundreds of cards and letters. Wogan realised that ad-libbing between records was something that came easily. It was the prototype for his BBC breakfast shows.

At the end of 1962 Telefis Eireann, the Irish television service, started, and he was soon reading the news. "Nobody knew what they were doing," he recalled, adding that "a lot of chancers" managed to get jobs there. The result was often a shambles but he quickly learnt to keep his head while all about him were losing theirs and he was cured of his nerves in front of the camera.

He took over a live quiz show, *Jackpot*, from another leading Irish broadcaster, Gay Byrne. Under Wogan, *Jackpot* continued to top the ratings, but Telefis Eireann decided to replace it with another quiz show. Wogan felt slighted and decided to look for opportunities in Britain. He sent a sample of his work to the BBC Light Programme and was offered a half-hour record programme called *Midday Spin* which he presented from Dublin.

In 1967 Wogan landed the job of presenting a nightly show, *Late Night Extra*, on the new Radio 1 and Radio 2 channels and soon joined the corporation full-time.

He had married Helen Joyce in 1965 – she was reputed to be one of the most beautiful women in the Emerald Isle. They had met at a party in Dublin. "She had been let down by a boyfriend which I found very extraordinary ... I gave her a lift home in my Morris Minor with the broken passenger seat. We went off and had some soup and sandwiches," he said, adding with a quip: "I know how to get round girls."

Their early married life was rocked by tragedy when their first daughter, Vanessa, died at three weeks. In his anguish, any remnant of his Catholic faith was extinguished. They went on to have two sons and a daughter. He joked that because he presented the breakfast show he escaped the morning chaos of getting them ready but by late afternoon he was on hand for the easier job of picking them up at the school gates. "I had the best of both worlds. It's no wonder I'm such a family man," he quipped. He was at his happiest at home in Berkshire enjoying his wife's cooking. After making a career out of his lighthearted take on life, he said the only thing he had really taken seriously was his family, because "It's the only important thing in life".

Tabloid hacks on the hunt for any whiff of scandal gave up on him. "There's nothing to be said for being famous," he said. "It's a pain. You can't be rude to people, it's inexcusable not to be nice."

Away from the camera and the airwaves, Wogan admitted to being a shy man who was the antipathy of the Irish notion of "craic". Curiously for someone who in his professional life was blessed with the gift of the gab, he confessed to being hopeless with small talk; he always left parties early, especially those of the BBC.

His passions were rugby and opera, dating back to his early days as an extra for the Dublin Opera Society during which he played an Assyrian slave and a Venetian doge. In later life he was involved in the Garsington Opera.

He wrote two autobiographies and a book of short stories, *Those Were The Days*, set in the Ireland of his youth.

Wogan is survived by his wife and three children. Appropriately for a family of "foodies", all his children ended up running restaurants.

WILLIAM TREVOR

22 NOVEMBER 2016

ONE OF THE GREATEST of all short story writers, William Trevor, who died on 20 November, aged 88, loved simple sentences that say something precise and suggest much more. A woman of 36 lives with her crippled father, who encourages her to go out dancing on a Saturday. "She'd cook him his tea and then he'd settle down with the wireless, or maybe a Wild West novel. In time, while still she danced, he'd stoke the fire up and hobble his way upstairs to bed."

This is pitiably out of step, as Trevor hints with the little words "In time". For although the woman may dance, her father can never be in time with her. Their lives are tragically unsynchronised. She can never escape to her own Wild West, and any stoking up of her fires is doomed not to end upstairs. She is already out of time, as she finds at the end of the story, when she realises she is too old to go dancing any longer.

Trevor specified the details of quotidian, often mundane lives to create a ground against which to paint the surprising secrets that people carry with them, whether they be conversations with ghosts, family shame, adultery, violence or some lively fantasy.

Praise from other writers was relentless. Graham Greene called *Angels at the Ritz* "surely one of the best collections, if not the best collection, since Joyce's *Dubliners*". Trevor's second novel, *The Old Boys* (1964), about schoolboy conflicts surfacing among a group of septuagenarians, was acclaimed by Evelyn Waugh as "uncommonly well written, gruesome, funny and original".

The Irish-born Trevor said that he simply wrote out of a curiosity about people's lives that was first awakened by his parents' "complete lack of respect for each other" and his wish to know "why these two very attractive people just couldn't put the thing together".

He was an intensely private man with a monkish pate and a mournful face that reminded one interviewer of a "faithful bloodhound". Others spoke of his serenity and aura of good nature and of his having the countenance of a "kindly schoolmaster".

He lived in an eighteenth-century house in Devon, where in 40 acres of seclusion he dedicated himself to the continuous production of stories, writing 3,000 words a day in front of a view of the rolling hills.

He professed himself uninterested in literary life, preferring to watch sport on television with a glass of Bushmills in his hand. "I've never gone in for the business of belonging to sets of people," he said. "I have friends because I like them. I hate the idea of groups."

At his best, Trevor could plot a whole story in an unobtrusive sentence. He could see the longings of ordinary people in their choice of clothes or furniture, the way they walked or smoked. And he had a wonderful ear for conversation and its mishaps.

" 'I tried to pacify Mrs Baxter,' Mr Thackeray said, 'but of course I didn't have a foot to stand on.' "

" 'If your mother hadn't died,' he'd say, not finishing the sentence."

" 'To the birthday girl,' my stepfather said, raising his glass of cider. 'Many happy returns, my best.' It was that I didn't care for in him: I wasn't his best, my mother was."

Plain spoken, with a dislike of the arty, Trevor wrote compassionately about people most of us scarcely notice: "Husbands and wives picked their way to the shops with a string bag each, to share the load." They are people to whom things happen, rarely as they would have wished. "Strange how people are allocated a life," he wrote. "If they are lucky they find someone with whom to share the load."

Some critics complained that his stories became dated and later work was less at home with the nuances of modern life. Others spoke of an "ungenerous and unkind morality" in his writing. He partly admitted to the charge. "I think there is a sort of God-bothering that goes on from time to time in my books."

Asked why he wrote short stories, he said that he drew on the Irish tradition of vocal storytelling that was borne out of the turbulence of its history – sectarianism and famine – when "there was no time for long novels", compared with the "tranquillity" of the nineteenth-century England of Trollope and Dickens, when "there was plenty of time to sit and read".

"A short story is like an impressionist painting," he said. "You cut down everything enormously and you get the effects from one big splash or explosion. You have to cut to the very edge. What excites me is to go as far as I can."

William Trevor Cox was born in Cork on 24 May 1928, a "lace-curtain" Protestant in de Valera's new Roman Catholic Irish Republic, and the son of a bank clerk who could just afford to keep a maid. As a young boy he went to a convent school at Loreto, where during prayers he withdrew to the kitchen and was entertained by the lay sisters, who treated him to pink marzipan. Retaining in later life what he called a "primitive belief in God", he remembered the kindliness of the nuns, and all his life he had a loving memory for details: what people wore, the colour of a room, the delicious taste of essence of lemon when eaten raw.

His family moved many times in his childhood, engendering in him a permanent feeling of being an "outsider and a loner". There was a succession of half-hearted tutoring arrangements, and for months at a time he was left to wander and dream.

His reading began with his sister's yellow-backed schoolgirls' tales, with titles such as *The Terrible Twins* and *Not-So-Simple Sophie*, and he was so carried away by these that in later years he used to buy *The Girl* to follow the stories.

His intelligent mother was unhappy and claustrophobic in a succession of small towns. Trevor and his two siblings felt the love of each parent, but knew that none was left between them.

Finally his schooling began in earnest in Dublin. At Sandford Park, he and a classmate would bunk off from cricket in their whites and go to the cinema. There were assignations with girls too, in the fourth row, but rather than kiss they agreed to scoff biscuits. His reading moved on to Gollancz crime thrillers, as he progressed to St Columba's College, where he edited the school magazine.

Going up to Trinity College Dublin, he first thought of studying medicine, but lasted only a day. He would have liked to read English, but was not allowed, so his degree, awarded in 1950, was in history. He loved Dublin: the dons, the pubs, the theatres and galleries, the nightlife that included a one-legged lady plying her trade on the quays.

He thought of working in advertising but was turned down by every agency in Dublin. He answered a newspaper ad for a tutor for a girl with learning difficulties, undeterred by the qualifying phrase "suit a nun".

He subsequently found himself teaching art in a prep school in Northern Ireland, but it went bust and to support himself while sculpting – which he had mistaken for his vocation – he took jobs in several others, particularly in the west of England.

Now that Trevor and his siblings had left home, their parents separated, job done, never to meet again. "They were victims of their innocence when chance drew them together and passion beguiled them," he wrote.

He won prizes for his sculptures but, over a decade or more, became dissatisfied. "My sculpture became more and more abstract, and finally I did not like it at all. There is hardly a worse thing could happen to an artist."

By the time he moved to England permanently in 1954 he was starting to write, and his first novel, *A Standard of Behaviour*, appeared in 1958. It had no success and has not been reprinted. He turned to advertising again but failed the writing test at J Walter Thompson. At the start of 1960 he was taken on by Notley's, which was known for employing poets, among them Edward Lucie-Smith, Peter Porter and Gavin Ewart. His boss had coined the slogan "Top people take The Times".

Although he enjoyed Sixties London – "mid-century breathing space between the world wars and Aids" – he never really caught up with it:

looking back 20 years later he would tell his readers the astonishing news that: "Popular music acquired significance, and the record companies a very great deal of money."

His job bored him, but left ample time for the writing he wanted to do. His second novel, *The Old Boys* (1964), won the Hawthornden prize, as did *The Boarding House*, published a year later. His first collection of short stories, *The Day we got Drunk on Cake*, was equally admired when it appeared in 1967. His wife, Jane Ryan, worked as his researcher and he dedicated most of his books to her because, he admitted, he could be "ratty" and "hard to live with". He said that growing up amid his parents' rows had given him "a great fear of quarrelling". His wife survives him with their two sons, Patrick Cox, a journalist based in Boston, Massachusetts, and Dominic Cox, a barrister.

He began at the typewriter in the early morning. "If for some reason I can't do it for a week, I can get very low. It's a kind of tonic." He wrote for an hour and a half before stopping for coffee and Rice Krispies and listening to the Irish news on RTÉ. He resumed for an hour, before spending the rest of the day mulling over ideas and observing people, beadily, as he always had.

He did not enjoy being interviewed, but submitted purgatorially from time to time, perhaps recalling that as a young writer he had once been asked to interview Anthony Powell, and had elicited very little beyond a wordless glare.

Trevor's typescripts became elaborate palimpsests as he rewrote, cut up pages and taped them together, groping towards utter clarity. Halfway through the process he would put a story away for a few months, until he had almost forgotten it, so that he could see its shape more clearly.

"Somerset Maugham said the only story worth telling is one that can be told after dinner on a boat," he once said of the writer, whom he greatly admired. "It's the opposite. You shouldn't be able to repeat it. The beauty is its shadow." He also contradicted the usual advice to write what one knows. One should, he said, write about what one doesn't know, so as to exercise the imagination. He spoke of feeling "schizoid" because when he wrote a story there was "nothing very much of yourself in there".

The Children of Dynmouth (1976) and *Fools of Fortune* (1983) both won Whitbread awards for fiction, and *Felicia's Journey* (1984) won the Whitbread overall. The novella *Reading Turgenev* (1991) was shortlisted for the Booker.

In 1992 the monumental, 1,200-page *Collected Stories of William Trevor* was published. He received an honorary knighthood in 2002. Late in life he discovered gardening. He was most proud of his potatoes – arguing that in shops they were "just not new enough".

He did not read much contemporary fiction, but reread Dickens, George Eliot and Jane Austen. "The test of literary admiration is whether or not you reread," he said.

Despite his inexhaustible curiosity about others, he never sought to explain his own gift. "If I didn't believe it was a mystery, the whole thing wouldn't be worthwhile. I don't know not just how something is going to end, but what the next couple of lines are going to be."

KEN WHITAKER

14 MARCH 2017

KEN WHITAKER, who died on 9 January, aged 100, was voted the "outstanding Irishman of the 20th century" in a poll conducted by Irish television in 2001.

In 1958, as head of the Republic of Ireland's finance department, he had formulated the plan credited with lifting the country out of an economic malaise that had made independence seem a failure. "If we cannot rectify this situation," Whitaker informed the veteran republican who was his minister, "we may be forced to beg to be taken back into the United Kingdom." Whitaker's plan proposed switching public investment from non-productive to productive purposes while dismantling the tariffs and restrictions on inward investment that had been the cornerstone of government policy since De Valera's Fianna Fáil party came to power in 1932.

To make the *volte-face* palatable to its followers the government asked Whitaker to publish the plan in the name of the Department of Finance, not its minister or the government. What emerged was a powerful exposition, lucidly expressed, that boosted national morale. It gave Whitaker public exposure that was unprecedented for an Irish civil servant. A year later, the economy took off, growing at twice the rate envisaged in the plan, albeit not in the way predicted. Ever after, Whitaker was acclaimed Ireland's economic saviour.

His other decisive intervention was in the late summer of 1969 when Northern Ireland was plunged into near anarchy after the police in Londonderry overreacted to a protest against the annual procession of the Protestant Apprentice Boys and bludgeoned stone throwers and peaceful demonstrators alike. In Belfast Catholics were left unprotected against the ensuing sectarian backlash. Under pressure from Charles Haughey and other hawkish ministers, the Taoiseach Jack Lynch went on television warning that his government would not stand by if

Catholic communities were attacked. In a menacing gesture Irish army posts were set up near the border.

Unhappy that he was being backed into a corner, Lynch turned to Whitaker, on whom he relied greatly. "Stay calm; don't add fuel to the fire" advised Whitaker, who then drafted a speech in which Lynch ruled out armed intervention in Northern Ireland and made clear that Irish unity could only ever be attained by persuading northern unionists to agree to it. Requests for arms to defend Catholic communities were rebuffed. All this set up a framework that, in its essentials, informed Irish government policy thereafter.

Thomas Kenneth Whitaker (known as Ken or TK) was born on 8 December 1916 in Rostrevor, Co Down, a part of Ulster included in what became Northern Ireland four years later. In 1922, his father, a manager in a linen mill, moved south of the new border to work in Drogheda. One of young Ken's abiding childhood memories was of horror when observing hostilities during the civil war that succeeded independence. An early manifestation of his later interest in economics was putting a halfpenny on a local railway line hoping that the engine's weight would turn it into a penny.

Whitaker was educated at the local Christian Brothers school. He shone academically but felt compelled by the family's financial circumstances to accept a post as a clerical officer in the civil service rather than compete for a university scholarship.

Within four years he had risen to administrative officer, the grade usually reserved for gifted graduate entrants. He took a master's degree in economics by correspondence course from London University. This dovetailed with his work at the Department of Finance where, in 1956, his exceptional performance was rewarded by appointment as head of the department. He was only 39.

As the Irish delegate at the International Monetary Fund, Whitaker became friendly with his counterparts in Northern Ireland, who were agreeably surprised that he was so understanding of their position. They engineered a meeting in Belfast in 1965 between Terence O'Neill, the new prime minister of Northern Ireland, and Taoiseach Seán Lemass.

It was the first such meeting since 1925. The thaw in relations was maintained after Lynch had succeeded Lemass in 1966. On a subsequent visit, Lynch and Whitaker were greeted by Ian Paisley carrying a placard "No Pope here". They wondered which of them Paisley thought was the Pope.

Lynch had appointed Charlie Haughey as minister for finance. It was a less happy experience for the authoritative Whitaker having such an unbiddable if able minister, as he disagreed with some of Haughey's policies, especially extravagant "spectaculars", such as free travel for all senior citizens and tax exemptions for artists. Early in 1969, averting further direct confrontation, Whitaker was appointed governor of the Central Bank. It was from this position that he advised Lynch to confront Haughey, who, in 1970, was dismissed from the government and charged unsuccessfully with conspiracy to import arms for use in Northern Ireland.

As governor of the Central Bank, Whitaker did not allow his closeness to Lynch to divert him from outspoken criticism of the government for borrowing to finance current expenditure. When Liam Cosgrave's coalition government, which took over in 1973, persisted in this policy over several years, Whitaker declined reappointment.

He became a non-executive director of the Bank of Ireland. This was the first time that a former governor had moved to the board of a commercial bank. In recent years, when the Central Bank failed in its regulation of the commercial banks with disastrous consequences for the Irish economy, it came to be seen as an unfortunate precedent. Another unfortunate legacy of Whitaker's term was the disposal of the Central Bank's substantial gold reserves at what was, in retrospect, a knockdown price.

While Whitaker was glad to experience the private sector from within for a few years, his heart was in public service. He was nominated as a senator when Lynch returned to government in 1977. Having stipulated that he must be free to speak his mind, Whitaker used the Senate to criticise the profligate policies pursued under Lynch and his successor Haughey that led to a decade of economic stagnation. Whitaker dismissed as quixotic the decision to break parity with sterling in 1978 and join the European Monetary System, after which the Irish pound floated downwards. He poured cold water on government demands that the British should declare their long-term intention of withdrawing from Northern Ireland, pointing out that the Republic could not match the subvention to the province provided by the British government.

A less spectacular but typically worthy public service undertaken by Whitaker was to assess individual long-term prisoners as suitable for early release. He chaired a committee on penal reform that recommended less imprisonment. Another committee he chaired made recommendations to preserve inland fisheries in which, as a keen fisherman, Whitaker had a special interest. Referring to his own passion for salmon fishing he quipped: "Everyone needs to have one irresistible temptation, preferably not an immoral one."

As chairman of these and other committees Whitaker had a light touch and jollied things along with the odd humorous remark. Impatient of drawn-out discussions, he liked to report back expeditiously. Experience had taught him that governments regarded the conclusions of such committees less as blueprints for policy than as a starting point in their deliberations.

Whitaker had a lifelong love of the Irish language. He served on bodies concerned with its preservation while distancing himself firmly from zealots whose aim was to replace English as the vernacular. Feeling at home among scholars, he was glad to give honorary service as chancellor of the National University of Ireland and as president of the Royal Irish Academy.

He had reservations about the 1985 Hillsborough Agreement negotiated behind the backs of the Ulster Unionists, which gave the government of the Republic an institutionalised consultative role in the governance of Northern Ireland under direct rule. Always more concerned to woo moderate unionists than to pander to the demands of the nationalist leaders in Northern Ireland, Whitaker criticized as needlessly provocative the location near Belfast of the secretariat for the consultative process.

Whitaker rejoiced when the Good Friday agreement 1998 removed this provocation and opened the way for the repeal of the territorial claim to Northern Ireland in the Irish Constitution. Cherishing Irish unity, even on a federal basis, as an ultimate objective, Whitaker believed it was feasible and desirable only if it had the willing consent of the Protestant majority in Northern Ireland. This was best pursued by promoting practical co-operation and building up mutual trust.

Throughout his long career Whitaker was ready to learn and adapt. As a young civil servant he transcended his training by transforming the department of finance from a cheese-paring watchdog into an engine for promoting economic growth. Similarly, as he approached his eightieth year, he transcended his religious convictions as a devout Catholic when, as chairman of a committee on the Constitution, he led the way in recommending the removal of its more confessional provisions.

Although much honoured and praised, Whitaker remained a modest man. "I must try to refrain from making an idol of myself," he joked on his 97th birthday. Possessed of a winning smile, he had, in his understated way, considerable charm and style. He was punctilious in observing proprieties and had a highly developed sense of pietas, one expression of which was the admirable appreciations he penned of deceased colleagues and friends. With his lucid prose style he was master of the art of the obituary.

Whitaker married Nora Fogarty, a fellow civil servant, in 1941 and they had five sons and one daughter. She died in 1994. In 2005 he married Mary Moore, who died three years later. He was predeceased by his only daughter, Catherine, and one son, Gerald, a banker. He is survived by four sons: Kenneth, an accountant, Raymond, a biochemist in the US, David, a dentist, and Brian, a solicitor.

THE MOST REV. EAMON
CASEY

16 MARCH 2017

EAMON CASEY, EMERITUS BISHOP OF GALWAY, died on 13 March aged 89. For many years, before the notorious scandal that brought him down, he had been the most popular and admired of Ireland's Catholic bishops – not only because of his tireless work for the poor and the homeless, but for his jovial, warm and gregarious personality.

He stood out from the run of bishops as an almost Rabelaisian figure, an extrovert showman and joker, a lover of song, drink and fast cars. He was also an exceptionally compassionate man, with an outsized social conscience and massive energy. In Britain he helped to found *Shelter*, the housing charity; in his aid work for the developing world he bullied governments to do more to combat poverty and deprivation; and in Central America he was an outspoken campaigner for human rights. He was the "embodiment of Catholicism's human face", declared *The Irish Times*.

All too human, it transpired. In 1992, when Casey was 65, news emerged of a love affair 18 years earlier, the existence of a teenage son and the money he had borrowed from diocesan funds to provide for his son. In May of that year he resigned and vanished to America.

At the same time Annie Murphy, an American from Connecticut who was 21 years his junior, made public her version of their relationship, which she said had been "magical . . . on gossamer wings. . . love at first sight". When she became pregnant, Casey pushed her to have the child adopted, but she refused; Peter was born in a home for unmarried mothers in Dublin, after which Murphy returned with him to the US. Casey made regular payments, but did not have anything to do with his son, who is now 42 and is a sales manager in Boston, Massachusetts.

Was Casey's human frailty a negation of his many virtues? Or in some way a part of them, for a priest who could not divorce his sexuality from his Christian humanism? Ireland was stunned and enthralled. Opinions were divided.

Some saw Casey as a humbug and hypocrite who had preached one moral code from the pulpit while practising something quite different. Others saw him as a victim of the church's own hypocrisy, of its rigid and outdated rules on celibacy. Since time immemorial priests in Ireland had enjoyed the company of secret mistresses, and in the 20 years previous 100,000 priests worldwide had left the church, many of them to get married.

The scandal intensified the debate over priestly celibacy and deepened a growing crisis within the Catholic church in Ireland. Many felt that a priest of his "vigour and radiant sexual magnetism", a phrase used of Casey, could hardly be expected not to love a woman. In *Forbidden Fruit*, the book that Murphy published the year after their relationship was revealed, she suggested that she might not have been Casey's first conquest. "He was a goddamn bishop. Where had he learnt all this?" she wrote of his athleticism between the sheets.

The Vatican maintained an embarrassed silence, but across the world there were banner headlines and, in Ireland, a storm of moral turmoil. This at a time when society and church were in crisis over abortion (there had been uproar over the case of a 14-year-old who had been raped, but was barred from travelling to England for a termination). Many clergy spoke with personal sympathy for Casey, including his archbishop, Joseph Cassidy of Tuam. Sister Maureen Murray, a liberal nun in Galway, said that the only thing Casey did wrong was to love a woman. "He's only broken church law, and we all know church laws can change," she said. Many good Irish Catholics quietly agreed.

Casey soon virtually corroborated Murphy's account of their relationship. "I have grievously wronged Peter and his mother," he said. "I have also sinned grievously against God." He had paid her partly out of his own salary, save for a sum of 70,000 Irish pounds in 1990, which he admitted having drawn from diocesan funds. This had since been paid back, with interest, by several donors but only after Casey's resignation. Urban myth suggested that he made his confession to Cardinal Jaime Sin, the Archbishop of Manila, with the words: "Forgive me Sin, for I have fathered." Graham Greene could not have written a more vivid scenario.

Eamon Casey was born on 23 April 1927 in Firies, in the rural west of Ireland near Tralee, Co Kerry, the son of a dairy manager, and always kept his thick Kerry brogue. He attended a seminary in Limerick, then the prestigious St Patrick's College, Maynooth, where he took a doctorate in philosophy. He is said to have agonised then about his vocation. He worked as a curate in Limerick, where the poverty sharpened his social conscience; he set up a marriage guidance council and other welfare schemes. He then moved to England as chaplain to the large Irish immigrant community in Slough, Berkshire. There he worked for the homeless and, in the 1960s, co-founded and later became chairman of *Shelter*, the organisation that did – and still does – so much to alert the British public to the plight of the homeless. His appearance in *Cathy Come Home*, Ken Loach's bleak TV drama about the homeless, made him a well-known figure.

In 1969, aged 42, Casey was appointed to his native Kerry as Ireland's youngest bishop. Some admirers felt it a waste to trap a firebrand inside a mitre in the distant west. Yet Casey continued his social activism; among much else he was popular for lifting the archaic ban on dances in Kerry church halls. He began to work for the developing world and, in 1973, was appointed chairman of *Trócaire*, the Irish church's new overseas aid agency. It became his passion, but not his only one. It was around this time that he began his affair with Murphy.

Casey was transferred to Galway in 1976, and three years later welcomed Pope John Paul II at a giant outdoor rally. During the next years Casey led the region's bishops in a campaign, without great success, to persuade Dublin and Brussels to help to halt economic decline in the west of Ireland. Still the head of *Trócaire*, he put even more energy into denouncing the selfishness of capitalism and its neglect of poverty in the developing world. He went to El Salvador and spoke out against the violence and human rights abuses of its US-backed right-wing regime. He even suggested that Ireland should break diplomatic ties with the US because of its support for such regimes and, in 1984, refused to meet President Reagan on his visit to Galway.

As bishop, Casey was far more outspoken than most of the Irish Catholic hierarchy against social injustice and inequality. It won him a few conservative enemies, but made him popular in Galway, as did his breezy persona. He was a man of the world: he smoked cigars, loved sport and music, and liked to lead a sing-song. He was a bit of an autocrat in his work, but very kindly to small children. On one occasion in London he was fined and banned from driving for 12 months after speeding while under the influence of alcohol. He apologised to his diocese, which made him even more popular; the Irish like a man who admits to his human weaknesses.

Some did find him a little too bland and plausible, perhaps too calculating. They pointed out that this political radical was theologically orthodox and, on moral questions, quite conservative. On matters such as abortion he kept a low profile, but was no dissenter. His public preaching against extramarital sex was soon to ring very hollow.

Although Casey was relatively little blamed for having an affair, he was criticised for the way that he had handled its consequences. Peter Hebblethwaite, the Jesuit priest and writer, described as "moral abortion" his attempts to persuade Murphy to have her son adopted. "He advised her to give it to God – how very convenient for him," he said. It was felt that Casey should have resigned when Murphy became pregnant and pursued his radical vocation as a layman. Instead, he put his episcopal career and the reputation of the church ahead of his human duty.

He spent the next months incognito in a monastery in the US, setting off the fire alarm with his smoking, after which, with Vatican permission, he moved to Ecuador, to devote the rest of his days to missionary work and making only occasional visits to his homeland. Eventually he took a post at a parish near Haywards Heath, West Sussex, ministering to the sick in a hospital, before returning quietly to Galway in 2006.

Casey's noble work for the underprivileged will be of lasting value. And so will his "sin" be. For, more dramatically than any other event of recent times, it spotlighted the ambiguities of the Catholic church's much-criticised attitudes to sexual morality. Casey may well have been a "great and generous" man, but in the church of his time he was probably in the wrong job.

He is survived by his son, Peter

MARTIN McGUINNESS

22 MARCH 2017

FEW MEN HAVE TRAVELLED AS FAR, personally and politically, as Martin McGuinness who died yesterday, aged 66. He failed his 11-plus and, after leaving school at 15, worked as a butcher's assistant in his native Londonderry. Within a few years he had become the scourge of the British state as one of the Provisional IRA's most senior and ruthless commanders, responsible for many deaths and acts of terror.

However, much later a very different McGuinness emerged. He embraced electoral politics and helped his close associate Gerry Adams bring most of the IRA's hard men on board. Not only that, but he was a principal architect of the peace process that led to the Good Friday Agreement of 1998 and became education minister in Northern Ireland's new power-sharing assembly, and later deputy first minister.

He formed a highly improbable partnership with Ian Paisley, the first minister and hardline Democratic Unionist leader who had formerly been his implacable enemy. The two men got on so well that they were dubbed the "Chuckle Brothers".

Once an international pariah and convicted terrorist, McGuinness was received in the White House by three successive American presidents – Bill Clinton, George W Bush and Barack Obama.

Most remarkable of all were his meetings with the Queen, the head of the very state against which the IRA had waged a vicious war that claimed more than 3,500 lives over three decades and ruined many more.

The first meeting took place at a Belfast theatre in 2012. The Queen shook McGuinness's hand in a powerful symbolic act of reconciliation. A later meeting with the Queen occurred at Hillsborough Castle in 2016 when she visited Northern Ireland as part of her 90th birthday celebrations. McGuinness asked how she was. The Queen, smiling, replied: "I'm still alive." She was probably referring to her longevity, but some commentators perceived a sly dig at a man who, in his younger days, had considered any member of the royal family a legitimate target for assassination.

The militant young Republican became in later life an amateur poet. He loved to go fly-fishing and supported Manchester United as well as following the traditionally Protestant sport of rugby. Stranger still, he was also a devotee of the England cricket team. Equally unexpected was his favourite television series, *Last of the Summer Wine*. He once said: "I sometimes wish I was one of the characters discussing the affairs of the world from a similarly idyllic background."

Non-smoking and teetotal, he was a family man too. He married Bernadette Canning in 1974 and lived with her in the heart of Londonderry's Bogside for the rest of his life. Together they raised four children. All survive him.

James Martin Pacelli McGuinness was one of seven children, born on 23 May 1950 to poor Catholic parents living in the deprived, overcrowded Bogside. He did not come from a conventional republican background, unlike Adams. His father, an iron foundry worker, disapproved both of republicanism's violence and its socialist tendencies. Living 50 metres from Celtic Park, the home of Derry's Gaelic Athletic Association, young Martin became a fan of the Derry Gaelic football and hurling teams, playing the sports while growing up.

He was educated at Hollybush Primary School and at the rough, tough Christian Brothers technical college. He left at 15 and became a butcher's assistant having been curtly rejected for other jobs because he was a Catholic.

McGuinness's baptism of fire occurred in 1969 when, along with many of the youths of his neighbourhood, he found himself throwing petrol bombs and stones at the Royal Ulster Constabulary (RUC), a police force local Catholics rejected as oppressive. He quickly graduated from stones to more lethal weapons. Although he originally joined the Marxist-inclined Official IRA, McGuinness was soon drawn towards the Provisionals, who took on the RUC and army much more aggressively.

Disciplined, ruthless and charismatic, he rose fast. As a leader of the IRA in Londonderry he masterminded its relentless bombing of the city, reducing much of its commercial centre to rubble. He and his accomplices then began targeting British soldiers, killing 26 in the city between August 1971 and December 1972. A British army officer who fought against McGuinness at that time described him as "excellent officer material".

By the time of Bloody Sunday in January 1972, when the army killed 14 unarmed civilians during a civil rights demonstration, he was second-in-command of the IRA's "Derry Brigade". The Saville inquiry reported 38 years later that McGuinness was engaged in paramilitary activity at that time, and was probably carrying a sub-machine gun that day, but had done nothing to justify the soldiers opening fire.

Later in 1972 McGuinness was part of an IRA delegation that was surreptitiously flown, in an RAF plane, to meet the home secretary William Whitelaw in a house in Cheyne Walk, Chelsea. "Whitelaw was a nice old man, but he didn't have a clue about Ireland," McGuinness later said. "But at least we were talking."

Whitelaw recalled: "The meeting was a non-event. They were still in a mood of defiance and determination to carry on until their absurd ultimatums were met."

After the London meeting McGuinness went on the run. He was, he later said, "fired at by the British army on countless occasions". In 1973 he was convicted in the Republic of Ireland and received a short prison sentence after being arrested near a car containing explosives. He told the court: "We have fought against the killing of our people. I am a member of Óglaigh na hÉireann (IRA) and very, very proud of it."

In the late 1970s McGuinness, Adams and other militant northerners seized control of republicanism, and McGuinness is widely believed to have served as the IRA's chief of staff between 1978 and 1982.

The two men denounced the southern old guard as soft and out of touch, and claimed that the army and police were gradually getting the upper hand. To counter this they pioneered a new "cell system" that made it far more difficult for the security forces to penetrate the IRA.

They transformed a run-down paramilitary outfit into a streamlined guerrilla force able to sustain its deadly if futile campaign.

For years McGuinness and Adams remained adamant that the IRA should no longer call ceasefires as it occasionally had in the past, maintaining that they would be regarded by Britain as signs of weakness. They developed the theory of "the long war", believing that violence would some day force a British capitulation.

"We don't believe that winning elections and any amount of votes will bring freedom in Ireland. At the end of the day, it will be the cutting edge of the IRA that will bring freedom," McGuinness insisted.

A new dimension developed in 1981 when ten republicans starved themselves to death in the Maze prison near Belfast. In the highly charged atmosphere support for Sinn Fein rose sharply, with the first hunger striker, Bobby Sands, winning a parliamentary by-election from his cell at the prison before he died.

After some hesitation, McGuinness and other IRA leaders decided to adopt a mix of violence and politics, the "Armalite and ballot box" strategy.

Veteran republicans argued at the time that this would divert their movement away from physical force and into politics, and eventually that is exactly what happened. But McGuinness heatedly denounced those critics at a 1986 Sinn Fein conference "Don't go my friends. We will lead you to the Republic."

The "struggle" went on, but McGuinness's Republic never arrived, and although the IRA killed dozens of people a year, it did not bring about a British withdrawal. Faced with a stalemate, McGuinness and Adams led the IRA and Sinn Fein ever more deeply into politics.

The two developed a "hard cop, soft cop" partnership. Hardliners in the IRA who felt that Adams was rather too political for their taste were reassured by the presence at his shoulder of the Londonderry republican who was viewed as a flinty icon of militancy.

The irony was that McGuinness, originally viewed as an uncomplicated militarist, would become the movement's most senior elected figure and its most personable politician.

By the early 1990s McGuinness was acting as the IRA's chief negotiator in ultra-secret contacts with government and intelligence representatives. These were followed by the IRA ceasefire of 1994, which broke down in 1996, but was reinstated in 1997 following the election in which McGuinness had become the MP for Mid Ulster – a position he held for almost 16 years and four elections, though he never took up his seat due to Sinn Fein's policy of abstentionism.

Negotiation followed, with Tony Blair, then prime minister, holding dozens of meetings with McGuinness and Adams, the heads of an organisation that had plotted to kill British ministers. The talks led to the 1998 Good Friday Agreement and the formation of a power-sharing administration. Jonathan Powell, who, as Blair's chief of staff, spent many hours closeted in negotiation with Adams and McGuinness, said it was "a remarkable act of leadership by them to talk the IRA into peace, and to persuade them to settle for something far less than they had demanded".

McGuinness initially served as minister of education in the new administration, though many Unionists were horrified at the thought of a man with his background being in charge of their children. His most radical act was to abolish the 11-plus exam in Northern Ireland.

The first power-sharing administration broke down in 2002, but when Ian Paisley emerged as the leader of unionism and first minister in 2007, McGuinness became deputy first minister. By that stage the IRA had put its weapons beyond use and announced that it was going out of business. Paisley's acceptance that McGuinness had truly abandoned the bomb and the bullet was sufficient to convince the world at large that the new arrangement was a genuinely historic breakthrough – and one that was a long way from the days when McGuinness regarded Britain, and the unionist Protestant population, as elements not to be negotiated with but to be defeated.

"My war is over. My job as a political leader is to prevent that war and I feel very passionate about it," he said.

In 2008 Peter Robinson, the first minister of Northern Ireland, replaced Paisley, but continued to work with McGuinness. In 2011 McGuinness ran as Sinn Fein's candidate for president of the Irish Republic, but came a distant third after a campaign in which he was dogged by questions about his IRA past.

In January 2016 Arlene Foster replaced Robinson as first minister, but her relationship with McGuinness was complicated by the fact that in 1986 he had delivered a graveside eulogy at the funeral of Séamus McElwaine, an IRA volunteer who had attempted to kill her father.

It ended badly when, in January 2017, McGuinness resigned over Foster's refusal to step down during an investigation of a bungled clean energy programme over which she had presided as minister. His resignation triggered the dissolution of the assembly and new elections, threatening to end a decade of relative stability in Northern Ireland.

At the same time, McGuinness resigned from politics, debilitated by the rare genetic disease – amyloidosis – that would go on to kill him.

Reactions to his death were predictably divided. Alastair Campbell, Blair's director of communications when the Good Friday Agreement was signed, called him "a great guy"; Lord Tebbit, whose wife, Margaret, was left paralysed by the Brighton bombing in 1984, condemned him as a "coward".

The Queen, meanwhile, reflected the journey he had taken in his life by writing a private message to his widow.

MAVIS ARNOLD

29 AUGUST 2017

ON FEBRUARY 23, 1943, fire broke out at St Joseph's, an orphanage run by nuns in Co Cavan, Ireland. Thirty-five girls were burnt to death. An inquiry at the time blamed the slow response of the emergency services.

Thirty years later Mavis Arnold, a determined Irish journalist with a natural talent for listening to people, began to piece together the full story: the girls had been locked in their dormitories by the sisters to avoid them being seen in public in their nightclothes.

Deciding to find out why a closed order of nuns, the Poor Clares, had been left in charge of a school, Arnold was warned at every turn: "It'll upset the good sisters. What's the point? Everything's different now."

She was told that State files did not exist. She was also refused interviews with medical and school inspectors from the era. One insisted: "The nuns did their best for the children". An official from the education department told her: "We'd better not delve into that."

Arnold had begun her research after a chance encounter at her own kitchen table in the house she shared with her journalist husband, Bruce Arnold, where she prepared two-course meals every night in between drafting chapters.

In 1970 she had offered to take care of an unmarried and pregnant 23-year-old woman, who would often sit quietly, "her shoulders hunched, rocking".

Over the next ten months the woman revealed to Arnold how, aged four, she had been put into St Joseph's. The school, which by this time had closed, stated that its purpose was to shelter, clothe, feed and morally instruct its destitute pupils. The girl told instead how she was virtually incarcerated and suffered punishments so severe that she still shuddered at loud noises.

Mavis Arnold

Arnold discovered how religious orders had often misused adequate State funds. She heard how, even as late as the 1960s, children had fought over the contents of the hens' bucket and the scrapings from the nuns' own generously covered table. At one school, children did not possess toothbrushes and were never seen by a dentist. They slept on foul bedding and contracted diseases from vermin. Most had an education that was so poor they were equipped only for menial tasks when they left the schools at 16. Many girls, like her young ward, soon became pregnant.

When Arnold's book, *The Children of the Poor Clares,* co-authored with Heather Laskey, was published in 1985 the reviews were disbelieving. However, Arnold was vindicated in 2009 when the government published the Ryan report, which found that since the 1940s, thousands of children in industrial schools had been subjected to systematic physical, sexual and emotional abuse. It also found that the perpetrators of this violence, such as the Cavan nuns, had been protected by their religious superiors.

Ysabel Mavis Cleave was born on 7 June 1937 in Mussoorie, a hill station in northern India. Her mother, Mary, was from Sligo in Ireland; her father, Major John Cleave, about 20 years older, was an Englishman. They met in India and married there.

Mary and her daughters returned to Ireland at the outbreak of the Second World War. Later they were mistakenly summoned back to India by the military authorities, who mixed up lists of wives, and had to be rescued when their ship was torpedoed. Major Cleave was reunited with his family at the end of the war, but died a year later.

Mavis grew up with her two sisters at Glen Lodge, a beautiful house in Sligo nestled between mountains and the shoreline. Her older sister, Maureen, also became a journalist, while her younger sister, Monica, was a horsewoman.

Mavis, after a local education and diploma in social sciences at Trinity College Dublin, became a social worker. She had met her husband at Trinity when they acted together in William Saroyan's *Jim Dandy.* They married in 1959 in Sligo and spent part of their honeymoon watching

Wagner operas at Bayreuth in Germany before settling in a large house called Rosney, near Dublin. She enjoyed knitting and weeding the garden. She could conjure up an excellent picnic in a matter of seconds – always with a chilled bottle of wine.

Taking her children to school, she began to bake cakes with other mothers to raise funds for a campaign to create multi-denominational education. This paved the way for the *Educate Together* charity, which now has 90 schools.

While writing her own book and occasional articles Arnold became a leading figure in creating the Women's Political Association, which campaigned to get women elected to the Dáil with the slogan: "Why not a woman?" After the collapse of the Soviet Union she led workshops in the new republics in Eastern Europe encouraging women to participate in democracy.

When it emerged in 1982 that the Irish government had tapped her husband's phone, believing his journalism to be a threat to national security, she joked that they would have to wade through hours of listening to her discussing women's strategy.

While Bruce, who survives her, was flamboyant in his bow ties and hats, Mavis had a practical nature that extended to her clothes. Rarely one to indulge in lavish purchases, she never wore heels and could not understand how anyone could walk in them. Small and pretty, she was comfortable proofreading her husband's prose or tending to one of the family's multiple pets.

Her greatest sadness was the death of their first child, Emma, from gastroenteritis as a baby in 1961. She had three more children: Hugo, a food consultant, Samuel, who died aged 49 after suffering a brain tumour, and Polly, a publisher who runs her own company.

She later took to mountain climbing with a group who liked to call themselves the B Team.

Although Arnold had Alzheimer's disease for the last years of her life, her "sisterhood" remained constantly in touch. Among those at her funeral following her death on 18 July aged 80, was the woman she had first helped at her kitchen table all those years ago.

LIAM COSGRAVE

6 OCTOBER 2017

A TRIM, BOWLER-HATTED FIGURE with a toothbrush moustache and a gravelly old-world Dublin voice, Liam Cosgrave, who died in hospital in Dublin on 4 October, aged 97, exuded an air of unpretentious, mild-mannered respectability and rectitude. Yet, as Taoiseach in the Republic of Ireland in the 1970s at the height of the Troubles, he proved himself capable of taking the gloves off, especially in his dealings with the IRA.

In December 1973, less than a year after he took office, Cosgrave brought off a diplomatic coup when he negotiated the historic Sunningdale Agreement with Edward Heath, the British prime minister, and Brian Faulkner, the Ulster Unionist leader, among others. It provided for a power-sharing executive in Northern Ireland, composed of unionists and nationalists, and a Council of Ireland to represent the two administrations on the island.

"There are no winners or losers," said Cosgrave, who hoped it would end the IRA campaign of violence. For most unionists, however, the agreement, especially its provision for a potentially powerful Council of Ireland, was several steps too far. Breaking with Faulkner, who was heading the power-sharing executive, they ran anti-agreement candidates who won all the unionist seats in the general election of February 1974 that brought the Labour Party under Harold Wilson back to power in the United Kingdom. Faulkner lost the leadership of the Ulster Unionist Party.

Although fatally wounded, the executive tottered on until confronted with a strike by the Protestant Ulster Workers' Council in May. Wilson turned a deaf ear to Cosgrave's entreaties to break the strike. The executive fell, brought down finally by the resignation of its unionist ministers. Direct rule from Westminster resumed. This lasted until power sharing (but not the Council of Ireland) was revived under the Good Friday Agreement of 1998.

Having watered down the Republic's irredentist claim to Northern Ireland by agreeing that its status in the United Kingdom would not be changed without the consent of the majority in the province, Cosgrave felt short-changed by Wilson. "An untrustworthy fellow," he remarked, contrasting him with Heath, whose visit to Dublin (the first ever by a serving British prime minister) to meet Cosgrave had opened the way to the agreement. Cosgrave, it must be said, was not blameless, having failed to appreciate soon enough Faulkner's difficulty selling the Council of Ireland to the unionist community.

Despairing of a quick fix for Northern Ireland, Cosgrave concentrated on putting down the IRA in the Republic. Their response was violent. Billy Fox, a Protestant senator from a border area, was murdered and members of the government and their families threatened with kidnapping. Cosgrave exhibited the steel behind his mild exterior, telling his cabinet that as long as he was Taoiseach there would be no ransoms. He banned all official contacts with republicans and was sharply critical when it was revealed that Wilson's government had been having secret meetings with them.

He had reason to be alarmed, as an exasperated Wilson harboured plans to cut and run in Northern Ireland so, in all probability, precipitating a sectarian war that would flow over into the Republic. Irresponsibly, Fianna Fáil politicians in opposition tried to recover their republican image with Anglophobe speeches demanding British withdrawal. Cosgrave was contemptuous, remarking: "Dying for Ireland, as usual, are they?"

If British ministers expected that Cosgrave's hostility to the IRA and general moderation would make him a pushover, they were doomed to be disappointed. He refused to countenance the extradition of IRA suspects to Northern Ireland or to abandon the case taken by the previous government in Strasbourg under the European Convention of Human Rights, alleging torture by the security forces in Northern Ireland.

Born in Templeogue on the outskirts of Dublin on 13 April 1920, Liam Cosgrave was the elder of two sons of William T Cosgrave, a reprieved veteran of the 1916 rebellion who, six years later, became the first head of government in an Irish Free State within the British Empire, and who oversaw putting down, with wholesale executions, armed republicans who took up arms to subvert the infant state.

Young Liam was educated at Synge Street Christian Brothers School and, as a boarder, at Castleknock College near Dublin. In 1943, while serving in the wartime army of neutral Eire, he was elected to the Dáil for Fine Gael, his father's party. Having studied law at King's Inns, he was also called to the Bar that year and practised, albeit not very actively, for a time; politics always came first, with horses a close second. His wife, Vera Osborne, whom he married in 1952, was from a horse-training family.

Cosgrave was Minister for External Affairs from 1954 to 1957 and, as such, spoke for the Republic after it was admitted to the United Nations in 1955. His outlook was a tad insular for this role; Rome was the only foreign place he enjoyed visiting. Conor Cruise O'Brien, then an official in the department, was exasperated when Cosgrave amended a draft speech prepared for him at the United Nations by inserting an appeal to Muslims and Jews to apply Christian principles to settle their differences. "That will go down well back home," he explained.

If Cosgrave was neither a sophisticated cosmopolitan nor a high-flier intellectually, he had compensating attributes as a politician. He had an enviable capacity to distil the political essence of a matter, however complicated. He was diligent in looking after constituents and had an uncanny memory for people and detail of their lives.

In 1965 he was elected leader of Fine Gael, then in opposition and with little prospect of being able to displace Fianna Fáil in government. But in 1970 his chance came. Information was leaked to him that several members of the government were involved in the illegal importation of arms to be used by the IRA. Cosgrave confronted Taoiseach Jack Lynch, privately, forcing him to sack two leading ministers, the future Taoiseach Charles Haughey and Neil Blaney.

Against the odds Lynch held his party together and survived with a reconstructed government. It was Cosgrave who almost became the victim of party dissidents. These were drawn from the left of the party. Cosgrave saw them off in an unusually impassioned speech calling them "mongrel foxes". "They are gone to ground," he continued, "but I'll dig them out and the pack will chop them when they get them."

At the end of 1972, however, he found himself at odds with almost all his parliamentary party when he refused to oppose a government bill facilitating proof of the offence of IRA membership. He was saved only by a bomb explosion in Dublin while the Dáil was debating the measure; this made further opposition impossible. Cosgrave had the nous to realise that his party, which prided itself on having founded the state in the teeth of republican violence, could not deny the government the means they considered essential to counter a renewed outbreak. On issues of state security he was not for turning, whatever the personal cost.

A few months later Jack Lynch sought to take advantage of the disarray in Fine Gael by calling a general election. Cosgrave reacted by negotiating an agreement with the Labour Party to fight the election as a coalition. Transfers between the two parties under proportional representation did the trick. Cosgrave became Taoiseach, receiving his seal of office from an unsmiling, aged president, Eamon de Valera, the man who had been his father's political nemesis. A reporter who had called on Cosgrave that morning had found him mucking out the stables.

The new government began well. Its ministers, who had been skilfully deployed, were more articulate and seemed more able than their predecessors. Cosgrave remarked in his self-deprecating way that there was so much talent in the cabinet that he was lucky to have found a place himself. Although not generally an eloquent speaker nor a good performer on television, he established an impressive mastery over the Dáil where his dry witticisms were much appreciated.

The government's credibility was somewhat dented in July 1974 when Cosgrave voted against a bill tabled by his Minister for Justice legalising the sale of contraceptives to married couples and so helped to ensure the bill's rejection; it emerged later that Cosgrave had not even notified cabinet colleagues of his intentions. "What would you expect from a fellow who was an altar boy until he was 24," wisecracked one wag in a sly reference to Cosgrave's piety – he attended Mass daily.

While IRA violence was widely deplored, Irish opinion, in its ambivalent way, was not prepared when, in response to the assassination in 1976 of the British ambassador Christopher Ewart-Biggs, Cosgrave's government had emergency legislation enacted allowing detention of suspects for up to seven days. The President, Cearbhall O Dalaigh, a former chief justice, referred the bill to the Supreme Court to rule on its constitutionality. At an army luncheon, an incensed Minister for Defence Patrick Donegan reacted by calling the President "a thundering disgrace." Cosgrave neither accepted the minister's proffered resignation nor offered an apology on behalf of the government. It was enough, he said gruffly, that the minister had apologised. O Dalaigh resigned. Cosgrave was not forgiven for his lack of respect for the presidency. It did not help that credible charges of police brutality emerged shortly afterwards, confirming that there was good reason for O Dalaigh's disquiet.

The episode epitomised a quality of personal loyalty in Cosgrave that was at once deeply attractive and, as on this occasion, potentially lethal. As he gave loyalty he also attracted it. Through it he welded together a coalition of diverse views with several *prima donna* personalities. He was content to act as chairman, and to let ministers and their civil servants get on with their business without interference. The short-spoken Cosgrave's quiet but firm authority over his colleagues secured reasonable cohesion.

The hike in oil prices in the wake of the 1973 Arab-Israeli war blew the economic plans of the government off course. In retrospect, they were to be faulted for their lavish social welfare bounty and consequent budget deficits that led Ken Whitaker, the governor of the Central Bank, to decline reappointment in 1976. But, at the time, it was a failure of presentation and insensitivity to public reactions, especially in relation to tax measures, that alienated supporters. The uncharismatic Cosgrave was the object of effective satire on a popular television series, depicted as a dry, grumpy Minister for Hardship telling people to grin and bear it...

Unwisely, Cosgrave went to the country before he had to. In the general election held in June 1977, the Fianna Fáil party produced a programme lavish in promises of financial benefits and capitalized on the discontent of sections of the community who felt let down by Cosgrave's government. Headed by the ever-popular Jack Lynch, Fianna Fáil were returned to power with a record majority.

In the weeks between the general election and the change of government, Cosgrave made a rash of public appointments from the ranks of well-tried followers who had stood by his party during their long wilderness years. It was the action of a man who did not expect to be back. Sure enough, shortly after he ceased to be Taoiseach, he resigned as leader of Fine Gael, so clearing the way for the election of Garret FitzGerald, his foreign minister, a long-time intriguer against his leadership.

Cosgrave remained in the Dáil, a silent member, until 1981, when he was succeeded in his constituency by his eldest son, also Liam, who subsequently became chairman of the Senate. His younger son, Ciaran, was sports psychologist to the Galway team who won the 2017 all-Ireland championship. His daughter, Mary, the eldest in the family, is an executive in the Irish tourist board; she lived with her parents and was her father's faithful companion after her mother became incapacitated years before her death in 2016.

Cosgrave left active politics behind with no apparent regrets. He indulged his passion for racing: he was a member of the Turf Club, the governing body of Irish racing. He rode out every morning on his farm on the outskirts of Dublin and hunted to hounds regularly, although in his thrifty understated way he steered clear of the High Society of the hunting world. He was an affable presence at State occasions. With his repertoire of political stories and penetrating observations he enlivened any gathering. But he made no public pronouncements apart from an occasional tasteful obituary or tribute on the death of someone who had served his party well.

The secular, flamboyant Ireland of recent decades was a far cry from the religious, austere society that Cosgrave reflected in his values and lifestyle. "You're great lads for vintages," he remarked drily to some affluent young barristers dining with him at the King's Inns. The traditional glass of Irish whiskey – Powers, the Catholic brand – was his only drink.

Punctilious to a fault, Cosgrave was an assiduous visitor to sick friends and seldom missed the funeral of an old associate or failed to write to the family.

His political reputation wore well, especially among the party faithful, although he did not enjoy a warm relationship with most of his successors. He continued to speak at book launches and other events well into his nineties, astonishing listeners by his accurate recall of past events and personalities.

INDEX